Medical Anthropology

Medical Anthropology

Regional Perspectives and Shared Concerns

Edited by

Francine Saillant and Serge Genest

Blackwell
Publishing

First published in Québec as Anthropologie médicale: Ancrages locaux, défis globaux
Copyright © Les Presses de l'Université Laval 2005
English translation © 2007 by Blackwell Publishing Ltd

BLACKWELL PUBLISHING
350 Main Street, Malden, MA 02148–5020, USA
9600 Garsington Road, Oxford OX4 2DQ, UK
550 Swanston Street, Carlton, Victoria 3053, Australia

First published 2007 by Blackwell Publishing Ltd

1   2007

Library of Congress Cataloging-in-Publication Data

Anthropologie médicale. English
    Medical anthropology : regional perspectives and shared concerns / edited by Francine Saillant and Serge Genest.
        p. cm.
    "First published in France as Anthropologie médicale: ancrages locaux, défis globaux."
    Includes bibliographical references and index.
    ISBN-13: 978-1-4051-5249-5 (hardcover : alk. paper)
    ISBN-10: 1-4051-5249-4 (hardcover : alk. paper)
    ISBN-13: 978-1-4051-5250-1 (pbk. : alk. paper)
    ISBN-10: 1-4051-5250-8 (pbk. : alk. paper)
1. Medical anthropology.   I. Saillant, Francine.   II. Genest, Serge.   III. Title.

    GN296.A627 2007
    306.4′61–dc22

                                                            2006014887

A catalogue record for this title is available from the British Library.

Set in 10.5 on 13 pt Minion
by SNP Best-set Typesetter Ltd, Hong Kong
Printed and bound in Singapore
by COS Printers Pte Ltd

For further information on
Blackwell Publishing, visit our website:
www.blackwellpublishing.com

CONTENTS

NOTES ON CONTRIBUTORS

Editors

Francine Saillant is a professor at Université Laval's Anthropology Department and Chief Editor of the journal *Anthropologie et Sociétés*. She has a Ph.D. degree from McGill University. She has conducted research on ethnomedicine in Québec and in France, on alternative medicine, on midwifery, and on women's knowledge of the body. She has also studied how globalization has affected health-care systems and households, especially women, in both Québec and Brazil. Her current research focuses on the anthropology of humanitarian aid. She has edited a number of books, including most recently *Transformations sociales, genre et santé*, with Manon Boulianne (PUL/l'Harmattan, 2003), *Identités, vulnérabilités, communautés*, with Michèle Clément and Charles Gaucher (Nota Bene, 2004), and *Communautés et socialités*, with Éric Gagnon (Liber, 2005).

Serge Genest has a Ph.D. degree from Paris V (Paris). He has conducted research on medical systems in Central and West Africa, in Southeast Asia, and in Québec. He has explored traditional systems of medicine in Africa, the encounter between local medicines and biomedicine, and AIDS. His current work deals more specifically with international development and health, as well as the connections between the environment and health.

Contributors

Gilles Bibeau is a professor at the Anthropology Department of the Université de Montréal. He is involved in directing an interuniversity research group on medical anthropology and ethnopsychiatry (GIRAME) and has edited two journals: *Psychotropes* and *Medical Anthropology Quarterly*. He directs an international network (Brazil, Peru, Nicaragua, Costa Rica, and Canada) within *El Colegio de las Americas* on the social determinants of health. His research covers a wide variety of areas: studies on biotechnologies, analyses of violence, drug addiction, and intercultural clinical practices, specifically in pediatrics, and mental health. He has written many books and articles, recently editing *Le Québec transgénique. Science, marché* *et nation* (Boréal, 2003) and, with M. Perreault, *Les gangs, une chimère à apprivoiser* (Boréal, 2002).

Carol H. Browner is a professor at the Department of Psychiatry and Behavioral Sciences and at the Anthropology Department of the University of California, Los Angeles. She has a Ph.D. from the University of California at Berkeley (1976) and a master's degree in public health (1977) from the same institution. She has conducted field research in urban Colombia, rural Mexico, and the United States. Her earlier research focused on fetal diagnosis. She is also interested in the proliferation of information in genetics and the use of genetics in the clinical practice of neurologists.

Roberto Campos-Navarro is a physician specializing in family medicine. He also has master's and Ph.D. degrees in social anthropology and is a medical anthropology researcher and lecturer at Mexico's Universidad Nacional Autónoma School of Medicine. He is a member of the Mexican society of medical history and philosophy, and of the support committee for the national council of indigenous healers, to which he also acts as an advisor. Dr Campos has written a number of books on traditional and lay medicine, and has given many courses and lectures on medical anthropology both in Mexico and at international meetings.

Arachu Castro has a Ph.D. in ethnology and social anthropology from the École des Hautes Études en Sciences Sociales (Paris), a Ph.D. in sociology from the University of Barcelona, and a master's degree in public health from Harvard's School of Public Health. She currently teaches social medicine at Harvard's School of Medicine where she directs the Program in Infectious Disease and Social Change. She has worked in the areas of infectious disease, reproductive health, and nutrition, both in Latin America and in Europe. She has also been much involved in producing public health documents on tuberculosis and AIDS in collaboration with WHO and the Pan American Health Organization. Her recent publications include: *Saber bien: Cultura y Prácticas Alimentarias en la Rioja* (Instituto de Estudios Riojanos, 1998) and, as editor, *Unhealthy Health Policy: A Critical Anthropological Examination* (Altamira Press, 2004). She is currently working on a book for the University of California Press: *AIDS in the Pearls of the Antilles: Rethinking Public Health from Haiti and Cuba*.

Josep M. Comelles (Barcelona, 1949) has a Ph.D. in anthropology from the École des Hautes Études en Sciences Sociales (Paris), and in psychiatric medicine from the University of Barcelona. He is a professor in social anthropology at the Universitat Rovira i Virgili (Tarragona, Spain), a visiting professor at Paris X, Lumière-Lyon 2, at CIESAS (Mexico) and at Università degli Studi di Perugia (Italy). His research interests focus on the history of psychiatry and anthropology, studies on health institutions, medical professions, and pluralism in health care. He has published *La Razón y la Sinrazón. Asistencia psiquiatrica y desarrollo del Estado en España* (Barcelona, 1988), *Enfermedad, sociedad y cultura* with

Angel Martínez (1993), and *Psiquiatría Transcultural* with Emilio González (2001).

María Beatriz Duarte-Gómez has a medical degree from the National University of Colombia. She also has degrees in public health from Antioch University and in sociology (public health management) from Birmingham University, and a Ph.D. in Public Health from Mexico's national public health institute. In addition, she is advisor to Colombia's Ministry of Health and consultant to the Pan American Public Health Organization. She has participated in research and program planning for indigenous groups.

Stefan Ecks studied anthropology, sociology, and philosophy at Göttingen, Berkeley, Paris (EHESS), and London (SOAS, LSE). He has a Ph.D. from the London School of Economics (2003). He is assistant professor at the Anthropology Department of the Institute of South Asian studies of Heidelberg, and specializes in the medical anthropology of South Asia. In 1999–2000, he carried out 18 months of field research in Calcutta on lay and professional representations of the body, self-image, and illness. He is currently carrying out research on social and medical anthropology theories and methodology, on suicide in South Asia, and on the use of drugs in mental health.

Sylvie Fainzang is a research director at Inserm, a member of Cermès (Centre de Recherche Médecine, Sciences, Santé et Société), and has a Ph.D. in ethnology and a Habilitation à Diriger des Recherches (EHESS, Paris). She encountered anthropology while translating a book by Marshall Sahlins for the publisher Gallimard (*Au cœur des sociétés. Raison pratique et raison utilitaire*, 1980). After her initial work in West Africa, she focused on French society where she has been working for twenty years. She has written a number of books, including: *L'intérieur des choses. Maladie, divination et reproduction sociale chez les Bisa du Burkina* (L'Harmattan, 1986), *Pour une anthropologie de la maladie en France. Un regard africaniste* (Ed. EHESS, 1989), and *Médicaments et société. Le patient, le médecin et l'ordonnance* (PUF, 2001). She is currently doing research on the role of lying in the doctor–patient relationship.

Didier Fassin is an anthropologist, sociologist, and physician, a professor at Paris XIII and research director at the École des Hautes Études en Sciences Sociales. He directs a research center on contemporary public health issues (Cresp, Inserm-UP 13-EHESS). His research is in the political anthropology of health, specifically the social production of inequality and the ways governments deal with health issues in both France and southern Africa. He has written a number of books, including: *Pouvoir et maladie en Afrique. Anthropologie sociale de la banlieue de Dakar* (PUF, 1992), *Antropologia y salud* (Abya Yala-IFEA, 1992), *Les enjeux politiques de la santé. Études sénégalaises, équatoriennes et françaises* (Karthala, 2000). He has also recently edited several books: *Les inégalités sociales de santé* (La Découverte, 2000) with A. Leclerc, M. Kaminski, and T. Lang, *Critique de la santé publique* (Balland,

2001) with J. P. Dozon, *Le gouvernement des corps* (Éditions de l'École des Hautes Études en Sciences Sociales, 2004) with D. Memmi, and *Afflictions. L'Afrique du sud, de l'apartheid au sida* (Karthala, 2004).

Paul Farmer, M.D., Ph.D., has been involved in infectious disease programs in the Americas for two decades. He is Director of the Maude and Lilian Presley Chair in medical anthropology at Harvard University's Department of Social Medicine. He has been a visiting professor at a number of institutions in the United States, France, Canada, Peru, Holland, Russia, and Central Asia. With his colleagues from Brigham and the Boston Women's Hospital, he has developed innovative strategies for community-based infectious disease treatment. He has conducted research mainly in Peru and Haiti, and has written a number of books, including: *Pathologies of Power* (University of California Press, 2003), *The Global Impact of Drug-Resistant Tuberculosis* (Harvard Medical School and Open University Institute, 1999), and *Infections and Inequalities* (University of California Press, 1998).

Usher Fleising is an emeritus professor at the University of Calgary. When he retired he was a professor at the Anthropology Department, and associate at the University of Calgary's Department of Community Health Sciences. He has degrees from McGill University and the University of New Jersey (Rutgers, Ph.D., 1976). His research and teaching link social and biological systems. In 2000, he became the principal researcher for a program on "Culture, society and health of Canadians" funded by the Social Sciences and Humanities Research Council of Canada (SSHRC). The project analyzed the subcultures involved in the discovery, marketing, and regulation of new drugs. He has published several articles on biotechnology and the culture of organizations in the biotech industry.

Ronald Frankenberg has a Ph.D. from the University of Manchester (England). He is an emeritus professor at Brunel University and a Fellow at Keele University in England. He is also an associate researcher at the Centre for Jewish Studies at the University of Manchester. He is a consultant for research in social anthropology and sociology.

Janice E. Graham has a Ph.D. from the Université de Montréal (1997) and specializes in the anthropology of medical systems. She has conducted postdoctoral research in neuroepidemiology and in medicine. Her research is focused on the construction of diagnoses, biotechnology, and technoscience. She was Chair of medical anthropology at the University of British Columbia from 1998 to 2000 with a fellowship from CIRH, and currently holds the Canada Research Chair in Bioethics (2002–2007). Her research focuses on an ethnography of the complex connections between science, industry, and government policies at Health Canada. It lies at the intersection between the study of sciences, technology and ethics, and analyzes how actors behave in contexts where the safety, effectiveness, and quality of new gene therapies raise moral issues.

Annette Leibing has a Ph.D. from Hamburg University in Germany. She works on topics such as aging, Alzheimer's disease, mental health, and memory. Formerly a professor at the Federal University of Rio de Janeiro, Brazil, she is currently a visiting professor at McGill University's Department of Social Medicine. Her two most recent books are *Thinking about Dementia: Culture, Loss and the Anthropology of Senility*, with Lawrence Cohen (Rutgers University Press, 2006), and *The Shadow Side of Fieldwork: Theorizing the Blurred Borders Between Ethnography and Life* with Athena McLean (Blackwell Publishing, forthcoming).

Margaret Lock is the Marjorie Bronfman Professor in Social Studies in Medicine at McGill University's Department of Social Studies of Medicine and Department of Anthropology. A Fellow of the Royal Society of Canada and an Officer of the Order of Québec, Margaret Lock received the Prix du Québec for the Humanities in 1997 and the Molson Award from the Canada Arts Council in 2002. She also was awarded the Wellcome Medal from Great Britain's Royal Anthropology Society. Her publications include *East Asian Medicine in Urban Japan* (University of California Press, 1980), *Encounters with Aging: Mythologies of Menopause in Japan and North America* (University of California Press, 1993), and *Twice Dead: Organ Transplants and the Reinvention of Death* (University of California Press, 2002), which have won several awards. Her current research focuses on postgenome biology and its impacts on clinical practice, families, and society in general.

Angel Martínez-Hernáez (Paris, 1964) is a professor in Social Anthropology at the Universitat Rovira i Virgili (Tarragona, Spain). He has a Ph.D. in Anthropology and a master's degree in social psychiatry (University of Barcelona). He is a professor at the University of Barcelona, and a visiting professor at UNAM (Mexico), at Università degli Studi di Perugia (Italy), at the Universidade Federal de Santa Catarina (Brazil), and at the University of California at Berkeley. His main research projects have focused on ethnopsychiatry, the biomedical system in Spain, and anthropological theory. He is currently working on social participation and health in Brazil. He has published *What's Behind the Symptom* (Harwood Academic Publishers, 2000).

Raymond Massé teaches the anthropology of health at Université Laval. He is a professor at the Department of Anthropology where he has been chair since 2002. From 1983 to 1994, he was a researcher at the Public Health Directorate for Montréal-Centre. From 1998 to 2002, he coordinated the public health ethics group in the clinical ethics network of the Fonds de recherche en santé du Québec. His fields of research include illness management in the French and English Caribbean, and social and cultural anthropology's contribution to disease prevention. His books include *Culture et santé publique. Les contributions de l'anthropologie à la prévention et à la promotion de la santé* (Gaëtan Morin, 1995), and *Éthique et santé publique. Enjeux, valeurs et normativités* (Presses de l'Université Laval, 2003).

Gustavo Nigenda (M.A., M.Sc., Ph.D.). After graduating in biology, he completed degrees in social anthropology at the Escuela Nacional de Antropologia e Historia (ENAH, Mexico), in financial planning and health systems at the London School of Hygiene and Tropical Medicine, and at the London School of Economics and Political Science where he completed his Ph.D. From 1986 to 2001, he was a researcher at Mexico's national public health institute. He has also occupied different consulting positions at the World Bank, the Interamerican Development Bank, and WHO, and since 2001 he has been a permanent consultant at the Mexican health foundation. Dr Nigenda is also an associate researcher at Sussex University's Institute of Development Studies. His research focuses on health systems reform, public–private partnerships in health care, and the connections between health sector reform and reproductive health programs.

Mariella Pandolfi is a professor at the Université de Montréal's Department of Anthropology. In 2004, she won the Montréal YWCA Foundation's Education Award. She is a visiting professor at McGill University in Montréal, the EHESS in Paris and Marseille, the CNRS, the University of Tarragona, Bergamo, Bologna (1999), and Milano Bicocca. She participates in several academic committees for anthropology journals (*AM: Anthropologia Medica* in Perugia, *Medicine and Anthropology* in London, *Cultural Anthropology* in Arlington, and *Ethnos* in Stockholm). Under the inspiration of the Italian ethnologist Ernesto De Martino, her work has helped to develop a critical medical anthropology of the body. Her writings include "Boundaries Inside the Body: Women's Sufferings in Southern Peasant Italy" (*Culture, Medicine, and Psychiatry* 14(2), 1990), *Itinerari delle emozioni: corpo e identità femminile nel Sannio campano* (Franco Angeli, 1991), "Le self, le corps, la crise de la présence" (*Anthropologie et Sociétés*, 17(1–2), 1993), *Perché Il Corpo? Utopia, Sofferenza, Desiderio* (Meltemi, 1996), and *Le arene politiche del Corpo* (2003). In them she has laid out a new model for analyzing suffering, narrativity, and embodiment. She is a consultant for several international organizations and foundations, and her current work in Albania and Kosovo (and more generally in the postcommunist Balkans) develops a critical reflection on humanitarian interventions, and a biopolitical interpretation of medical anthropology.

Enrique Perdiguero is a medical doctor and professor in the history of science at Miguel Hernández University (Alicante, Spain). After completing his studies in medicine he presented a Ph.D. dissertation on writings on home care during the Spanish Enlightenment (1989). Most of his research focuses on lay medicine, pluralism in health care, and the history of public health. He is the author of *Medicina y Cultura. Estudios entre la antropología y la Medicina* with Josep M. Comelles (Bellaterra, 2000).

Ilario Rossi has a Ph.D. in anthropology and sociology. He teaches the anthropology of health at the University of Lausanne's Faculty of Social and Political Sciences and is a project manager at the Polyclinique médicale universitaire (Department of Medicine and Community Health). He has written many articles and a book entitled *Corps et chamanisme. Essai sur le pluralisme médical* (Armand Collin, 1997). His research focuses on health systems policies in Western nations and in the South, highlighting the relationships between health practices, knowledge production, and civil society.

Carolyn Sargent has a Ph.D. in anthropology from Michigan State University and a master's degree in social anthropology from the University of Manchester (England). Currently she is a Professor and Chair of feminist studies at Southern Methodist University. Her research deals with gender and health, reproduction, and medical ethics. She has conducted research in Benin, Jamaica, and France, where she is currently studying representations of family and reproduction among migrants from the Senegal River valley living in Paris. She has co-edited two books, *Gender in Cross-cultural Perspective* (Prentice-Hall, 4th edition, 2005) and *Medical Anthropology: Contemporary Theory and Method* (Praeger, 1996), and has recently co-authored "Polygamy, Disrupted Reproduction, and the State: Malian Migrants in Paris, France" (*Social Science and Medicine* 56, 2003).

Johannes Sommerfeld studied anthropology, sociology, and economics at the University of Hamburg (Germany). After completing a Ph.D. based on field research in Haiti in the area of medical anthropology, he obtained a master's degree in public health from the University of South Florida. He is currently directing social, economic, and behavioral research within the special research and training program on tropical diseases (UNICEF/UNDP/World Bank/WHO) at WHO headquarters in Geneva, Switzerland. He was formerly an associate at Harvard University's International Development Institute and at Heidelberg University's School of Medicine. He has conducted research in Mali, Burkina Faso, and Haiti and has published a number of books on infectious diseases within a perspective linking the social sciences of health, medical anthropology, and research on international public health.

Sjaak Van Der Geest is a professor of medical anthropology at the University of Amsterdam. He has conducted research in Ghana and Cameroon and has published many articles and books on a wide variety of subjects, including contraceptive perceptions and practices, field research, Ghanaian popular music, missionaries, and anthropologists, and a broad range of issues in medical anthropology, most notably the reinterpretation and use of Western pharmaceuticals in non-Western societies, hospital ethnography, attitudes towards death, and perceptions of hygiene and waste management. He is currently conducting research on the social and cultural meaning of ageing in Ghana.

Angelika Wolf studied anthropology, sociology, and psychology at the Free University of Berlin. She is an associate researcher at the Department of Medical Management and Health Sciences at the University of Bayreuth, in Germany, and is a Professor in the Department of Social Anthropology at the Free University.

She has conducted research in medical anthropology on HIV/AIDS in sub-Saharan Africa. Her research mainly focuses on local conceptions of sexually transmitted diseases, on children who have become heads of household in the context of HIV/AIDS in South Africa, and on social security systems in Africa.

PREFACE

Given our great good fortune in bringing on some of medical anthropology's luminaries to write this book, we hope, as one early reviewer of the manuscript wrote: "With such a line-up, one might well feel embarrassed not owning the volume." Flattering as that is, our hope is that this collection will not just end up on the shelves of our colleagues but will allow us as researchers, practitioners, and instructors to reach out to students and others interested in learning about medical anthropology. Our intent has been to offer a multi-vocal overview of the various paths followed by medical anthropology in Europe and in the Americas. Since, as we discuss at greater length in our introduction, the robust field of medical anthropology is a composite of national traditions and disciplinary subfields, we need to consider how best to do justice to the wide range of practices, traditions, concepts, and theories of medical anthropologists and to the individuals and societies they study and that have shaped them.

Our answer is this book: a volume that is both a synthesis and a prospectus. Our objective, to broaden views of medical anthropology beyond the rich tradition in the United States, which is well established and imposing even today and in so doing to include a wider spectrum of traditions both in the Americas and in Europe which have contributed to the development of medical anthropology.

We asked the authors – all of whom are uncontested leaders in the field – to give a localized and situated interpretation of the discipline, to present both established and emerging practices, and to draw attention to the issues they see on the horizon, both locally and globally. Only by reading these perspectives side-by-side can we grasp the forms, interpretations, and trends that define the "world of medical anthropology."

ACKNOWLEDGMENTS

The editors wish to thank several people and organizations for their help and support in completing this book.

First, we would like to thank all the contributing authors for their patience and commitment. Through the course of our work together we needed to contact each other dozens of times by email and telephone all over the world, including at times while doing fieldwork in difficult conditions. We particularly appreciated their genuinely warm response to the project, their enthusiasm, and the quality of their contributions and suggestions.

We also are grateful to those who helped to prepare the manuscript: Mary Richardson, for the French–English translations; Richard Whelan, for revising the manuscript from beginning to end; Fabiola Stoi, Florina Gaborean, and Agnès Blais, all graduate students in anthropology at Université Laval, for their support in editing the texts and in checking the bibliographies; and Caroline Savoie, secretary of Université Laval's Centre de recherches sur les lettres, les arts et les traditions (CELAT), for preparing the version that was sent to the publisher.

We also thank CELAT and the Anthropology Department of Université Laval for their financial and logistic support, as well as the Québec Population Health Research Network of the FRSQ (Fonds de la recherche en santé du Québec), for the academic publications grant they provided.

Francine Saillant and Serge Genest

INTRODUCTION

Francine Saillant and Serge Genest

This book is an answer to a simple question: how has medical anthropology developed since the first manuals were published in the United States in the 1970s and 1980s (Eisenberg and Kleinman 1981; Foster and Anderson 1978; Logan and Hunt 1978; McElroy and Townsend 1979; to name but a few). They were followed by a plethora of works by as many authors in the field (Lindenbaum and Lock 1993; Nichter 1989; Sargent and Johnson 1996; Van Der Geest 1998; among others). But how has medical anthropology developed in some other countries – to what extent have diversified intellectual traditions, rooted in continental, regional or national environments, contributed to the elaboration of concepts and theories, often linking together the specificity of one tradition to the more general concerns of the international scientific community? Some may protest that the answer is so obvious as to make the question hardly worth asking. Are over one hundred journals and thousands of publications each year, professional associations all over the world, general and thematic conferences and symposia, and educational programs in the best universities not sufficient to prove the vitality and reach of this disciplinary crossroads?

However, there is no clear-cut answer to those questions. A closer look at the various paths followed by medical anthropology in Europe and in the Americas, be it through the institutions where it expresses itself or through its most current debates, makes us leave behind a more linear history and shift to a kaleidoscopic vision of multiple elements. But again, this never prevents all those traditions agreeing on major fieldwork or theoretical issues in a global context.

Yet medical anthropology remains fragmented by its myriad national traditions and the many disciplinary subfields that have emerged and developed within it, many which admittedly reproduce categories of medical specialties (e.g. nutrition, childbirth, psychiatry). It has been substantially re-shaped from within by the debates over the sovereignty of the body, of cultures and of professions, or the implementation of technologies in all spheres of life, even into the farthest recesses of the body where issues of intimacy and functionality appear to have been laid bare, and by the ethical debates over what is most "worthy" of consideration or "humane" in situations of medical uncertainty.

Issues of justice in the realm of life and death are not always framed by medicine: when policies become biopolitics that favor the lives of certain groups or individuals at the expense of others, the decision-makers are often politicians, civil servants, administrative agents, or company managers. Physicians are one group of "actors" in such decisions, but only one. The consequences of unfavorable decisions for the health of various groups of people do of course fall in the scope of medicine; but instead of focusing here on medical practice or medical events, it is the mechanisms by which some people are considered more deserving of a life of dignity, or simply a life, that are the focus. This new anthropology in the making often goes far beyond the borders of the therapeutic arena, while still dealing with the issues of life and death that are of concern both to the medical world and to anthropology: many studies instead take us to the streets, and to prisons, laboratories, industries, factories, morgues, courts, scholarly journals, and conferences. Although the debates are highly varied, the question of who "deserves to live" comes to the forefront each time a decision needs to be made regarding a host of questions: the viability of the fetus (abortion); the birth of extremely premature infants (neonatology); access to health care in slums (what are the public health standards?); how to eradicate the disparities revealed by the "political epidemiology" of AIDS (should we still be calling it epidemiology, or even sociocultural epidemiology?); the spaces of humanitarian intervention (what causes are noble? what groups deserve aid? what level of violence is intolerable?); and how the rejects of society living off drugs and street prostitution should be considered, guilty as they are in the eyes of politicians because of their "responsibility" for their problems.

As medical anthropology moves in new directions, we need to consider how to do justice to the many different practices, traditions, concepts, and theories of anthropologists and to the societies and groups they study and that have shaped them. How do we do justice to the extraordinary productivity of the authors, the variety of their worksites, but also to the academic traditions that have influenced how they have carried out their research in the countries where they work? Is it possible, in a book that is both a synthesis and a prospectus, to broaden our field of vision beyond the United States, whose presence is established and imposing even today (e.g. Ember and Ember 2004), bringing into view traditions both in the Americas and in Europe which have contributed to its development? How do we review the history of medical anthropology while at the same time showing where it is headed, what the different issues are in different locations, its histories and traditions, and the new questions it is addressing? How do we shift medical anthropology away from its usual circles, at the same time honoring each person's space and contribution? The ambitious project behind this book was to re-examine the field of medical anthropology by offering readers a glimpse of the many different perspectives of those within it and who are in a privileged position because of their impact on how it has been defined and on the directions it has taken. Our intention was also to reflect on how the major social issues facing us are coloring the way it is being expressed, and to put its founding concepts into perspective.

We had to ask ourselves whether the admittedly impressive vitality of medical anthropology is leading to a certain form of institutionalization and routine in academic practices, or perhaps even to a subtle loss of stamina as a certain conformism takes over. Paradigms have shifted: more empiricist and positivist at the outset, then more textualist, and now clearly headed in the direction of a multiflavored critical anthropology.

Although certain trends tend to dominate, it is striking to what extent all the paradigms that have left their mark on the field since the 1970s remain alive and well, often overlapping as some fade while others take their place. National questions and social issues, as well as the places where medical anthropologists practice (anthropology departments in different centers and institutions connected to the world of health care), admittedly have considerable influence over research programs. While the question of migration may be relevant in Paris and Montréal, the issues of violence and inequalities will echo more loudly in Brazil, and Aboriginal issues will be more prominent in research in Mexico and in Canada. An anthropologist working in public health units may focus more on epidemiology, taking a more empiricist approach, while another who works in an anthropology department next to a comparative literature department may feel comfortable meandering through the textualist and hermeneutic trends in the discipline.

Is it possible to take a fresh look at the history of medical anthropology, showing its many places of birth, and if so, would that not create new theoretical and methodological spaces?

This book is therefore an invitation to explore the poly-vocal, multi-sited history of medical anthropology, to a plural reading of the field. Is anthropology (in this case medical anthropology) capable of applying to itself the approach it has taken to other cultures, that is, respecting the plurality of societies and local worlds in its interpretations? Is it willing to give up the center? Of course, referring to "national medical anthropologies" (Diasio 1999) is a first step in that direction, but certainly not a last step.

Another question that has haunted medical anthropology since its beginnings is the question of its dangerous liaison with a profession that represents the establishment, biotechnological capitalism and pernicious forms of biopolitics, all too often to gain credibility, and sometimes accepting a role as a pale sociocultural variable in certain collaborations with medical professions. Doing so has often watered it down and undermined its innovative potential. Will medical anthropology lose sight of the goals of anthropology as a whole as it becomes overspecialized and fragmented? What fresh perspectives and what contraints will emerge from the transformations taking place in the world, characterized as they are by the omnipresence of technologies, by the shifting and fluid nature of the boundaries of politics, identity, and the body, and by the AIDS epidemic and the fear of bioterrorism, to name but a few salient contemporary phenomena? Are the categories that medical anthropology developed during the 1970s and 1980s showing signs of aging? For example, where are we at in our reflections on the illness/sickness/disease triad, health-seeking behavior, medical pluralism, the notion of medical systems, or even the term "medical anthropology"?

We have asked the authors of the following chapters, all of whom are uncontested leaders in the field, to give a localized and situated interpretation of the discipline, to present both established and emerging practices, and to draw attention to the issues they see on the horizon, both locally and globally. Only by reading these viewpoints and perspectives side by side with an open mind can we grasp the forms, interpretations, shifts, and postures that may help clarify what the "world of medical anthropology" might be today.

Changes in Scale

In its beginnings, medical anthropology was influenced by general anthropology in its view of field sites as islands: closed communities on a circumscribed territory, pure forms, bounded cultures, suspended time. The study of ethnomedical practices and medical systems was influenced by that mind-set, with an emphasis on the more classical area in which diverse therapeutic practices were classified and interpreted along holistic lines. From the early 20th century until the 1950s, the anthropologist had to integrate into village life, be it African or Asian, become acquainted with its symbolic and religious world, and discover how the therapeutic objectives of certain practices were what gave them meaning through their power to attend to matters of living, caregiving, and dying. The people studied were endowed with culture, but also with bodies; they were born, suffered, and died, and that was taken seriously. The entire academic tradition of anthropology has accustomed us to exploring the links between religious cosmologies and medical cosmologies, be they religious worlds, theodicies of evil and affliction, or moral paradigms that connect evil and misfortune, good and harmony. The most in-depth studies of non-Western scholarly medicine, such as Chinese, Tibetan, Ayurvedic, or Unani medicine, were used as examples for studying non-Western lay medicines or medicines with no written tradition. The first medical anthropology, before it was known as such, was a symbolic and religious anthropology.

In the 1950s and 1960s, with the new concern for development, this interest in the symbolic and religious became instrumentalized. Extraordinary indigenous systems of thought were conceptualized as beliefs to be studied so that biomedicine could be more effectively enrolled in the service of improving people's health. Anthropological research opened the way for what would later become the anthropology of public health.

It was only towards the 1970s that medical anthropology was named. In the beginning it was very empiricist, with the paradigms of ecology and sociocultural epidemiology (McElroy and Townsend 1979); then it took up its interest in the symbolic, becoming increasingly textualist and hermeneutical (Kleinman 1988); and more recently, it has become a multi-faceted critical enterprise with Foucauldian, feminist, deconstructionist, and political economy influences that we feel are well represented in this book. On both sides of the Atlantic a political view of medical anthropology has emerged with contributions from Baer et al. (1997), but also from Fassin (1996, 2000, 2004) and Farmer (2003). It should not be forgotten that this political, critical outlook was preceded by an entirely different tradition developed by Italian colleagues (see Pandolfi and Bibeau in this volume, Chapter 7).

The shifts in medical anthropology paradigms have been abundantly commented on by several authors before us (Augé 1986; Augé and Herzlich 1984; Colson and Selby 1974; Fabrega 1972; Lieban 1973; Scotch 1963; to cite but a few historical markers). However, we feel it is important to emphasize that what put anthropology and classical medical anthropology on the map was the study of how medical systems are embedded in cosmologies and religious worldviews. During the 1960s and 1970s, given the importance of biomedicine and its expansion throughout the world, attention was focused more on the phenomena of contact, resistance, transformation, and the adaptation of local practices, narrowing the focus to more and more specific aspects of treatment practices, whether biomedical or not, in the name of "efficiency." That was the first reduction.

In the 1970s, the writings of anthropologists were increasingly critical of what they perceived as the dehumanization of biomedicine, its biological reductionism, its technicization, its hegemony, its collusion with the establishment and with corporations, and its insensitivity to other forms of knowledge. There were three major influences on that critical trend: the place that the World Health Organization gave to traditional medicine in 1978, the social movements advocating demedicalization, including the women's movement (Saillant 2003), and Michel Foucault's work on the medical gaze and medical power (1988). Research focused more on the clinical relationship (the "clinical gaze") and on power and the subjection of "patients" (in obstetrics and psychiatry for instance), not only in the clinics and hospitals of different countries in the North, but also in the South where studies explored local knowledge, indigenous knowledge, the indifference to or manipulation of that knowledge, and the reification of subjects. That anthropology remained fairly restricted to the confines of the clinic, the health center, or the village, taking up the metaphor of the island without necessarily naming it. But of course the realities of *métissage* eroded a hole in the dike of bounded worlds and the encounters between systems and practices inherited from different ontologies had to be taken into account.

It was the Foucault of biopolitics (2004) that gave the strongest impetus to the change in scale. The shift in his analyses from the world of the clinic to biopolitics and governmentality, and his viewpoints on subjectivation and resistance, were highly influential in anthropological research on medical systems, particularly in North America. Michel Foucault's work has been avidly read in the United States, amongst others through the writings of Rabinow (1984) and Dreyfus and Rabinow (1983).

From Ethnomedicine to "Medicoscapes"

Ethnomedicine has been one of the preferred objects of medical anthropology (Benoist 1996); it has even studied biomedicine as an "ethnomedicine" among others, although the status, cultural and economic power, and expansionism of biomedicine make it somewhat different from the medical systems found in the

Amazon or in a rural population of Eastern Europe. However, it has been largely shown not only that its values, cosmology, and rationality are well embedded in the *episteme* of the Enlightenment and "Western reason" and that they are contingent to them, but also that there are considerable variations depending on where biomedicine is practiced (different medical specialties, institutions, or places in the world). The claim of universalism does not stand up easily to such diversity. Indeed, the applications and models, including modes of reasoning, cannot continue unchanged from an emergency unit to a geriatric ward, from a humanitarian medicine to a street medicine, from Sri Lanka to the American Hospital in Paris, or among the Inuit of the Canadian North. This move towards the study of Western biomedicine was important and has rescued anthropologists from exoticism, folklorism, and the ethnography *ad nauseam* of all the ethnomedicines of the world. They are now free to study biomedicine as any other medical system with its share of "beliefs" and irrationality. But there was an undesired and undesirable effect to that: medical anthropology was linked all the more closely to the study of "Medicine" making it appear more "medical" than ever.

On the other hand, it created unforeseen openings: not only did medical anthropology distance itself from the folklore that originally characterized it, but it also moved away from sociologism and diehard empiricism by going beyond the clinical space and the favored object of interactionism (the doctor–patient relationship) and by restricting itself less and less to clinical hermeneutics (the flow of meaning in the doctor–patient relationship). Instead it moved into some of the least visible territories. Some anthropologists took a genealogical approach to the study of medical practices (Fassin 1996), others left the bedside and entered the morgue, and still others took the path of translocality and the study of the connections between transnational organizations and local organizations (Pandolfi 2002) to understand practices as a flow of meaning carried by networks of actors.

In the same spirit, research has been done upstream from the clinic where certain treatment "choices" are determined: in pharmaceutical, vaccine, and genetic laboratories, but also in the medical journals and conferences where debates are held (Franklin and Lock 2003; Lock 2002). A host of work has also demonstrated that the biomedical body is not the fixed and immutable object that we might have thought it was: the study of medical imaging reveals the many bodies that coexist in medical practice, how uncertain the body's most obvious boundaries can be, and the ontological questions on how to define the inside and outside, matter and spirit, human and nonhuman (Franklin and Lock 2003). Throwing the ballast of folklorism and sociologism overboard, anthropology has changed scales and, in the words of Marcus (1995), is free to follow the object wherever it may lead, far from empirical evidence and a representation of the clinic as the bedside, to encounter the intrinsic strangeness and plurality of ever-changing clinical worlds. The homogeneity of the Western model has been a mere illusion. And the successive shifts in the anthropological gaze have of course had a role to play in the transformation of medical practice itself.

As we have mentioned, medical anthropology has emphasized the issue of medical hegemony. As biomedicine has sought to extend its reach, as it has moved into the most improbable places on the planet and into spheres of life unimaginable only fifty years ago, it has been cloaked in an aura of modernity and progress. Yet it has been "transported" by means other than drug bags and tent hospitals. Like Coca-Cola, jeans, and Céline Dion CDs, its most effective ambassadors have been the electronic media through advertising, video clips, television series, and news-entertainment. The coverage of Yasser Arafat's death was a striking example of how biomedicine can mutate from an ethnomedicine to a mediascape, and even a "medicoscape" (on medicoscape, see in this volume Chapter 8 by Wolf *et al.*, p. 151). It is not only its practices and means that travel, but also its imagery of truth, success, and power over life and death.

The updates of Yasser Arafat's state of health were a particularly successful medicoscape in that only his closest relatives had access to the images of his death, all else rested on rumors, hearsay, and imagination. Television chains announced Arafat's death, and then retracted; more than ever, the questionable nature of the criteria for death became apparent. The updates became the object of discussion between families, civilizations, and politics. Never before had a medically assisted death been so political and so contested. At the same time, the highest medical authorities orchestrated a share in the end of the Raïs. Leaving the camps of Palestinian desolation, Arafat boarded an airplane waving farewell to his people to be treated in a place where medicine is accessible and more "neutral" than in neighboring Israel. He arrived in the place of medicine-as-entertainment where diagnosis merges with news bulletin, and where medical discretion is confused with State secret. Allah was no longer the only One able to save the legitimate representative of Palestine; other saviors were watching over this faceless death, sending out the paradoxical image of the medicine of power and control brought down to its only admission of powerlessness: to certify that death has occurred and can no longer be warded off. Thus, medical hegemony combined with the notion of medicoscape opens new perspectives for anthropology in the study of new ritualities, cosmologies and symbolism of life at the beginning and end, even in contemporary times.

The Languages of the Body

The study of the representations of the body is at the heart of all medical anthropology (Le Breton 1990, 1999). However, studying the body does not necessarily imply studying health or illness. Over the past thirty years, one of medical anthropology's main challenges has been to find a different language for speaking about the body and naming its realities. The challenge has been considerable because of medical hegemony and the authority of medical institutions, of course, but also because the languages of the other medicines were unable to develop concepts that would open onto another "scientific" language for the body. It was not enough to understand the role of breath, or of *chi*, or to draw the cultural cartography of bodies. To speak of breath or *chi*, one has to be situated where biomedicine thinks it is situated without playing the same game: a "true" or at least "credible" language for the body had to be found so that the dominant epistemology of Western rationality concerning the body could be radically exploded. Csordas's notion of embodiment (1994, 2002), Bourdieu's concept of habitus (1992), and Foucault's theory of biopower (2001a–c) all helped to crack the surface of generally accepted ideas.

Whereas 18th-century medicine sought to banish the environment, interiority, and subjectivity from the medical gaze, these are precisely what sociology, anthropology, philosophy, and history have tried to reintroduce. First they took on the body as an object of analysis, which gave them access not only to the body but also to society and culture, and then they situated their disciplines at the heart of several new theories: a new existential theory of culture (Csordas 1994, 2002); a new theory of the relationship between interiority and exteriority and spatial positions represented by habitus (Bourdieu 1994); and a new theory of power based on power/knowledge and disseminated power (Foucault 2004; Saillant 2004, 2005).

The development of these theoretical approaches meant that biomedicine was no longer the only empirical field in which such theories and concepts were being elaborated. Medical anthropology took note of these developments and rapidly integrated them into its vocabulary on the body. The multiple forms of embodiment represented by culture and the self, society and social relations, and the many forms that power takes on, changed the dominant representations of a biological body whose appropriations and distinctions social scientists had to translate into lay terms. Those authors undertook an in-depth re-examination of the category of the body, decentering it as others had previously done for the categories Man and Universe. In the new academic program of "embodiment," the biological body was no longer taken as a category, a truth, and an incontestable set of facts; instead, to study the realities surrounding affairs of the body, researchers placed themselves on the ever-shifting terrain of the many ways in which the social, the subjective, and the biological interpenetrate one another. Recent questions on how "long memory" is embodied, such as the memory of extreme forms of subjection, or of slavery and colonization (see comments by Fassin on Farmer's article (2004) in *Current Anthropology*), radicalize that perspective, for the point in speaking of embodiment should not be to restrict it to a specific time and place, but rather to encompass the many mediations of *history made flesh*. To what extent are disturbances that show up on the biological level the product of a series of mediations that are invisible clinically, that cannot be adequately measured by the tools of epidemiology? The idea of embodiment not only re-opened the body as a locus of the social, but it re-introduced debates that had been suspended by techno-scientific rationalism: what body are we now speaking about, what role do emotions and the psyche play as keys to the various forms of embodiment?

The language of the body changed significantly as it extricated itself from "sociocultural influences" and their underlying functionalism, a legacy of epidemiology that turned culture and the social arena into a series of variables that all too often reduced the complexity of relations to simple dualities (space–time, body–emotion, body–environment, biology–society, science–nonscience). While this new language of the body did not really seep into the institutions most invested in scientific truth and evidence-based medicine, it did infiltrate some of the less conventional fringes and the areas where there was the most debate over presumed truths, most notably under the influences of social scientists and anthropologists.

The debates over the language of the body have helped to redefine how the body's boundaries are represented. But whosoever questions inequalities in the face of life and death also raises the serious issue of who truly owns the body. As discussed by Hannah Arendt and later Giorgio Agamben (1997, 1999, 2003), the casualties of globalized capitalism are seen in the useless bodies of those who have become superfluous, those who are too old to be productive, those who have been worn to the bone and who have lost a part of their lives working and producing wealth for others, and those who will die for lack of access to basic health care or treatments that are routine in wealthy nations. When they are left to their own devices, to their "biological fate" as it were, other bodies and body parts will simply be commoditized and sold on the market. Such is the reality of migrant workers, sex workers, child slaves, and child soldiers: who owns the body and can the body be converted into mere biological and energy matter to be used until death, not only through medicine, but also in a society that worships things? In the 1960s, feminists addressed the issue of the sovereignty of the body in the slogan "Our bodies, ourselves." They demanded the right to use their bodies and their reproductive abilities as they saw fit, thus rejecting the idea that biology is social destiny. That question must be taken up again and broadened. The productive and reproductive body should be of serious concern as we reflect on its dignity and on what we want it to be for the future of humanity (Bibeau 2004; Franklin and Lock 2003). On such matters, we should shirk neither humanism nor the search for justice (Farmer 2003; Fassin 2004; and articles in this book).

Intellectual property is a central issue for anthropological reflection and practice. Questions surrounding the ownership of the body are part of the broader issue of property over forms of life, which is a hotly debated topic in the field of biotechnologies. It is now becoming important in a less visible but equally sensitive area: local knowledge. In the past, the theme of intellectual property rights was not covered in research into the local knowledge of diverse medical systems studied by anthropologists, since it was considered natural and uncontroversial to study and describe cultures and knowledge in the name of making their contributions available to all as part of humanity's universal heritage. The anthropologist's task was to bring such knowledge to light, to have it recognized, and to make it part of academic understandings by defending the principles of diversity and legitimacy. Several factors have complicated this simplistic scenario: first, certain intellectual approaches, in particular postcolonialism (Ashcroft et al. 1995; Spivak 1999) and postmodernism, have loudly denounced the ways in which anthropologists "stole" cultural property and knowledge, reifying and reinventing them, delocalizing them and redirecting them towards various institutions such as museums. In the area of ethnomedical knowledge, plants were integrated into Western pharmacopoeias without local people receiving any compensation from the pharmaceutical companies that took the credit for "discovering" them. In many countries, such as Brazil, government and local authorities have become extremely concerned about biopiracy, fearing that their green heritage will be stolen from them, even though the scale of the problem remains difficult to assess. Debates are currently being held on the subject of opening the Amazon to researchers. Clearly, ethnomedical research can no longer be conducted without remaining aware of what is at stake when knowledge of life forms, which has been handed down and constantly enriched for generations, can be owned. If we are to question the ownership of the body in the face of biotechnology or the excesses of triumphant capitalism, in the perspective of a symmetrical and postcolonial anthropology, we must also re-examine our (anthropological) practices in terms of what is done with the knowledge gathered, as it too is knowledge of life forms.

From Illness to Suffering

Current research on the anthropology of social suffering, which was initiated by Arthur Kleinman, Veena Das, and Margaret Lock (Das et al. 2000, 2001; Kleinman et al. 1997), gives "illness" the potential status of social suffering. For many years pain was a subject of much debate: how are we to understand the connections between the biology of pain and the environment in which pain is experienced? Anthropologists had already made significant contributions to these debates. However, the notion of social suffering is something else entirely. Although several authors had emphasized that pain is not strictly biological and that it implies a moral suffering, the current theme of social suffering is not really related to earlier debates in anthropology on the connections between pain and suffering. The question currently being debated brings us back onto the terrain of "illness" as a category, of illness as an experience of suffering, and of the work of professionals who can potentially reduce an experience of suffering to (biological) illness, reify it and do violence to individuals by subjectivizing them in the role of a sick person with no history. It is interesting to note that it is medical anthropologists who have developed the field of the anthropology of suffering by questioning the various forms of structural, political, institutional, professional, and historical violence that produce various forms of suffering: sometimes distress, sometimes profound inequalities, and in a significant number of cases, illness.

This is not to say that "diseases" no longer exist as categories. Rather, this anthropological approach helps us to step back from medicocentrism by refusing to take medical categories and their various meanings as givens, by leaving more room for the loci and experiences of suffering, of which illness may or may not be an expression, and by redefining the boundaries of the political, corporeal, and subjective. The cut-off point between the macro and the micro is defined somewhat differently here than it is in a political economy approach to critical medical anthropology (*à la* Singer and Baer 1995). In this new approach to suffering, the hermeneutics of illness developed by an interpretative medical anthropology undergoes a series of mutations. Henceforth, it takes not illness, but subjectivity and its movements as the object of study (subjectivation and de-subjectivation). It explores experiences in their historical and existential depth, and not as the sole result of power relations between groups, although it does acknowledge that these exist. Regimes of historicity (Hartog 2003) are considered to produce social suffering. This new approach to suffering attempts to grasp different levels of construction, from the regime of historicity itself to the specific social relations it engenders and to the various mediations (such as the action and discourse of administrative, professional, and political agents) that categorize the experience (by pathology, by administrative unit, by ethnic group), thus dispossessing the subject of his or her power to speak and ability to act.

Social suffering is a not a new way to talk about illness; it is a tool for medical anthropology as it continues to put medical language into perspective and to find other ways of speaking about "diagnosis–disease treatment–recovery," which the anthropological categories of "disease classification–healing ritual–forms of healing" copy, and in so doing remain ensnared in medical rationality. Work on social suffering provides alternatives to the language of disease that do not simply add a little social into the pathological, but take suffering as a social phenomenon. Suffering no longer appears merely as a moralized and culturalized form of pain, and illness is viewed as a possible consequence of suffering (not simply its cause). As such, medical anthropology is to some extent becoming an anthropology of affliction that announces a new critical medical anthropology.

Right to Life and Social Justice

A series of shifts are demedicalizing medical anthropology: a shift in the boundaries of the medical realm, and the boundaries of the body, and a new perspective on the categories of medical system, disease, treatment, and healing. Medical anthropology is also being called on to work on scales that go far beyond the strictly therapeutic: without renouncing therapy groups, health-seeking behavior, medical systems, or healing rituals, medical anthropology is dealing with new realities that at times involve the infinitely small and the invisible in treatment practices (e.g. biotechnologies, trading on the gene market, and medical imaging), and at other times involve intercontinental realities such as multilateral organizations, corporations, transnational and humanitarian organizations (see the special issue of *Les temps modernes*, 2004). It also extends from the private, family, and domestic spheres of certain aspects of "lay" and local medicine to networks of researchers, activists, and patients, as is the case with AIDS.

Classical medical anthropology focused on the right for other forms of medicine to exist and be recognized as legitimate in the context of an economic and symbolic battle for the right to other forms of treatment and the recognition of alternative epistemologies (Saillant 1989; Saillant and O'Neill 1987). Now it would appear that the issue of other forms of care, while not completely obsolete, has been replaced by another concern, shared not only by many medical anthropologists but also by other categories of observers in civil society, international organizations, rights-based associations, and various disciplines. Medical issues have become easily associated with the issue of rights since many of the people studied by anthropologists live in conditions of extreme poverty. Researchers are therefore witness to a large array of deprivations that are all the less justifiable in so much as many of them are part of the multiple processes of colonization initiated by the West, the consequences of which are being felt in the form of violence and structural inequalities that lead to suffering and mental and physical illness.

In the 1970s, anthropologists were somewhat ambivalent concerning universal access to medical care, as it appeared to be yet another means for medicine and technique to colonize people who had already endured their share of colonization, to further undermine their cultures and their material and symbolic treasures. However, the question of universal access is being interpreted quite differently today. Several events have sounded the alarm and changed the consciousness of both local people and social scientists. The first is the AIDS scandal and the blatant inequalities in access to treatment, which are turning the disease into a genocidal risk in some parts of the world, particularly in the South and in Africa. Second, in the general atmosphere of neoliberalism, the harmful effects of decreases in public funds for health-care services in both the North and South, and which have a disproportionate effect on the poorest and most at risk, are obvious. The problem of access could therefore no longer be viewed as geographic, cultural, or economic, but as political and moral. The economic policies of multilateral organizations, and the ideology of governments who have adopted, or been forced to adopt, neo-liberal policies that have emptied social programs of their substance, have created new problems for entire social groups, the return of old epidemics such as tuberculosis, and the most pessimistic statistics on morbidity and mortality. Admittedly biomedicine is not the only remedy; rather, the issue is improving living conditions for all, and remembering that for some people the choice to save a life cannot be compared to the possibility of opting for one type of medicine or another. At the heart of this new anthropology in the making are the criticism of anthropology's strictly culturalist tropicalism, the ethical urgency of reflecting on health care for all, and the idea that some groups respond positively to what biomedicine has to offer, considering it important to save themselves and their loved ones, while preserving their zones of influence and resistance to that model.

Regional Expressions and Shared Concerns in Medical Anthropology

As we have seen, the medical anthropology of the 21st century lies at the crossroads of broader issues and changes in scale. In undertaking this project, we wagered on the originality of another shift away from seemingly central tradition: viewing medical anthropology through a broader variety of national and continental intellectual traditions. In fact, terms like national or continental traditions must be placed in context: science, including anthropology of course, is constructed with a universalistic perspective, but at the same time, it must rely on a "social demand for knowledge," which is often connected to national interests (Diasio 1999:26). We therefore felt that social phenomena as they unfold in the context of globalization could not be adequately understood unless the anthropological tradition was apprehended through the various components of its local expressions (Copans 2000), nor could the problems, theoretical trends, and methodologies used to interpret them be properly identified.

This explains why the book is divided into two main parts. The first part deals with medical anthropology in Canada, the United States, Brazil, and Mexico. Anthropology benefits from a long intellectual tradition in those four countries and this provided medical anthropology with favorable conditions to develop: leaders, genuine institutions, and sociolinguistic specific arenas. Medical anthropology in Canada is then examined in two complementary sections in Chapter 1. The first one (Section 1, Bibeau, Graham, and Fleising) deals with the rather limited unity of medical anthropology in the country, showing at the same time the present focus on biotechnologies and the leading role played here by anthropologists in Canada and elsewhere in the world. The second section focuses on the mainly francophone medical anthropology in Québec (Section 2, Massé), mixing together the intellectual traditions from France and the United States, and putting forward pragmatism and interdisciplinary researches. Next to this, Castro and Farmer (Chapter 2) give an overview of medical anthropology in the United States through authors and the main theoretical trends first, but also through programs, institutions, and journals. Medical anthropology in Brazil and Mexico (Chapters 3 and 4) complete this picture of this regional and continental space, opening on a plural and multilingual perspective of the subdiscipline (English, French, Spanish, and Portuguese). It could be noticed that our Brazilian colleagues are much inspired by the European tradition, due to the role played by some French scholars in the development of universities (Claude Lévi-Strauss and Roger Bastide being good examples of this). Representations of the body and the individual as subject have become central themes of the researches in Brazil. On their part, Mexican scholars draw much influence from Spain and the United States, but keep also a focus on applied anthropology and Aboriginal issues.

The second part of the book deals with the European traditions. Spain (Chapter 6, Comelles, Perdiguero, and Martinez-Hernáez), Italy (Chapter 7, Pandolfi and Bibeau), and France (Chapter 5, Fainzang) shed a clear light on the differences which exist between the various traditions in medical anthropology. It is worth noting that the deep intellectual roots of those countries partially explain why medical anthropology in the "latin" space grew up without any reference to medicine or public health over a long period of time, in a rather parallel mood from the English-speaking traditions. This specific orientation tends to increase with medical anthropology becoming more politically engaged (see Chapter 13 by Fassin) on the one hand, and to decrease through the many linkages with the English-speaking international science (see comments on that topic in Chapter 7,

Pandolfi and Bibeau). Chapters from Germany (Chapter 8, Wolf, Ecks, and Sommerfeld), from Switzerland (Chapter 11, Rossi), from Holland (Chapter 9, Van der Geest), and from Great Britain (Chapter 10, Frankenberg) open up on a remarkable variety of researches, institutions, and publications each year adding to an already huge corpus of local and international anthropological knowledge. All those articles give the reader a new look at medical anthropology since they all give the opportunity to go beyond the linguistic barriers to scientific knowledge. The chapter on the United Kingdom deals with various details on the building up of this local tradition; it shows both the solid link which exists between colleagues from this country and the United States and the many differences in their intellectual itineraries and networks.

The third part of this book, including the conclusion, gives the opportunity to look at medical anthropology from cross themes. Two of them stemmed from specific historical and social contexts, diffused on both continents, contributing to bring changes to the subdiscipline as a whole. The gender approach (Chapter 12, Browner and Sargent) gives information on feminists researches in the United States and Canada who first had an influence on European colleagues who had become more sensitive to these issues, namely in the "latin" countries. The chapter on the anthropology of life politics (Chapter 13, Fassin) which links Foucault's and, more recently, Agamben's works to the development of medical anthropology, goes the other way around. In that case, European works inspired the Foucauldian analyses in the Americas, North and South. Then, the conclusion (Margaret Lock), which comes as a counterpoint to this introduction, offers a genuine synthesis which helps read the history of medical anthropology from a new perspective, pinpointing elements of convergence, beyond its local expressions.

References

AGAMBEN G., 1997, Homo sacer I. Le pouvoir souverain et la vie nue. Paris: Seuil.

——, 1999, Homo sacer III, Ce qui reste d'Auschwitz. Paris: Rivages.

——, 2003, État d'exception, Homo Sacer II. Paris: Seuil, L'Ordre philosophique.

ASCROFT B., G. GRIFFITHS and H. TIFFIN, 1995, The Post-Colonial Studies Reader. Pp. 242–243. London: Routledge.

AUGÉ M., 1986, L'anthropologie de la maladie. L'Homme 26(1/2):81–90.

AUGÉ M. and C. HERZLICH, eds, 1984, Le sens du mal. Anthropologie, histoire, sociologie de la maladie. Paris: Éditions des Archives contemporaines.

BAER H. A., M. SINGER and I. SUSSER, 1997, Medical Anthropology and the World System. Westport: Bergin & Garvey.

BENOIST J., 1996, Soigner au pluriel. Essais sur le pluralisme médical. Paris: Karthala.

BIBEAU G., 2004, Le Québec transgénique. Montréal: Boréal.

BOURDIEU P., with the contribution of L. WACQUANT, 1992, Réponses. Pour une anthropologie réflexive. Paris: Seuil.

COLSON A. C. and K. E. SELBY, 1974, Medical Anthropology. Annual Review of Anthropology 3:245–262.

COPANS J., 2000, Mondialisation des terrains ou internationalisation des traditions dis-
ciplinaires? L'utopie d'une anthropologie sans frontières. Anthropologie et Sociétés
24(1):21–42.

CSORDAS T. J., 1994, Embodiment and Experience. The Existential Ground of Culture
and Self. Cambridge: Cambridge University Press.

——, 2002, Body/Meaning/Healing. New York: Palgrave Macmillan.

DAS V., A. KLEINMAN, P. RAMPHELE and P. REYNOLDS, 2000, Violence and Subjectivity, Berkeley: University of California Press.

DAS V., A. KLEINMAN, M. LOCK, M. RAMPHELE and P. REYNOLDS, 2001, Remaking
a World. Violence, Social Suffering and Recovery. Berkeley: University of California
Press.

DIASIO N., 1999, La science impure. Anthropologie et médecine en France, Grande-
Bretagne, Italie, Pays-Bas. Paris: PUF.

DREYFUS H. L. and P. RABINOW, eds, 1984, Beyond Structuralism and Hermeneutics,
Chicago: Chicago University Press.

EISENBERG L. and A. KLEINMAN, 1981, The Relevance of Social Science for Medicine.
Boston: Reidel.

EMBER C. R. and M. EMBER, eds, 2004, Encyclopedia of Medical Anthropology. 2 vol.
New York, Kluwer Academic/Plenum.

FABREGA H., 1972, Medical Anthropology. Biennial Review of Anthropology 167–229.

FARMER P., 2003, Pathologies of Power. Health, Human Rights and the New War on the
Poor. Berkeley: University of California Press.

——, 2004, An Anthropology of Structural Violence. Current Anthropology
45(3):305–325.

FASSIN D., 1996, L'espace politique de la santé: essai de généalogie. Paris: P.U.F.

——, 2000, Les enjeux politiques de la santé: études sénégalaises, équatoriennes et françaises. Paris: Karthala.

——, 2004, L'Afrique du Sud, de l'Apartheid au sida. Paris: Karthala.

FOSTER G. and B. ANDERSON, 1978, Medical Anthropology. Chichester, Sussex, UK:
Wiley & Sons.

FOUCAULT M., 1988 (1st edition 1963), Naissance de la clinique. Paris: Presses universitaires de France.

——, 2004, Naissance de la biopolitique. Paris: Seuil.

FOUCAULT M., D. DEFERT, F. EWALD and J. LAGRANGE, 2001a (1994 edition), Les
rapports de pouvoir passent à travers le corps. In Dits et écrits II, 1976–1988. Pp. 228–
236. Paris: Gallimard.

——, 2001b (1994 edition), Biohistoire et biopolitique. In Dits et écrits II, 1976–1988. Pp.
95–97. Paris: Gallimard.

——, 2001c (1994 edition), Naissance de la biopolitique. In Dits et écrits II, 1976–1988. Pp.
815–825. Paris: Gallimard.

FRANKLIN S. and M. LOCK, 2003, Remaking Life and Death: toward an Anthropology
of the Biosciences. Santa Fe: School of American Research Press.

HARTOG F., 2003, Régimes d'historicité. Paris: Seuil.

KLEINMAN A., 1988, The Illness Narratives: Suffering, Healing, and the Human Condition. New York: Basic Books.

KLEINMAN A., V. DAS and M. LOCK, 1997, Social Suffering. Berkeley: University of
California Press.

LE BRETON D., 1990, Anthropologie du corps et modernité. Paris: Presses universitaires
de France.

——, 1999, L'adieu au corps. Paris: Métailié.

LES TEMPS MODERNES, 2004, Special issue, L'humanitaire. (627) April–June:1–188.

LIEBAN R. W., 1973, Medical Anthropology. *In* Handbook of Social and Cultural Anthropology. J. Honigman, ed. Pp. 1031–1072. Chicago: Rand McNally.

LINDENBAUM S. and M. LOCK, 1993, Knowledge, Power and Practice: The Anthropology of Medicine and Everday Life. Berkeley: University of California Press.

LOCK M. M., 2002, Twice Dead: Organ Transplants and the Reinvention of Death. California Series in Public Anthropology. Berkeley: University of California Press.

LOGAN M. H. and E. E. HUNT, 1978, Health and the Human Condition: Perspectives on Medical Anthropology. Duxbury: Duxbury Press.

MARCUS G., 1995, Ethnography in/of the World System: the Emergence of Multi-Site Ethnography. Annual Review of Anthropology 24:95–117.

MCELROY A. and P. K. TOWNSEND, 1979, Medical Anthropology. Duxbury: Duxbury Press.

NICHTER M., 1989, Anthropology and International Health: South Asian Case Studies. London: Kluwer Academic Publishers.

OMS, 1978, Promotion et développement de la médecine traditionnelle. Report of an OMS meeting. Technical Report, 622. Genève.

PANDOLFI M., 2002, Moral Entrepreneurs, souverainetés mouvantes et barbelés. Le biopolitique dans les Balkans postcommunistes. Anthropologie et Sociétés 26(1):29–52.

RABINOW P., 1984, The Foucault Reader. New York: Pantheon Books.

SAILLANT F., 1989, Les thérapies douces au Québec: l'émergence d'une nouvelle culture thérapeutique. *In* Comprendre le recours aux médecines parallèles. M. Moulin, ed. Pp. 168–175. Centre de sociologie de la santé, Université Libre de Bruxelles.

——, 2003, Le mouvement des femmes, la transformation des systèmes de santé et l'enjeu des savoirs. *In* Transformations sociales, genre et santé. Perspectives critiques et comparatives. F. Saillant and M. Boulianne, eds. Pp. 263–282. Québec/Paris: PUL/L'Harmattan.

——, 2004, Constructivismes, Identités flexibles et communautés vulnérables. *In* Identités, vulnérabilités, communautés. Saillant F., Clément M. and Gaucher C., eds. Pp. 19–42. Québec: Nota Bene.

——, 2005, Corps, médiations, socialités. *In* Communautés et socialités. Pp. 169–186. F. Saillant and É. Gagnon, eds. Montréal: Liber.

SAILLANT F. and M. O'NEILL, 1987, Accoucher autrement. Repères historiques, sociaux et culturels sur la grossesse et l'accouchement au Québec. Montréal: St-Martin.

SARGENT C. and T. JOHNSON, 1996 (1st edition 1990), Medical Anthropology: Contemporary Theory and Method. Westport: Preager.

SCOTCH N. A., 1963, Medical Anthropology. Biennial Review of Anthropology 30–68.

SINGER M. and H. BAER, 1995, Critical Medical Anthropology. Amityville: Baywood.

SPIVAK G. C., 1999, A Critique of Postcolonial Reason. Routledge: New York.

VAN DER GEEST S., 1998, The Art of Medical Anthropology: Readings. Amsterdam: Het Spinhuis.

Part I

Perspectives from the Americas

Chapter 1

CANADA

Section 1

Bioscience and Biotechnology Under Ethnographic Surveillance: Where Do Canadian Medical Anthropologists Stand?

Gilles Bibeau, Janice E. Graham, and Usher Fleising

In a 1992 article on the "Practice of Medical Anthropology in Canada," Lock and Bibeau endeavored to assess the specificity of Canadian anthropology against the background of the identity of Canadian history and culture. They wrote:

> The persistence of fundamental debates in Canada around problems such as language, national identity, and multiculturalism have played a major role in supplying social scientists with specific themes for research, teaching, and social involvement. It should not come as a surprise that issues considered central in Canadian anthropology parallel those thought of as central to the country as a whole. It is true that there is no such thing as a genuine "Canadian" paradigm in contemporary anthropological theory, and this absence no doubt reflects the fact that Canadian anthropology shares the never ending, recurrent identity crisis characteristic of the Canadian society. (1992:150)

Lock and Bibeau highlighted the eclecticism, the multiplicity of topics, and the plurality of theoretical frames that one finds in Canadian anthropology. These features were viewed as a healthy sign of vitality and openness and proof that Canadian anthropology can adjust to the social topics that prevail at a given time in society. They concluded that Canadian anthropologists "sought to interpret discourses and actions with respect to medically related issues in social and cultural context" (1992:171). It is remarkable that all of the studies reviewed by Lock and Bibeau concentrated on Amerindian communities or immigrant groups in a multicultural Canada. However, topics of power, political action, and militancy were present and paved the way for the notions of biopolitics, biopower, and biosociality which are central to medical anthropology today.

These decades have been characterized as an intellectual era during which cultural, postcolonial, feminist, and multicultural studies generated a flush of creativity in the humanities and social sciences, particularly in anthropology. The "culture wars" of that era were an outcome of the introduction of cultural studies, gender issues, and postcolonial perspectives in the curricula of humanities and social science departments. Perhaps this was done out of ignorance of a distinctly anti-reductionist interpretation of culture by anthropologists. The word "culture" was then appropriated by scholars of numerous disciplines who redefined what they deemed to be an essentially static entity into a more dynamic and flexible concept for their own purposes. Despite such redefinitions, many progressive anthropologists have purged the use of the word "culture" from their vocabulary. And "science wars" have now succeeded those "culture wars": a new context has propelled "new" (biotechnologies, health, the environment, intellectual property, and privacy as it relates to the accessibility and merging of information in computerized databases) to the forefront of social, legal, and ethical debates.

Bioscience and biotechnology were not top priorities when Lock and Bibeau penned their overview, but by the late 1990s they drove debates in Canada. "Canadian Biotechnology Advisory Committee" reports issued in 1998 and 2001 illustrate the shift: experts were now recommending to the government to support the Canadian bioindustry, pushing Canada to develop more expertise in biotechnologies. Noting a new area for critical study, anthropologists have adjusted their research agendas, albeit with a more deeply structured critical analysis and a slower reaction than that of the bioethicists and lawyers who currently hold the lion's share of genomics research funding (Graham and Brunger 2003).

Until the early 1990s, Canadian medical anthropologists focused on patient groups. Their areas of study included: patient health-care-seeking behaviors and analysis of patient complaints; doctor–patient co-construction of explanatory models and treatments; the semantics of disease representations; and comparative medical systems.[1] Lock and Bibeau illustrated Anglo-Canadian directions by exploring how Patricia Kaufert and John O'Neil (1990a,b) studied obstetric conditions and informed consent among Inuit women on the west coast of Hudson Bay; how Linda Garro (1990) undertook research into the lay medical knowledge of the Ojibwa of Manitoba; how Naomi Adelson (2000) studied the cultural construction of the concept of health among the Cree of Northern Québec; how Joseph Kaufert and John O'Neil (1990a,b) reviewed the use of "cultural brokers" and "linguistic interpreters" in the Cree communities; and how Margaret Lock and Pamela Wakewich-Dunk (1990) interpreted the "propensity for somatization" among immigrant Greek women.

In this chapter, we have chosen to examine recent Anglo-Canadian practices by concentrating on the work of a few people, including the co-authors of this essay. This work centers on the political, economic, and commercial aspects of bioscience and biotechnology and their social, ethical, clinical, and philosophical dimensions. Our selection is deliberately biased to emphasize one of the most promising directions that the field of medical anthropology has recently taken.

To explore these developments, we have organized our chapter around the following four issues: (1) ethnographies of scientific cultures; (2) biosciences, markets, banking, and venture capital; (3) social and ethical issues of biobanks, technology assessment, clinical trials, regulation, and marketing of therapeutic (pharmaceutical, biologic, and genetic) products; (4) genetic testing, breast cancer genes, and clinics.

Ethnographies of Scientific Cultures

During the last two decades of the 20th century, anthropologists developed theories and concepts to map and critique contemporary societies, cultures, and technoscience. New anthropological approaches appear to be more attuned to the global restructuring of the world economy, to the increasing fusion of cultural horizons that are reorganizing Canadian cities along multicultural lines, and to the profound reshaping of our everyday life by bioscience and biotechnology. The so-called "third industrial revolution" (computer science, molecular biology, internet and communication systems) has transformed our world in association with neoliberal dogma, economic globalization, and the human rights agenda being imposed on all nations around the world. This "new world order" has generated an ideological discourse of legitimization, firstly in inventing biopolitical narratives anchored in our increasingly technologized world and secondly in universalizing an ethical regime based on Western values.

Social scientists have convincingly demonstrated that we live in a time in which "biopolitics" constitutes the key strategy utilized for the maintenance of post-industrial societies. "Biopower," a concept coined by Michel Foucault (1980) and reshaped by Giorgio Agamben (1997), is also central to our society, subjecting individual bodies and communities to sophisticated techniques of surveillance at the service of political control. A number of critical discourses propose alternative scenarios to the dominant paradigms: the quest for a less profit-oriented economy by antiglobalization organizations (Beck 2000); the engagement of society in its demand for more democratic participation; the critique of industries which create increasing risk for ecological systems and individuals (Brown 2001); the denunciation of the growing production of toxins, genetically engineered crops, and invasive biotechnological products. In these discourses, anthropologists have captured the uncertainties, contingencies, and ambiguities generated by our increasingly complex and controlling societies. Their writings address transnational companies, environmental movements, civil governance, NGOs, international organizations, the World Bank, human rights, democracy, war, and terrorism.

Biotechnologies seduce us with fantasies of the abolition of disease and the utopia of immortality. The rhetoric of biotech companies suggests strategies to discipline bodies and minds. Increasingly, organizations within society are demanding active governance and controls to establish transparency and public accountability for the strategies being advanced by technoscientists and owners of biotech firms. Anthropologists have accurately noted that our world has become much more intrusive, elusive, and controlling.

Without losing sight of clinical and scientific settings, the attention of Canadian medical anthropologists has turned toward a science studies approach. This is seen in their ethnographies of the production sites of bioscientific research and in their assessment of the impact of technoscientific commodities on the lives of people. Current ethnographies of biotechnology operate in a "set of third spaces" to use the analogy proposed by Michael Fischer (2003). Their terrains are complex and multiple, no longer restricted to dualisms of North/South, primitive/civilized, science/magic, raw/cooked. They concentrate on three main areas:

1   The ethnography of science laboratories, high-tech research firms and biotech-nological companies, involving interviews and participant-observation among research scientists and technicians working with high-tech instruments to manufacture science.

  This science studies approach is largely inspired by Bruno Latour, whose work, (with Stephen Woolgar) *Laboratory Life: the Social Construction of Scientific Facts* (1979), revised in 1986 when "social" was discarded from the title to make way for the wider, even more heterogeneous term, "performance of actors." This work was soon followed by historically situated ethnographies on topics such as the world of high-energy physics (Traweek 1988), proto-oncogene cancer research (Fujimura 1996), and clinical trials of interleukin 2 (Löwy 1996).

  To date, the most complete comparative ethnography of the international variations of the "cultures of technoscience" that we have at our disposal comes from our McGill colleague Margaret Lock (2002). In a remarkable study, she has demonstrated how the dominant values in Japanese and North American societies model the world of bioindustries in strikingly different ways. The study compared practices of organ transplantation, almost nonexistent in Japan but increasingly widespread in North America. Lock demonstrated how differences in determining the time of death presented a different configuration of the cultures of technoscience that prevail in North America in relation to those found in Japan: in attitudes regarding organ donation and their implantation in another body, in the establishing of boundaries between body and machine, and more broadly, in Japanese and North American representations of the person, life, and death. In her work, Lock stresses the Japanese refusal "to recognize brain death as the end of life"; their definition of death induces them to deny that technology penetrates into the space surrounding death.

  The "philosophy of life" that structures Japanese society penetrates their biotechnical practices to the core. This philosophy provides the ethical markers which allow them to judge both lawful and unlawful actions, sets the criteria which define the time of death, and determines, in the final analysis, the ambivalent relationships of how they regard organ donations and transplantations. The "techno-medical culture" that has developed in Japan, notably around death and organ transplantation, differs radically from what is found in North America; not for reasons of greater or lesser technological capacity but because different cultural values determine the uses a society makes of biotechnologies.

2 The ethnography of the complex connections that link biotechnological corporations, governments, universities, markets, banks, and venture capital.

Researchers have documented how the forces of capital make life-and-death decisions concerning high-tech companies, pushing them to compulsive commercial competitiveness in a sort of shell game where finance and corporate maneuvers matter more than the value of the company's portfolio. In disclosing the hidden connections between biotechnological research, government policy, and private interests, anthropologists have questioned the construction of the biopolitical order that controls groups and individuals in our society.

3 The ethnographic assessment of the cultural and ethical consequences for society and individuals of the massive deployment of biotechnologies and biosciences.

Medical anthropologists have testified, through the ethical dimension of their questioning, that we have entered a society in which the notion of risk has taken over (Douglas 1992) and must therefore be taken seriously (Beck 1992). Their ethical questions are many and vary in form and content from those of traditional philosophical and legal scholars: Who decides on and ultimately owns the biological information contained in biobanks? What is the meaning and effect of the structural sources of these inequalities? In what circumstance, and by whom, is genetic testing advocated, accessed, and applied? How do biotech companies establish the professional and public platforms and markets which allow them to do whatever is technically possible in the domain of reproductive technologies? In what ways do the public accommodate or resist the power of the biotech industries? What does informed public consent mean in the face of the media hype and the promises made by biotechnology companies? Do people realize and accept that science and technology construct the world differently compared to how people live and die?

Medical anthropologists are currently documenting what is happening in different scenarios: the recognition of patents on life-forms; the increased control of the female body at all stages of birth, reproduction, and menopause; the ill effects of medical technologies like genetic testing and pharmaceutical interventions (e.g., hormone replacement therapies, vaccination, and public health programs); the merging of venture capital, public funds, and private money to advance bioscience research; the blurring of boundaries between academic research and private laboratories; the efforts made by governmental agencies and private firms to contain debates over social and ethical issues related to biotechnologies; the drive of research toward marketable products; the marketing of unremarkable and undesirable products; the uncontained compulsivity of start-up companies in the *dot.com* world; the swallowing of small companies by larger firms that buy the development rights of future products.

Medical anthropologists are examining new kinds of contextually sensitive ethical dilemmas, turning their gaze to governance, research ethics, security, privacy and accuracy of data in biobanks, genetic and reproductive technologies, genetic testing and technology assessment, patents, genomics and genetic engineering, biotechnological commodities, configured diagnostic imaginaries, conflicts of interest, reliability issues related to pharmaceutical company-sponsored research, pharmaceutical rhetoric and publications, machine–human hybrids, xeno-transplantation, and pharmacogenomics. Their eyes pan the perceived rights of a plurality of societies, national, international and transnational interests, and the different avenues taken in attempting to regulate the emerging products of biotechnologies.

Biosciences, Market, and Venture Capital: Usher Fleising

At the Universities of Calgary, British Columbia and Dalhousie, research on the anthropology of biotechnology and new pharmaceuticals has been conducted in recent years under the leadership of Usher Fleising.[2] The purpose of the multisited project is to increase the understanding of the commercialization and regulation of new medicines in the context of rapidly developing scientific technologies. By exploring "the pipe" (the 10- to 13-year cycle and $400- to $800-million cost of moving from drug discovery to market approval), this study has probed the moral basis of profit by asking what it means when disease is defined as a "market opportunity." The research team is investigating the complex interrelationships between scientific, industrial, clinical and policy communities, as well as surveying the general population that must ultimately sanction and benefit from pharmaceuticals.

Attached to and complementing "the pipe" SSHRC project is a CIHR(Canadian Institutes of Health Research)-funded study on knowledge translation. The goal of this study is to increase understanding of the knowledge translation activities currently employed by health researchers and the cultural factors that condition these activities. The project borrows the concept of boundary objects from the SSST literature, mapping the cognitive domains that connect the bench to the bedside. Ideally, this information will serve as a foundation for larger scale inquiry into the differences between clinical science and basic research, and the common concepts that link these different fields together. Currently, they are narrowing their focus to how technological innovations from science (in the form of magnetic resonance imaging, MRI) are altering clinical practice, thus translating knowledge from physics and mathematics into patient care and medical research settings.

Fleising (2003) has used ethnohistorical reconstructions of social change on the Great Plains to demonstrate that the disruptive innovation of recombinant technology is also characterized by social and ideological continuity via processes of alliance formation and the distribution of authority. The distribution of authority is also a theme in his study of the organizational culture of biotechnology organizations. Fleising (2002) demonstrates that the founders of modern biotechnology companies, in an effort to avoid the demonization that was attached to the nuclear industry, delegated authority for regulatory negotiation and risk management to senior positions in their firms.

In a forthcoming publication on the culture of finance in biotechnology, Fleising (2005) examines the traffic between technologies (DNA-based medicine), the economic structures of production (the capital markets), and ideology (the culture of therapeutic intervention). His theoretical framework concentrates on the symbology of power and a meaning-centered representation of therapeutic intervention. "A symbology of power," writes Fleising, "is assigned to DNA and genetics both in the media and in scientific publications, where it is said that molecular and DNA-based medicine is how allopathic medicine will confront cancer, AIDS, Alzheimer's, genetic diseases and most other challenges to the body, including baldness, obesity and certain mental health problems" (2001a:239). The power symbol has been operationalized by adopting a sociopsychological definition for ideology derived from Geertz (1973). Therapeutic intervention provides the justifications which drive the financing of biotechnology in the capital markets of the United States. An examination of metaphor and rhetoric employed in the banking arenas where companies are displayed to potential investors shows how biotechnology exaggerates the societal tensions created by the boundary between the organic and the socio-moral.

Beginning with the question "where does medicine come from?" Fleising and colleagues locate (pharmaco)genomics within the corporate metaphor of the drug pipeline and describe the exchange relationship between biotechnology firms, the capital markets, and the pharmaceutical industry. In the finance model for the medical pipeline, disease is viewed as a market opportunity and medicine comes from a continuous cycle of deal flow. Framed in this way, the tendency for a firm to commodify (pharmaco)genomics is counterproductive in a market culture that is defined by the uncertainty of genomic science, the risk profile of a development industry, and an insatiable appetite for capital. A clean picture of the social arena and *habitus* produced at the intersection of body, technology, and (pharmaco)commodity must distinguish the science of genomics from the business of genomics. Market culture in genomics (including pharmacogenomics) is constantly reproduced through exchange relations that are highly vulnerable to uncertainty, risk, and change.

Usher Fleising's work on the social, economic and political dimensions of biotechnologies is highly innovative. In articles in *New Genetics and Society* (2001a), Fleising stresses two concepts, "genohype" and "genetic essentialism," to discuss the risks attached to the commercial objectives of biotechnological companies where DNA is considered a commodity. Fleising shows provocative insight concerning biotechnologies by taking the commercial and economic dimensions of the bio-industry seriously and by demonstrating how the merchandization of stockpiled body products has been prioritized in the hegemonic reductionist biological model.

Fleising's biosocial approach to biotechnologies (DNA as a commodity, genetic testing, property rights, and nuclear risks) is becoming more widespread in anthropological circles and has changed a number of common views on bioethics and health-care biotechnology. His timely work demonstrates the risks attached to the dominant reductionistic frame currently used in genomic companies, which overemphasize the genetic aspects (genohype) of health problems. Fleising's research places him among the most prestigious biosocially grounded specialists who are studying the expanding field of genetics and DNA-based medicine. The research model he advocates is based on solid evidence that connects genotype to phenotype (genetic signatures with the living and environmental conditions of individuals), and laboratory activities with the commercialization of genetics. Fleising's critical stance has been worked out as a reaction to two dominant paradigms, namely the "deterministic approach in genetics" that dominates North American DNA companies and the "market model" which is at the very core of research activities in genetics.

According to Fleising, the objective of biotechnology companies is clear: to manufacture marketable, innovative and competitive products. It is thus easily understood why anything resembling a "discovery" is immediately turned into a media event. These days, companies apparently have no other choice, if they are to survive, than to keep up with the ratings from an applauding press. Their part in the market depends on it, government support defers to it, and bank credit and capital risk adjusts to it.

Anthropologists have pointed out that bioscience is caught between the triumphalist discourses of the large laboratories and their star researchers, and a society eager to hear that science is responding to the challenge of medicine. Biotechnology ethnographers are showing how the ideological genetic rhetoric opportunely serves the purposes of ambitious bioentrepreneurs, bankers, and politicians. Financial logic leads them to seize these simplistically inflated discourses by arbitrarily putting the genome at the center of biology and dictating the political orientation of the research. Bioscience has always been, and still is, a matter of research; and for some time now, it has also been a matter of marketing. More recently, it has become an affair of state and international commercial competition. Research and development in the biotechnology industry is more than ever inundated by political, economic, commercial and legal considerations.

Cultural–Ethical Issues of Biobanks and the Regulating and Marketing of Therapeutic Products: Janice Graham

Janice Graham[3] takes a science studies approach to aging, dementia and cognitive impairment, diagnostic imaginaries, databases as cultural texts, and the technological assessment of emerging therapies. Her research explores the cultural relations and technologies used by scientists, industry, government regulators, and policy-makers in the evaluation and regulation of pharmaceuticals, biologics and genetic therapies.[4] Graham has turned her gaze toward the creation, effectiveness, and marketing of purportedly *therapeutic* product. Her doctoral research, examining dementia diagnostics and the databases where epidemiological and clinical information are stored, was carried out in a genetic epidemiology laboratory in Montreal as it made the transition from a university-based research group to a dot.com biotechnology company.

Her initial interest in the formation of the subdiagnoses of dementia (Graham et al. 1996a, 1996b) led to postdoctoral work in geriatric medicine and neuroepidemiology (Graham et al. 1997, 1999), and later to an examination of the technologies of critical appraisal and treatment assessment in industry-sponsored clinical trials and pharmaceutical research (Graham 2003a). Driven by an interest in the expectations and effects of treatment for people affected by dementia, she developed qualitative clinimetric ethnographic techniques to assess individually defined symptoms. This interest was critically triggered when the techniques developed were later used to show "improvements" and to further market drugs whose actual efficacy was less than convincing (Graham et al. 2000, Graham 2001b).

Clinical trials are largely funded by the pharmaceutical industry. Medical journals continue to devote entire issues to industry-sponsored research results, whose consistently positive findings foreshadow hope for record sales to large markets. Potential treatments for dementia, which affected some 8% of Canadians aged 65 and over during the 1990s, could well be assigned to the wider diagnostic category (and market) of cognitive impairment, affecting 25% of seniors (Graham et al. 1997). As public support declined, clinician-researchers were encouraged to meet directly with industry to form university–industry and public–private research partnerships. While evidence mounts that these social relationships are fraught with conflicting interests, the research results have claimed special space in key journals and remain largely uncontested. These results, with carefully designed recruitment strategies, innovative methodological approaches and sophisticated, if sometimes enigmatic, biostatistical analytical wizardry, safely speed these drugs through regulatory approval (Graham 2003a).

Graham had developed an ethnographically sensitive, patient- and caregiver-centered approach to assess treatment effects, taking into consideration the everyday life and social world of those affected by an illness. However, this approach was used to promote sufferers' expectations and, consequently, drug sales, rather than treat the original symptoms which marked the illness. In the meantime, the language and superficially exercised practice of determining "qualitatively meaningful treatments" has moved into clinical trial research design and drug company marketing rhetoric (Graham 2001b). But how do these questionable therapies get market approval?

Graham is currently studying efficacy in scientific regulatory practices and policy, where she explores the complex interrelations between science, industry, government, and policy stakeholders. This research questions the moral basis of profit and the cultural meanings of disease in the life history of pharmaceuticals and biologics. To this end, she has been conducting fieldwork in the Biologics and Genetic Therapies Directorate at Health Canada to examine the approval process and evidence based knowledge used to evaluate and regulate pharmaceuticals, biologics, and emerging genetic therapies. Her ethnography of the regulatory cultures and moral encounters involved in evaluating the safety, efficacy and quality of new and emerging products in Health Canada's regulatory directorates follows teams of research scientists, biologists, medical officers, and technicians, equipped with state-of-the-art technologies and instrumentation, as they liaise with industry sponsors, policy analysts, and bureaucrats to tweak basic science in response to regulatory needs. Scientists, clinical evaluators, and bureaucratic advisors review submissions, sample consistency, conduct often extensive chemistry and manufacturing confirmatory tests, balance legislated deadlines with partial data, and public health needs with public and industry desires.

Substances approaching the porous walls between science and society, culture and nature, human and nonhuman, industry and government are weighed, scaled, and assayed into existence. Whether pharmaceuticals or biologics in origin, these substances are translated and transformed into everyday life-soothing market products, or negotiated and clarifaxed into withdrawal. Graham attempts to articulate the complex scientific, commercial and political processes involved in the regulation of pharmaceuticals, biologics, and genetic therapies at Health Canada. In the process, she encounters the management of risk-benefits and the rhetoric of openness, transparency, and accountability in an atmosphere of increased industry–university–government research partnerships actively being promoted by the new Canadian Institutes of Health Research (CIHR) and Health Canada. Issues of conflict of interest among clinician-scientists funded by industry have arisen frequently and have been extensively covered in major medical journals over the past two years.

While there is a growing critique of the relationships between research, universities, and industry that raises ethical flags, and while the work of John Abraham in the UK has examined European pharmaceutical regulation, Graham's work stands alone in anthropological studies that examine the regulatory process using an ethnographic approach within the actual regulatory system.

The balancing of social and health risks with economic benefits as well as the increasing role of risk assessment and issue management in the regulation of novel therapeutic products requires careful ethnographic inquiry. Graham's work examines the strategic management of the multiple stakeholder interests in the practice of public policy decisions. How is the precautionary principle evoked and how is the science that is meant to ensure safety, quality and efficacy of therapeutic products used to arrive at these decisions? The role of the expert has long been contested in the anthropological literature, where the long-term effectiveness of local pragmatic knowledge may be favorable to a sustainable community. The degree of uncertainty among scientific experts may well be similar to that of the general public. How do the relationships among the safe, effective, moral and profitable aspects of these issues play out when individuals expect health and safety, when communities expect jobs and livelihoods, and when shareholders expect profit? In strategically directing profit-driven research, the role of the Canadian government, and in particular, Industry Canada and the funding agencies, does not go uncontested.

Graham and Brunger (2003) examined the ethical, cultural and social aspects of Genome Canada, which received $300 million from the Canadian government to develop and implement a national strategy in genomics and proteomics research for the benefit of all Canadians. Encouraged to foster public–private partnerships, the five genome centers established across Canada have a mandate to ensure that

Canada becomes a world leader in genomic research. Research includes agriculture, bioinformatics, environment, fisheries, forestry, health and technology development. Following the Ethics Legal and Social Issues (ELSI) initiative at the National Institutes of Health in the United States, Genome Canada also supports research projects aimed at studying and analyzing the ethical, environmental, economic, legal, and social issues related to genomic research (GE3LS). But how critical can these studies be in light of the mandate and funding source from Industry Canada? "Can risky technology be stopped?" asks Graham.

Margaret Everett provides an excellent overview of how the attempt to transform genes into commodities bore witness to the complex building of legal arguments and precedents surrounding property rights. She highlights conflicts of interest which arise, and how interest groups self-servingly exploit individualized informed consent by using the argument of presumed consent in order to maximize the catchment group. These databases can then be sold to biotechnology companies. Both sides may differentially use arguments whereby body parts – organs, genes, and blood seen as metaphors for individual property rights – serve to fragment and objectify the body and cause these interest groups to arrive at somewhat contradictory impasses. Everett (2003) makes clear that there is a "cultural resistance to turning [body] parts into marketable products" despite the drive to establish economic value for those parts.

Genetic Testing, Breast Cancer Genes, and Clinics: Patricia Kaufert

In an era where the culture of science is being questioned by the scientists themselves, a "deep cultural ambivalence" that arises with the commodification and commercialization of the body and disease and its treatment by emerging therapies has been noted by social scientists in the United Kingdom, United States, and Canada, who have been examining the new genetics (Kaufert 2000a; Kerr and Cunningham-Burley 2000; Everett 2003; Glassner and Rothman 2001). As Rapp (1999:37) argues, "choice is market driven" and various tactics are used by an aggressive industry to institute presumed consent, from direct to consumer advertising (Mintzes et al. 2002) to Big Pharma co-opting of patient advocacy groups (Batt 1994, 2002).

Recent developments in biotechnology have generated a new reality in which a multitude of diverse body products, genes, blood, gametes, and tissue are extracted from humans, linked to medical files and family pedigrees, and stored away in biocollections. Within the frame of their genetic-based research on illness, university laboratories, geno-proteomic research companies, as well as biotechnological companies have created new commodities: genealogies; individual genetic records/ cards containing SNPs(single nucleotide polymorphisms) and haplotypes; typical genomes collected from those suffering from the same illness; regional and national genomes.

Biotechnologies comprise a large range of techniques, practices, and products which are increasingly thought of as actual merchandise. The unconventional nature of these new objects of exchange has led jurists to redefine the ownership rights of all that affects living organisms, of the derivatives of living organisms, of all types of biocollections, and of techniques and practices used in modifying or creating products. Products found mainly in the health, pharmaceutical, food, cosmetic and environment sectors have been patented by biotechnology companies in order to guarantee their rights. It will doubtless be difficult to avoid the growing merchandizing of stockpiled products however much researchers are opposed to the genetic essentialism of more complex biological models.

Patricia Kaufert worked in women's health issues including menopause, midwifery, and mammography. In the late 1990s she turned to health policy with particular emphasis on genetic testing for hereditary breast cancer. Sharing a concern for how reproductive and genetic technologies affect women's health, Kaufert is a member of the Working Group on Women and the New Genetics, an offshoot of the National Network on Environments and Women's Health (NNEWH). They address research needs and provide policy advice related to federal government initiatives. Kaufert's feminist activism is underscored in both her own activities (Kaufert and Kaufert 1996; Goel et al. 1998; Mustard et al. 1998; Kaufert 2000a, 2004b) and in the edited volume *Pragmatic Women and Body Politics* (Lock and Kaufert 1998). She recognizes that issues of consent, commercialization, patenting, insurance, equity, access, and justice raised by new genetics are not of interest to the public health and epidemiology communities (Kaufert 2000b). In the 1990s she endeavored to raise "a lot of questions" and awareness, if not "an alarm bell," in the social science community (Kaufert 2004b), holding that a "new language" and new methodologies are needed. As with Rapp, at the core of this work is a grounding of the individual's experiences of biotechnologies (Kaufert 2000b). Kaufert, however, also evaluates the importance of other forms of information such as the statistics and epidemiological and public health data used by policy-makers.

For Kaufert, the exclusion of vulnerable women from the decision-making process in the new genetic models, at the same time that their disembodied bodies are tested without the available technological capacity to determine penetrance or susceptibility, is a problem. Who has control and who has access to health-care technologies for screening? Testing and treatment remain critical issues, as are the differential costs and benefits to the public and private sectors. Kaufert highlights how the debates surrounding the interests of insurance companies in genetic data and their insistence on the right to select who can and cannot be insured, link medicine, law, and commerce in US society, creating "an ideal set up for an analysis of power and politics" (2000b:827). Knowledge and money together drive biotechnology. While Kaufert suggests that "the health insurance industry is probably the most difficult to target" (2000b:828) for anthropologists, we would argue that the multinational pharmaceutical industry, with its countless subsidiaries and their researchers creating their own research data, likely prove more illusive than does the insurance sector.

Risk issues arise when emerging products with potentially enormous social and health consequences enter the Canadian regulatory system. While risks are often linked with health and safety, there are also social and ethical risks associated with less stringent controls for treatment efficacy and effectiveness. In a society with publicly funded health services, should technologies with limited benefit be regulated in the same way as those with more widespread benefits? As the potential for targeting known molecular structures is now upon us, new drug submissions, specific to a few but accessible to even fewer, may well escalate. High cost individual therapies, instead of population-based approaches, may attract greater venture capital for their R&D and find their way to regulatory approval faster. How are risks assessed in regulatory submissions? How are they anticipated in policy-making? And more importantly, how can unforeseen risks be managed when the regulatory doors are opened to novel therapies and new technologies, as they must be in a TRIP- (Trade-Related Aspects of Intellectual Property rights) enforced global free trade environment? Can and should risk be managed? How do the uncertainties that define a risk fluctuate under the constraints of stakeholder inequalities, biopower, marginalized knowledge, and varying interpretations (Lock 1998; Sjöberg 2002)?

Conclusion: the "Rainbow Colors" of Canadian Medical Anthropology

Whether or not they use the language explicitly, most medical anthropologists have been "community-based," working among groups who have been coping with mobilities, often associated with "the other." There is no doubt that shared knowledge directs successful grant-writing, as new avenues for funding social science health research have opened up with the passing of the *Canadian Institutes of Health Research Act* in 2000.[5] This act "encourages interdisciplinary, integrative health research."

While there has been understandable resistance by anthropologists to uncritically adopt the language of CIHR (e.g., "community-based research," "vulnerable populations," and "social inequalities,"), those doing so have found funding for their projects. While CIHR works through its transition from the Medical Research Council, which had a decidedly biomedical and bench-science focus, it is developing a common language, albeit painfully, that will accommodate the critical work of anthropology.

The significance and usefulness of the work by medical anthropologists in wider projects examining the social determinants of health is, perhaps, more obvious to those in biomedicine. As a result, over the past several years, many medical anthropologists are finding homes outside of traditional anthropology departments in faculties of medicine embracing interdisciplinary approaches, and in community, public health, epidemiology, and bioethics programs. Combined with interdisciplinary and women's studies programs and psychology departments, a majority of

Canada's medical anthropologists have primary appointments outside of anthropology departments. The slowness of many anthropology departments to respond to the legitimacy of the ethnographic examination of scientific cultures should be a cause for reflection.

Canadian medical anthropologists working in the previously outlined fields are still, like their American colleagues (Marcus 1995a, 1995b; DelVecchio Good 1995; Rabinow 1996, 1999; Fischer 2001, 2003; Young 1995; Rapp 1999), using ethnographic fieldwork and case studies as their primary tools. They utilize techniques of multilocal or multisited ethnography (Marcus 1995a, 1995b, 1998) and the techniques of multivocality in order to elicit the voices of the different actors, both the dominant and the oppressed. The critical approaches provided by Foucault, Bourdieu and Agamben are at the core of the ethnographic accounts produced by Canadian scholars, particularly among those who study the changing relations between state, academia, bank and market, the conflicts of interest between partners in biotechnologies and life sciences, and the complexities of power structures and commercial alliances.

They study the positions taken for and against genetic testing, as well as those whose interests are actually served. They follow the public funding of research activities undertaken by private companies and the types of results obtained when private funding supports evidence-based medicine. Anthropologists tend to link their examination of the many ethical debates that take place in society to biopolitics and biosocialities and to various forms of cultural critique. Anthropologists are often perceived as ethical agents, sometimes as subversive militants; in most cases they are acute observers of the social scene and tools of the nature-cultures in which ethical dilemmas take place. The positioning of anthropological work is contrasted with a normative ethics that is mired in the canonical principles of philosophers and legal scholars. Anthropologists engage a critical social science studies approach to science and biotechnology that respects both structural global political economies and locally sited instantiations of accommodation and resistance.

We think the key characteristics of the practice of medical anthropology in Canada may be summarized as follows. Canadian anthropologists show an increasing taste for the critique of past social theories and have also embarked on the construction of cultural, postcolonial and critical theories in which the concepts of biopolitics, biopower, and biosocialities dominate. Canadian medical anthropologists practice their profession using a community-based applied model that incorporates an action-geared perspective with some militancy and a strong commitment to social justice and bioethics (this may reflect the sociopolitical aspect of the Canadian identity). They develop and provide both conceptual and methodological tools to help articulate their critique of biotechnology with institutions at work in society. Over the past decade, authors have become more ready to consider themselves as genuine "actors" involved in the scientific environments which they describe in their writing of ethnographies. It is also intriguing to see how the use of personal anecdotes and case histories engage the reader in issues with larger stakes.

Notes

1. See Allan Young (1982) for an excellent identification of the main topics studied in classic medical anthropology.
2. The project involves coinvestigations with the University of British Columbia (Michael Burgess, Center for Applied Ethics) and Dalhousie University (Janice Graham, Bioethics and Anthropology), and collaboration with the University of Alberta (Tim Caulfield, Health Law).
3. Graham holds a research chair in bioethics in the Faculty of Medicine at Dalhousie University. She held an endowed research chair in medical anthropology at the University of British Columbia (1998–2002) and a CIHR New Investigator award. Her recruitment to a Canada research chair in bioethics at Dalhousie continues a trend among Canadian medical anthropologists who leave anthropology departments for faculties of medicine and health sciences.
4. Two doctoral students working with Graham at Dalhousie are engaged in cutting edge SSHRC- and CIHR-funded ethnographies of bioscience that focus on the regulation of scientific practices. Christina Holmes' (2003) multi-sited ethnography explores the cultural process of agricultural biotechnology by asking how, why, and by whom the scientific development of genetically engineered plants is influenced in developed and developing countries. Working at Health Canada and at international crop centers, Holmes studies how scientific and technological development interacts with trends in science, scientific goals, scientific funding, the social construction of society's needs, and trade imperatives and restrictions. Sharon Batt examines the ethical and policy issues arising from the pharmaceutical industry funding of patient advocacy groups. Drawing from personal experience as a former breast cancer patient who spent 15 years engaged in patient advocacy, Batt (1994, 2002) witnessed how patient advocacy organizations become heavily funded by the pharmaceutical industry, raising conflict-of-interest questions.
5. http://www.parl.gc.ca/36/2/parlbus/chambus/house/bills/government/C-13/C-13_4/90094bE.html#1, accessed February 4, 2004.

References

ADELSON N., 2000, Being Alive Well: Health and the Politics of Cree Well-Being. Toronto: University of Toronto Press.
AGAMBEN G., 1997, Homo Sacer 1. Le pouvoir souverain et la vie nue. Paris: Seuil.
BANQUE MONDIALE, 2002, Global Economic Prospects and The Developing Countries. Washington: Banque Mondiale.
BATT S., 1994, Patient No More: The Politics of Breast Cancer. Charlottetown: Gynergy Books. Published simultaneously in the UK – London: Scarlet Press. Australia and New Zealand edition – Melbourne, Spinifex, 1996. French translation: 1998, À bout de patience: les enjeux de la lute au cancer du sein. Montreal: Remue-ménage.
——, 2002, Perfect People: Cancer Charities. In Women and Health: Power, Technology, Inequality and Conflict in a Gendered World. K. Strother Ratcliff, ed. Pp. 57–74. Boston: Allyn and Bacon.
BECK U., 2000, What is Globalization? London: Blackwell. (Original in German, 1997.)

——, 1992, Risk Society: Towards a New Modernity. Thousands Oaks, CA: Sage. (Original in German, 1986.)

BIBEAU G., 2004, Le Québec transgénique. Science, marché, humanité. Montréal: Boréal.

BROWN O., 2001, Transnational Companies in the Global Economy. Oxford: Oxfam.

DELVECCHIO GOOD M.-J., 1995, Cultural Studies of Biomedicine: An Agenda for Research. Social Science and Medicine 41(4):461–473.

DOUGLAS M., 1992, Risk and Blame: Essays in Cultural Theory. London: Routledge.

EVERETT M., 2003, The Social Life of Genes: Privacy, Property and the New Genetics. Social Science and Medicine 56(1):53–65.

FISCHER M. M. J., 2001, Ethnographic Critique and Technoscientific Narratives: The Old Mole, Ethical Plateaux, and the Governance of Emergent Biosocial Polities. Culture, Medicine and Psychiatry 25:355–393.

——, 2003, Emerging Forms of Life and the Anthropological Voice. Durham, NC: Duke University Press.

FLEISING U., 2001a, In Search of Genohype: A Content Analysis of Biotechnology Company Documents, New Genetics and Society 20(3):239–254.

——, 2001b, Genetic Essentialism. Mana and the Meaning of the Body. New Genetics and Society 20(1):43–57.

——, 2002, The Legacy of Nuclear Risk and the Founder Effect in Biotechnology Organizations. Trends in Biotechnology 20(4):156–159.

——, 2003, The Horse and the Molecule: Reflections on Biotechnology and Social Change. International Journal of Biotechnology 5(2):57–169.

——, 2005, From Bank to Bench to Pharmacy Shelf: Biotechnology and the Culture of Finance. *In* Proceedings Crossing Over: Genomics in the Public Arena. E. Einsiedel, ed. Kananaskis, Alberta, April, 25–27. Calgary: University of Calgary Press.

FOUCAULT M., 1980, Power/Knowledge. New York: Pantheon.

FUJIMURA J. H., 1996, Crafting Science: A Sociohistory of the Quest for the Genetics of Cancer. Cambridge, MA: Harvard University Press.

GARRO L., 1990, Continuity and Change: The Interpretation of Illness in an Anishinaabe (Ojibway) Community. Culture, Medicine and Psychiatry 14:417–454.

GEERTZ C., 1973, The Interpretation of Cultures: Selected Essays. New York: Basic Books.

GLASSNER P. and H. ROTHMAN, 2001, New Genetics, New Ethics? Globalization and Its Discontents. Health, Risk and Society 3(3):245–259.

GODBOUT M. and P. L'ARCHEVÊQUE, 2001, Science et éthique. Protéger la recherche en génomique, Le Devoir. décembre, 17.

GOEL V., M. COHEN, P. KAUFERT et al., 1998, Assessing the Extent of Contamination in the Canadian National Breast Screening Study. American Journal of Preventive Medicine 15(3):206–211.

GRAHAM J. E., 2001a, Harbinger of Hope or Commodity Fetishism: Re-cognizing Dementia in an Age of Therapeutic Agents. International Psychogeriatrics 13(2): 131–134.

——, 2001b, If Meaning Counted: Measuring E/Affect in Antidementia Therapies. Gerontologist 47(suppl. 1): 572–573.

——, 2003a, Anthropology of Biotechnology and Pharmaceuticals. Humankind/Nature Interaction: Past, Present, Future. Florence, Italy: International Union of Anthropological and Ethnological Sciences (IUAES).

——, 2003b, Creating Hope and Commodifying Disease: Redefining Dementia. International Psychogeriatrics 15(suppl. 2): 90–91.

GRAHAM J. E., K. ROCKWOOD, B. L. BEATTIE, I. MCDOWELL, M. R. EASTWOOD and S. GAUTHIER, 1996a, Standardization of the Diagnosis of Dementia in the Canadian Study of Health and Aging. Neuroepidemiology 15:246–256.

GRAHAM J. E., A. B. MITNITSKI, A. J. MOGILNER, D. GAUVREAU and K. ROCKWOOD, 1996b, Symptoms and Signs in Dementia: Synergy and Antagonism. Dementia 7: 331–335.

GRAHAM J. E., K. ROCKWOOD, B. L. BEATTIE, R. EASTWOOD, S. GAUTHIER, H. TUOKKO and I. MCDOWELL, 1997, Prevalence and Severity of Cognitive Impairment with and without Dementia in an Elderly Population. Lancet 349:1793–1796.

GRAHAM J. E., A. B. MITNITSKI, A. J. MOGILNER and K. ROCKWOOD, 1999, The Dynamics of Cognitive Aging: Distinguishing Functional Age and Disease from Chronological Age in a Population. American Journal of Epidemiology 150(10):1045-1054.

GRAHAM J. E., R. BASSETT and K. STADNYK, 2000, A Twist of the Prism: Family and Clinical Measures of Alzheimer's Disease Treatment. Neurobiology of Aging 21(1S):S91.

GRAHAM J. E. and F. BRUNGER, 2003, *Examining the Ethical, Cultural and Social of Genome Canada.* Joint conference of the Canadian Anthropology Society and the Society for Anthropology in North America. Halifax, Nova Scotia.

HOLMES C., 2003, Hazarding the Knowledge Maize: Expert Knowledge and Risk in the Controversy over Transgenic Food Genome, Canada GELS Symposium, Montreal.

KAUFERT P., 2000a, Screening the Body: The Pap Smear and the Mammogram. *In* Living and Working with the New Medical Technologies. M. Lock, A. Young and A. Cambrosio, eds, Pp. 165–183. Cambridge: Cambridge University Press.

——, 2000b, Health Policy and the New Genetics. Social Science and Medicine 51(6):821–829.

——, 2004a, From the Laboratory to the Clinic: The Story of Genetic Testing for Hereditary Breast Cancer, in Penny Van Esterik (Ed), Head, Heart and Hand. Partnerships for Women's Health in Canadian Environments. Toronto, Ontario: National Network on Environments and Women's Health.

——, 2004b, Belling the Cat: Learning to Know (But Not Necessarily Trust) the New Genetics, http://www.cwhn.ca/groups/biotech/availdocs/3-kaufert.pdf, accessed February 10, 2004.

KAUFERT P.A. and J. M. KAUFERT, 1996, Anthropology and Technoscience Studies: Prospects for Synthesis and Ambiguity. Medical Anthropology Quarterly 10(4): 686–690.

KAUFERT P. and J. O'NEIL, 1990a, Cooptation and Control: The Reconstruction of Inuit Birth. Medical Anthropology Quarterly 4:427–442.

KAUFERT J. and J. O'NEIL, 1990b, Biomedical Rituals and Informed Consent: Native Canadians and the Negotiation of Clinical. *In* Social perspectives on Medical Ethics. G. Weisz, ed. Pp. 41–63. Philadelphia: University of Pennsylvania Press.

KERR A. and S. CUNNINGHAM-BURLEY, 2000, On Ambivalence and Risk: Reflexive Modernity and the New Human Genetics. Sociology 34(2):283–304.

LATOUR B. and S. WOOLGAR, 1986, Laboratory Life: The Social Construction of Scientific Facts. Princeton, NJ: Princeton University Press (1979 Beverly Hills, CA: Sage Publications).

LEEMING W., 1999, Medical Specialization and Medical Genetics in Canada (1947 and After). Unpublished doctoral dissertation, York University, Canada.

LOCK M., 1998, Breast Cancer: Reading the Omens. Anthropology Today 14(4):7–16.

——, 2002, Twice Dead. Organ Transplants and the Reinvention of Death. Berkeley: University of California Press.

LOCK M. and G. BIBEAU, 1992, Healthy Disputes: Some Reflections on the Practice of Medical Anthropology in Canada. Health and Canadian Society/Santé et société canadienne HCS/SSC 1(1):147–175.

LOCK M. and P. KAUFERT, eds, 1998, Pragmatic Women and Body Politics. Cambridge: Cambridge University Press.

LOCK M. and P. WAKEWICH-DUNK, 1990, Nerves and Nostalgia: Expression of Loss Among Immigrants in Montreal. Canadian Family Physician 36:253–258.

LÖWY I., 1996, Between Bench and Bedside. Cambridge, MA: Harvard University Press.

MARCUS G., 1995a, Technoscientific Imaginaries: Conversations, Profiles, Memoirs. Late Editions 2. Chicago: University of Chicago Press.

——, 1995b, Ethnography in/of the World System: The Emergence of Multisited Ethnography. *In* Annual Review of Anthropology. W. Durham, E.V. Daniel, and B. Schieffelin, eds. Pp. 95–117. Palo Alto: Annual Reviews.

——, 1998, Ethnography Through Thick and Thin. Princeton NJ: Princeton University Press.

MINTZES B., M. L. BARER, R. L. KRAVITZ, A. KAZANJIAN, K. BASSETT, J. LEXCHIN, R. G. EVANS, R. PAN and S. A. MARION, 2002, Influence of Direct to Consumer Pharmaceutical Advertising and Patients' Requests on Prescribing Decisions: Two Site Cross Sectional Survey. British Medical Journal 324:278–279.

MUSTARD C. A., P. KAUFERT, A. KOZYRSKYJ et al., 1998, Sex Differences in the Use of Health Care Services. New England Journal of Medicine 338:1678–1683.

RABINOW P., 1996, Making PCR. Chicago: University of Chicago Press.

——, 1999, French DNA. Chicago: University of Chicago Press.

RAEL., 2004, Welcome to the Realian Revolution. Electronic document, http://www.rael.org/, accessed February 4, 2004.

RAPP R., 1999, Testing Women, Testing the Fetus: the Social Impact of Amniocentesis in America. New York: Routledge.

SJÖBERG L., 2002, The Allegedly Simple Structure of Experts' Risk Perception: An Urban Legend in Risk Research. Science, Technology and Human Values 27(4):443–459.

SOKAL A., 1996, Transgressing the Boundaries. Social Text 46/47:217–252.

TRAWEEK S., 1988, Beamtimes and Lifetimes. Cambridge, MA: Harvard University Press.

YOUNG A., 1982, The Anthropologies of Illness and Sickness. Annual Review of Anthropology 11:257–285.

——, 1995, The Harmony of Illusions. Inventing Post-Traumatic Stress Disorder. Princeton, NJ: Princeton University Press.

Further reading

BELMONT REPORT ORGANISATION MONDIALE DE LA SANTÉ (OMS), 1997, Proposed International Guidelines on Ethical Issues in Medical Genetics and Genetic Services, Genève. Electronic document, http://www.who/gl/eth/98, accessed February 7, 2004.

BOURDIEU P., 2001, Science de la science et réflexivité. Paris: Éditions Raisons d'agir.

CANADIAN BIOTECHNOLOGY ADVISORY COMMITTEE, 2004. Electronic document, http://cbac-cccb.ca/epic/internet/incbac-cccb.nsf/vwapj/F448_IC_CBAC_Annual_E.pdf/$FILE/F448_IC_CBAC_Annual_E.pdf, accessed February 7, 2004.

COMITÉ CONSULTATIF CANADIEN DE LA BIOTECHNOLOGIE (CCCB), 1998, Assumer le leadership au prochain millénaire. Ottawa, Industrie Canada, Electronic document, http://www.cbac.cccb.ca, accessed February 7, 2004.

COMITÉ CONSULTATIF CANADIEN DE LA BIOTECHNOLOGIE (CCCB), 1998, Assumer le leadership au prochain millénaire. Ottawa, Industrie Canada, Electronic document, http://www.cbac.cccb.ca, accessed February 7, 2004.

——, 2002, Brevetabilité des formes de vie supérieures et enjeux connexes. Ottawa, Industrie Canada. Electronic document, http://www.cbac.cccb.ca, accessed February 7, 2004.

COMITÉ D'ÉTHIQUE DE HUGO, 1999, Déclaration relative aux principes devant guider la conduite en matière de recherche génétique, Les Cahiers du Comité consultatif national d'éthique, 24, avril.

EVANS ROBERT G., M. L. BARER and T. R. MARMOR, eds, 1994, Why are Some People Healthy and Others Not? The Determinants of Health in Populations. New York: Aldine de Gruyter.

FLEISING U. and A. SMART, 1993, The Development of Property Rights in Biotechnology. Culture, Medicine and Psychiatry 17(1):43–57.

FOUCAULT M., 1966, Les mots et les choses. Archéologie des sciences humaines. Paris: Gallimard. (Translation: The Order of Things. New York: Pantheon, 1970.)

FRANKLIN S. and M. LOCK, eds, 2003, Remaking Life and Death: Toward an Anthropology of the Biosciences. Santa Fe: School of American Research.

GLASS K. C. and J. KAUFERT, eds, 2001, Continuing The Dialogue: Genetic Research with Aboriginal Individuals and Communities. Vancouver: National Council on Ethics in Human Research.

GOVERNMENT OF CANADA, 2001, A Canadian perspective on the precautionary approach/principle. Discussion Document. Electronic document, http://www.pco-bcp.gc.ca/raoics-srdc/docs/Precaution/Discussion/discussion_e.pdf, accessed February 10, 2004.

HOEKMAN B. and M. KOSTECKI, 1995, The Political Economy of the World Trading System: From GATT to WTO. Oxford: Oxford University Press.

KELLER E. F., 2000, The Century of the Gene. Cambridge, MA: Harvard University Press.

KNOPPERS B. M., ed., 1998, Socio-Ethical Issues in Human Genetics. Cowansville: Les Éditions Yvon Blais.

LIPPMAN A., 1992, Prenatal Genetic Testing and Screening: Constructing Needs and Reinforcing Inequities. American Journal of Law and Medicine 17:15–50.

LOCK M., 1993, Encounters with Aging: Mythologies of Menopause in Japan and North America. Berkeley: University of California Press.

LOCK M. and P. KAUFERT, 2002, Menopause, Local Biologies, and Cultures of Aging. American Journal of Human Biology 13:494–504.

LOCK M., A. YOUNG and A. CAMBROSIO, eds, 2000, Living and Working with the New Medical Technologies. Intersections of Inquiry. Cambridge: Cambridge University Press.

MASSÉ R., 2000, Les limites d'une approche essentialiste des ethnoéthiques. Pour un relativisme éthique critique. Anthropologie et Sociétés 24(2):13–30.

NATIONAL COMMISSION FOR THE PROTECTION OF HUMAN SUBJECTS ON BIOMEDICAL AND BEHAVIOURAL RESEARCH, 1978, Belmont Report (French translation: 1982, Le rapport Belmont. Les Cahiers de bioéthique 4:232–250. Québec, Les Presses de l'Université Laval).

ORGANISATION MONDIALE DU COMMERCE, 1994, Accord sur les aspects des droits de propriété intellectuelle qui touchent au commerce: annex 1 C of Accord de Marrakech instituant l'Organisation mondiale du commerce, Marrakech. Electronic document, http://www.wto.org/indexfr.htm, accessed February 7, 2004.

REID R. and S. TRAWEEK, eds, 2000, Doing Science + Culture. New York: Routledge.

ROCK M., 2002, Sweet Blood and Power: Making Diabetics Count. Ph.D. thesis, Anthropology Department, Montreal, McGill University.

ROSS R. A., 2001, The Raelians. Electronic document, http://www.rickross.com/groups/raelians.html, accessed February 4, 2004.

STRATHERN M., 1992, Reproducing the Future: Essays on Anthropology, Kinship and the New Reproductive Technologies. New York: Routledge.

UNESCO, 1997, Déclaration universelle sur le génome humain et les droits de l'homme, Paris: 11 novembre. Electronic document, http://www.unesco.org/ibe/fr/genome/projet, accessed February 7, 2004.

WILLIAMS-JONES B. and J. E. GRAHAM, 2003, Actor-network Theory: A Tool to Support Ethical Analysis of Commercial Genetic Testing. New Genetics and Society 22(3): 271–296.

WORKING GROUP ON WOMEN'S HEALTH AND THE NEW GENETICS, 1999, Shifting Connections: A Report on Emerging Federal Policy Relating to Women's Health, The New Genetics and Biotechnology. Electronic document, http://www.cwhn.ca/groups/biotech/availdocs/macintosh.PDF, accessed February 10, 2004.

Chapter 1

CANADA

Section 2

The Anthropology of Health in Québec: Toward a Blending of Approaches and Methods

Raymond Massé

The anthropology of health holds a special place within Québec anthropology. Its development has been fostered by collaborations that French-speaking anthropologists have developed with their English-speaking colleagues in Québec, but also with American and English Canadian Anglo-Saxon anthropology. Most likely some unique features have emerged from both traditions, perhaps less in the research topics than in the theoretical and methodological approaches. The goal here is not to highlight these specificities; however, as we will see, much of the research done by French-speaking anthropologists has been colored by their interest in semiotics, phenomenology, and European hermeneutics.

This text cannot do justice to all of the Québec anthropologists who have carried out research on issues related to illness and health. Instead, our aim will be to identify some of the main threads running through (in particular the interest in transcultural psychiatry) and some contemporary research topics. We will also highlight Québec's contributions to broader theoretical debates (Genest 1978), such as those related to the tension between violence and asceticism in interpretative anthropology, or to the risk of decontextualization in a critical anthropology of diagnostic categories. Anthropology's contributions to public health and to a research practice in which qualitative and quantitative methods complement each other also are original. The importance of these last two points is related to the focus on applying concepts and research findings to planning and programming among Québec anthropologists of health. Québec anthropology is marked by its openness to transdisciplinary collaborations not only with the medical world and with public health, but also with community groups. This chapter concludes with some thoughts on the dangers of medicalizing the anthropology of health.

Brief History of Medical Anthropology in Québec

In two texts that present an exhaustive review of the research on the social and cultural dimensions of health and illness, Marc-Adélard Tremblay (1982, 1983) dates the first research to the 1960s and 1970s. In the 1950s, Tremblay was associated with the work on mental health conducted by Alexander H. Leighton's team in Nova Scotia. Starting at the beginning of the 1960s, Tremblay contributed directly to the beginnings of medical anthropology in Québec through his teaching and research at Laval University. During the 1960s, researchers from the universities of Montréal and Laval, but most of all McGill, carried out a series of studies on sociocultural epidemiology and psychological disorders. At the time, research focused mainly on forest workers and First Nations communities, but also on comparing the nature and causes of mental illness in French- and English-speaking communities in Québec from a transcultural psychiatry perspective (Murphy 1974). At the beginning of the 1980s, a new field of research opened up under the influence of anthropologists interested in women's health issues (De Koninck et al. 1981; De Koninck and Saillant 1981; Saillant 1985). Other fields of research from that pioneering period included the social living conditions of the ill, health professionals, social representations of health and illness, sociocultural epidemiology, and education and prevention. Prevention and health promotion have been some of the most significant areas to which the anthropology of health has been applied in Québec. At the same time, beginning in the early 1970s, anthropologists were being hired by some of the new health institutions (regional health and social services centers, local community health centers, community health departments), paving the way for interdisciplinary collaborations. However, Tremblay (1982) drew attention to the fact that Québec anthropologists were not very interested in analyzing how health institutions work and how patients feel about health care. Although the former is still largely understudied, some people have taken an interest in how immigrant populations (Bibeau 1992), refugees (Rousseau 2000), and Aboriginal communities (Roy 2002) view health-care services.

Research activities in the anthropology of health have mainly gravitated around the dynamic *Groupe Interuniversitaire de Recherche en Anthropologie Médicale et en Ethnopsychiatrie* (GIRAME). The group was formed in response to a need for dialogue expressed by researchers from various disciplines involved in the *Transcultural Psychiatric Research Review* that Eric Wittkower founded at McGill University in 1956. The interdisciplinary review not only gained an international reputation in transcultural psychiatry, but also fostered dialogue between medicine, psychiatry, psychology, and anthropology. From 1974 to 1983, a total of 89 monthly seminars were organized with a steadily increasing number of participants. The journal *Santé, Culture, Health* (which was first published as the *Bulletin d'information en anthropologie médicale et en psychiatrie transculturelle*) played a major role in the development of the anthropology of health as one of the field's leading journals. Until 1994, when it was discontinued, it was a channel for the motivations of a generation of anthropologists interested in the field of health.

Current Research Themes

Before discussing the key themes of public health and the sociocultural construction of psychiatric diagnostic categories, I will illustrate the wide diversity of fields of interest among Québec anthropologists with a few examples.

The Anthropology of Illness

Many researchers have focused on AIDS. In a recent issue of *Anthropologie et Sociétés* (1991) co-edited by Gilles Bibeau and Ruth Murbach, the authors review research on the social, cultural, legal, and political dimensions of AIDS. They approach HIV status as a litmus test of the contradictions in the discourse of professionals and ordinary people that make certain social subgroups into scapegoats. The reflection broadens to include inequalities in access to antiretroviral drugs in developing countries, leading to a critical review of how the anthropology of health has helped to question the classical theories used to explain the cause and effect relationship between socioeconomic inequalities and people's health (Nguyen and Peschard 2003). The authors show how AIDS fosters the emergence of new forms of sociability through the interfaces between social and biomedical changes in a global context.

Some authors are exploring some very innovative lines of thinking in addition to classical approaches to risk factors for AIDS (Godin et al. 2002). For instance, Joseph Lévy is interested in the cultural aspects of homosexual and bisexual relations connected with the transmission of AIDS and other STDs. He has an original approach to high-risk sexual practices, exploring sexual "scenarios." This is an example of multidisciplinary collaboration (involving anthropologists, philosophers, public health doctors, and community workers) in analyzing how vulnerable groups view HIV–AIDS and prevention programs. But Lévy goes furthest off the beaten track in his work with Alexis Nouss (Lévy and Nouss 1994) on how AIDS is portrayed in American and French novels. In an interesting example of how narrative analysis and the ethnology of illness can be combined, they depart from the empirical approach to research, instead doing what they call "novelistic anthropology," which goes straight to the heart of the multiple meanings of illness in its connections to death, sex, and text, often doing this better than empirical research can.

Still in the area of physical illness, Francine Saillant's work on the anthropology of cancer in Québec (1988, 1990b) is one of the first systematic applications of interpretative anthropology concepts such as explanatory models and semantic networks of illness. Her work is another good example of Québec anthropology's concern with combining a subtle analysis of the meaning of illness and a phenomenology that is respectful of the day-to-day experience of illness both in the overall society and on hospital oncology wards. The author blends the semiotics of cancer and the construction of meaning both in biography and in the wider society where mythical heroes do battle with this symbol of death. The critical constructivist perspective later found in Lock's work on menopause (1993) and, more recently, Roy's research (2002) on diabetes in First Nations communities was only just being sketched out at the time.

Bioethics and Anthropology

As the social sciences are being increasingly called on to contribute to debates on bioethics, various colleagues have begun reflecting on the sociocultural dimensions of the values and principles that guide North American bioethics. Leigh Turner (1998) has formulated an anthropological and sociological critique of bioethics and is currently editing an anthology on methods and theories in bioethics. Lock's work on organ transplantation and brain death (2002) as well as Bibeau's work on the genome (2003) tackle the ethical issues raised by new biotechnologies. In an issue of the journal *Anthropologie et Sociétés* on anthropology's contribution to bioethics, Massé (2000) invited various colleagues to discuss the topic, particularly through the concept of cultural relativism. Anthropologists in Québec have taken an interest not only in curative biomedicine, but also in the issues raised by prevention and health promotion programs. Out of a concern for a public health ethics that is sensitive to the many different values found among target populations, Massé (2003) identifies a variety of emerging ethical issues related to social labeling, discrimination, and the abuse of power that comes out of conflicts opposing the dominant values of public health institutions to "popular" values widely shared in the population. He proposes a model for identifying and analyzing such issues based on the dominant values in contemporary society and the notion of common morality. A sensitivity to cultural and ethnic realities and a concern for contextualizing moral worlds are at the heart of his model.

Anthropology and Humanitarian Aid

Humanitarian aid is also approached from two angles. First, some studies focus on the connections between refugees' migratory experiences and their mental health. Rousseau has focused specifically on women refugees who have been victims of violence (Atlani and Rousseau 2000) and on humanitarian (particularly medical) assistance in the context of international violence towards women and children (Rousseau 2000). Going beyond the simple analysis of risk and protection factors related to mental disorders and school achievement, Rousseau et al. provide information to government authorities on how service needs vary from one ethnic group to another, questioning the relevance of the prevention policies and strategies implemented by schools and by the health system for immigrants as a whole. In the Québec "tradition," these studies are conducted in close collaboration with those concerned and with public institutions, in particular with "issues tables." In a more critical perspective, Québec anthropology has more recently approached humanitarian assistance as a form of interference by Northern nations in world governance via transnational NGOs who have often given their allegiance to financial power holders (International Monetary Fund) and the UN (Pandolfi 2002). In reference to Brazilian and Québec NGOs, Saillant and Paumier (2003) and Saillant et al. (2005) have analyzed the discourse of humanitarian organizations working with handicapped persons and refugees. They suggest that the world of humanitarian aid is a plural, polysemic, heterogeneous field with different stakes and definitions depending on the actors, organizations, and locations.

Anthropology, Home Caregivers, and Home Care

The anthropological view of caregiving focuses in part on noninstitutional practices. Saillant (1999) has encouraged anthropology to turn its attention to an anthropology of home care in the context of medical pluralism and the combination of a wide range of nurturing practices, including informal practices in the domestic sector generally considered to be women's work. An issue of *Anthropologie et Sociétés* (1999) edited by Saillant and Gagnon argues for an anthropology of caregiving, not as a subdiscipline of anthropology, but as a new path for exploring individuality, alterity, gender relations, and new forms of sociality. Of particular interest are the everyday experience of caregivers, spouses, children, and other relatives who provide day-to-day care to persons with illnesses living at home (Gagnon and Saillant 2000), and the ways in which social norms influence caregivers' views of responsibility. Inspired by the theories of responsibility developed by Ricoeur and Lévinas, as well as by a feminist reading of "reproductive work," the authors present a nuanced analysis of the construction of responsibility toward sick relatives that interweaves notions of emotional attachment, choice, and duty. Their analyses of home care among community organization workers (Gagnon and Saillant 2000) are a springboard for more in-depth reflections on changes in social ties in modern societies characterized by professionalized and institutionalized care. This anthropological perspective on the complementary services provided by a host of "intermediary" organizations (social economy businesses, volunteer community groups, users' cooperatives, etc.) – which are characterized by proximity with the sick, the eradication of hierarchical relations, mutual aid, generosity, and the rejection of professional neutrality – raises the issue of what role these new forms of sociality and mutual assistance play in the management of vulnerable groups made all the more fragile by transformations in social ties within couples, families, and neighborhoods. An anthropology of health cannot overlook these reconfigurations in the relationships between dependent persons and communities (Saillant and Gagnon 2001).

A quick overview of the field would not be complete without reference to the work done on alternative therapies (Rousseau et al. 1990; Saillant et al. 1990), on lay medicine among Québec families in the early-20th century (Saillant 1990a), on the sociocultural construction of physical handicaps (Fougeyrollas 1995), and on ethnomedicine, which were the object of a stimulating issue of *Anthropologie et Sociétés* edited by Saillant and Genest (1990).

A Rich Collaboration with Public Health

The anthropology of health in Québec has been particularly open to developing constructive collaborations with the world of biomedicine. Research in public health has played a key role in such encounters. Work environments have been receptive to anthropologists, and many now work in local community service centers (CLSCs), regional public health departments (DRSPs), organizations that manage workplace health and safety, Québec youth centers, and even the ministry of health and social services. Several university anthropologists have also fostered dialogue by carrying out research with some of these institutions. Such collaborations now cover the overall population, going far beyond the specific issues raised by First Nations and immigrants, which are more classical topics for anthropologists to study. Examples include work on adapting public health programs to Montréal's multiethnic reality (Gravel and Battaglini 2000), work among the Inuit on issues such as childbirth and ear infections (Dufour 1988, 1989), work on the sociocultural causes for mental disorders in remote regions (Corin et al. 1990), and the ethnoepidemiology of psychological distress (Massé 1999).

However, it is important not to idealize such collaborations. The task has generally been extremely difficult; the rift between the two fields in both epistemology (empiricism versus interpretivism, prediction versus explaining behavior) and methods (qualitative versus quantitative), as well as the resolutely critical discourse of anthropologists with regards to the categories, concepts, and theoretical models of preventive medicine, all constitute barriers to communication. In addition, some anthropologists (Bibeau 1997) believe that in North America at least, collaborations with public health may distort the anthropological approach (we will come back to this point later). Nonetheless, the encounter has played a key role in developing an anthropology of health that strives to overcome oppositions between fundamental and applied research, qualitative and quantitative methods, academic circles, and public institutions.

Anthropology's contribution to prevention and health promotion was summarized in a book by Massé (1995). It is based on several empirical studies and defends the idea that high-risk behavior is rooted in the social practices and culture of the populations targeted by public health programs. The author suggests that since people's health is clearly influenced by culture and social relations, public health must cooperate with the social sciences, including anthropology, as they are the disciplines best able to decode sociocultural factors. The theoretical concepts and methodological approaches put forward by the anthropology of health are essential. The concepts of lay knowledge, networks of meaning, explanatory models of illness, illness behavior, and illness narratives, among others, are highly relevant for grasping the meaning people give to sickness, symptoms, high-risk behavior, and even preventive interventions themselves. In summary, anthropology has succeeded in raising awareness within public health circles regarding multiethnic realities, community aspects, local knowledge, and the need for a contextualized approach to high-risk behavior (Bibeau 1997).

This interest in public health and its research questions and methods does not however mean that anthropologists endorse a medicalization of the anthropology of health. Bibeau (1997), for example, deplores the fact that some anthropologists working in public health neglect their training as fieldworkers and adopt the rationalist models of epidemiology and the economics of health and their prediction models of health behavior without the necessary critical distance. We can only reiterate his warning that anthropologists who uncritically adopt the work agenda, epistemological postulates, and methodologies prevalent in public health, risk encouraging a medicalization of the discipline. Through its analysis of how behavior is rooted in beliefs, values, and ideologies, anthropology must counteract the commoditization of behavior prediction models that simplify the factors determining high-risk behavior to the extreme (in a cognitivist and behavioralist framework) (Bibeau 1997:250). We have also reiterated warnings about naïvely adopting psychosocial models for predicting high-risk behavior (Massé 1995).

In particular, anthropology has denounced the simplistic use of the notion of rationality on which prevention models in public health are based. Allan Young (1981) made an important theoretical contribution when he pointed out that rationalized knowledge is only one manifestation of lay knowledge, which also includes prototypical, empirical, intersubjective, and other types of knowledge. There is a large noncognitive space between popular explanations for illness that individuals construct logically and coherently, and the cognitive structures that are assumed to have guided such constructions. If we ignore that, we fall into a textualization that leads us to believe that illness narratives are the exact reflection of the language structures of a given culture. Some authors have continued such critical reflections on public health interventions, suggesting that we recognize the coexistence of many different logics of knowledge and rationalities regarding health behavior (Massé 1997), that the postulate of rationality in public health practices results in oversimplification (Bibeau 1997), and that it is important to acknowledge the twists and turns of reason in any semiotics of illness (Corin 1993). This critique of rationality leads Young to underline the dangers of equating explanatory models of illness with cognitive models reified with explanatory beliefs for illness, and with individual models that are projected onto the entire population targeted by prevention or health promotion programs (Young 1990).

Bibeau is no less radical in his criticism of the liaison between anthropology and public health, pointing out that:

Despite their declared intention to break with the dominant public health models, most anthropologists are not really willing to distance themselves from the methodology and theorizing of what is perceived as "real" science in public health: survey questionnaires; focused studies of specific health problems such as tuberculosis, diarrhea, malaria, and so on; quantitative analyses and probability statements of causality; and theories represented as models. (Bibeau 1997:247)

He suggests that medical anthropologists must take their critiques further rather than "deliberately refuse to question the foundations of the public health enterprise as it exists in developing countries" (Bibeau:247). This criticism seems too radical to be applied to anthropologists employed by public health institutions who must deal with the constraints of multidisciplinarity. Here, the object of criticism is a demonized public health system. In our view, anthropology can only truly contribute to public health if anthropologists drop their knee-jerk reflex of approaching public health as a means for subjugating people to political, medical, and economic powers, and to globalization.

On the other hand, anthropologists must remain critical of the political, ideological, and economic ways prevention programs are used. We cannot debate the issue any further here for lack of space; suffice it to say that in Québec, the tradition of cooperation between anthropologists and public health stimulates much debate over the difference between collaborating "with" public health (which leaves more leeway and more space for independent and critical thinking), and collaborating "in" public health (which implies integrating the methods and goals of public health, but not abdicating criticism).

A Concern for a Complementary Use of Qualitative and Quantitative Methodologies

In Québec, the theoretical reflection and critical questioning of medicine's categories and epistemology are generally based on empirical research combining classical ethnographic methods and quantitative methods. Most researchers have divided their work between empirical research along the lines of sociocultural epidemiology, using quantitative methods (random samples, questionnaires, standardized measurement tools, statistical analyses, etc.), and theoretical reflections inspired by critical anthropology. They generally maintain a specifically anthropological analysis of the interfaces between the meanings of illness and care practices, and continue their own field research. This assertion is worth illustrating with a few examples.

In her critical work on menopause in Japan, Lock (1993) combined quantitative and qualitative approaches, blending classical fieldwork with a more epidemiological type of survey. The data collection techniques she used included group interviews, individual interviews, excerpts from life histories, documentary analysis, and closed questionnaires with 1,316 Japanese women regarding menopausal symptoms. The combination of methodologies was intended not only to provide a cross-cultural basis for comparing the symptoms associated with menopause, but also to analyze the contradictions between the subjective experience described by Japanese women and the ideologies communicated by the media and physicians regarding menopause.

Most of the work by Cécile Rousseau (e.g., Rousseau et al. 2000, 2001) on mental health among refugees is empirical, comparing immigrants from different ethnic groups. In several studies, Corin has combined statistical analyses with hermeneutical and phenomenological approaches. In her research on the lived world of schizophrenics, Corin (1990) used data from standardized measures on social connections with qualitative analyses based on observations and repeat research interviews. She too is interested in studying to what extent methods that in the end are partially incommensurable may complement each other. In his research on the experience and expression of psychological distress in Québec, Massé (1999) shares the same concern with combining the quantitative analysis of closed questionnaires with phenomenological, hermeneutical, and semantic analyses. In order to identify how episodes of psychological distress are manifested cognitively, physically, emotionally, and behaviorally, he carried out an ethnosemantic analysis of accounts given by Quebeckers. This phenomenological approach was then combined with a process of designing and validating epidemiological tools for measuring distress in the overall population.

This predisposal to combining quantitative and qualitative methodologies is not without controversy. Based on an analysis that opposes quantitative methods and "real anthropology," sometimes a bit radically, certain authors claim that the cohabitation between ethnographic and quantitative methods risks distorting the anthropological approach (Lock and Bibeau 1993).

An Anthropology of Health that Blends Hermeneutics with Phenomenology and Ethnographic Contextualization

One of the main trends in the anthropology of health in Québec is its openness to mixed approaches marked by a concern for ethnographic contextualization. Ellen Corin's work on the social and institutional integration of schizophrenics (1990) is a perfect illustration of that trend. She draws both on phenomenology, which focuses on the analysis of the "specific lived worlds" of the ill, and on critical anthropology's concern with the sociocultural construction of such disorders. As in the study she codirected on mental health in northwestern Québec (Corin et al. 1990), here too she combines an anthropological approach to the construction of meaning, Ricoeur's hermeneutics, and European psychiatric phenomenology that explores ways of being in the world. This hybrid approach takes her beyond the analysis of the predictors of the revolving door syndrome; her objective is to understand from the inside the new forms of sociality that psychiatric patients develop. Anthropologists must not subordinate their research to a normative, decontextualized definition of what might constitute an acceptable form of social integration for patients, or a "good" treatment outcome. The patients speak for themselves; they define their sociability as "general," meaning that it involves a dose of strategic social withdrawal varying in intensity and in nature from one former psychiatric patient to another, and according to their everyday needs and their respective tolerance for social pressure created by "normal" sociability. Research shows that the difference between patients who are not re-admitted to hospital and those who are is that the former are better able to remove themselves socially; this "positive withdrawal" is a protective factor. The latter experience isolation as a form of imposed social "exclusion" whereas the former experience it as a form of detachment that they seek out, welcome, and accept. Corin speaks of this "social withdrawal" as an icon of people's social isolation in Western societies (Corin 1990:183). She argues for an anthropology that strives to grasp this "thick-ness of being" (Corin 1998c) among the ill through their experiences, their identity strategies, and the ways they manage their relationship to sociability. This concern for an anthropology that remains attentive to the context and meaning of the illness experience must not be confined to theoretical reflections; it must be expressed through empirical studies that draw on a variety of different methodologies.

A Concern for Balance between Asceticism and Violence of Interpretation

A criticism of the excesses of textualist approaches is partly responsible for the fact that Québec anthropologists take care to analyze the meaning of illness in context; over the past two decades, these approaches have tended to reduce culture to a text, and the interpretations of illness and caregiving practices to "sub-texts." When drawing on hermeneutics and the construction of meaning, culture must be ana-lyzed in constant tension between an inevitable interpretative violence and a true concern for an ascetic reading of culture as text, as Bibeau and Corin (1995) con-vincingly argued in a classic text. Anthropology's uniqueness lies in this "dialectics of proximity and distance, submission and violence" (Bibeau and Corin 1995:5). Consequently, when anthropological methods imitate textualist analyses, it can only bring discredit to the discipline. Culture is not the equivalent of a series of texts. We must defend a credible and reliable interpretative anthropology in which anthropologists retain an optimal distance between experience and discourse, between context and meaning. Intersubjectivity is not only in the heads of indi-viduals; it exists in collective, social, and community practices. The authors give as an example their study on mental health in rural Québec to illustrate a "con-textual semiotic interpretation" that shows that "popular models used in the three milieus [forest, mining and farming communities] for identifying, explaining and reacting to mental health problems cannot be understood independently of the social context of each of the three subcultures and the specific value system that prevails in it" (Bibeau and Corin 1995:41). They highlight the specificity of the three "systems of signs, meanings and actions" for each case. French-speaking anthropologists in Québec clearly are interested in combining hermeneutics, semantics, and ethnography in order to grasp the meaning behind locally situated social practices. The community is therefore more than the place to which information belongs, more than the far-off context; it is a true coauthor that participates in the interpretative enterprise.

Constructivism, Deconstructivism, and Diagnostic Categories

Medical anthropology is no longer concerned only with the descriptive analysis of therapeutic knowledge and practices in various ethnomedicines, but more radically "the focus is shifted to the way in which all knowledge relating to the body, health, and illness is culturally constructed, negotiated, and renegotiated in a dynamic process through time and space" (Lock and Bibeau 1993:149). In other words, it takes an interest in decision-making, medical praxis in its interrelations with patients and society, and especially, the ways in which the values and interests of physicians and researchers shape how illness is defined. Medical anthropology has taken this role very seriously, in particular with respect to diagnostic categories.

Lock (1993), for example, shows that beyond the physiological reality of the end of menstruations, menopause is a historically situated social, cultural, and professional construction. Menopause appears to be influenced by the cultural conceptions of women's social roles (in particular, during the middle and end of their reproductive lives), by the economic consequences of menopause, and by national policies on aging. Similar questions have been asked regarding the definition of brain death and the debates on how to determine the moment of death for the purpose of organ transplants (Lock 1989). Following an analysis of the positions of North American and Japanese nurses and doctors, Lock (2000a) deplores the fact that European and American societies have accepted the concept of brain death without any real debate, unlike Japan which opposed it in 1997 (Lock 2000b). She refers to this as a form of "cultural anesthesia" that is encouraged by the fact that such debates are "well masked by the persuasive metaphors about saving lives associated with the transplant industry" (Lock 2000a:238). Through such work, anthropology has been able to question why organ transplantations are not authorized on vegetative patients, even though they too no longer have any conscious life (Lock 2000a:259).

Critical constructivism has, however, been applied mainly to the field of mental health. In an issue of *Transcultural Psychiatry* on the relationship between culture and the DSM IV, Kirmayer (1998) asked various authors to discuss to what extent the editors of the *Diagnostic and Statistic Manual* are able to take the suggestions of the *Culture and Diagnostic* working group into consideration. In a harsh editorial, Kirmayer denounced their inability to consider culture's influence on the incidence and prevalence of health problems, the limits to the universality of diagnostic categories, and the ways in which symptoms are expressed through local idioms. His critical approach is echoed by Corin's research (1996) on the variations in diagnostic boundaries, by Kirmayer and Young's work (1998) on how culture influences the somatic manifestations of mental disorders, and how the notion "mental disorders" is constructed, in particular, anxiety disorders (Kirmayer 1994;

Kirmayer et al. 1996), and by the sociocultural construction of post-traumatic stress (Young 1995a). Yet culture clearly influences not only the ways in which symptoms are expressed, but also health-seeking processes, ways of communicating suffering, and the way in which the sufferer and his or her relatives understand and interpret the symptoms.

Allan Young's work (1995b, 2000) on post-traumatic stress disorders (PTSD) also illustrates this criticism of the empiricist pretenses of psychiatry. As an anthropologist and historian, Young conducts an archaeology of the presuppositions that have guided research on PTSD over the past century. His work is part of a critical approach to psychiatric categories as sociocultural constructions and historical products. For instance, PTSD is viewed as a techno-phenomenon that is as much the result of the "work" of construction set in motion by diagnostic and clinical practices and biomedical research technologies, as it is the result of demands made by interest groups and institutions that have used it as a moral argument. In short, biomedical resources are used to construct a diagnostic category for disorders that, while they involve real suffering, are only labeled as such when contemporary interests and means come together. Young (2000) argues that American and British medical authorities are unable to establish any direct connection between incidents, toxins, viruses or other factors that could explain the Gulf War syndrome, for instance. The etiological models for all post-traumatic stress syndromes (related to war, past physical or sexual abuse, etc.) cannot be validated. Psychogenic models (psychological causes related to hysteria), somatogenic models, and mixed models cannot be proven. The critical implications of this are major. Unlike some who point to an epidemic of hysteria in the West, Young does not see any connections between the Gulf War syndrome, multiple personality disorders or chronic fatigue syndrome. However, these disorders do have one etiological factor in common: memory. A constructivist approach to hysteria and PTSD must include an analysis of the social construction of memory as a mechanism by which an individual selects meaningful episodes, perhaps even as a "grammar of forgetting and remembering." This refers to the various processes of selectively forgetting or remembering that direct an individual's reconstruction of past experiences. In all these syndromes, there are histories of the origin of the trauma, ideologies defined as "standardized explanatory accounts routinely employed by clinicians, researchers, patients, and writers to translate (reduce, simplify, homogenize) patients' lifeworlds into patterns (generally sequences) connecting stock causes with effects. It is published under the heading of post-traumatic stress disorder in the diagnostic manual of the American Psychiatric Association" (Young 2000:143).

Limits of Critical Medical Anthropology

Medical anthropology in Québec, especially in English, has actively critiqued the empiricism underlying the construction of diagnostic categories and etiological models. By highlighting the influence both of the epistemological postulates of biomedicine and the sociopolitical uses of its categorizations, it demonstrates that concepts and categories are not what they may seem; they are the products of self-interested and biased constructions. In doing so it has helped to move beyond ethnosemantic, hermeneutical, semiotic approaches and other culturalisms that emphasize the patient's, the family's, and society's search for the meaning of illness to the detriment of a critique of how biomedical diagnostic and etiological categories are constructed. This critical constructivism, however, has its own limits. As Ian Hacking (2001) has pointed out, without denying the reality of the constructed object (e.g., illness), constructivism deconstructs the "essentialist" nature of an object. The object is no longer approached as being determined by the nature of things; it is evitable, and should even be eliminated from scientific discourse.

But can this kind of deconstructivism, which reduces culture to ideologies for justifying various social, political, and corporate uses of the objects of study, truly take the weight of culture into consideration? Does it not limit culture to a source of bias in the anthropological study of illness? Have contemporary critical anthropologists invented a notion of culture only to reject it, as Brightman has suggested (1995)? Should we not deplore the fact that this critical anthropology discredits the idea of a supranarrative symbolic web on which both interpersonal relations and the notion of subject and its relationship to others are based (Corin 1998b:14–15)? Québec anthropology is concerned with the way culture "works" on health, while avoiding the abuses of overinterpretation perpetrated by constructivism and a certain critical anthropology (which subordinates culture to intertextuality, to the co-construction of meaning, and to an opposition to science). Like all those who identify with a hermeneutical and interpretative approach, Québec anthropologists seem critical of any meta-interpretative system that may impose a meaning on cultural reality from the outside rather than allow it to arise out of a careful examination of the relationships between cultural elements within a given context (Corin 1998a:38).

Hacking (2001) asks another fundamental question regarding certain forms of constructionisms: do they not simply voice a rage against reason and a powerless hostility towards science, especially among people who do not have a rudimentary knowledge of science (2001:97)? Of course, this is not the case of the authors discussed in this chapter. Nonetheless, the constructivist critique in anthropology is part of a trend that criticizes the scientific pretensions of the discipline. The future of the anthropology of health certainly will need to combine a purely empiricist critique of diagnostic categories and etiologies with a concern for the "scientific" analysis of symptoms, causes, and health-seeking processes. The challenge of medical anthropology will be to establish a scientific anthropology in which the work of culture is reconciled with a concern for empirical studies; as Kuznar (1996) and Lett (1997) have shown in their work, which is receptive to the contributions of constructivism, this reconciliation should lead to a comparative anthropology, but most of all, a healthy complementarity with the biomedical sciences.

Various empirical studies (Massé 2001a; Roy 2002) have tried to reconcile an analysis of the way in which people give meaning to illness with a critical analysis of the influence of social and political structures on the production of illness. More or less implicitly, these studies are a response to Bibeau's call (1997) for an analysis of the interfaces between, on the one hand, the macrosociological forces that condition the semiological construction of reality, the historical contexts, and power relations in which cultural values have developed and, on the other hand, the intermediary levels by which cultural codes are linked to the macrosocial context. Without claiming that the anthropology of health in Québec succeeds in transcending the opposition between the interpretation of meaning and the deconstruction of biomedical categories and explanations, we believe that it is characterized by a special concern for combining, even truly linking, different approaches.

Québec Resists the Medicalization of Medical Anthropology as Best It Can

Has Québec anthropology managed to avoid the traps of a medicalization of the anthropology of health? Has it been able to avoid the insidious medicalization of its research objects and agendas, by which research language and practices are imported from medical science, a trap that Browner (1999) has called "going native"? Is Québec anthropology in danger of disengaging itself from the field and of overproducing empty concepts and decontextualized theories, despite the fact that it has made a significant contribution to an anthropology of complexity and strives to blend different methods and to link the various levels of reality in the area of health? The risk is real, as it is in Anglo-Saxon medical anthropology, which is increasingly wrapped up in popular themes such as medical technologies, organ transplantation, gene therapy, and other facets of an anthropology of biomedicine. Does the urgent call for a critical anthropology, which is often equated with a political economy of health, not justify refocusing on a critical anthropology of biomedicine, raising the issue of how it differs from the sociology of health, philosophy, or political economy? I have reiterated Browner's warning (Massé 2001b) regarding a certain tendency to abandon classical field sites in favor of an "ethnography" of locations such as hospitals (where organ transplantations are carried out), hospital emergency rooms, research laboratories, and other institutional settings. This turn towards biotechnologies, organ transplantations, and gene therapies as research objects calls for a methodology in which open interviews and documentary analysis are often the only data collection techniques. However pertinent such approaches and objects may be, do they not express a biomedicalization within the discipline?

This trend is evident in the work by Lock et al. (2000) on the way in which biomedical technical innovations (scientific instrumentations and technical procedures) transform medical practices, in research projects on the emergence of new representations of the body related to progress in molecular genetics, on the ethical issues raised by the *Human Genome Diversity Project* (Lock 1999); or

Bibeau's recent research (2003) on genetic modification in which he examines the role played by geno-proteomics in health research and its interfaces with Québec's nationalist ideologies and politics.

One of the difficulties that critical anthropologists have a difficult time avoiding when they study biotechnologies is how to separate their ideological positions and the data on which they base their critiques. All too often, there is an implicit criticism which is left largely unexplained, yet the reader cannot help but be aware of a bias against biomedicine and for traditional or alternative medicines. It is rare to encounter a clear statement of the limits or abuses of biomedical practice, though there are many. Its shortcomings are simply postulated without an articulate argumentation that hinges on identified objects of criticism or clearly identified criteria for evaluation. Readers may often feel uncomfortable as they try to distinguish between what is related to the author's editorial position, intuitions, or moral values, and what is based on a demonstration grounded in observation. It is easier to follow Joralemon (1999) when he implores anthropologists interested in engaging in ethical debates to go beyond assertions and to systematically demonstrate how anthropology can contribute to debates in ethics on the acceptability of certain practices. Unfortunately, several publications in critical medical anthropology seem to base their credibility on critical engagement, denunciation, and the deconstruction of research objects instead of grounding it in a systematic and well-supported analysis of verifiable data based on identified methods of analysis.

Conclusion

This brief incursion into research in the anthropology of health in Québec reveals what we see as two significant trends. The first is related to anthropologists' openness to dialogue and collaborations with government institutions and health professionals. Through its interest in blending diverse methodologies and in grounding theoretical reflections in empirical research, Québec anthropology is manifestly concerned with applying its findings, as we have seen in the fields of public health and community health. However, it is essential that we consider the limits of collaboration, the integrity of the discipline, and the risks of medicalizing an anthropology whose main focus is on health. The second trend is an openness to blending approaches. While many Québec anthropologists recognize the relevance of moving beyond a disengaged culturalism to present a structured critique of biomedicine's concepts, categories, and postulates, they view as essential a multidimensional approach that draws on phenomenological, semiotic, and hermeneutical perspectives. The deconstruction of biomedical categories goes hand in hand with a concern for understanding what illness and caregiving means to people. In Québec, the anthropology of health in the 21st century will be shaped by the merging of these two trends.

References

ATLANI L. and C. ROUSSEAU, 2000, The Politics of Culture in Humanitarian Aid to Refugees. Transcultural Psychiatry 37(3):435–449.

BIBEAU G., ed., 1991, L'univers du Sida. Anthropologie et société 15:2–3.

——, 1992, La santé mentale et ses visages: un Québec pluriethnique au quotidien. Boucherville: Gaëtan Morin.

——, 1997, At Work in the Fields of Public Health: The Abuse of Rationality, Medical Anthropology Quaterly, 11, 2:246–252.

——, 2003, Le Québec transgénique. Science, marché, nation. Montréal, Les Éditions du Boréal.

BIBEAU G. and E. CORIN, 1994, From Submission to the Text to Interpretive Violence. In Beyond Textuality. Ascetism and Violence in Anthropological Interpretation. G. Bibeau and E. Corin, eds. Pp. 3–54. New York: Mouton de Gruyter.

——, 1995, Culturaliser l'épidémiologie psychiatrique. Le système de signes, de sens et d'action en santé mentale. In La construction de l'anthropologie québécoise: mélanges offerts à Marc-Adélard Tremblay. Y. Breton, P. Charest and F. Trudel, eds. Québec: PUL. Electronic document, http://www.bibl.ulaval.ca/doelec/pul/tremblay.html

BRIGHTMAN R., 1995, Forget Culture: Replacement, Transcendance, Relexification. Cultural Anthropology 10(4):509–546.

BROWNER C. H., 1999, On the Medicalization of Medical Anthropology. Medical Anthropology Quarterly 13(2):135–140.

CORIN E., 1990, Facts and Meaning in Psychiatry: An anthropological Approach to the Lifeworld of Schizophrenics. Culture, Medicine and Psychiatry 14:153–158.

——, 1993, Les détours de la raison. Repères sémiologiques pour une anthropologie de la folie. Anthropologie et Sociétés 1–2:5–20.

——, 1996, Cultural Comments on Organic and Psychotic Disorders. In Culture and Psychiatric Diagnosis. A DSM IV Perspective. J. E. Meezing, A. Kleinman, H. Fabrega and D. L. Parron, eds. Pp. 63–69. Washington, DC: American Psychiatric Press.

——, 1998a, Refiguring the Person: The Dynamics of Affects and Symbols in African Spirit Possession Cult. In Bodies and Persons: Comparative Perspectives from Africa and Melanesia. M. Lambecket, A. Strathern, eds. Pp. 80–102. Cambridge: Cambridge University Press.

——, 1998b, Le rapport à l'autre. In Résonances. Dialogues avec la psychanalyse. S. Harel, ed. Pp. 11–58. Montréal: Éditions Liber.

——, 1998c, The Thickness of Being: Intentional Worlds, Strategies of Identity, and Experience Among Schizophrenics. Psychiatry 61(2):133–146.

CORIN E., G. BIBEAU, J-C. MARTIN and R. LAPLANTE, 1990, Comprendre pour soigner autrement. Montréal: Les Presses de l'Université de Montréal.

DE KONINCK M. and F. SAILLANT, 1981, Situation des femmes et stéréotypes chez les soignants: perspectives féministes. Santé Mentale au Québec V:2.

DE KONINCK M., F. SAILLANT and L. DUNNIGAN, 1981, Essai sur la santé des femmes. Québec: Conseil du Statut de la femme.

DUFOUR R., 1988, Femme et enfantement. Sagesse dans la culture Inuit. Québec: Éditions Papyrus.

——, 1989, Prêtez-nous l'oreille. Anthropologie de l'otite moyenne chez les Inuit. Ph.D. thesis, Département d'Anthropologie, Université Laval.

FOUGEYROLLAS P., 1995, Le processus de production culturelle du handicap: contextes sociohistoriques du développement des connaissances dans le champ des différences corporelles et fonctionnelles. Lac-Saint-Charles, Québec: CQCIDIH/SCCIDIH.

GAGNON É. and F. SAILLANT, 2000, De la dépendance et de l'accompagnement. Soins à domicile et liens sociaux. Paris and Québec: L'Harmattan and Les Presses de l'Université Laval.

GENEST S., 1978, Introduction à l'ethnomédecine. Essai de synthèse. Anthropologie et Sociétés 2(3):5–28.

GODIN G., J. LÉVY and G. TROTTIER, eds, 2002, Vulnérabilités et prévention VIH/Sida: enjeux contemporains. Québec: Les Presses de l'Université Laval.

GRAVEL S. and A. BATTAGLINI, 2000, Culture, santé et ethnicité. Vers une santé publique pluraliste. Montréal: Régie Régionale de la santé et des services sociaux.

HACKING I., 2001 [1999], Entre science et réalité. La construction sociale de quoi? Paris: Éditions La Découverte.

JORALEMON D., 1999, Exploring Medical Anthropology. Boston: Allyn and Bacon.

KIRMAYER L. J., 1994, Is the Concept of Mental Disorder Culturally Relative? In Controversial Issues in Mental Health. S. A. Kirk and S. Einbinder, eds. Pp. 1–20. Boston: Appleton-Century-Croft.

——, 1998, Culture in DSM-IV. Transcultural Psychiatry 35(3):1–3.

KIRMAYER L. and A. YOUNG, 1998, Culture and Somatization: Clinical, Epidemiological, and Ethnographic Perspectives. Psychosomatic Medicine 60(4):420–430.

KIRMAYER L., A. YOUNG and B. C. HAYTON, 1996, The Cultural Context of Anxiety Disorders. Psychiatric Clinics of North America 18(3):503–521.

KUZNAR L., 1996, Reclaiming a Scientific Anthropology. London: Altamira Press.

LETT J., 1997, Science, Reason, and Anthropology. The Principles of Rational Inquiry. New York: Rowan and Littlefield Publishers.

LÉVY J. and A. NOUSS, 1994, Sida-fiction. Essai d'anthropologie romanesque. Lyon: Presses Universitaires de Lyon.

LOCK M., 1989, Reaching Consensus about Death: Heart Transplants and Cultural Identity in Japan. Society-Societe 13(1):15–26.

——, 1993, Encounters with Aging. Mythologies of Menopause in Japan and North America. Berkeley: University of California Press.

——, 1999, The HGDP and the Politics of Bioethics. Politics and the Life Sciences; 18(2):323–325.

——, 2000a, On Dying Twice: Culture, Technology and the Determination of Death. In Living and Working with the New Medical Technologies. M. Lock, A. Young and A. Cambrosio, eds. Pp. 233–262. Intersections of Inquiry. Cambridge: Cambridge University Press.

——, 2000b, The Quest for Human Organs and the Violence of Zeal. In Violence and Subjectivity. V. Das., A Kleinman., M. Ramphele and P. Reynolds, eds. Pp. 271–295. Berkeley, California Press.

——, 2002, Twice Dead: Organ Transplants and the Reinvention of Death. Berkleley: University of California Press.

LOCK M. and G. BIBEAU, 1993, Healthy Disputes: Some Reflections on the Practice of Medical Anthropology in Canada. Health and Canadian Society/Santé et société canadienne 1(1):147–175.

LOCK M., A. YOUNG and A. CAMBROSIO, 2000, Living and Working with the New Medical Technologies. Intersections of Inquiry. Cambridge: Cambridge University Press.

MASSÉ R., 1995, Culture et santé publique. Les contributions de l'anthropologie à la prévention et à la promotion de la santé. Boucherville: Éditions Gaëtan Morin.

——, 1997, Les mirages de la rationalité des savoirs ethnomédicaux. Anthropologie et Sociétés 21(1):53–72.

——, 1999, Les conditions d'une anthropologie sémiotique de la détresse psychologique. Recherche Sémiotique/Semiotic Inquiry 19(1):39–62.

——, 2000, Qualitative and Quantitative Analysis of Idioms of Distress: Complementarity or Incommensurability of Ethnosemantic, Content and Confirmatory Factor Analyses. Qualitative Health Research 10(3):411–423.

——, 2001a, Pour une ethnoépidémiologie critique de la détresse psychologique à la Martinique. Sciences sociales et Santé 19(1):45–73.

——, 2001b, Contributions and Challenge of Medical Anthropology to Anthropology: Integration of Multiple Dimensions of Social Suffering and the Medicalization of Medical Anthropology. Rivista della Società Italiana di antropologia medica 11–12:41–60.

——, 2003, Éthique et santé publique. Enjeux, valeurs, et normativités. Québec: Les Presses de l'Université Laval.

MURPHY H. B. M., 1974, Differences of Mental Disorders between French Canadians and British Canadians. Canadian Psychiatric Association Journal 19:247–253.

NGUYEN V-K. and K. PESCHARD, 2003, Anthropology, Inequality, and Disease: A Review. Annual Review in Anthropology 32:447–474.

PANDOLFI M., 2002, Moral Entrepeneurs, souverainetés mouvantes et barbelés. Le biopolitique dans les Balkans postcommunistes. Anthropologie et Sociétés 26:29–51.

ROUSSEAU C., 2000, Refugees to Our Land: Organized Violence and Social Suffering; Les Réfugiés à notre porte: violence organisée et souffrance sociale. Criminologie 33(1):185–201.

ROUSSEAU C., A. DRAPEAU and R. PLATT, 2000, Living Conditions and Emotional Profiles of Cambodian, Central American, and Quebecois Youth. Canadian Journal of Psychiatry 45(10):905–911.

ROUSSEAU C., A. MEKKI-BERRADA and S. MOREAU, 2001, Trauma and Extended Separation from Family among Latin American and African Refugees in Montréal. Psychiatry 64(1):40–59.

ROUSSEAU N., F. SAILLANT and D. DESJARDINS, 1990, Les thérapies douces au Québec: Portrait des praticiennes et praticiens. Research document. Québec: Centre de Recherche sur les Services Communautaires, Université Laval.

ROY B., 2002, Sang sucré, pouvoirs codés, médecine amère. Diabète et processus de construction identitaire: les dimensions socio-politiques du diabète chez les Innus de Pessamit. Québec: Les Presses de l'Université Laval.

SAILLANT F., 1985, Le mouvement pour la santé des femmes. In Traité d'anthropologie médicale. L'institution de la santé et de la maladie. J. Dufresne, F. Dumont and Y. Martin, eds. Pp. 743–762. Montréal: Presses de l'Université du Québec/Institut québécois de recherche sur la culture/Presses Universitaires de Lyon.

——, 1988, Cancer et Culture. Produire le sens de la maladie. Montréal: Éditions Saint-Martin.

——, 1990a, Se soigner en famille: Les recettes de médecine populaire dans les familles québécoises du début du XXième siècle. Research document. Québec: Centre de Recherche sur les Services Communautaires, Université Laval.

——, 1990b, Discourse, Knowledge and Experience of Cancer: A Life Story. Culture, Medicine and Psychiatry XIV(1):81–10.

——, 1999, Femmes, soins domestiques et espace thérapeutique. Anthropologie et Sociétés 23(2):15–39.

SAILLANT F. and E. GAGNON, 1999, Présentation. Vers une anthropologie des soins. Anthropologie et Sociétés 23(2):5–14.

——, 2001, Responsabilité pour autrui et dépendance dans la modernité avancée. Le cas de l'aide aux proches. Lien social et politique XLVI:55–69.

SAILLANT F. and S. GENEST, 1990, Culture et clinique. Anthropologie et sociétés 4(1).

SAILLANT F. and M. PAUMIER, 2003, L'Humanitaire, le corps, la citoyenneté. Imaginaire universaliste, transnationalismes et métissages. Conference papers on Brasil, Montréal: CELAT/UQAM (publication on CD).

SAILLANT F., ROUSSEAU, N. and D. DESJARDINS, 1990, Thérapies douces et quêtes de sens. Revue internationale d'action communautaire 24(64):63–72.

SAILLANT. F., COGNET M. and M. RICHARDSON, 2005, Représentations de l'accueil et de l'Humanitaire dans les sites internet des organisations transnationales, nationales et locales reliées à l'intervention auprès des réfugiés. Anthropologica 47(1):115–127.

——, 1983, L'anthropologie de la santé: une réponse aux innovations dans le système médical québécois. Santé, Culture, Health 1(2):14–42.

TREMBLAY M. A., 1982, L'anthropologie de la santé en tant que représentation. *In* Imaginaire social et représentations collectives. Mélanges offerts à Jean-Charles Falardeau. F. Dumont and Y. Martin, eds. Pp. 253–274. Québec: Les Presses de l'Université Laval.

——, 1983, L'anthropologie de la santé: une réponse aux innovations dans le système médical québécois. Santé, Culture, Health 1(2):14–42.

TURNER L., 1998, An Anthropological Exploration of Contemporary Bioethics: the Varieties of Common Sense. Journal of Medical Ethics 24:127–133.

YOUNG A., 1981, When Rational Men Fall Sick: An Inquiry into Some Assumptions Made by Medical Anthropologists. Culture, Medicine and Psychiatry 5(4):317–335.

——, 1990, (Mis)applying Medical Anthropology. Multicultural Settings. Santé, Culture, Health VII(2–3):197–207.

——, 1995a, Reasons and Causes for Post-Traumatic Stress Disorder. Transcultural Psychiatric Research Review 32(3):287–298.

——, 1995b, The Harmony of Illusions: Inventing Post-Traumatic Stress Disorder. Princeton: Princeton University Press.

——, 2000, History, Hystery and Psychiatric Styles of Reasoning. *In* Living and Working with the New Medical Technologies. Intersections of Inquiry. M. Lock, A. Young and A. Cambrosio, eds. Pp. 135–162. Cambridge: Cambridge University Press.

Chapter 2

THE UNITED STATES

Medical Anthropology in the United States
Arachu Castro and Paul Farmer

Although it was not until the 1960s that the label "medical anthropology" came to describe a subfield in the United States (see Scotch 1963), the history of the anthropological study of health and illness is as old as the discipline itself. As early as in 1881, the contents of the presentations at the meetings of the Anthropological Society of Washington, founded two years earlier – and which would become in 1902 the American Anthropological Association (AAA)[1] – reveals that some anthropologists were including the study of illness and medical practices in their ethnographical observations (Fletcher 1881; Petroff 1881).

From the outset, anthropological studies of health have been contextualizing, insisting on the embeddedness in the social world of all that may be observed or elicited. The early interest of North American anthropologists in non-Western medical systems – an area of study that later became to be known as ethnomedicine – gained momentum after the work of British physician-anthropologist W. H. R. Rivers, who began his fieldwork in India in 1901. With Rivers, illness representations first became the object of systematic and sustained investigation, as reflected in his book published simultaneously in London and New York (Rivers 1906). Rivers established basic concepts that maintained that indigenous medical systems are social institutions and that indigenous medical practices are rational and follow an internal logic. Nonetheless, Rivers also instilled a stereotype of non-Western medical systems that inextricably linked magic, religion, and medicine, a stereotype which was adopted by most anthropologists during the first half of the 20th century (Foster and Anderson 1978).

The continuing influence of Rivers' interest in concepts of disease causation is reflected in Clements' *Primitive Concepts of Disease*, which appeared in 1932 (Clements 1932) and which documented the first worldwide comparative survey of beliefs about disease etiology, citing over 200 sources that were mainly ethnographic. The study fitted neatly into the already discredited paradigm of historical particularism, which attempted to place various "culture traits" – in this case, etiological concepts – into larger frameworks of geographical diffusion and chronological sequences (Farmer and Good 1991).

During the Second World War, Ackerknecht began to publish his more influential investigations. His work – that of a historian and a physician heavily indebted to functionalist anthropology – reified the primitive-modern distinction: "Primitive medicine is primarily magico-religious, utilizing a few rational elements, while our medicine is predominantly rational and scientific employing a few magic elements" (Ackerknecht 1946:467). This radical and frequently repeated distinction did not prevent Ackerknecht from deploying Western categories (e.g., surgery, psychotherapy, obstetrics) to describe "primitive" responses to illness and necessarily impoverished his understanding of the illness categories of other cultures. Also in the 1940s, culture and personality studies flourished under the leadership of Ruth Benedict, Gregory Bateson, and Margaret Mead (Benedict 1946; Mead 1942), with the exploration of behavior, instinct, schizophrenia, and other psychiatric conditions in specific populations.

Anthropological research, oriented toward practical problems, represented the humanitarian ideology of anthropology of that time, under the impetus of people such as Margaret Mead. While the 1940s were characterized by efforts to find solutions to health problems, this sense of compromise was diluted with the end of the Second World War, after which many anthropologists who did work on health and nutrition opted for positions in academia or in areas of North American military occupation. With the expansion of academic departments and an increase in university budgets, there was a return to tribal ethnology and to postwar theoretical interests. This was a time of disappointment with public matters, which served to distance anthropology from contemporary politics.

The 1950s and 1960s saw the rapid growth of medical anthropology as an applied practical discipline in the field of international public health, which is attested by some reviews of the existing anthropological literature (Caudill 1953; Paul 1963; Polgar 1962; Scotch 1963). Since the 1950s, anthropologists have collaborated with public health professionals, some of them with the recently created World Health Organization (WHO),[2] in a wide variety of projects designed to bring services to populations in developing countries and in the United States. These programs were linked to the idea that technology would solve the economic underdevelopment of poor countries.

Applied medical anthropologists were engaged in international public health to examine "cultural barriers" to health promotion and health campaigns and to design health programs that would be deemed culturally appropriate by local populations ("the natives"). The stated goal was to understand why biomedical ideas and therapies were not readily accepted (Foster and Anderson 1978), and to interpret community structures and help foreign or foreign-trained health technicians to implement top-down development programs (Farmer and Good 1991:137) – which George Foster later called the "ethnocentric or silver platter approach" (Rockafellar and Adams 2002).

There was, at the time, little critical reflection on the purpose of such programs or on the perceived needs of the populations the programs sought to serve (Jordan 1989; Taussig 1980). Studies of traditional healers, including birth attendants, proliferated at this time. Later, the anthropologists who produced such work were criticized as being handmaidens of biomedicine (Greenwood et al. 1988; Singer and Baer 1995:5) – similar to what they had earlier been to colonial powers (Scheper-Hugues 1990) – and cheerleaders of the Western "medical industrial complex." Much of this work focused on a deceptively complex problem: how to get local populations to alter their behavior in a fashion that would improve their health. Wells can be dug, vaccinations offered, birth control devices or medications provided, oral rehydration therapies made available, but if these services and technologies are not used or not used appropriately, they will be of little value. Public health officials saw resistance to such obviously effective behaviors as irrational, the result of ignorance, superstitions, or traditional views that conflicted with modern medical knowledge and required change.

When top-down biomedical efforts failed to yield results, anthropologists George Foster and Benjamin Paul developed a sociocultural model to comprehend native cosmologies and local understandings of health and healing (see Foster 1951; Paul 1955). George Foster, along with a group of his young students and research associates at the Smithsonian Institution, began active collaboration with public health specialists in the Institute of Inter-American Affairs (Foster 1951), merging international public health and anthropology – which has led some to attribute Foster with the invention of medical anthropology as we know it today (Rockafellar and Adams 2002). By explaining to health personnel how non-Western beliefs conflicted with biomedical assumptions and practices and by offering suggestions on how to improve the delivery of health care, Foster and his colleagues were "able to demonstrate the practical utility of their knowledge" (Foster and Anderson 1978:8).

Anthropologists addressed the problem by analyzing health beliefs in relation to a local culture, as Benjamin Paul wrote in the introduction to the most important early collection of studies in this tradition:

> What appears from the outside as irrational belief and behavior becomes intelligible when viewed from within. Perceiving the connections between items of belief and behavior as the people themselves perceive them enables us to make better sense of the seemingly capricious pattern of acceptance and rejection, of successful and unsuccessful education efforts. (Paul 1955:5)

Indigenous "items of belief," Paul argued, must be understood from the natives' point of view. Only then can the seemingly irrational be understood, and only then can programs of education be developed that work within the local frame of reference. Illness representations, from this perspective, are beliefs with a logic to be uncovered by ethnographic research. As American foreign aid and international agencies supported public health efforts in the developing world – the US International Cooperation Administration, launched in 1964, was the predecessor of the Agency for International Development (USAID) – anthropologists began to find positions in schools of public health and a variety of governmental and nongovernmental organizations. Several of Benjamin Paul's students at the Harvard School of Public Health continued careers in schools of public health or medicine.

Medical anthropology as an applied discipline has continued to grow and has become increasingly specialized, focusing on health education, nutrition, infectious diseases, diarrheal disease, infant mortality, and primary health-care systems, as well as on more classic public health interventions. The contributions of anthropologists to the development field were enhanced by improvements in the theory and methodology of anthropology, mainly: the emergence of subfields devoted to problem-solving in the areas of health, nutrition, education, or agriculture. Studies of how central decisions about health and social policies impacted on poor or otherwise marginalized groups were also initiated.

"Ethnoscience," or "ethnosemantics," which contributed to the eventual emergence of the cognitive sciences (Gardener 1985), used medical phenomena as one source for the analysis of cognitive representations. Disease nosologies elicited in the field were construed as hierarchically structured taxonomies held to represent the informants' mental representations of disease. It was asserted that inclusion criteria were largely the presence or absence of distinctive attributes or "features." Frake, for example, borrowed the technique of componential analysis from linguistics to analyze the diagnostic terms for skin disorders used by members of one small, nonliterate society (Frake 1961). Although few of the early cognitive anthropologists would consider themselves medical anthropologists, cognitive studies have emerged as one important approach to the study of illness representations within medical anthropology.

In the 1960s, while "it was something of an embarrassment to be identified as a medical anthropologist" (Good 1994:4) due to its practical nature, medical anthropology began to take new shape as the comparative study of medical systems (Rubel 1960, 1964), particularly focusing on those societies in which the "great traditions" of non-Western professional medicine have flourished alongside diverse popular medical traditions. Foster argues that 1963 marked the point in time where "American anthropologists fully appreciated the implications of health and illness research for anthropology" (Foster and Anderson 1978:3), as reflected mostly by the work of Scotch (1963) and Paul (1963). At around this time, *Medical Anthropology*, the first scholarly journal in the field, was founded by Pertti Pelto. With time, "the diverse issues that concern medical and psychiatric anthropologists have moved ever closer to the center of the discipline, and have become ever more prominent in the social sciences and humanities at large" (Good 1994:4).

In the 1960s, most courses in medical anthropology were being offered at medical schools and schools of public health: Case Western Reserve University, Columbia University School of Public Health, Harvard School of Public Health, Harvard University, Stanford University, and the Universities of California at Los Angeles School of Public Health, California Medical Center, Colorado, Kentucky, Michigan School of Public Health, North Carolina at Chapel Hill School of Public Health, Pennsylvania, Pittsburgh School of Public Health, Puerto Rico Medical Sciences Campus, Vermont, and Washington at Seattle (Weidman 1968; Scott 1969).

It was within this context that the Organization of Medical Anthropology was formed in 1967 by a group of persons interested in social sciences and medicine, which had earlier founded the "Roster of Anthropologists, Physicians, and Others Who Have Special Interests in Medical Anthropology." The Organization first met in Berkeley, California, in April 27, 1968, at the 27th Annual Meeting of the Society for Applied Anthropology (SfAA), during which the *Medical Anthropology*

Newsletter was conceived, and first published in October 1968 with 53 subscribers (Weidman 1968). A month later, on November 22, the Organization held its first medical anthropology workshop at the American Anthropological Association (AAA) Annual Meeting, which took place in Seattle, Washington, and became the Group for Medical Anthropology (GMA). Thereafter, medical anthropology meetings have met regularly both at the SfAA and AAA meetings.

At the AAA Annual Meeting in San Diego, California, in November 1970, the GMA became the Society for Medical Anthropology (SMA) and adopted its Constitution, of which its first objective was "to promote study of anthropological aspects of health, illness, health care, and related topics" (Leighton 1970). In 1971, the SMA became a section of the AAA. That same year, with the support of the Wenner–Gren Foundation, Charles Leslie organized the first major research conference on Asian medical systems (Leslie 1976). For the first time, anthropologists tackled the ethnographic study of the classical traditions – Ayurveda and Yunani medicine in India, Chinese medicine in several Asian societies, Galenic medicine in both Islamic and Hispanic societies – as well as the interrelations among professional, folk, and popular medical traditions. This research took its place alongside more traditional studies of healing systems of small, nonliterate societies, providing a new focus on medical pluralism and on the plurality of care-seeking strategies that organize behavior in relation to alternative resources. Multiple and often highly contested interpretations of illness and medical authority thus emerge as central issues in the study of illness representations. These studies of plural medical systems have also provided many of the basic concepts and methods for anthropological studies of health care in the United States.

The mid and late 1970s saw the development of a new self-consciousness of theorizing in medical anthropology – beginning, notably, with Horacio Fábrega (Fábrega 1972; Fábrega and Silver 1973). Hazel Weidman's (Weidman 1978) study of health culture in Miami led to the creation of mental health services targeted to culturally distinct groups. Steven Polgar, who did extensive work on fertility and its regulation, worked with the WHO and taught at a school of public health (see Polgar 1972; Weidman 1982).

Long criticized in the academy for being applied and atheoretical (Colson and Selby 1974:257), anthropologists with an interest in medical systems, illness experience and healing, and illness representations have developed an increasingly sophisticated theoretical discourse, bringing medical anthropology to the center of the discipline at large. Arthur Kleinman's work, beginning in the late 1970s, marked the emergence of medical anthropology as a systematic and theoretically grounded field of inquiry within the larger discipline. Kleinman designated the medical system a "cultural system," and thus a distinctive field of anthropological inquiry (Kleinman 1978). His work combined an interest in complex medical systems following the Leslie tradition, detailed ethnographic analyses of illness and healing in Chinese cultures, theoretical development linked to symbolic, interpretive, and social constructivist writing, and the study of applied medical anthropology (Kleinman 1975, 1980).

In 1978, the WHO and UNICEF organized an international conference on primary health care (PHC) with the stated aim of bringing health indices, rather than GDP, to the center of the development process. The PHC movement, based on community involvement and the concept of human rights, sought to promote community-based responses to common health problems, especially maternal and child health, nutrition, family planning, water and sanitation, control of infectious diseases, and health planning. This movement opened the door for participation on the part of anthropologists in the design, implementation, and evaluation of PHC programs (Pillsbury 1991:66) – which, by the 1980s, became one of the primary recipients of funding from donors in North America and Europe. Foster encouraged the involvement of anthropologists in the health-policy arena by studying the bureaucratic structures and personnel of the development agencies themselves (see Foster 1977; Tendler 1975).

The development of an anthropological interest in nutritional studies occurred in the 1970s due to the exhausting of tribal studies and to university budget cuts in parallel with the worldwide crisis:

> Nutritional anthropology, like the many recent hyphenated anthropologies, has emerged in a transitional period in which anthropologists desire to move into the study of contemporary society, or are compelled to do so by the loss of traditional tribal subject matter. The process of becoming a hyphenated anthropologist has become largely one of seeking support wherever it can be found, for in the current job crisis, cross-disciplinary anthropologists must locate new employment niches.[3]

In addition to the centrifugal effect that this context offered the discipline came the opportunity of incorporating highly specialized basic research groups, in which the practical or political orientation was lost. A point was reached when commonplace definitions were accepted and health and nutritional data were accumulated with no concern for theory.[4] It was not until the 1980s that a debate was initiated on how to study the cultural bases of food practices. Today, most of the work in nutritional anthropology stems from members of the Council on Nutritional Anthropology, a section of the AAA. This organization is working to devise a systematic methodology to gather qualitative data on food practices and to quantify them, as shown in the manuals for the anthropological study of nutrition that have been published (Fitzgerald 1976; Jerome et al. 1980; Pelto et al. 1989; Quandt and Ritenbaugh 1986). The multiple publications of nutritional anthropologists since the 1970s gave recognition to the subspecialty of nutritional anthropology in the United States, and in particular in applied research for public health projects.

From the 1970s on, several departments of anthropology started to offer courses in medical anthropology: University of California at Berkeley (early 1970s),[5] University of Illinois at Urbana (1970), University of Hawaii (1971), University of Massachusetts (1972), University of Iowa (1974), Brown University (1975), University of Michigan (1976), University of Kansas (1976), Emory University (1978), University of Alabama (1978), University of Arizona (1980), University of Missouri at Columbia (1987), and Yale University (1995). Some graduate programs in medical anthropology had started even earlier, and exist today in several departments of anthropology: University of Connecticut (mid 1960s, founded by Pertti Pelto), University of Kentucky (late 1960s), Hunter College at City University of New York (early 1970s), Michigan State University (early 1970s, founded by Arthur Rubel), University of South Florida (1973), University of California at Berkeley and San Francisco (1975, founded by George Foster and Margaret Clark), Case Western Reserve University (1977), University of Memphis (1978), Harvard University (1982), University of Arizona (1986), University of Alabama (2002), and Wayne State University.[6]

In February 1983, the official publication of the SMA was renamed *Medical Anthropology Quarterly* (Johnson 1983), which is one of the leading journals in the field, together with *Medical Anthropology, Culture, Medicine and Psychiatry* (founded in 1977), and *Social Science and Medicine*, which has a section on medical anthropology.

In the 1980s, the participatory approach, enhanced by the primary health care movement, became a cornerstone of many public health and development programs designed to be equitable. It was based on the idea that the lived experience of people, ("putting people first") and not GDP indicators, needed to be central to the conduct and evaluation of development programs (Cernea 1985). People-centered development became one anthropological approach to economic development (Pillsbury 1986:22), a heterogeneous social process often informed by an interest in human rights (Bennett 1996:S32) or by redressing gender inequalities (see Boserup 1986).[7] By then, it had become increasingly clear that many of the health and social problems facing poor populations in the world were not in fact due to endogenous cultural factors but rather to a complex series of push-pull forces that were undermining rural and small-scale economies, leading to urbanization and a decline in health status even as poor people took up wage labor. Furthermore, it also became clear that the integration of poor communities into national and international economies does not necessarily improve their living conditions, and that economic prosperity and the ability to become consumers in a global market are not universal human goals.

Within the disquietude of the post-Vietnam War period, some medical anthropologists (Baer et al. 1986; Frankenberg 1988; Janzen 1978; Leslie 1989; Morgan 1987; Singer 1986, 1989) called for the development of a critical medical anthropology which was grounded in a political economy of health (Navarro 1985; Waitzkin 1981; Young 1976) and which focused more explicitly on the representation of power relations and social inequalities within illness discourse, ideas that gained momentum in 1990 (Morsy 1990; Scheper-Hughes 1990; Singer 1990; Singer et al. 1990). Critical medical anthropologists started to explore current and past socio-economic and political processes, to examine how illness representations serve to represent and misrepresent power relations within a society, to identify and expose structural forces that undermine the health of poor and marginalized groups, and to document how the growing social inequalities between and within countries have, in the absence of a social justice agenda, proven to be formidable barriers to the promotion of modern sanitation and health care (see Baer et al. 1997; Bourgois 1995; Castro 2003; Castro and Farmer 2002, 2003a, 2003c, 2003d; Castro and Singer 2004; Donahue 1989, 1990; Farmer 1992, 1999, 2002, 2003; Farmer and Castro 2004; Farmer et al. 1996; Kim et al. 2000; Morgan 1998; Nichter 1996; Pfeiffer 2003; Singer 1997; Stebbins 1993; Whiteford 1993; Whiteford and Manderson 2000). Anthropologists also began to study the international role of health and health care in "managing inequality" rather than in addressing the growing gap between rich and poor and the "outcome gap" necessarily associated with growing inequality (Castro and Farmer 2003b). At the close of the last century, there was often more interest in studying inequalities of access to technologies than in remediating them.

After a few years of internal debate, critical medical anthropologists have reunited in a revitalized Critical Anthropology of Health Caucus, and share this mission statement:

> By exploring current and past socioeconomic and political processes, we seek to identify and expose structural patterns that undermine the health of poor and marginalized groups wherever they reside. Further, we seek to understand the international role of health and health care in maintaining and furthering systems of inequality. As anthropologists, we are concerned with the impact of structure on local experience, behavior, and meanings. At the same time, we seek to understand how local and broader initiatives about health issues can have an impact on the encompassing social structures. (Castro and Millen 2000)

Critical Anthropology of Health members are currently concerned with the effect on health of political economic issues such as: the effects of corporate-led globalization; poor-country debt; structural adjustment policies such as the deregulation of labor; privatization of health services in particular; trade-related issues, especially between vastly unequal trading partners; the health impacts of for-profit health care; the exportation of US-style, for-profit health companies; the changing face of international aid, sanctions, and embargoes; and the effects of armed conflict and military intervention. Critical Anthropology of Health members also examine the effects on health of past and ongoing processes such as: wealth and income disparities within and between countries; the unequal distribution of health resources; colonialism; institutional racism; sexism and homosexism; slavery; entrenched poverty; and structural violence and social suffering.

In 2003, the SMA, with its 1,400 members, is the largest nongeneralist section of the AAA,[8] and encompasses a growing number of interest groups. These are: AIDS and Anthropology, Alcohol and Drug Study, Andean Health Research, Bioethics, Biological Weapons, Clinically Applied Medical Anthropology, Council on Anthropology and Reproduction, Council on Nursing and Anthropology, Critical Anthropology of Health Caucus, Disability Research, Global Health and Emerging Disease, and Pharmaceuticals.

Undoubtedly, the longstanding theoretical and methodological contributions of medical anthropology have informed and inspired the larger discipline, and larger disciplinary debates concerning culture, power, representation, and social structure, and other issues increasingly reflect advances stemming from medical anthropology research and practice. This reverse in the flow of ideas marks medical anthropology's move from the margin into the mainstream of the field. (Sobo 2003:5)

Medical anthropologists have long participated in national and international efforts to improve health, have worked with epidemiologists to explain disease patterns, and have collaborated extensively with public health providers to promote successful, "appropriate," and "culturally sensitive" health interventions. But with few exceptions, medical anthropologists in the United States have focused most of their efforts on analyzing, improving, or evaluating specific problems within health programs, such as discrepancies of beliefs and values between implementers of health initiatives and their targeted recipients.

Rarely have medical anthropologists stepped back to examine the wider socio-economic constraints placed on those who control the budgets of national and international health policies. Yet, if medical anthropologists are to get to the heart of why some health initiatives succeed in terms of improving health outcomes, while others fail or even worsen health problems, medical anthropologists must also examine these constraints and the core principles that guide national level and international efforts to eradicate or control disease.

Are the principles guiding health policy based on beliefs that health is a human right and a public good? Are they tied to notions of health equity, with an ethical imperative to protect the poor and other vulnerable groups? Or are they driven more by fear and less benign ideological and geopolitical objectives? What are the implications for poor people of health policies generated from nonhealth concerns? Even when sound epidemiological findings, considerations of equity, and health as a fundamental human right form the core of bilateral and international health policy, well-intentioned health efforts are often undermined at the implementation stage when the interests of capital and the interrelated trilogy of fear, ideology, and geopolitics come to take precedence over public health concerns (Castro and Millen 2001).

With deep knowledge of the local health effects of many political and economic development endeavors and approaches, as well as of local systems of meaning, medical anthropologists are in a position to encourage novel ways of promoting equity in access to health care. The dimensions of the global AIDS pandemic, which has in the course of the past two decades become the leading single infectious cause of young adult death in much of the world, and the persistence or "re-emergence" of diseases that had been previously slated for eradication, bring the shortcomings of past approaches into sharp relief.

Medical anthropologists are well positioned to critically examine alleged barriers to health care. Should anthropologists: Continue to document the suffering of those living with untreated disease? Try to shed light on the processes that contribute to the decrease of stigma and discrimination associated with disease, such as the introduction of effective therapy? Devote greater attention to the practical considerations of scaling up prevention and treatment in public health programs? Become advocates for those living with disease who as yet have no access to treatment? Incorporate a human-rights approach to disease? Or finally, concentrate on developing mechanisms for effective, appropriate, and community-enhancing delivery mechanisms for public health programs?

Anthropologists' greater participation in research that will contribute to preventing infections and alleviating the enormous suffering wrought by disease can contribute to making anthropology a more vibrant and relevant discipline through debate and action in response to the greatest health challenges of our time.

Acknowledgments

We are indebted to Yasmin Khawja for her invaluable assistance searching and reviewing documents, and contacting every department of anthropology in the United States on our behalf. We are also grateful to all the anthropologists who undusted their files to tell us about the history of the teaching of medical anthropology in their departments.

Notes

1. The AAA is currently the largest professional association of anthropologists, with more than 11,000 members (Carlo Simpao, AAA Membership Services, personal communication, August 2003).
2. The Pan American Health Organization, headquartered in Washington, DC, was created in 1902 and, with the creation of the World Health Organization, became the Regional Office for the Americas.
3. The term nutritional anthropology includes all the studies that seek to understand sociocultural and/or biological variability of the human species through the analysis of differences in food and nutrition within and between human groups. The first anthropological studies on food and nutrition did not analyze nutrition as a central theme, rather they were incorporated into studies of economic anthropology (exchange of food) and studies of kinship and its associated food practices. Anthropological studies particularly dedicated to nutrition had begun in the 1930s, with the pioneer work of Audrey Richards (Richards 1932, 1939), a student of Bronislaw Malinowski who followed the functionalist approach of the British school.
4. The early anthropological studies of food and nutrition were isolated, ignored the work of others, and lacked an explicit theoretical framework and dialogue. With the exception of some edited volumes, these studies formed part of a fragmented and little developed subdiscipline. This academic orientation, distanced from contemporary themes and present in the United States since the 1950s, is, according to some authors, the cause of the secondary statute of the anthropological interests in food and nutrition. In the 1940s the concept of *food habits* was adopted. "But only the *concept* was grasped, while the effort to situate the work at the *theoretical* level in academic anthropology – through the theory of cultural patterns formulated by Margaret Mead and her collaborators – was not successful" (Montgomery and Bennett 1979:127). The trend of North American research is characterized by a quantitative focus that

prioritizes the pragmatism of fieldwork and statistical analysis of data. Its pragmatism, which reflects the Boasian tradition according to which anthropological research is basically ethnographic and that all synthesis is premature, renders it difficult to be used to formulate theories. The quantification of sociocultural variables related to food and nutrition allows for the contribution of anthropology in numerous studies of nutritional public health. Normally, data are gathered with an idea of problem-solving – rather than with theoretical references pertaining to anthropology – and the data is analyzed to the extent to which they will be utilized – and financed. The lack of elaboration of theories impedes at the same time the results of applied research from being reinvested into basic anthropology, and maintains anthropology's subordination to nutrition and to public health (Castro 1996).

5.   In 1930, the systematic study of the humanities in medicine was institutionalized at the University of California at San Francisco, when the Regents of the University of California established a Department of History in the Medical School in San Francisco (Bourgois 2003). The Department of History of the Medical School was the second freestanding history program located in a medical school in the United States. After merging with the Division of Medical Anthropology, formerly located in the Department of Epidemiology and Biostatistics, it became the Department of Anthropology, History and Social Medicine in 1999, under the leadership of Philippe Bourgois.

6.   This information is based on the SMA website (www.medanthro.net/academic/grad/namerican.html, accessed August 2004), on the websites of departments of anthropology, and on e-mail and telephone exchanges with Vincanne Adams, Mary K. Anglin, Florence Babb, David Barondess, Philippe Bourgois, Peter Brown, Nancy Buffone, Thomas J. Csordas, Nina L. Etkin, Anne Ferguson, Ruthbeth Finerman, Mark Flinn, Katherine Grimaldi, Penn Handwerker, David Hess, John M. Janzen, Peter Little, Jim Moore, Lorna Moore, Lynn Morgan, Michael Dean Murphy, Mark Nichter, Holly Peters-Golden, Linda-Anne Rebhun, Lorna Rhodes, Nancy Rockafellar, Nancy Scheper-Hughes, Elisa Sobo, Alan Swedlund, Janelle Taylor, and Linda Whiteford.

7.   The study of reproduction and sexuality has grown exponentially within medical anthropology since the late 1970s, first as a reaction to biomedicine and later through the incorporation of gender perspectives (Bledsoe et al. 2000; Browner and Sargent 1990; Davis-Floyd 1992; Ginsburg and Rapp 1991; Jordan 1978; Layne 2000; Lock 1993; Lock and Kaufert 1998; Inhorn 1994, 2002; Martin 1987; Morgan and Michaels 1999; Ragone 1994; Rapp 1999).

8.   The largest sections of the AAA are: General Anthropology, American Ethnological Society, Cultural Anthropology, Society for Medical Anthropology, and Archeology Division, in this order (Carlo Simpao, AAA Membership Services, personal communication, August 2003).

References

ACKERKNECHT E. H., 1946, Natural Diseases and Rational Treatments in Primitive Medicine. Bulletin of the History of Medicine 19:467–497.
BAER H. A., M. SINGER and J. JOHNSEN, 1986, Introduction: Toward a Critical Medical Anthropology. Social Science and Medicine 23:95–98.
BAER H. A., M. SINGER and I. SUSSER, 1997, Medical Anthropology and the World System. Westport: Bergin & Garvey.

BENEDICT R., 1946, The Chrysanthemum and the Sword: Patterns of Japanese Culture. Boston: Houghton Mifflin.

BENNETT J. W., 1996, Applied and Action Anthropology: Ideological and Conceptual Aspects. Current Anthropology 36:S23–S53.

BLEDSOE C., S. LERNER and J. I. GUYER, eds, 2000, Fertility and the Male Life Cycle in the Era of Fertility Decline. Oxford: Oxford University Press.

BOSERUP E., 1986, Woman's Role in Economic Development. Vermont: Gower.

BOURGOIS Ph., 1995, In Search of Respect: Selling Crack in El Barrio. New York: Cambridge University Press.

——, 2003, University of California, San Francisco, School of Medicine, Department of Anthropology, History and Social Medicine. Academic Medicine 78:1060–1061.

BROWNER C. and C. F. SARGENT, 1990, Anthropology and Studies of Human Reproduction. *In* Medical Anthropology: Contemporary Theory and Method. C. B. Sargent and T. M. Johnson, eds. Pp. 219–234. New York: Praeger.

CASTRO A., 1996, Les implications socioculturelles des pratiques alimentaires dans la région de la Rioja (Espagne du Nord). Ph.D. Thesis, École des Hautes Études en Sciences Sociales, Paris.

——, 2003, Determinantes socio-políticos de la infección por VIH: Violencia estructural y culpabilización de la víctima. Conferencia plenaria. [Socio-political Determinants of HIV: Structural Violence and The Blaming of the Victim. Plenary lecture.] 2nd Latin American Forum on HIV/AIDS and STIs, Havana, Cuba, 2003, pp. 22.

CASTRO A. and P. FARMER, 2002, Anthropologie de la violence: La culpabilisation des victimes. Notre Librairie: Revue des Littératures du Sud 148:102–108.

——, 2003a, El sida y la violencia estructural: La culpabilización de la víctima. Cuadernos de Antropología Social 17:31–49

——, 2003b, Health and Economic Development. *In* Encyclopedia of Medical Anthropology: Health and Illness in the World's Cultures. C. R. Ember and M. Ember, eds. Pp. 164–170. New York: Kluwer/Plenum.

——, 2003c, Infectious Disease in Haiti: HIV/AIDS, Tuberculosis, and Social Inequalities. EMBO Reports 4(6S):S20–S23.

——, 2003d, Violence structurelle, mondialisation et tuberculose multirésistante. Anthropologie et Sociétés 27(2):23–40.

CASTRO A. and J. V. MILLEN, 2000, Critical Anthropology of Health Interest Group in collaboration with the Institute for Health and Social Justice. Anthropology Newsletter.

——, 2001, Praxis, Policy and the Poor: Critical Ethnography of International Health Policies, Anthropology Newsletter, January.

CASTRO A. and M. SINGER, eds, 2004, Unhealthy Health Policy: A Critical Anthropological Examination. Walnut Creek, CA: Altamira Press.

CAUDILL W., 1953, Applied Anthropology in Medicine. *In* Anthropology Today: An Encyclopedic Inventory. A. L. Kroeber, ed. Pp. 771–806. Chicago: University of Chicago Press.

CERNEA M. M., 1985, Putting People First: Sociological Variables in Rural Development. New York: Oxford University.

CLEMENTS F., 1932, Primitive Concepts of Disease. University of California Publications in Archeology and Ethnology 32:185–252.

COLSON C. and K. E. SELBY, 1974, Medical Anthropology. Annual Review of Anthropology 3:245–262.

DAVIS-FLOYD R., 1992, Birth as an American Rite of Passage. Berkeley: University of California Press.

DONAHUE J. M., 1989, Rural Health Efforts in the Urban Dominated Political Economy: Three Third World Examples. Medical Anthropology Quarterly 11:109–125.

——, 1990, The Role of Anthropologists in Primary Health Care: Reconciling Advocacy and Research. *In* Anthropology and Health Care. J. Coriel and J. D. Mull, eds. Pp. 79–97. Boulder, CO: Westview.

FABREGA H., 1972, Medical Anthropology. *In* Biennial Review of Anthropology. B. Siegel, ed. Pp. 167–229. Stanford: Stanford University Press.

FÁBREGA H. and D. B. SILVER, 1973, Illness and Shamanistic Curing in Zinacantan: An Ethnomedical Analysis. Stanford: Stanford University Press.

FARMER P., 1992, AIDS and Accusation: Haiti and the Geography of Blame. Berkeley, CA: University of California Press.

——, 1999, Infections and Inequalities: The Modern Plagues. Berkeley: University of California Press.

——, 2002, La violence structurelle et la matérialité du social. Leçon inaugurale. Paris: Collège de France.

——, 2003, Pathologies of Power: Health, Human Rights, and the New War on the Poor. Berkeley: University of California Press.

FARMER P. and A. CASTRO, 2004, Pearls of the Antilles? Public Health in Haiti and Cuba. *In* Unhealthy Health Policy: A Critical Anthropological Examination. A. Castro and M. Singer, eds. Pp. 3–28. Walnut Creek, CA: Altamira Press.

FARMER P. and B. J. GOOD, 1991, Illness Representations in Medical Anthropology: A Critical Review and a Case Study of the Representation of AIDS in Haiti. *In* Mental Representation in Health and Illness. J. A. Skelton and R. T. Croyle, eds. Pp. 132–162. New York: Springer-Verlag.

FARMER P., M. CONNORS and J. SIMMONS, eds, 1996, Women, Poverty, and AIDS: Sex, Drugs, and Structural Violence. Monroe, MN: Common Courage Press.

FITZGERALD T. K., ed., 1976, Nutrition and Anthropology in Action. Amsterdam: Van Gorcum.

FLETCHER R., 1881, Cranial Amulets and Prehistoric Trephining. 35th Regular Meeting of the Anthropological Society. Washington, DC, pp. 47–51.

FOSTER G., ed., 1951, A Cross-Cultural Anthropological Analysis of a Technical Aid Program. Washington, DC: Smithsonian Institution.

——, 1977, Medical Anthropology and International Health Planning. Social Science and Medicine 11:527–534.

FOSTER G. and B. G. ANDERSON, 1978, Medical Anthropology. New York: Wiley.

FRAKE C., 1961, The Diagnosis of Disease among the Subanun of Mindanao. American Anthropologist 63:113–132.

FRANKENBERG R., 1988, Gramsci, Marxism, and Phenomenology: Essays for the Development of Critical Medical Anthropology. Medical Anthropology Quarterly 2(4):324–337.

GARDENER H., 1985, The Mind's New Science. New York: Basic Books.

GINSBURG F. and R. RAPP, 1991, The Politics of Reproduction. Annual Review of Anthropology 20:311–343.

GOOD B. J., 1994, Medicine, Rationality, and Experience: An Anthropological Perspective. Cambridge: Cambridge University Press.

GREENWOOD D., S. LINDENBAUM, M. LOCK and A. YOUNG, 1988, Introduction. Theme Issue: Medical Anthropology. American Ethnologist 15(1):1–3.

INHORN M., 1994, Quest for Conception: Gender, Infertility, and Egyptian Medical Traditions. Philadelphia: University of Pennsylvania Press.

——, ed., 2002, Infertility around the Globe: New Thinking on Childlessness, Gender, and Reproductive Technologies. Berkeley, CA: University of California Press.

JANZEN J., 1978, The Comparative Study of Medical Systems as Changing Social Systems. Social Science and Medicine 12:121–129.

JEROME N. W., R. F. KANDEL and G. H. PELTO, eds, 1980, Nutritional Anthropology. Pleasantville, NY: Redgrave.

JOHNSON T. M., 1983, SMA Business. Medical Anthropology Quarterly 14(2):24.

JORDAN B., 1978, Birth in Four Cultures: A Cross-Cultural Investigation of Childbirth in Yucatan, Holland, Sweden and the United States. Montréal: Eden Press.

——, 1989, Cosmopolitical Obstetrics: Some Insights from the Training of Traditional Midwives. Social Science and Medicine 28(9):925–944.

KIM J. Y., J. MILLEN, A. IRWIN and J. GERSHMAN, 2000, Dying for Growth: Global Inequality and the Health of the Poor. Monroe, MA: Common Courage Press.

KLEINMAN A., 1975, Explanatory Models in Health Care Relationships. In Health of the Family. National Council for International Health, ed. Pp. 159–172. Washington, DC: NCIH.

——, 1978, Concepts and a Model for the Comparison of Medical Systems as Cultural Systems. Social Science and Medicine 12:85–93.

——, 1980, Patients and Healers in the Context of Culture. Berkeley: University of California Press.

LAYNE L., 2000, Transformative Motherhood: On Getting and Giving in a Consumer Culture. New York: New York University Press.

LEIGHTON D. C., 1970, From the Editor's Desk. Medical Anthropology Newsletter 2(6):1–5.

LESLIE C., 1976, Asian Medical Systems. Berkeley, CA: University of California Press.

——, 1989, Indigenous Pharmaceuticals, the Capitalist World System, and Civilization. Kroeber Anthropological Society Papers (69–70):23–31.

LOCK M., 1993, Encounters with Aging: Mythologies of Menopause in Japan and North America. Berkeley: University of California Press.

LOCK M. and P. A. KAUFERT, eds, 1998, Pragmatic Women and Body Politics. New York: Cambridge University Press.

MARTIN E., 1987, The Woman in the Body: A Cultural Analysis of Reproduction. Boston: Beacon Press.

MEAD M., 1942, And Keep your Powder Dry. New York: Morrow.

MORGAN L. M., 1987, Dependency Theory in the Political Economy of Health: An Anthropological Critique. Medical Anthropology Quarterly 1(2):131–154.

——, 1998, Latin American Social Medicine and the Politics of Theory. In Building a New Biocultural Synthesis: Political-Economic Perspectives in Biological Anthropology. A. Goodman and T. Leatherman, eds. Pp. 111–134. Ann Arbor: University of Michigan.

MORGAN L. and M. W. MICHAELS, 1999, Fetal Subjects, Feminist Positions. Philadelphia: University of Pennsylvania Press.

MORSY S. A., 1990, Political Economy in Medical Anthropology. In Medical Anthropology: A Handbook of Theory and Method. T. M. Johnson and C. F. Sargent, eds. Pp. 22–46. New York: Greenwood.

NAVARRO V., 1985, US Marxist Scholarship in the Analysis of Health and Medicine. International Journal of Health Services 15:525–545.

NICHTER M., 1996, The Primary Health Care System as a Social System: Primary Health Care, Social Status, and the Issue of Team-Work in South Asia. *In* Anthropology and International Health: Asian Case Studies. M. Nichther and M. Nichte, eds. Pp. 111–134. Amsterdam: Gordon and Breach.

PAUL B., ed., 1955, Health, Culture, and Community: Case Studies of Public Reactions to Health Programs. New York: Russell Sage.

——, 1963, Anthropological Perspectives on Medicine and Public Health. Annual of the American Academy of Political and Social Sciences 346.

PELTO G. H., P. J. PELTO and E. MESSER, eds, 1989, Research Methods in Nutritional Anthropology. Tokyo: United Nations University.

PETROFF I., 1881, Amphibious Aborigenes of Alaska. 35th Regular Meeting of the Anthropological Society 1:33–39.

PFEIFFER J., 2003, International NGOs and Primary Health Care in Mozambique: The Need for a New Model of Collaboration. Social Science and Medicine 56(4):725–738.

PILLSBURY B., 1986, Making a Difference: Anthropologists in International Development. *In* Anthropology and Public Policy: A Dialogue. W. Goldschmidt, ed. Pp. 10–28. Washington, DC: American Anthropological Association.

——, 1991, International Health: Overview and Opportunities. *In* Training Manual in Applied Medical Anthropology. C. E. Hill, ed. Pp. 54–87. Washington, DC: American Anthropological Association.

POLGAR S., 1962, Health and Human Behavior: Areas of Interest Common to the Social and Medical Sciences. Current Anthropology 3(2):159–205.

——, 1972, Population History and Population Policies from an Anthropological Perspective. Current Anthropology 13:203–211.

QUANDT S. A. and C. RITENBAUGH, eds, 1986, Training Manual in Nutritional Anthropology. Washington, DC: American Anthropological Association.

RAGONE H., 1994, Surrogate Motherhood: Conception in the Heart. Boulder: Westview Press.

RAPP R., 1999, Testing Women, Testing the Fetus: Amniocentesis in America. New York: Routledge.

RICHARDS A. I., 1932, Hunger and Work in a Savage Tribe: A Functional Study of Nutrition among the Southern Bantu. London: Routledge.

——, 1939, Land, Labour and Diet in Northern Rhodesia: An Economic Study of the Bemba Tribe. London: Oxford University Press.

RIVERS W. H. R., 1906, The Todas. London: Macmillan.

ROCKAFELLAR N. and V. ADAMS, 2002, The Legacy of George Foster and the Invention of Medical Anthropology. University of California at Berkeley Anthropology Centennial Conference, Berkeley, California.

RUBEL A. J., 1960, Concepts of Disease in Mexican-American Culture. American Anthropologist 62:795–814.

——, 1964, The Epidemiology of a Folk Illness: Susto in Hispanic America. Ethnology 3:268–283.

SCHEPER-HUGUES N., 1990, Three Propositions for a Critically Applied Medical Anthropology. Social Science and Medicine 30(2):189–197.

SCOTCH N., 1963, Medical Anthropology. Biennial Review of Anthropology 3:30–68.

SCOTT C., 1969, Social Science Involvement in Schools of Public Health. Medical Anthropology Newsletter 1(5):4–5.

SINGER M., 1986, Developing a Critical Perspective in Medical Anthropology. Medical Anthropology Quarterly 17(5):128–129.

——, 1989, The Coming of Age of Critical Medical Anthropology. Social Science and Medicine 28:1193–1203.

——, 1990, Reinventing Medical Anthropology: Toward a Critical Realignment. Social Science and Medicine 30(2):179–187.

——, ed., 1997, The Political Economy of AIDS. New York: Baywood.

SINGER M. and H. A. BAER, 1995, Critical Medical Anthropology. New York: Baywood.

SINGER M., H. A. BAER and E. LAZARUS, 1990, Critical Medical Anthropology in Question. Social Science and Medicine 30(2):v–viii.

SOBO E., 2003, Theoretical and Applied Issues in Cross-cultural Health Research: Key Concepts and Controversies. *In* Encyclopedia of Medical Anthropology: Health and Illness in the World's Cultures. C. R. Ember and M. Ember, eds. Pp. 3–11. New York: Kluwer/Plenum.

STEBBINS K., 1993, Constraints upon Successful Public Health Programs: A View from a Mexican Community. *In* Health and Health Care in Developing Countries: Sociological Perspectives. P. Conrad and E. B. Gallagher, eds. Pp. 211–227. Philadelphia: Temple University.

TAUSSIG M., 1980, Reification and the Consciousness of the Patient. Social Science and Medicine 14:3–13.

TENDLER J., 1975, Inside Foreign Aid. Baltimore: Johns Hopkins University Press.

WAITZKIN H., 1981, A Marxist Analysis of the Health Care Systems of Advanced Capitalist Societies. *In* The Relevance of Social Science for Medicine. L. Eisenberg and A. Kleinman, eds. Pp. 333–339. Dordrecht: Reidel.

WEIDMAN H., 1968, From the Editor's Desk. Medical Anthropology Newsletter 1:1–8.

——, 1978, Miami Health Ecology Project Report: A Statement on Ethnicity and Health. Miami, FL: University of Miami, Department of Psychiatry.

——, 1982, Research Strategies, Structural Alterations and Clinically Relevant Anthropology. *In* Clinically Applied Anthropology. N. Chrisman and T. Maretski, eds. Pp. 201–241. Boston: Reidel.

WHITEFORD L. M., 1993, International Economic Policies and Child Health. Social Science and Medicine 37(11):1391–1400.

WHITEFORD L. M. and L. MANDERSON, eds, 2000, Global Health Policy, Local Realities: The Fallacy of the Level Playing Field. Boulder, CO: Lynne Rienner.

YOUNG A., 1976, Some Implications of Medical Beliefs and Practices for Social Anthropology. American Anthropologist 78:5–24.

Chapter 3

BRAZIL

Much More than Medical Anthropology: The Healthy Body and Brazilian Identity

Annette Leibing

This article addresses Brazilian contributions to the field of medical anthropology, although the diversity in topics and methodologies makes it difficult to write about it as a unified field. The local aspect cannot be described separately from transnational fluxes of knowledge, but some elements can nevertheless be highlighted in order to better understand the specific context of a national production within this subdiscipline. First of all, in Brazil, it is rarely even called medical anthropology (*antropologia médica*), but more often "the anthropology of health," "– of the body," and so on. Medical anthropology has been criticized by some Brazilian scholars as returning to studies of local or so-called alternative forms of medicine, while generally pointing out the shortcomings within biomedicine, but nevertheless arguing within the same criticized positivistic framework of much of biomedical thinking. An aversion to a perceived American hegemony in the field underlies this argument, while European, mainly French, German, and British sources, have been more influential for some leading Brazilian scholars. The reason the expression "medical anthropology" is maintained in the title of this essay is that I want to focus on the above-mentioned "so on" in the Brazilian context, where very fine scholarly work exists that often goes unnoticed by anthropologists abroad.

Antropologia médica connotes for many a restricted scope of the field. This is why I would suggest applying this expression to the international field and using (the more optimistic sounding) anthropology of health to indicate a *Brazilian* way of doing medical anthropology, which is loosely linked to the former but is not subordinate to it.[1] Having said that – and this is meant as a unifying proposal and not as a final truth – some general reflections on Brazilian health politics and anthropological topics will be followed by a more specific analysis of the origins of the field (whatever its designation). These are embedded in a more generalized discussion of Brazilian national identity – an important issue in Brazilian social sciences.

Topics of Reflection

It is not by coincidence that the question of identity is intimately linked to the problem of popular culture and the State; ultimately, to speak about

Brazilian culture means to discuss the political destinies of the country. (Ortiz 1999:13)

In Brazil, those health problems traditionally linked to poverty go hand in hand with the typical problems of rich nations. Infectious and degenerative diseases, subnutrition, and a high rate of obesity form the specific paradoxical scenario with which the Brazilian health system has to deal. It is based on the division between a high tech private sector and a public sector which provides, although with strong regional variations, only basic care with long waiting lists, shortages of materials and health professionals, and a concentration in urban centers.[2] While this situation is not atypical for developing countries, what is specific to Brazil is the extreme preoccupation with health within the population. Indeed, Brazil holds the rank of second per capita highest rate worldwide for plastic surgery (Statistics (ISAP) 2001), a fact that has already lead some to call the country a "hypochondriac nation" (*Jornal do Brasil* 1999). In the state of Rio de Janeiro, there exists one pharmacy for every 2,648 inhabitants, while the World Health Organization (WHO) recommends one for every 8,000 (*Jornal do Brasil* 1999,5).

Brazilian body politics must be seen in the background of this immense market. The following observations from the US Department of Commerce accurately reflect the situation:

> Brazil is the largest, most populous and most industrialized country in Latin America. The Brazilian GDP reached approximately US$700 billion in 1996, the 8th largest in the world. [. . .] Overall US-Brazil trade reached US$21.5 billion in 1996, with US exports representing US$12.7 billion of the total trade figure. As a result of Brazil's market opening, the US–Brazil balance of trade currently represents the 7th most important trade surplus for the United States economy worldwide. [. . .] According to 1990 figures, Brazil invested the lowest percentage of per capita spending in the public health care sector in Latin America, with US$19.1 billion, or 2.76% of the national GDP dedicated to the sector, averaging US$127.50 per capita.
>
> [. . .] A survey conducted by the Ministry of Health concluded that the total number of patients hospitalized in Brazil during 1994 (latest information available), is as follows: private entities: 40%; philanthropic entities: 32%; public entities: 17%; and university hospitals: 11%.
>
> [. . .]
>
> Brazil is a top consumer of pharmaceuticals worldwide. Brazilians consume a wide variety of medicines, varying from analgesics to amphetamines. [. . .] Since 1994, the stabilization of the economy increased the purchasing power of the lower class. Average monthly inflation declined from 50 per cent in 1994 to its current average of less than 1 per cent. Since 1994, 13 million new consumers entered the market. Also, the opening of the market allowed different kinds of products to enter Brazil, such as the full range of vitamins and food supplements. People from the middle and upper classes, comprising 52 per cent of the market, comprise the principal consumer case of these products. Even though this group has had access to basic medicines, they now consume a wider variety of products, including weight loss products. Another factor influencing the market growth is cultural. The Brazilian pharmacies do not always require doctor's prescriptions to sell medicines. Anyone can buy almost any type of medicine in Brazil, without prescriptions.

According to official statistics, 80 million Brazilians are accustomed to purchasing medicines without prescription. In fact, for every three boxes of medicine sold in Brazil, only one is prescribed by a doctor. The most consumed drugs are analgesics, antiphlogistic and vitamins, but, since the past three years, amphetamines are increasingly being used. Brazil now is the world largest consumer of amphetamines, approximately 20 million tons are consumed per year. Drugs such as Prozac increased 43% over the last two years. (Strategis Canada 2002)

What are the current topics that Brazilian anthropologists of health work on? In the 1980s, as Ana Maria Canesqui (1994) observed, the main topics were nutrition, and health and disease in relation to the urban working classes (see Duarte 1986, a "classic" in Brazilian anthropology of health) or to other minority groups. In particular, these topics included clinical practice, the specialists and institutions, and criticisms of the shortcomings of biomedical knowledge and its practices in comparison to the more "holistic" framework of native models of health intervention.

Carrara (1994), in the beginning of the 1990s, describes the changing focus of the anthropological gaze from more "primitive" doctrines as practiced by Indian and ethnic groups to a more modern description of urban marginalized populations, where madness and sexuality are but two of the main topics that go hand in hand with a shift from spiritual topics to more material, organic matters like disease categories or new technologies (e.g., Salem 1997). In doing so, social scientists have increasingly made inroads into areas that had previously been only occupied by medical professionals, who are sometimes working in the same institutions – a situation rarely seen outside of Brazil. At the same time, anthropological analysis became more abstract, at least for some, and less centered on traditional ethnography, leading to more sophisticated epistemological reflections. It is interesting to note that in Brazil, feminist or "critical" approaches have rarely been adopted, nor has economic background data been used, something that can be found more frequently in either public health studies or other social sciences like sociology or urban studies. This is not to say that Brazilian researchers in the anthropology of health are not critical, but critique here is the result of analysis, not a starting point.

Beside conference programs organized by various scientific organizations[3] that give a good overview of topics in the field, several edited volumes (Alves and Minayo 1994; Alves and Rabelo 1998; Duarte and Leal 1998; Leal 1995; Leibing 1997, 2004) also highlight some of the themes chosen by Brazilian (and some foreign) anthropologists of health. These volumes began to be published in the 1990s, but except for *The Medical Anthropologies in Brazil* (Leibing 1997), they are all in Portuguese. However, more and more Brazilians are publishing in other languages, as well as studying and working abroad.[4]

Medicine and Anthropology – Defining the National

[Brazil] . . . is of course not a sick society, but rather a disturbed one (*perturbação*). [. . .] Besides its very high rates of diseases, Brazil suffers a moral suffering, from missing perspectives and from disenchantment about the missing perspectives of the Nation. (Duarte 1998)

In the introduction to a recently edited volume on Brazilian anthropology of health and medical anthropology (both terms are used), carrying the subtitle *Tracing Identity and Exploring Boundaries*, the authors, Paulo César Alves and Miriam Rabelo (1998), state that there is no unifying methodological or theoretical understanding demarcating the boundaries of the field (see also Leibing 1997). This is not surprising given the diversity of backgrounds and theoretical orientations within this ever-growing field in Brazil. The first studies were undertaken by scholars working in the public health field, mainly epidemiologists, but in recent years social anthropologists have founded a parallel discipline in the wider field of health and society.[5]

What can be shown within the variety of contexts and theoretical approaches is a certain approved way of thinking, which is inseparable from some influential groups in the anthropology of health. This kind of knowledge is often but not exclusively linked to the diffusion of ideas stemming from the *Museu Nacional*, the graduate program in anthropology of the Federal University of Rio de Janeiro (PPGAS). Though the *Museu* does not represent the whole of Brazil,[6] it is an important influence that is often used to define "good anthropology."

Brazilian anthropologists, including those who work within the subfield discussed here, rarely – though this is changing – study topics outside of their national boundaries. The reason – not enough funding, as some pragmatically argue – can also be understood as an ongoing preoccupation with the Nation's identity (Ortiz 1998, 1999; DaMatta 1983; Duarte n.d.; Leibing and Benninghoff-Luehl 2001; Lesser 1999; and others). This can be described as a constant awareness or preoccupation with what is considered Brazilian versus the Other, or the authenticity of the Brazilian in negotiation with or in controversy with foreign elements. This preoccupation with the boundaries between national and international medicine, as well as a Brazilian national body, can be traced to early medical texts. For example, at the First Brazilian Medical Congress in 1888, the lead speaker and *Tropicalista* Júlio de Moura stated that Brazilian doctors should ask themselves, "What do we want? What are our ideas? What [future] directions do we envisage?" and to which Moura himself answered: "What preoccupies us now is . . . tropical pathology . . . There is no other area of medicine in which we can so readily . . . establish . . . the value of [Brazilian] research . . . The French have already instituted the study of exotic disorders . . . to improve the health of their naval personnel. Such an initiative should have begun in our country . . . How great would the reputation of Brazilian medical professors grow" (Peard 1999:81).

Another example is the nationalization of a disease like syphilis, as described in a fine analysis by Sérgio Carrara (1996, 1997). He shows how at the beginning of the 20th century a "foreign disease" like syphilis became an important site for formulating a national modern identity which "attempted to value the country's non-European heritage rather than seeing Amerindian and African roots as the sole source of all the nation's evils" (1997:93). Throughout Brazilian history, ethnicity and race have been important markers of the national discourse. Sometimes this has been formulated in a positive sense – by locating the "soul" of Brazilian culture and its authenticity and even superiority[7] in poorer populations, while endlessly repeating the mantra of the democracy of the three races (black, white, native Indians).[8] The shadowy side of this discourse is that it often masks an intrinsic racism of the mainly white upper classes (see Fry 2001; Maio and Santos 1996; Sheriff 2001), maintaining in a "cordial" way the strong hierarchical thinking of Brazilian society.[9]

The relationship between race (sometimes climate) and the national body, especially within psychiatry at the beginning of the 20th century, has been extensively analyzed, as in Jurandir Freire Costa's description of the eugenics movement in Brazil (Costa 1981). At that time, scientists discussed the danger facing the Brazilian race stemming from nonwhite immigrants; "mixture of blood" became an important means of conceptualizing Brazilian identity (Lima and Hochmann 1996; Peard 1999; Schwarcz 1993; and others).

As Jane Russo (2000) has noted, one instrument of the Brazilian "civilization process" was psychoanalytical theory, which was eagerly adopted by Brazilian psychiatrists in the first half of the 20th century, in part because it was able to explain and channel Brazilian sexuality – sometimes seen in a positive light as sensuality, sometimes as primitive or uncivilized. For Brazilians, sexuality is the source of never-ending jokes and playful ways of communication, while at the same time provoking anxiety and strong moral judgments and rules (Goldstein 1999; Parker 1991). It is no wonder that sexuality (as deviance, or as related to AIDS or to gender and reproduction, etc.) is a common topic in Brazilian anthropology of health.

The "national" within Brazilian anthropology of health is sometimes described in contrast to a US hegemony with its theoretical reductionism[10] and pragmatism; drawing inspiration from Europe for theory is common (and elegant). Classical theories in the social sciences, applied in a contemporary way, entangle foreign-derived theory with local topics and elevate it to a higher level of a national anthropology. This does not mean an adherence to the fashionable "new hope from Europe" as is happening these days in North America, but mainly the old Europe and its theorists such as Max Weber, Walter Benjamin, Georg Simmel, Marcel Mauss, Louis Dumont, and others who are evoked in formulating and understanding Brazilian health phenomena.

Cecília Minayo (1998), in a lucid overview of the field, states that "[a]n important counterpoint to the American hegemony in the field comes from French anthropology" (1998:33). This observation is not limited to anthropology, since historically, members of the elite in Brazil spoke French.[11] This language was also understood and sometimes spoken by the relatively small middle class, who were by the 1920s considered "the social embodiment of progressive modernity" (Owensby 1999:4). Through the mass media, ideas of modernity were "imported" from metropolises like New York, London, or Paris and incorporated into Brazilian value systems and hierarchies. Renato Ortiz (1998) describes the "classical discussion" of Brazilian intellectuals on the authenticity of Brazilian culture as revolving round the penetration of foreign ideas into Brazilian thinking and the question of imitation, a concern which was most markedly formulated at the influential "Modern Arts Week" in 1922. However, as Ortiz has argued, foreign ideas were mainly used to legitimize national concerns and were not a simple importation. This is similar to Minayo's (1998) observation that the anthropology of health is an "adolescent science" – a science in the making, temporarily being sustained by arguments from abroad and in need of more intense dialogue *within* the Brazilian scientific community.[12]

There are also other authors who have made an impact on Brazilian anthropology of health, though they cannot all be mentioned here. For example, Michel Foucault and Ludwik Fleck are important sources for discussing medical epistemologies, and authors influenced by them often provide a critique of the medical establishment. Other authors, most of them based on European intellectual schools (Mary Douglas' work), or others like Adam Kuper, are important, as are North American works like Allan Young's *The Harmony of Illusion* (1995) or Byron Good's *Medicine, Rationality, and Experience* (1994), which both critically analyze the making of medical knowledge.[13]

This does not mean that North American sources are "banned" from Brazilian work, since they are probably the most often quoted (Minayo 1998). What I am describing here – again – is how one could situate a specifically Brazilian way of doing what is considered there to be good anthropology by leading anthropologists. What one can observe today with increasing frequency is a self-confident exchange with a diversity of foreign and national sources, without the initial insecurity regarding authenticity.

National Topics: Psychiatry and Native Brazilians

> The sociologist who wants to understand Brazil often has to transform himself into a poet. (Bastide 1957:15)

Two topics should serve in the following to illustrate the discussion on national medical anthropology: psychiatry and native Brazilians. Both are topics which have their origins in the European gaze on the "exotic Brazilian," especially going back to Claude Lévi-Strauss who helped to found the University of São Paulo and taught there between 1934 and 1937. His book *Tristes Tropiques* (1976) formed a milestone for ethnographic texts on Brazilian Indians.[14]

Research on native medical systems is often about *ethnomedicines* which relate strongly to the otherness of the described system. As in many other contexts, native medicine in Brazil is also mostly described as holistic (as opposed to reductionist biomedicine) and as operating in a psychological system of personhood (socially embedded) as opposed to the so-called Western individualistic thinking. Newer approaches look at Indian medicine and health as being interwoven with the wider Brazilian social and political landscape and the people as suffering from a marginal status which directly influences health and dignity (e.g., Ferreira 2004). Langdon (1999), in a short overview of the field, writes that after the Second World War social scientists, and especially anthropologists, started to reflect on and to intervene in indigenous health practices which were conceived as "ignorant practices" or as obstacles to official health interventions. Langdon also states that after 50 years the general conditions, including health, of most indigenous populations are still precarious. Related to this is the field of *ethnobotanics* with the Amazon forest as its central symbol. The local aspect of most "ethno" approaches has been transcended by the international discussion on the preservation of the Amazon and the national preoccupation of bio-piratery and the defense of national boundaries.

Francine Saillant (2004) writes about the complex inside–outside position of gazing native Brazilians and provides a description of practices of caring within *caboclo* communities living in the Amazon. These persons, who are the descendents of whites and Indians and mostly poor, are practically invisible because they do not have the exotic charm of Indian tribes, nor are they part of the mainstream Brazilian society; they are "beings in-between."

In 1938, Roger Bastide became the successor of Lévi-Strauss at the University of São Paulo and his interest in psychiatry opened another path for anthropological inquiry: ethnopsychiatry. As in the case of native medicine, two approaches exist side by side. In a simplified form, there is the holistic approach of traditional, shamanistic healing practices and the search for culturally sensitive models which implicitly or explicitly criticize biomedical thinking. These approaches are used to try to reach disadvantaged groups within Brazilian society: for example, healing rituals for persons living in marginalized communities in the northeastern part of the country have been developed by the psychiatrist Adalberto Barreto, who studied ethnopsychiatry in France. This approach is more praxis-oriented, as is the Brazilian Association of Ethnopsychiatry, whose members are mainly psychiatrists.

A second school is focusing more on the penetration of mainstream psychiatric medicine into Brazilian society, analyzing its values and truth claims. This more theoretical approach transcends the local–global division and provides valuable information about how certain forms of knowledge became institutionalized in Brazil (e.g., Carrara 1998; Duarte 2000).

Conclusion

In order to present some of the richness of Brazilian contributions to the field of medical anthropology/anthropology of health, I have provided a partial "picture" by focusing on the definition of national boundaries and identity. This being said, in conclusion, how can one describe the "Brazilian-ness" of the national anthropology of health? Two overlapping definitions of the "national" are conceivable from what has been discussed above: first, the specificity of local Brazilian topics no doubt distinguishes Brazilian anthropology of health from other contexts. There are, for example, the body politics of the Afro-Brazilian religions (Caroso et al. 1997; Monteiro 1985), the richness of the "tropical pharmacy" (Elisabetsky and Nunes 1990), the (not so) native Indian notions of the body and health (Ferreira 2004; Forline 2004), and structural violence as a factor in social suffering (Scheper-Hughes 1992). While these topics have often been linked to the interest of foreign anthropologists in the "exotic" part of Brazilian culture, and therefore are less fashionable in today's intellectual climate, some of these topics – which for a while were almost excluded from the anthropology of health and were seen as belonging to the anthropology of religion or to general anthropological scholarship concerning Indians – are now being taken up in a new way. Certain phenomena are no longer perceived as folklore apart from mainstream national and international culture, but as the result of a continuous historical process of negotiations and institutionalizations.

A second point is the refusal to accept a North American hegemony in delimitating a theoretical scope (although this does not apply to all social scientists working in the field) and the self-confident choice of European sources, without completely ignoring important scholars in Canada, the United States, and other countries. The result, an often elegantly written analysis of the roots and origins of cultural phenomena, definitely adds to and expands upon much of what one can read in medical anthropology.

Echoing Moura's preoccupation from 1888 – "What [future] directions do we envisage?" – we might return to one more observation from Minayo's article (1998): "I am . . . defending . . . a correspondence between anthropology and the most relevant questions for a population, the system and its sanitary politics" (1998:43). Minayo sees a danger in isolating anthropology into its own academic niche if it is unable to establish a dialogue with other health-related disciplines. She is correct. Some hold the notion that more applied work is often methodologically insufficient, while others believe theoretical work is becoming increasingly "abstracted from the 'real' world."

Many ways of looking at health have a place in Brazil; theoretical and applied work cannot be seen as mutually exclusive, but rather as complementary. Accordingly, the difficulty could rather come from a division between the two orientations which would deny the insights gained from multiple approaches and the will to accept each others limits and complementarities. "We are living in a specially remarkable period," wrote Sigmund Freud in 1939, when he saw that science had become one-sided and aversive to "the other": "We find to our astonishment that progress has allied itself with barbarism" (Canguilhem 1998). Anthropology *can* be part of this kind of barbarism if scholars move too far away from political, economic, and phenomenological factors related to disease and health, or likewise acknowledge only the applied approaches with their often unrecognized "pastoral powers" being seen as "good science." Putting barbarism and other "-isms" into context is an ongoing task for all medical anthropologists – in Brazil this is happening through fine analysis, not by simply through being "critical."

Acknowledgments

I would like to thank my Brazilian colleagues from whom I have learned much and the two anonymous reviewers. I regret that I had to leave out many references due to space restrictions.

Notes

1. An alternative stems from Carrara (1994:41) who suggests using anthropology *and* health/medicine/the body/AIDS, etc. This would emphasize that culture is but one element in understanding the biocultural phenomena of health.
2. A popular joke is about a mother who asks her little daughter:

   > Where have you been?
   > In my room, playing doctor with Joãozinho.
   > Doctor??? screams the horrified mother.
   > Doctor from the SUS (public system), mummy . . . He did not even touch me.

3. For example: ABA, the Brazilian Anthropological Association, *Abrasco*, the Brazilian Association of Public Health, or *Anpocs*, the Brazilian Society for Graduate Studies in Social Sciences.
4. The way in which the impression of non-Brazilians (Gilles Bibeau, Marilyn Nations, Francine Saillant, Richard Parker, Nancy Scheper-Hughes, and many others) differs from a Brazilian one on health-related topics in Brazil would make interesting research for another article. It would be worth considering why certain topics which seem to be in the foreground when looking at Brazil from abroad – such as the extreme plasticity of the Brazilian body (plastic surgery, fitness, etc.) or the use and abuse of psychotropic medication even by "normal" people in order to be able to lead a "normal" life – do not seem to be part of the research agenda. Another subject could be the choice of "exotic" topics by foreigners versus a tendency to analyze mainstream medicine by Brazilians.
5. For the history of anthropology in Brazil, see Corrêa (1995), Peirano (2000), and Neiburg (2002).
6. The Rio de Janeiro group studying the wider field of suffering is multi-institutional. Other more visible research groups are linked to the Anthropology Department of the Federal University of Rio Grande do Sul and the Public Health School (*Escola de Saúde Pública*) of the Federal University of Bahia, beside a number of smaller groups and single researchers.
7. One example would be Brazilian flexibility (*jeitinho*) which reveals Brazilian superiority in comparison to the stiff (and unsensual) foreigners (Leibing 2002).
8. Race and ethnicity are used as interchangeable here since both are used to designate hierarchies or, as Immanuel Wallerstein (2000:84) wrote on "peoplehood": "[It] resolves one of the basic contradictions of historical capitalism – its simultaneous thrust for theoretical equality and practical inequality."
9. In an interesting study on the Afro-Brazilian religion Xangô, Beatriz Góis Dantas (1988) shows how in a paradoxical way practices of "whiteness" are incorporated into a discourse on the superior "authentic African."

10. Examples would be Luiz Fernando Duarte's critique of North American discussion on *nerves* (Duarte 1993) or Fabíola Rohden's comments on Emily Martin's approach in *The Woman in the Body* (Rohden 1998). Also, the article by psychiatrist Octavio Domont da Serpa Jr on culture-bound syndromes includes an early critique of North American medical anthropology (Serpa Jr 1994).

11. On the formation of the Brazilian elite at the end of the 19th century, marked by European, especially French, influences, see Needell (1987).

12. Needell (1987:199) also writes (about the *fin-de-siècle* French literature) that as "Brazilians kept *au courant* with these trends, they naturally assimilated and adapted them; there was no simple copying. The new schools found echoes among Brazilian writers seeking to make reputations by reworking fashionable trends in their own way."

13. In a superficial way, one could describe the common ground of the newer theoretical references in the leading schools in the field as emphasizing a socio-history of cultural phenomena.

14. It is revealing that Lévi-Strauss, at the beginning of "Tristes Tropiques," describes New York poetically, where its streets are compared to shady valleys in which colorful cars look like flowers. Right afterwards he describes, with a certain shame, Rio de Janeiro and its famous hills, which he compares to stumps in a toothless mouth. It is the good savage he is expecting and not the urban world. And, beside the shock about the misery he finds in the native Brazilian communities, it is nevertheless the beauty and authenticity of the people and nature that overwhelms Lévi-Strauss and lets him talk again in the most poetic metaphors.

References

ALVES P. and M. C. S. MINAYO, eds, 1994, Saúde e Doença, Um olhar antropológico. Rio de Janeiro: Fiocruz.

ALVES P. C. and M. C. RABELO, 1998, Introdução 7–12. *In* Antropologia da Saúde, Traçando identidade e explorando fronteiras. Rio de Janeiro: Relume Dumará.

BASTIDE R., 1957, Brésil: terre de contrastes. Paris: Hachette.

CANESQUI A. M., 1994, Notas sobre a produção acadêmica de antropologia e saúde na década de 80. *In* Saúde e Doença, Um olhar antropológico. P. Alves and M. C. S. Minayo, eds. Pp. 7–12. Rio de Janeiro: Fiocruz.

CANGUILHEM G., 1998, The Decline of the Idea of Progress. Economy and Society 272/3:313–329.

CAROSO C., N. RODRIGUES, A. F. NAOMAR, E. CORIN and G. BIBEAU, 1997, When Healing is Prevention: Afro-Brazilian Religious Practices Related to Mental Disorders and Associated Stigma in Bahia, Brazil. *In* The Medical Anthropologies in Brazil. A. Leibing, ed. Pp. 195–213. Berlin: VWB Verlag.

CARRARA S., 1994, Entre Cientistas e Bruxos – Ensaios sobre dilemas e perspectivas da análise antropológica da doença. *In* Saúde e Doença, Um olhar antropológico. P. Alves and M. C. S. Minayo, eds. Pp. 33–46. Rio de Janeiro: Fiocruz.

——, 1996, Tributo a Vênus, A luta contra a sífilis no Brasil, da passagem do século aos anos 40. Rio de Janeiro: Fiocruz.

——, 1997, The Symbolic Geopolitics of Syphilis: An Essay in Historical Anthropology. *In* The Medical Anthropologies in Brazil. A. Leibing, ed. Pp. 81–95. Berlin: VBW.

——, 1998, Crime e Loucura, O aparecimento do manicômio judiciário na passagem do século. Rio de Janeiro: Eduerj/edusp.

CORRÊA M., 1995, A Antropologia no Brasil (1960–1980). *In* História das Ciências Sociais no Brasil, vol. 2. S. Miceli, ed. Pp. 314–333. São Paulo, Sumaré.

COSTA J. F., 1981, História da Psiquiatria no Brasil. Rio de Janeiro: ed. Campus.

DAMATTA R., 1983, Carnavais, Malandros e Heróis, Para uma sociologia do dilema brasileiro. Rio de Janeiro: Zahar.

DANTAS B. G., 1988, Vovô Nagô e Papai Branco, Usos e abusos da África no Brasil. Rio de Janeiro: Graal.

DUARTE L. F. D., 1986, Da Vida Nervosa nas Classes Trabalhadoras Urbanas. Rio de Janeiro: Jorge Zahar.

——, 1993, Os Nervos e a Antropologia Médica Norte-Americana: Uma revisão crítica. Physis 3(2):43–74.

——, 1998, Interview: A Antropologia Médica Pede Passagem. Colóquio 13:33–38.

——, ed., 2000, Antropologia e História dos Saberes Psicológicos. Cadernos IPUB VI (18).

——, n.d., La nature nationale: entre l'universalisme scientifique et la particularité symbolique des nations. Civilisations 52(2):21–44.

DUARTE L. F. D and O. F. LEAL, eds, 1998, Doença, Sofrimento, Perturbação: Perspectivas etnográficas. Rio de Janeiro: Fiocruz.

ELISABETSKY E. and D. S. NUNES, 1990, Ethnopharmacology and its Role in Third World Countries. Ambio 19:419–421.

FERREIRA M. L., 2004, Atração Fatal: Trabalho escravo e o uso de psicotrópicos por povos indígenas de São Paulo. *In* Tecnologias do Corpo. Uma antropolgia das medicinas no Brasil. A. Leibing, ed. Pp. 81–111. Rio de Janeiro: NAU.

FORLINE L., 2004, Contato Iminente, Saúde Desamparada: Consequências dos contatos interétnicos com os índios Guajá no Maranhão. *In* Tecnologias do Corpo. Uma antropolgia das medicinas no Brasil. A. Leibing, ed. Pp. 249–275. Rio de Janeiro: NAU.

FRY P., 2001, Feijoada e Soul Food 25 Anos Depois. *In* Fazendo Antropologia no Brasil. N. Esterci, P. Fry and M. Goldenberg, eds. Pp. 35–56. Rio de Janeiro: DP&A.

GOLDSTEIN D., 1999, Interracial Sex and Racial Democracy in Brazil: Twin Concepts? American Anthropologist 101(3):563–578.

GOOD B. J., 1994, Medicine, Rationality, and Experience. An Anthropological Perspective. Cambridge: Cambridge University Press.

Jornal do Brasil, 1999, Falsa hipocondria. June 1, 5.

LANGDON E. J., 1999, Saúde e Povos Indígenas. Os desafios na virada do século, Congreso Latinoamericano de Ciencias Socialess y Medicina, Isla de Margarita, Venezuela, 7 June.

LEAL O. F., ed., 1995, Corpo e Significado, Ensaios de antropologia social. Porto Alegre: UFRGS.

LEIBING A., 2002, Flexible Hips? On Alzheimer's Disease and Aging in Brasil. Journal for Cross-Cultural Gerontology 17:213–232.

LEIBING A., ed., 1997, The Medical Anthropologies in Brazil. Berlin: VWB Verlag.

——, 2004, Corpo, Vulnerabilidade e Tecnologia. Uma antropolgia das medicinas no Brasil. Rio de Janeiro: NAU.

LEIBING A. and S. BENNINGHOFF-LUEHL, ed., 2001, Devorando o Tempo, Brasil, o país sem memória. São Paulo: Mandarim.

LESSER J., 1999, Negotiating National Identity: Immigrants, Minorities, and the Struggle for Ethnicity in Brazil. Durham, NC: Duke University Press.

LÉVI-STRAUSS C., 1976 [1955], Tristes Tropiques. Paris: Plon.

LIMA N. T. and G. HOCHMAN, 1996, Condenado pela Raça, Absolvido pela Medicina. O Brasil descoberto pelo movimento sanitarista da Primeira República. *In* Raça, Ciência e Sociedade. M. C. Maio and R. V. Santos, eds. Pp. 23–40. Rio de Janeiro: Fiocruz.

MAIO M. C. and R. V. SANTOS, eds, 1996, Raça, Ciência e Sociedade. Rio de Janeiro: Fiocruz.

MINAYO M. C. S., 1998, Construção da Identidade da Antropologia na Área de Saúde. O caso brasileiro. *In* Antropologia da Saúde, Traçando identidade e explorando fronteiras. P. C. Alves and M. Rabelo, eds. Pp. 29–46. Rio de Janeiro: Relume Dumará.

MONTEIRO P., 1985, Da Doença à Desordem, A magia da umbanda. Rio de Janeiro: Graal.

NEEDELL J. D., 1987, A Tropical Belle Epoque, Elite Culture and Society in Turn-of-the-century Rio de Janeiro. Cambridge: Cambridge University Press.

NEIBURG F., 2002, A Propósito de Mana, Espaços Nacionais e Circulação Internacional de Idéias. Mana 8(1):165–179.

ORTIZ R., 1998, Cultura Brasileira e Identidade Nacional. São Paulo: Brasilense.

——, 1999, A Moderna Tradição Brasileira, Cultura brasileira e indústria cultural. São Paulo: Brasilense.

OWENSBY B. P., 1999, Intimate Ironies, Modernity and the Making of Middle-class Lives in Brazil. Stanford: Stanford University Press.

PARKER R. G., 1991, Corpos, Prazeres e Paixões, A cultura sexual no Brasil contemporâneo. São Paulo: Best Seller.

PEARD J. G., 1999, Race, Place, and Medicine, The Idea of the Tropics in Nineteenth-century Brazilian Medicine. Durham: Duke University Press.

PEIRANO M. G., 2000, A Antropologia como Ciência Social no Brasil. Etnográfica 4(2):219–232.

ROHDEN F., 1998, Ensaio Bibliográfico, O Corpo Fazendo a Diferença. Mana 4(2):127–141.

RUSSO J. A., 2000, A Psicanálise enquanto Processo Civilizador. Um projeto para a nação brasileira. Cadernos do IPUB VI(18):10–20.

SAILLANT F., 2004, Saber e Itinerários de Cuidados na Amazônia Brasileira. O doméstico na encruzilhada do espaço terapêutico. *In* Tecnologias do Corpo.Uma antropolgia das medicinas no Brasil. A. Leibing, ed. Pp. 227–247. Rio de Janeiro: NAU.

SALEM T., 1997, As Novas Tecnologias Reprodutivas. O estatuto do embrião e a noção da pessoa. Mana 3(1):75–94.

SCHEPER-HUGHES N., 1992, Death Without Weeping, The Violence of Everyday Life in Brazil. Berkeley: University of California Press.

SCHWARCZ L. K. M., 1993, O Espetáculo das Raças, Cientistas, instituições e questões racial no Brasil, 1870–1930. São Paulo: Companhia das Letras.

SERPA Jr, O. D., 1994, Culture-bound syndromes e a natureza das classificações psiquiátricas. Jornal Brasileiro de Psiquiatria 43(9):483–491.

SHERIFF R. E., 2001, Dreaming Equality, Color, Race, and Racism in Urban Brazil. New Brunswick: Rutgers University Press.

STATISTICS (ISAP), 2001, website http://www.isaps.org, accessed August 2001.

STRATEGIS CANADA, 2002, website http://strategis.ic.gc.ca/SSG/dd76139e.html, accessed June 23, 2002.

WALLERSTEIN I., 2000, The Construction of Peoplehood. Racism, Nationalism, Ethnicity. *In* Race, Nation, Class, Ambiguous Identities. E. Balibar and I. Wallerstein, eds. Pp. 71–85. London: Verso.

YOUNG A., 1995, The Harmony of Illusions, Inventing Post-Traumatic Stress Disorder. Princeton: Princeton University Press.

Chapter 4

MEXICO

Medical Anthropology in Mexico: Recent Trends in Research and Education

María Beatriz Duarte-Gómez,
Roberto Campos-Navarro, and Gustavo Nigenda

Introduction

Our objective in this chapter is to illustrate the development of medical anthropology in Mexico. The chapter will be divided into three sections. The first is a review of the history of the development of anthropology as an academic discipline interested in the health/illness/caregiving process among different peoples. In it, we will present a historical summary from the beginnings of medical anthropology to the second decade of the 20th century, under the critical influence of Anglo-Saxon anthropology. Then, we will analyze its consolidation around the second half of this century with the institutionalization of *indigenism* as a public policy guiding government action with respect to American Indian communities. Lastly, we will focus on the past few decades during which it has diversified, broadening the range of research to include peasant and urban communities.

In the second section, we will examine the subjects and institutions that use anthropology as a tool for analyzing and understanding the health/illness/caregiving process. Medical anthropology increasingly draws on disciplines other than anthropology, for example from the field of health, and has been greatly enriched through that encounter.

In the third section, we will describe how medical anthropology developed teaching and training for the country's technical and professional managers beginning in the 1930s when the Escuela Superior de Medicina Rural (school for rural medicine, ESMR) was created to secure doctors trained to work in rural communities and able to understand American Indian cultures. In the 1980s and 1990s, graduate-level programs in medical anthropology were set up. Recently, the Department of Health has adopted a policy that encourages its employees to take training in intercultural relations; it is only just being implemented and is limited to a few locations. Some concluding remarks will follow.

The Anthropology of Health and Illness in Mexico:
A Brief Historical Summary

Although medical anthropology in Mexico is not solely restricted to the sociocultural aspects that affect the health/illness/caregiving process among American Indian groups, we will nonetheless highlight indigenous people in this summary as they were the main object of research until the mid-20th century.

The arrival of the Spanish in the mid-16th century on what is now Mexican soil marked the beginning of the conquest of indigenous groups. It also instigated a range of genetic, biological, and cultural exchanges that included the introduction of diseases against which Native groups had no immunity and for which they had no therapeutic resources.

Over the following centuries, what we will call biomedicine (also referred to as Western, modern, scientific, or Galenic medicine) developed mainly to the advantage of dominant groups, while local medicines remained the main resource for American Indians (Aguirre-Beltrán 1994). In the extremely rare cases in which American Indians received biomedical treatment, it was administered by members of religious orders who had created health posts or infirmaries for the exclusive use of Native Mexicans. In these posts, a sort of intercultural medicine developed involving adaptations such as using Native languages, serving local foods, incorporating traditional therapeutic methods by local healers, and hiring local personnel (Campos-Navarro and Ruiz-Llanos 2001).

At the end of the colonial Spanish regime, American Indians lived mainly in what were referred to as "refuge zones" (Campos-Navarro 2003) where institutional health activities were later concentrated. Indigenous culture was considered to hinder the progress of capitalism, which was met with strategies for integrating American Indians through education and intermarriage (Aguirre-Beltrán 1994). The governments of the Republic never took much interest in the health of Native peoples; on the contrary, they closed hospitals such as the Real Hospital de San José de los Naturales, considered to be the best hospital for Indians in New Spain (Campos-Navarro and Ruiz-Llanos 2001). Patients were sent to the San Andrés hospital in Mexico City, which became the Hospital General de México in 1904. Nonetheless, several other hospitals continued to be administered by the Church. During the period known as the "Porfiriato" (1879–1910), the government did not adopt any real health policy, seeking only to "correct the scientific delay and catch up to the large nations" by creating several urban hospitals (Brachet 2003).

We will analyze the policies regarding indigenous people in Mexico in three phases, beginning with the Revolution of 1910.

The first phase (1910–1933) witnessed what could be considered to be the beginning of medical anthropology in Mexico, with Gamio's work (1916) on the connection between development and nutrition. This was also the period when what is known today as *indigenism* began with Gamio's book *Forjando Patria* (1916), which became a grassroots book for integrating indigenous peoples into Mexico's political and social system (Aguirre-Beltrán 1994; Campos-Navarro 2003; Gamio 1916; Pozas and Pozas 1976).

In a quest for unity in the population and the abolition of inequality, the Mexican Revolution continued an assimilationist form of indigenism, with a few nuances depending on the group of ideologues (Pozas and Pozas 1976). For example, Gamio proposed a positive exchange of values from which a national culture would emerge, and he suggested that healers and midwives be incorporated and trained instead of being attacked. At the other end of the spectrum, there were those who proposed the complete Westernization, or even extermination, of Indians (Aguirre-Beltrán 1994).

The services of scientific medicine were made available to the general population through campaigns for eradicating endemics and epidemics. Since it was a private medicine reserved for individual care, not only was it economically inaccessible for American Indians, it was also culturally and geographically beyond reach (Bonfil 1994). Meanwhile, American Indians preserved their own traditions for dealing with health and illness, reinterpreting, assimilating or rejecting elements of the new medical culture. In 1926, Robert Redfield was already speaking of a transition model by which patients and practitioners resorted to one medicine or another (Aguirre-Beltrán 1994). Certain indigenous practices, such as the use of medicinal plants described by chroniclers and academics from the Conquest to the present day, were considered useful.

The second phase (1934–1967) is noteworthy for the institutionalization of indigenism as an official policy, and the implementation of development projects through the Instituto Nacional Indigenista (National Indigenist Institute, INI). Indigenism was designed as a policy of liberation, but did not take into account those it was intended to liberate. Its objective was the nonviolent assimilation of indigenous peoples into a society that, presumably, would offer them a better standard of living through education (in Spanish), health care, and land redistribution (Aguirre-Beltrán 1994; Aguirre-Beltrán and Pozas 1973; Flores 1998; Gamio 1916; Hernández et al. 1993; Pozas and Pozas 1976).

The reflections of the First National Conference on Rural Health, in 1936, resulted in obligatory social service for all medical students. In addition, the Escuela Superior de Medicina Rural (ESMR) was created as part of the Instituto Politécnico Nacional (national polytechnic institute, IPN). These measures were intended as strategies for guaranteeing the availability of doctors able to work in rural communities and to understand Native cultures, but they were short-lived. It was during that period that medical anthropology developed under the influence of Gonzalo Aguirre-Beltrán and Miguel Othón de Mendizábal.

As a public policy, indigenism was adopted during the discussions and declarations of the First Interamerican Indigenist Congress, held in Patzcuaro in 1940. On that occasion, cultural relativism and the importance of cooperation between anthropology and the biological sciences were discussed for the first time (Aguirre-Beltrán 1994). The indigenist policy was implemented by specialized organizations such as INI, created in 1948 to oversee development in indigenous regions through coordination centers, which in turn set up health centers to be overseen by doctors and indigenous advocates. Their objective was to introduce Western medicine and to "change attitudes and beliefs that might prevent people from accepting the benefits of scientific medicine" (Campos-Navarro 2003).

The idea of intercultural medicine put forward by Aguirre-Beltrán, who is considered to be the pioneer of medical anthropology in Mexico, was even more assimilationist in its character and goals: to break down the cultural barriers to public or socialized medicine. He suggested that health care should be mainly preventive, including residences where family members could stay and traditional healers would work. He also promoted multidisciplinary teamwork and wanted anthropological research findings to be used to guide health workers (Aguirre-Beltrán 1994). Moreover, he believed that biomedicine should be made available to Indians whether or not they asked for it, adapting it to the cultural context of communities through health training, and integrating it into the intercultural context (Campos-Navarro 2003). Critical anthropology, on the other hand, was opposed to imposing forms, contents and values on indigenous peoples and argued in favor of an intercultural medicine based on knowledge of Native cultures, whose goal would be to produce biological, cultural, social, and environmental changes. It also questioned the idea that culture was the main cause of the problems facing American Indians; a more critical perspective instead laid the blame on social and economic difficulties.

In the third phase, from 1968 on, the Ministry of Health (SSA) consolidated its role as the entity responsible for the health of American Indians. The treatment models excluded all options that deviated from scientific medicine, despite the fact that in its discourse the government supported ethnic pluralism (Pozas and Pozas 1976).

During this period, health-care services gradually increased in indigenous communities with the arrival of medical personnel from INI, SSA, and the Instituto Mexicano de Seguro Social (Mexican social security institute, IMSS) in cooperation with IMSS-COPLAMAR (later IMSS-Solidaridad, and today IMSS-Oportunidades). The latter was created in 1979 as part of a program that interfaced with traditional medicine and that still exists today (Campos-Navarro 2003). However, the program has been criticized for having a weak sociocultural orientation, which is essential for understanding the health/illness/caregiving process process and for planning services properly (Aguirre-Beltrán 1994).

A number of international agreements and declarations have been signed that, while they have not ensured the necessary changes in relations between Aboriginal peoples and Western societies, they have served, and still do serve, as a way to move towards guaranteeing American Indians' right to health care. These agreements include, for instance: the Declaration of Alma Ata, ratified in 1978; the International Labor Organization's Convention 169 on Indigenous and Tribal Peoples (1989); the Hemispheric Workshop on Health and Indigenous Peoples signed in Winnipeg, Canada in 1993; the Health of Indigenous Peoples Initiative of the Pan American Health Organization (PAHO) and the World Health Organization (WHO), in 1992; and the Declaration of the International Decade of the World's Indigenous People beginning in 1994. In spite of the commitment of the world's nations, these agreements have not met all the objectives they set out to achieve.

Starting in 1968, critical anthropology, represented most notably by Eduardo Menéndez, Arturo Warman, Guillermo Bonfil, and Margarita Nolasco, clashed with Aguirre-Beltrán's culturalist orientation, taking some research and institutional projects in new directions. At the beginning of the 21st century, interculturality in official Mexican health services is still just in its inception. There are exceptions in certain projects and programs that integrate aspects of intercultural care, such as having traditional therapists present in some of the health units run by INI, SSA, or IMSS-Oportunidades, or making some local adaptations such as using hammocks instead of hospital beds (Campos-Navarro 1997). In addition, two hospitals were created where traditional therapists can offer consultations in an allopathic context: one is in Cuetzalán, Puebla, and the other in Jesús María, Nayarit. Although this initiative on the part of INI gives American Indians access to two medical approaches, the lack of awareness and training among Western health employees with regards to intercultural work makes it difficult to adequately develop the potential of these hospitals for teaching, research, and care.

Over the last ten years, health services, which were the responsibility of INI in indigenous regions, have been gradually transferred to the health services of individual states (Servicios Estatales de Salud or SESA) as part of a process of decentralization and extended health coverage. During the last decade of the 20th century, as a result of the revitalization of the indigenous movement in its battle to recover dignity and autonomy, "Indigenous peoples have moved into the political space as subjects with alternative proposals to make" (Aguirre-Beltrán and Pozas 1973) and the theme of indigenous peoples can be heard in all official speeches in Mexico.

In this new scenario of international and national proposals and pressure from indigenous and nonindigenous groups, the current government (2000–2006) has created an institution that advises the executive branch of the government and must represent the interests of indigenous peoples to the government. In addition, the government has proposed that institutions of the same level as ministries be created to promote an ethnic and intercultural vision in all its programs. In 2001 moreover, SSA set up the Health and Nutrition for Indigenous Peoples Coordination. It lasted only two years, but its traditional medicine department (which still exists and is in its beginnings) promotes training in intercultural relations. INI has disappeared and its place is now occupied by an intersector national commission for the development of Indigenous peoples.

Furthermore, on June 15, 2001, the Presidents of Mexico and the Central American countries signed the Plan Puebla Panamá (PPP), one of the eight basic objectives of which is human and social development, including a regional health project. The state of Puebla took advantage of the context in which the Plan was approved to create five hospitals with traditional medicine components to them (Hospitales Integrales con Medicina Tradicional) (Secretaría de Salud de Puebla 2003). Their impact on people's health will be assessed in the future.

There are other attempts at intercultural health-care models used by NGOs, some of which originated with the beginnings of the Zapatista movement. The Zapatista movement has demanded social changes to improve the poor material living conditions that often result in deaths due to curable and preventable diseases. The current Zapatista strategy is to avoid using government health services as much as possible. Instead, with the help of NGOs, the movement has set up independent disease prevention and health recovery projects.

In spite of the progress made, either through acceptance or tolerance of traditional medicine in specific programs or projects (Nigenda et al. 2001) and a more open attitude to dialogue and cooperation, the official health system has not yet integrated in its practices the principle according to which the therapeutic effectiveness of drugs is linked to the symbolic and emotional context that is meaningful only in a given culture. Neither has it allowed communities to fully participate in decisions regarding health services (Pozas and Pozas 1976).

Research

Between 1990 and 2000, Mexican medical anthropology diversified its subjects of interest and entered a new phase of theoretical and methodological research. On the one hand, this is the product of new institutions devoted to rural development located in remote regions. On the other, it can be traced to the influence of public health as an intermediary in knowledge production.

During the entire period when indigenous medicine was the focus of study, most of the institutions and researchers interested in medical anthropology were in Mexico City and very few of them were located in the regions. It seems that the Universidad Veracruzana where Aguirre-Beltrán carried out the final phase of his research was the only exception. Prior to 1990, most of the institutions interested in the development of medical anthropology were government institutions, universities, and research centers funded by the Department of Education.

More recently, private and civil nonprofit organizations, known as nongovernmental organizations (NGOs), came onto the scene, giving the field greater diversity.

Public health, as a field that studies people's health needs and the socially developed mechanisms for fulfilling them, has had a significant impact on today's view of medical anthropology. Public health concepts and methods have been used to forge strong connections with medical anthropology, and a considerable amount of scientific research has consequently been generated.

Although Gonzalo Aguirre-Beltrán was a physician and his work had an enormous influence on the development of Mexican medical anthropology, prior to the 1990s, medicine took very little interest in medical anthropology. Medical anthropology was mainly the domain of anthropologists, and their professional perspective colored both the approach to research and the subjects discussed at the time. Today, there is clearly another element in play: a growing number of researchers trained in the biological, medical and social sciences are involved in the development of the field. This is fundamental for the future of medical anthropology. Although the discipline theoretically defines specifically anthropological themes in the area of health, illness, and death, as well as methods of fieldwork and analysis, it is difficult to draw a clear line between the academic production in the field of medical anthropology, and research in subdisciplines close to it, such as medical sociology or social medicine. In itself, the difference can be as important for assessing academic production and its achievements in related subdisciplines, as it is for identifying the gaps that need to be filled in the future.

It is important to emphasize the fact that over the course of its history, medical anthropology has been able to use its research outcomes to help design and implement government policies for improving health conditions and providing services. From the outset, medical anthropology research in Mexico was conducted in government institutions, not universities. Again, it was Aguirre-Beltrán who made the connection between the two. Over the years, medical anthropology has probably become a more academic than pragmatic activity. However, it is clear that providing government services requires a knowledge of issues that are not yet well understood, such as the connection between culture and service use, or the interaction between service users and providers. And this is despite the fact that these aspects constantly change as new programs and services are offered.

A significant part of the reason that medical anthropology has become more focused on research is that universities have become more open to the field. Yet in many cases universities have not succeeded in establishing a good working relationship with the government institutions responsible for providing the population with health services. To some extent, this is because researchers are the biggest critics of public institutions, which can have the effect of distancing them, but it is also because the institutional differentiation in the Mexican public sector has not developed a workable strategy for interacting. It is worth remembering that Aguirre-Beltrán was both a renowned academic and a civil servant involved in government actions. A critical view of society is no doubt one of the researcher's tasks, and medical anthropology should be no exception. Nonetheless, it is also important to actively encourage dialogue with decision-makers in order to negotiate the value and practical use of research results.

There have also been ethnological and ethnographic phases in the development of medical anthropology. In the periods prior to 1990, both the development of theoretical proposals and data collection in the field (and its application) went hand in hand. In the past few years, the vast majority of work has been based on field data and has been interpreted with predefined theories. Recently, although theoretical formulations have been more limited and have been concentrated in a few institutions, their influence has been no less significant. The work of Eduardo Menéndez may well be the most important in that regard. His theoretical proposals have received support among a large number of contemporary medical anthropologists, both in Mexico and elsewhere in Latin America and in Europe.

There have been many contributions to Mexican anthropology by foreign researchers (such as Robert Redfield, Oscar Lewis, and George Foster, to name those most well known) and they have been vital to its development. A large portion of the theoretical academic production that is influential in Mexico comes from foreign countries, in particular the United States, France, and England. Recent work in Mexican anthropology has been based on these theories, and ethnographies continue to be conducted in large part by researchers who do not work in Mexican academic institutions.

Lastly, it is important to point out that Mexican anthropology is in an expansion phase and that the participation of researchers who also have training in other areas has enriched the discipline. The boundaries originally set by indigenist anthropology have been transcended. We have gone from studies in traditional medicine to health issues of the day, such as institutions and chronic diseases. The pioneering era is over, and we now have a critical mass to influence the development of medical anthropology, as well as a greater regional and institutional diversity.

Institutions and Themes

As mentioned in the previous section, over the past few years there has been an institutional diversification in the production of information based on scientific research. Most of the institutions are governmental and they are mostly located in the south of the country, but there are also some in the northern states, such as Sonora (Table 4.1). Private or social institutions also play a role in producing research-based publications. However, most of the work is done in just a few institutions: the Centro de Investigaciones y Estudios Superiores en Antropología Social (CIESAS), the Faculty of Medicine at the Universidad Nacional Autónoma de México (UNAM), and the Instituto de Investigaciones Antropológicas, which also is part of UNAM. Most of the institutions that support research in medical anthropology are universities, both in the capital and in the rest of the country.

As we can see, research themes still revolve around indigenous medicine, in both its practical and ideological aspects; for instance, the use of medicinal plants, concepts regarding sexuality, and reproduction. However, equally interesting approaches, for example those developed by Arthur Rubel, Rolando Collado-Ardón, and others regarding the epidemiological view of traditional illnesses such as *susto* (magical fright), have not been continued and remain simply a part of the historical legacy of research in the country.

It is important to point out that one of the key moments in the history of modern medical anthropology in Mexico occurred in 1994 when INI published the Biblioteca de la Medicina Tradicional. It was the result of an enormous amount of work on traditional medical practices and concepts among Mexico's First Nations, and took almost ten years to complete.

Recently, other themes have come to the forefront. One of them is the study of alcoholism in indigenous communities directed by Eduardo Menéndez at CIESAS. Health program assessments carried out by public institutions have also increased. They have shown that the programs are not always as culturally sensitive as they could be, despite efforts to adapt them to local conditions. Evidently, the adjustments have been insufficient in both quantity and quality, and an in-depth knowledge of community preferences is needed so they can be adapted to each group. Because government programs are based on criteria that place priority on the effectiveness, not quality, of health care (which is particularly relevant to interactions between users and providers), the programs tend to be the same from one area to another.

Studies on the connection between programs and how they are used has opened up many different lines of research. The theme that has received the most attention

Table 4.1 Institutions where Research in Medical Anthropology is Conducted in Mexico.*

Institution	Type	Belongs to	Themes
Centro de Estudios Superiores en Antropología Social	Public	Secretaría de Educación Pública	Theoretical developments, medical models, home care, alcoholism
Instituto Nacional Indigenista	Public	Secretaría de Desarrollo Social	Traditional and indigenous medicine
Instituto Nacional de Antropología e Historia	Public	Secretaría de Educación Pública	Health and religion, traditional medicine
Instituto de Investigaciones Antropológicas	Public	Universidad Nacional Autónoma de México	Medical ideology, the body, traditional medicine
Centro Universitario de Ciencias de la Salud	Public	Universidad de Guadalajara	Chronic disease, family health, health institutions
Facultad de Medicina	Public	Universidad Nacional Autónoma de México	Traditional medicine, intercultural health, chronic disease
Facultad de Ciencias Antropológicas	Public	Universidad Autónoma de Yucatán	Indigenous medicine
Facultad de Ciencias Sociales	Public	Universidad Autónoma de Sonora	Traditional medicine, herbalism
Escuela de Medicina	Public	Universidad Veracruzana	Indigenous medicine, HIV/AIDS
El Colegio de la frontera sur (ECOSUR)	Public	Consejo Nacional de Ciencia y Tecnología	Mental health
Instituto Nacional de Salud Pública	Public	Secretaría de Salud	Medical models, health services use, health-care quality, AIDS

(Continued)

Table 4.1   *(Continued)*

Institution	Type	Belongs to	Themes
El Colegio de México	Public	Secretaría de Educación Pública	Reproductive health
El Colegio de Sonora	Public	Secretaría de Educación Pública	Occupational health
El Colegio de Michoacán	Public	Secretaría de Educación Pública	Traditional medicine, healers
NGO	Private/ social	Independent	Reproductive health in indigenous villages
Fundación	Private/ social	Independent	Alternative medicine, health conditions and health care in indigenous villages
Mexicana para la Salud			

*Compiled by the authors, 2004.

is sexual and reproductive health, mainly because the largest number of consultations and hospitalizations in the Mexican health-care system is related to pregnancy and childbirth. In many of the marginalized regions of the country, maternal and infant mortality rates remain high, and over the decades, inadequacies in the quality of reproductive health care and violations of reproductive rights have been observed.

AIDS has become an important research theme because of the epidemiological scope of the problem. Research has shown that society in general, and health service providers in particular, stigmatize those infected with AIDS. AIDS is probably the area where the connection between research and policy-making is the most direct.

Research on alternative or complementary medicine is also worth mentioning. It is very topical and its impact has yet to be assessed in many countries. In spite of the fact that nearly 8 percent of urban-dwellers frequently use complementary medicines, formal health systems deny their existence; what is more, there is much confusion over what exactly alternative medicines are. Although most of the approaches have been imported recently, the health system tends to classify them with traditional medicine, meaning they are considered to have a rational basis that cannot be scientifically proven, and therefore are viewed as relatively ineffective and difficult to defend. Nevertheless, people use them more and more, and an in-depth understanding of their logics and how they interact with the health-care system is imperative.

In short, current medical anthropology research in Mexico is the product of a series of historical events that helped to construct its initial conceptual foundation, which was focused on the study of American Indian groups. Various different approaches were then added to that base, enriching the vision of medical anthropology and making it into an essentially academic activity. Medical anthropology has taken very little interest in directly applied research or health program assessments. Currently, there are a number of health programs (both federal and state) that need performance assessments. Given that they need the anthropological perspective to understand quality of care, patient satisfaction, patients' perspectives on programs, and many other aspects that apply to indigenous and non-indigenous populations, the field may well experience rapid expansion in the future.

Teaching Medical Anthropology in Mexico

As the field of study has grown, developed, and been consolidated in Mexico, so has teaching. It began piecemeal as early anthropologists who had studied, directly or indirectly, the health/illness/caregiving process began to teach.

As mentioned earlier, Mexican medical anthropology began with the avant-garde work of M. Gamio on improving the living conditions of people in the Teotihuacán valley (1922), in which he emphasized food and its nutritional value. Later, under the direction of M. Sáenz in Cañada de los Once Pueblos, efforts were made to introduce medical care into Purépecha communities in the state of Michoacán (1932–33). In the 1940s and 1950s, Gonzalo Aguirre-Beltrán, the theoretician of cultural relativism in Mexico and disciple of Melville Herskovits and of Gamio, came onto the scene. He published books that have become classics in Mexican medical anthropology, including *Los programas de salud en la situación intercultural* (1994), *Magia y Medicina. El proceso de aculturación en la estructura colonial* (1963), and *Antropología Médica. Sus desarrollos teóricos en México* (1986).

In 1939, Aguirre-Beltrán with Miguel Othón de Mendizabal, Julio de la Fuente, and a few others gave the first systematic lessons on medical anthropology at the Escuela Superior de Medicina Rural (ESMR), which was part of IPN. The philosophy underlying the institute was to transfer scientific and technological knowledge to peasants and the working class and to offer an alternative to what was perceived to be university elitism. At ESMR, in Mexico City, they tried to train young doctors from peasant families so that they would return to their communities to practice medicine in accordance with biomedical concepts. Their efforts did not bear fruit for a variety of reasons that are not entirely clear. The demand for doctors was increasingly located in cities as the State set up and funded health institutions. It should not be forgotten that in 1943 the government created the Instituto Mexicano de Seguro Social and the Department of Health, which employed large numbers of physicians trained both in universities and at the Instituto Politécnico Nacional.

Undergraduate courses with some emphasis on ethnomedicine and traditional medicine are still being offered sporadically at the Escuela Nacional de Antropología e Historia (ENAH). In 1985, following an initiative by Eduardo Menéndez and the support of Roberto Campos-Navarro as teacher, a master's seminar in medical anthropology was begun. After 1996, the seminar had grown enough to form a group of Ph.D. students. The biannual courses, based on a critical medical anthropology perspective, established a conception of the health/illness/caregiving process that goes beyond strictly culturalist dimensions, introducing explanatory models of a more sociopolitical nature. By distancing themselves from the dominant cultural relativism, they shaped a different view that highlights the theoretical presentation of the medical models that E. Menéndez had been developing since the 1960s in important works such as *Poder, estratificación y salud. Análisis de las condiciones sociales y económicas de la enfermedad en Yucatán* (1981), *Morir de alcohol. Saber y hegemonía médica* (1990), and *La parte negada de la cultura. Relativismo, diferencias y racismo* (2002).

On account of political and administrative differences with the academic authorities of the ENAH, all three professors who directed the master's and PhD seminar had to quit in 2000, and the seminar disappeared.

In the 1990s in Mexico City, the Centro de Investigaciones y Estudios Superiores en Antropología Social (CIESAS) set up M.A. and Ph.D. programs in medical anthropology where a large number of students have been trained. Today, there are regular courses in medical anthropology at the campuses in the cities of Oaxaca and San Cristobal de las Casas, Chiapas. The professors include E. Menéndez, M. E. Módena, R. M. Osorio, S. Lerín, P. Sesia, and G. Freyermuth, and they too work within a critical medical anthropology perspective.

At the Escuela de Salud Pública (which was changed to the Instituto Nacional de Salud Pública in the 1990s), courses that are close to medical anthropology are offered. Many of the theses presented by graduate students are strongly influenced by anthropology. The professors who have worked there over the years include G. Aguirre-Beltrán, H. García Manzanedo, R. Loewe, E. Menéndez, M. Bronfman, and R. Castro.

Since the 1970s, there have been a few courses in the anthropology of medicine for residents specializing in family medicine at the Instituto Mexicano de Seguro Social under an agreement with UNAM. Currently, however, similar efforts are few and far between.

In 1985, UNAM's Faculty of Medicine included the first obligatory courses in medical anthropology in its curriculum. In an effort to give medical training a more humanistic inclination, a decision was made to include ethics and medical anthropology in the history and philosophy section. Because of the number of registrations (an average of 800 undergraduates a year), professors had to be hired who were either physicians with additional training in anthropology or else anthropologists with experience in the health/illness/caregiving process. In the beginning, the course content dealt with the origin, development, and use of medical anthropology, systems of beliefs and values in the Mesoamerican area regarding the health/illness/caregiving process, medical models, traditional Mexican lay medicine, biocultural processes (pregnancy, childbirth, post-partum care, feeding, aging, and death), anthropological aspects of the doctor–patient relationship, medical practice in intercultural contexts, and human beings as a whole.

Degrees in medical anthropology were organized along the same lines. In 2000, UNAM set up a degree in intercultural health in coordination with the Tomás Frías University in the city of Potosí, Bolivia. The curriculum stood out by its theoretical and practical character, as it allowed students to complete their degree by making a public presentation of an applied research project. Currently, B.A. programs in anthropology are being developed at the Universidad Autónoma de Guerrero, and there are master's and Ph.D. programs in intercultural health at the Universidad Mayor de San Cristobal de Huamanga in Ayacucho, Peru. The books used in UNAM courses include *La antropología médica en México* (1992) by R. Campos-Navarro and *Antropología y Práctica Médica* (1987) by Viesca et al.

Although UNAM's Instituto de Investigaciones Antropológicas does not offer graduate courses specifically on medical anthropology, it does have courses such as the anthropology of the body, the ethnology of health and illness, the anthropology of medicine and others, giving students whose research lies within the field of medical anthropology a theoretical basis. Although they do not have medical anthropology programs as such, the University of Guadalajara, the Colegio de Michoacán, the Escuela de Salud Pública/Instituto Nacional de Salud Pública, the Universidad Autónoma de Yucatán, the Colegio de Sonora, and the Universidad Autónoma del Estado de México do offer regular or occasional courses.

The Federal Department of Health, through its traditional medicine and intercultural development section, has recently tried to introduce medical anthropology into the schools of medicine and nursing. It remains to be seen how much impact its efforts will have and how long they will last. The Faculty of Medicine at the Universidad Veracruzana deserves special attention since it has an obligatory course in anthropology for which R. M. Lara y Mateos edited a textbook called *Médicina y Cultura. Hacia una formación integral del profesional de la salud* (1994).

The new government policies have created opportunities for civil society to become involved in intercultural approaches to health. For example, an NGO named Yolpahtli (intercultural health services in American Indian villages), made up of anthropologists and biomedical specialists, has designed courses to raise awareness and provide training for civil servants at the Department of Health in states where there is a significant indigenous population, in an effort to introduce an intercultural approach into health programs for Native Mexicans.

Concluding Remarks

As we have seen, medical anthropology has developed rapidly in Mexico over the past 70 years. Because of the large number of phenomena involving intercultural relations in the area of health, Mexican medical anthropologists have been able to develop their own professional identity. It is no coincidence that the same period has witnessed the foundation of government health institutions that are at the core of health services in Mexico today. In the beginning, health institutions were a reflection of the Mexican government's integrationist policy with regards to the country's indigenous peoples. Many studies focused on understanding how to achieve access to and acceptance of government health services. Once that goal was reached, they then began studying the relationship between American Indian patients and health workers, in particular doctors.

The increase in intercultural interactions gave momentum to the discipline as an important field of research, not only for producing new knowledge on the expression of interculturality in the area of health, but because that knowledge could also be applied to defining government policies and adapting programs to local realities.

It is worth emphasizing the important role that researchers from other countries have played in the development of medical anthropology in Mexico. International influence has helped to consolidate a discipline that is original, theoretically diverse, and methodologically sound, producing findings that are extremely relevant. There are many publications in medical anthropology based on studies conducted in Mexico, both by Mexicans and by foreigners, and some of them can be considered true classics nationally and internationally.

Teaching is probably the area where development has been the slowest and most disjointed. It was only in the 1980s that the Escuela Nacional de Antropologia e Historia (ENAH) set up a seminar on the health/illness relationship. Following that initiative, other institutions set up educational and on-going training programs, but they are still unable to meet the demand.

Mexican medical anthropology has gone from a foundation period during which it gained recognition, to a stage where there is a critical mass of researchers and teachers. It has moved from the almost exclusive study of traditional indigenous medicine to a wide variety of themes related to the health of the overall population. The recent thematic diversification is a sign of maturity, and the coming years will be crucial in reinforcing the discipline. In order to pool the efforts of the various institutions that foster its development, the main players need to be identified, be they universities, institutions for higher learning, health institutions, or NGOs.

References

AGUIRRE-BELTRÁN G. and R. POZAS, 1963, Magia y medicina. El proceso de aculturación en la estructura colonial. Mexico DF: Instituto Nacional Indigenista.
——, 1986, Antropología Médica. Sus desarrollos teóricos en México. Obra Antropológica XIII. México DF: FCE.
——, 1994[1955], Programas de salud en la situación intercultural. Obra Antropológica V. México DF: FCE.

——, 1973, La política indigenista en México. Métodos y resultados, vol. II, chap. 5. Medicina y Salubridad. Instituciones indígenas en México actual. Mexico DF: INI-SEP.

BONFIL G., 1994, México profundo. Una civilización negada. México DF: Ediciones Grijalbo.

BRACHET V., 2003, Nacimiento, auge del estado benefactor mexicano (1823–2000). Paper presented at a seminar on Social Policy in Late Industrialization: A Comparative Study of Latin America. Universidad de Santiago de Chile, August 13–15, 2003.

CAMPOS-NAVARRO R., 1992, La antropología médica en México. México DF: Instituto Mora/Universidade Autonóma Metropolitana.

——, 1997, La hamaca: historia, etnografía y usos médicos de un mueble americano, IMSS 35(4):287–294.

——, 2003, Una visión general sobre la medicina intercultural. Capítulo primero. Introducción a la medicina Intercultural. Mexico City: Ediciones Trillas.

CAMPOS-NAVARRO R. and A. RUIZ-LLANOS, 2001, Adecuaciones interculturales en los hospitales para indios en la Nueva España. Gaceta Médica de Mexico 137(6): 595–608.

FLORES J., 1998, La revuelta por la democracia. Pueblos indios, política y poder en México. Mexico DF: Ediciones El Atajo.

GAMIO M., 1916, Forjando Patria. México.

HERNÁNDEZ J, L. PARRA and M. MATUS, 1993, Etnicidad, nacionalismo y poder. Tres ensayos. Oaxaca: Universidad Autónoma Benito Juáre de Oaxaca.

LARA Y MATEOS R. M., 1994, Médicina y cultura. Hacia una formación integral del profesionial de la salud. Mexico DF: Ediciones Plaza Y Valdés.

MENENDEZ E., 1981, Poder, estratificacion y salud. Analisis de las condiciones sociales y economicas de la enfermedad en Yucatan. Mexico DF: CIESAS.

——, 1990, Morir de alcohol. Saber y hegemonía médica. México DF: Ediciones Patria.

——, 2002, La parte negada de la cultura. Relativismo, diferencias y racismo. Barcelona: Ediciones Bellaterra.

NIGENDA G., G. MORA, S. ALDAMA and E. OROZCO, 2001, La práctica de la medicina tradicional en América Latina y el Caribe: El dilema entre la regulación y la tolerancia. Salud Pública de México 43(1):41–51.

POZAS R. and I. POZAS, 1976, Los indios en las clases sociales de México. 5th edition. México DF: Siglo XXI.

SECRETARÍA DE SALUD DE PUEBLA, 2003, Hospitales Integrales con Medicina Tradicional. Puebla: Secretaría de Salud de Puebla.

VIESCA L., 1987, Antropología y Práctica Médica. México DF: Facultad de Medicina, Universidad Nacional Autonóma de Mexico.

Part II

Perspectives from Europe

Chapter 5

FRANCE

Medical Anthropology in France: A Healthy Discipline

Sylvie Fainzang

Presenting how the anthropology of health has developed in France and how it has contributed to international research in the field is a difficult task, since any discipline necessarily evolves in synergy with what is taking place in other countries. As we know, science has no borders, though particular national and social contexts (academic choices, political constraints, institutional changes, etc.) may leave their imprint on scientific endeavors. This is all the more true in today's world where the social context tends to be increasingly uniform under the impact of globalization. Nonetheless, in this chapter we will attempt to paint a picture of French medical anthropology, presenting its directions and dynamics, and showing how the questions that it has addressed over time must be connected to more general issues implied by social realities, and therefore by specific political, economic, cultural, and pathological situations.

Medical Anthropology: A Guaranteed Vintage?

The field of medical anthropology emerged in France in the 1980s at an intersection between different paths: it crystallized a stream of interests in the medical system and illness management in other cultures among researchers from religious anthropology, on the one hand, and biological anthropology, on the other. This period saw the emergence of different labels: medical anthropology, the anthropology of illness, and ethnomedicine. Those designations were connected to "schools" that formed around figures such as Marc Augé, Andras Zempléni, and Jean Benoist, each of whom encouraged different types of research.

Some studies have focused on biomedical issues, attempting to draw connections between the biomedical facts and processes and the sociocultural phenomena found in specific settings. These fields of research have had strong ties to other disciplines such as epidemiology. They tend to explain biomedical facts by sociocultural factors, and it is the connection between the two that makes the approach part of medical anthropology. For example, the study on the carcinogenic action of substances found in dried fish eaten by certain Chinese ethnic groups (Hubert Baré and de Thé 1988) is an example of an interdisciplinary collaboration where research in the ethnology of food was essential. As Sindzingre and Zempléni (1982) have noted, that research demonstrated a connection between lifestyle and given pathologies, and was an example of a complete medical anthropology study in that an understanding of eating strategies required a study of their socioeconomic, ecological, and political determinants. Ethnomedicine, on the other hand, has focused more on lay knowledge of illness and its treatment, with a particular interest in pharmacopoeias. Such research has been criticized for setting phenomena related to illness and medicine apart from the broader context.

The anthropology of illness developed in counterpoint both to ethnomedicine and, most particularly, to medical anthropology, with Marc Augé (1984) as its leading spokesman. In his view, the anthropology of illness could not be separated from social anthropology. For him, illness is a specific empirical object of general anthropology, and a concrete example of the links between the biological order and the social order. Taking the path laid out by Anglo-Saxon work on the importance of social control in treating illness, specifically the British school (around Evans-Pritchard and Turner) which highlighted the tactical role of healing practices in social processes, French research (Augé 1984; Zempléni 1985) has emphasized that local theories of power (theories of the person and explanatory theories of illness) are immanent in the social structure, and therefore that social processes and interpretative and therapeutic processes are dynamically linked. This approach to the anthropology of illness has sometimes led to cooperation between anthropology and other disciplines such as psychology, psycho-analysis, and psychiatry (in particular, work by Zempléni (1982) on the persecution process behind systems for interpreting illness in African societies).

Medical anthropology and the anthropology of illness thus tend to cover quite different objects, issues, and purposes (Fainzang 1990). The former tends to use anthropology to shed light on illness phenomena through knowledge of cultural realities in an effort to enrich medical research, while the latter considers that research on illness is an exceptional opportunity for reflecting on the problems raised by social and cultural anthropology. Although the notion of "the anthropology of illness" has somewhat declined in favor of the expression "medical anthropology," for the simple reason that the latter, borrowed directly from the English, is most commonly used in the international literature, nonetheless, the anthropology of illness has had a strong impact on how the field has developed in France, particularly through its holistic approach taken from its direct connection with social anthropology.

Later on, the notion of "the anthropology of health" was coined, and though it gradually gained in popularity, never completely took the place of "medical anthropology." For some, "the anthropology of health" expresses their support for social anthropology's project of studying the economic, social, and cultural changes affecting societies; for others, it conveys their desire to play an active role in both debates and actions concerning Third World development. In keeping with Marc Augé's view that the anthropology of illness should remain firmly rooted in social anthropology in general (1986), some researchers have proposed a more social and political interpretation of the basis for the relationship between health and individuals or groups. Fassin (2000b) has defined the anthropology of health as "the relationship between the physical and psychological being, on the one hand, and the social and political world on the other," making it "both something other than, and much more than, the flip side of illness to which it is often reduced, or than the idea of well-being promoted by health institutions" (2000b:96, our translation). Instead, he suggests the notion of *biologics*, that is, "social logics that put life forms *and* life itself to the test of the political." Thus, he stresses the fact that the anthropology of health, unlike medical anthropology, cannot be understood without a dual historical and political interpretation, since health is conceived as a product of society and politics.

As we can see, these different notions and designations are sometimes based on a specific theoretical foundation, and are sometimes a matter of convention; over time, the ecumenical use of the expression "anthropology of health and illness" has come to be used to refer to the field. Nowadays, the use of these notions tends to be less dogmatic, and sometimes almost no distinction is made between medical anthropology and the anthropology of health, as if to adapt to the terms most commonly used in other countries, most notably in North America and Northern Europe.

While this distinction may have seemed sterile to some foreign observers, its merit has been in reminding us not to lose the epistemological contributions of anthropology, and not to allow medical anthropology to serve only medical purposes. In many cases, the way the field has been named has implicitly questioned whether medical anthropology researchers were doing anthropology or medicine; in other words, whether they aimed to increase the profitability of health programs or to improve our understanding of man in society.

The issue of the relationship between anthropology and medicine has remained problematic, because when anthropology takes illness or medicine as its object, it has sometimes tended to identify with medicine, not managing to free itself sufficiently from the snare of biomedical categories. Francis Zimmermann (1995) maintained "we cannot completely reject the medical point of view for fear of doing no more than a history of religions," yet one might respond that it is possible to pay attention to the phenomenological dimension of illness (and its implications in terms of bodily experience and suffering) without endorsing the medical "point of view." In fact, we are increasingly coming to the conclusion that Western medicine itself is an object for anthropology, and not simply a scientific discourse that cooperates with anthropology in examining illness. Medical anthropology has wagered on its ability to use its analytical tools to study biomedicine; in other words, medical anthropology must be able to consider the biomedical system (its practices and discourses) like any other secular social practice or exotic phenomenon. This implies that medical anthropology must not be founded on the medical paradigm, epistemologically speaking. The field of illness and medicine can be examined perfectly well with categories that lie completely outside the field of medicine, that is, with truly anthropological categories. The biomedical point of view must be studied with the same critical distance as the religious point of view. But to do so, our discipline has had to renew its observational framework; most significantly, it has had to consider the possibility of studying our own society, and not just others.

The Dynamics of Fieldwork and Research Themes

In 20 years of existence, the discipline has focused on a wide variety of topics. For some, the choice has been linked to academic research itineraries, while for others it has been dictated by their desire to respond more directly to social needs.

Anthropology at Home

Although for many years anthropology defined itself as a discipline that studied the Other, research gradually turned towards Western society, in our case, French society, as its proponents became convinced that not only could the same questions be asked "at home," but that the confrontation between work abroad and work at home could help to shed light on social reality. Thus, research in France on illness and medicine that addressed the same questions as research in so-called "exotic" locations needed to be encouraged.

That is what I set out to do, borrowing not only the objects and research issues from exotic field studies, but also the methodology, in particular concerning models for interpreting illness (Fainzang 1989). The findings of that research highlighted different accusation models set in motion when illness strikes. In addition, it demonstrated both the cultural diversity of explanatory models, and the universality of the logics underlying them. "Anthropology at home" has since continued the effort to transpose questions that have been explored by anthropologists in "exotic" fieldwork settings (symbolic systems, representations of the body, the relationship between patients and health-care institutions, etc.) onto French society. In such research there has been a pronounced interest in observing practices and not just conducting interviews and collecting discourse (Fainzang 1996). The methodological, epistemological, and theoretical issues raised by practicing "anthropology at home" in the field of health and illness have been the subject of much debate in Europe, most notably concerning the conditions under which such research is possible. Those debates were formalized through the international *Medical Anthropology At Home* network, with headquarters at the University of Amsterdam (Van Dongen and Fainzang 1998).

An Unavoidable Topic: AIDS

There have been a large number of studies on AIDS for reasons that are obviously related to the development of the epidemic and the large sums of money earmarked for research on the syndrome. This has stimulated thinking on issues such as contagion, discrimination, risk, etc., which are relevant to many situations other than AIDS, but had not yet been explored as systematically (although they had been the object of the odd study). Many research projects have focused on AIDS both in African societies (e.g., Gruénais 1993; Gruénais et al. 1997; Raynaut and Muhongayire 1993), and in Western societies (Calvez 1989; Rosman 1999). Some researchers have taken a more specific interest in the illness experience and the individual, community and institutional reactions to AIDS, in particular the issue of informing others that one has the disease and the social consequences of doing so (Dozon and Vidal 1993; Hassoun 1997; Vidal 1996). These researchers have analyzed how persons with AIDS construct their experience of the illness and interpret its occurrence and manifestations, which raises issues of screening and its social implications, of information sharing with significant others, of physical and moral suffering, of how loved ones rally around the AIDS sufferer, etc.

Others have focused on the relationship between the different health-care institutions, directly in line with reflections on situations of medical pluralism most often observed in Third World societies where biomedicine has penetrated the social fabric. Researchers have sought to identify the mechanisms underlying the therapeutic itineraries of the ill in many different circumstances, specifically, how they choose from among the many treatment options, and in what order they do so, a question that is particularly germane in societies that have evolved through multiple creolizations (or *métissages*) and that are connected to postcolonial France (Benoist 1996). As AIDS has spread, some anthropologists have studied the relationship between traditional healers and biomedicine, which was largely powerless in the face of this new disease (Dozon 1996). This opened onto some central questions, for example: "can anthropological research help fight discrimination against persons with AIDS?" (Desclaux 1996:267); or "how can and must our discipline collaborate with medicine" (Raynaut 1996)? These questions were gathered together in a publication by Benoist and Desclaux (1996) who favor a more "engaged" rather than applied anthropology. They believe that anthropology has an important role to play in AIDS research, and that a neutral distance is neither possible nor acceptable. They question the distinction between fundamental and applied research, and believe that the term "engaged" can advantageously replace the word "applied," which they feel expresses a form of dominance and an "instrumentalization" of the discipline. On that point, Fassin is delighted that things are different today with AIDS, given French anthropology's longstanding mistrust of applied research. As his work has amply demonstrated, he has always questioned the borderline between the academic and the political.

While many studies have dwelt on the upheavals caused by AIDS (Cook 1996; Desclaux and Taverne 2000), others have taken a more nuanced view of its impact. Stéphane Teissier (1996), for instance, has shown that AIDS has had more the effect of exposing the world of health and medicine than of disrupting it. Other researchers have examined the social context both before and after the emergence of HIV in an effort to understand the causal relationship between the destructuring of societies and the exponential increase in AIDS in Africa. Desclaux and Raynaut (1997) have drawn attention to the responsibility of African authorities in the AIDS tragedy, showing how injustice and violence result in greater individual vulnerability, both physical and psychological. Thus, AIDS must be seen as a consequence of precarious living conditions. Fébronie Muhongayire (1997) has underlined how already fragile social situations are made worse by the upheaval in family structures. Much work has also been done on women's particular social vulnerability, particularly through studies on how the disease upsets the balance in the family structure. These studies as a whole show just how inseparable the responses to the illness are from the social treatment of fertility, the body, and the family, but also femininity, masculinity, and gender relations.

One of the more popular themes in the field of medical anthropology, which has come to the forefront through this epidemic, is risk. Aware of the wide gap between scientific knowledge and lay perceptions of health risks, researchers have taken on the task of elucidating how individuals perceive and manage risk, both in Africa and in France, and not only for AIDS (Calvez 1989, 2001; Zonabend 1989). Within an anthropological approach, risk is viewed as part of a given social context and is managed within that context. In the case of AIDS, current research shows that health issues are integrated as resources in the service of relational issues, and that risk-taking is not unconscious: it is rational, since it is a means to an end, for example in the area of relationships. Taking risks can procure significant relational benefits that may appear much more important than health concerns. Risk management involves a personal and collective assessment of one risk in comparison with others (Vidal et al. 1997). Health risks defy other risks such as social, family, and emotional risks, and an individual may manage risks by choosing the lesser of two evils. For example, the risk of losing a lover by expressing mistrust or of jeopardizing one's social recognition by not procreating may weigh heavier in the balance than the risk of losing one's health. It is quite clear that most of the time people's choices are less about taking one risk than about refusing to take another. From that standpoint, anthropology's contribution is in paying close attention to the social context surrounding risk management.

Studies have also developed around issues such as prevention and contagion (Vidal 1999). The complex debates that have taken place among health professionals regarding whether AIDS is "contagious" or "transmitted" point to more than a technical problem. The use of notions of "contagion" or "transmission" itself is an object for anthropologists because it involves reasons and social implications. Work on these notions has enriched reflections on representations of contamination, which of course is pertinent to situations other than AIDS (Bonnet and Jaffré 2003), as they speak both of the relationship to the body and the relationship to others.

Reflections on risk have led to resurgence in work on rationality. Clearly, examining care-seeking behavior strictly in reference to a medical logic is no longer possible. In the West, as in developing countries, health-seeking behavior more often obeys a social logic. However, the problem is that there may be a gap between a person's perception of his or her illness and how he or she chooses to deal with it (Fainzang 1997). Not only is this question valid in our societies (as non-Western societies do not have a monopoly over irrational behavior), but studying the behavior of those closest to medical rationality and knowledge, either professionally or culturally, gives the issue of rationality a new dimension. Understanding patients' choices is important, not in order to show how far they are from medical rationality, but to grasp the symbolic logics from which they arise. While it is clear that any analysis must take into account the reality of health policies and the social conditions in which people live in order to understand their health problems, studying behavior is nonetheless of utmost relevance when we realize that very knowledgeable people often behave in apparently irrational ways.

The topics in this nonexhaustive list have been explored not only in France but in other countries as well. The fact that it is impossible to separate the development of research in France from what is being done elsewhere is obvious in the case of the anthropology of pharmaceuticals. The field of research initiated by Van der Geest and Whyte (1988) (thus outside France) on the basis of research conducted in developing countries has led to a number of studies in the areas of drug prescription, distribution, and use. The anthropology of pharmaceuticals is being developed in English-speaking countries and in France on a wide variety of questions related to major public health problems found in countries in both the North and South: overmedication, access to prescription drugs, failure to follow prescriptions, misuse of drugs, commercial strategies, self-medication, and compliance (Haxaire 2002). The anthropological approach to pharmaceuticals is also based on an analysis of their social uses and the categories and social relations surrounding their production and distribution. Here again, like the argument that the anthropology of health and illness must remain firmly rooted in social anthropology, the anthropology of pharmaceuticals must not cut itself off from the overall anthropological project: the goal is not only to understand how prescription drugs are used, but also to see what drug use can tell us about individuals and society (Fainzang 2001).

Theoretical Orientations

The Question of Meaning

French anthropology has been deeply marked by the search for meaning, both the meaning that anthropologists give to individual behavior and social practices, and the meaning that individuals and groups themselves find in illness, the former being strongly influenced by the latter. For many anthropologists (Augé 1984; Fainzang 1986; Sindzingre 1984; Zempléni 1985), the emphasis on meaning expresses their conviction that illness representations and care-seeking are necessarily embedded in an overall symbolic system from which they cannot be separated; when illness and misfortune strike, people search for the meaning in the event and for an understanding of its causes, this search taking place within the overall symbolic system. Benoist (1996) has pointed out that the counterpart to the search for meaning is the search for care. He believes that it is not the former but the latter that guides therapeutic itineraries, and that anthropologists must pay close attention to pragmatic logics and the "social experience of illness." We are in complete agreement that the ill do not "seek meaning" from institutions or specialists in treating illnesses, since they quite often have already found a meaning in the social and cultural context of their lives. Moreover, the search for care is no doubt the most important factor in shaping therapeutic itineraries. Still, the importance of the meaning on which their behavior is based should not be denied. Meaning appears to influence not only to whom they turn, but also their choice of treatment options and their compliance with prescriptions (Fainzang 1989, 1996). Jaffré and Olivier de Sardan (1999) have suggested that we should be wary of overinterpreting illness, a position that is based more on a phenomenology of illness, but from a different perspective. Their methodological and theoretical position is that the question of meaning should be addressed differently, that is, by reasserting the primacy of emic conceptions of illness. They believe that the materiality of illness must be reintroduced into analyses and more emphasis must be placed on the language of symptoms. As anthropology endeavors to understand the search for meaning, it cannot be concerned solely with local constructions of the meaning of illness, nor with semantic networks and explanatory models of illness. In doing so, it risks masking the socioeconomic dimensions of illness, unequal access to care, and power relations within medical practice (as some would criticize a certain interpretive anthropology of doing).

Towards a More Political Outlook

French medical anthropology has been partly influenced by the critical medical anthropology developed on the other side of the Atlantic, that is, by the critical analysis of the sociomedical context in which medical anthropology has developed. One of the contributions of critical medical anthropology has been to encourage a growing number of anthropologists to systematically take into account issues of medical ethics (e.g., reflecting on medical testing in developing countries) or to study objects more distantly related to medicine, such as "humanitarian assistance."

Generally speaking, in the past few years, medical anthropology has become known for its critical outlook, even when it has not chosen that label. One of medical anthropology's main targets for criticism has been the idea that people's poor health is due to their ignorance of medical concepts and inappropriate behavior. As the field has developed across the Atlantic, anthropologists have realized the importance of not confining themselves to the study of beliefs and behavior. In their anthropological analyses, they must take into account the uneven distribution of health care, social inequalities, and industrial policies that contribute to health problems in minority communities and among the disadvantaged, as well as international policies responsible for underdeveloped health-care systems. Anthropology has been increasingly criticized for having ignored the fact that the obstacles to health-care access are more the result of medical practices than individual behavior. The development of medical anthropology here and elsewhere has enabled researchers to critically reconsider the conceptual paradigms they use and to formulate new anthropological questions.

Stepping through the opening created by North American authors such as N. Scheper-Hughes and M. Lock (1987), French authors are focusing more on political issues, sometimes taking this dimension of medical anthropology further still. Rather than follow Scheper-Hughes and Lock in their typology of the body (individual, social, and political body), Fassin (1996) argues that the individual body is also always a social and political body. He prefers to speak of a "political space of health" integrating, for instance, the embodiment of inequality and the inscription of the social order on the body. He feels it would be better to build a political anthropology of health with three dimensions: the political anthropology of the body, of medicine, and of public health. Fassin (1999) suggests linking the local and the global in the area of biopolitics and speaking in terms of the global-ization of health, making his work part of a critical anthropology perspective. He does not, however, reject involvement in health programs. He encourages greater attention to the global interdependence of the determining factors in health, which he feels is lacking in many studies in medical anthropology. Using his fieldwork in Senegal, Ecuador, and France as examples, Fassin (1999) sees health as the "litmus test" of the political realm. His work is rooted in a criticism of an exclusively cultura-list anthropology, advocating instead for a repoliticization of research in the field.

It is interesting to note that the development of work influenced by critical medical anthropology partly revives the initial vocation of the anthropology of illness, in that it proposes an analysis of medicine as the expression of domination and an approach to illness as a manifestation of the social order. While it often sets aside the cultural variable in favor of more sociological variables such as the role of medical institutions and power relations underlying medical practice, and shows greater interest in the political issues related to health, it also re-emphasizes that the concerns of medical anthropology cannot possibly be dissociated from those of general social anthropology. However, as a broader spectrum of anthro-pologists are advocating that anthropology be more applied, its more political orientation is evident both in the choice of new objects (precarious living situa-tions, health conditions, inequalities) and by a new research goal, borrowing from what medical anthropology used to be.

In this perspective, Dozon and Fassin (2001) have undertaken a criticism of public health: analyzed as a cultural phenomenon, public health involves opera-tions aimed at judging and classifying, thus revealing its status as a normative enterprise (a criticism initiated by English-speaking writers). But there is more: in addition to these "political cultures of public health," the authors point to the "cultural politics of public health," that is, the ways in which public health con-structs its relation to other cultures. These Others are considered responsible for the ineffectiveness of public health interventions and prevention programs because of their high-risk behavior and their cultural characteristics. Essentially, anthro-pology's role here is to denounce the misuse of culture, in cases where it is applied without any reference to the social and political context in which target popula-tions live. These authors have shown that public health rhetoric, which lays blame on individuals and their culture, serves to remove responsibility from political institutions for taking urgent political action to enable people to effectively gain access to care. As Massé (2002) has pointed out, although these authors may not have chosen to analyze the ethical and political implications of prevention pro-grams, unlike their Anglo-Saxon counterparts, they both defend and illustrate the criticisms that anthropology has historically made of public health.

It would not be fair, however, to conclude that the anthropological approach to public health is exclusively a critical one. Other work has examined the relevance of development projects (in West Africa, in particular), with an explicit view to helping to reform health-care systems (Jaffré and Olivier de Sardan 2003).

Should We Do Away with Culture?

Given ethnology's current interest in immigrant populations and the often problematic transition from one society to another, some authors have examined aspects that had previously been viewed solely from an ahistorical viewpoint in a new light, and have criticized work referred to as ethnopsychiatry. These criticisms have created an opportunity for some much-needed clarifications (Andoche 2001; Fassin 2000a; Rechtman 1995) regarding the ways in which the notion of culture can be used and abused, for example hiding the sociopolitical behind the psychopathological, with a tinge of the cultural.

Today, both in our own societies and elsewhere, the variation in social (historical, political, and sociocultural) contexts remains at the heart of anthropological analyses. Dozon (1997) has praised anthropologists working on AIDS in Africa for avoiding the stumbling block of culture, and Bonnet (2000) has shown in the case of drepanocytosis (sickle cell anemia) that among immigrant patients, the culture of origin is not *de facto* an obstacle to understanding a Western scientific discourse; patients' actions cannot be attributed to their culture alone, nor does their social identity boil down to a purely ethnic identity. Olivier de Sardan (1999) also argues that the analysis of the social context must remain a central axis to the anthropology of health, which he considers to be part and parcel of the anthropology of development.

Currently, the notion of culture is in crisis in the field of anthropological research. Many writings are motivated by the necessary criticism of the essentialist approach to culture, and consequently of the culturalism that sometimes tends to dominate on the other side of the Atlantic. How can culture be freed from culturalism? is a question that has also been asked by Olivier de Sardan (2001) and Fainzang (2001) amongst others.

But do we necessarily need to choose between culture and politics? I, for one, have refused to separate the cultural from the social and political, proposing rather an approach to culture that takes into account social, historical, and political dimensions (Fainzang 2001). Both culturalism and the essentialization of phenomena related to it can be challenged without rejecting all attempts to understand the cultural variables that shape social practices, alongside social and economic variables. Indeed, in the case of the cultural realities related to behavior towards doctors and prescription drugs, I felt that it was necessary to pay attention to what has historically shaped these realities, and to interpret the information in social and political terms. Culture must be viewed dynamically in its inevitable connections with history and politics, connections that shape many of the characteristics of doctor–patient relationships, for example, the practice of lying (Fainzang 2002).

The Subject as Object

Medical anthropology has also benefited from broader theoretical contributions in the social sciences that do not necessarily study illness – for example, the work of Bourdieu – which has shown to what extent problems related to health and illness are connected to structural constraints regardless of whether or not subjects are aware of them. As Dressler (2001) has shown, work that takes into account both how individuals are constrained by social structures and how they give meaning to the world around them contains elements of Bourdieu's thinking, in particular the attempt to reconcile the antinomy between structuralism and constructivism. Although Bourdieu (1987) maintains that there are objective structures which are independent of the consciousness and desires of agents, and which are capable of guiding or shaping their practices and representations (structuralism), there is also a social genesis of models of perception, thought and action, and social structures (constructivism).

It seems to me that the field of health lays out the question of the subject with particular acuity. Following a trend attributable to an enthusiasm in the social sciences for theories of action, many anthropologists tend to consider the individual as an entirely conscious, self-willed actor responsible for his or her choices and actions. However, when individual behavior is examined, it is clear that individuals are constrained not only by social structures, but also by a whole set of factors that, combined with acts over which they have real decision-making power, reveal the true complexity of social behavior. The term that best conveys that complexity is without a doubt "subject." It does not suggest that patients are passive beings, completely incapable of playing the role as actors that the social sciences now ascribe to them, nor does it imply that they are totally independent. Instead, its aim is to acknowledge the fact that individuals both act and are acted on, meaning that the role they play is partly chosen and partly imposed. The individual is a *subject*, just like the *subject of* the verb, that is, he or she is the author, and sometimes master, of his or her actions; but the individual is also a subject like the *king's subject*, in that he or she is partly subjugated or *subject to* forces beyond his or her self, specifically, social factors, the political context, and cultural influences, in other words, other laws and other rules than those of his or her making (Fainzang 2001).

The goal of this chapter was to present an overview of the anthropology of health and illness in France, its development, the different schools of thought, the fields of research, and the issues it has examined, in an attempt to identify what makes it unique. In spite of the many bumps along the way, which were in part related to quarrels among different schools, and which I choose to believe have been enriching in that they have stimulated valuable debates regarding the objects of our discipline, medical anthropology has emerged stronger and better for all these contributions, increasingly dynamic and growing exponentially. However nowadays, we must admit that the issues addressed increasingly tend to be the same in different countries and, as we can see in the international literature, research carried out in one country soon finds an echo in the others, a situation that is encouraged by a contemporary context of economic, political, and cultural globalization.

References

ANDOCHE J., 2001, Culture et santé mentale: les avatars français de l'ethnopsychiatrie. *In* Critique de la santé publique. J. P. Dozon and D. Fassin, eds. Pp. 281–308. Paris: Balland.

AUGÉ M., 1984, Ordre biologique, ordre social: la maladie, forme élémentaire de l'événement. *In* Le sens du mal. Anthropologie, histoire, sociologie de la maladie. M. Augé and C. Herzlich, eds. Pp. 35–91. Paris: Editions des archives contemporaines.

——, 1986, L'anthropologie de la maladie. L'Homme 97/98:81–89.

BENOIST J., ed., 1996, Soigner au pluriel, Essais sur le pluralisme médical. Paris: Karthala.

BENOIST J. and A. DESCLAUX, eds, 1996, Anthropologie et sida. Bilan et perspectives. Paris: Karthala.

BONNET D., 2000, Au-delà du gêne et de la culture. Hommes et Migrations 1225: 23–38.

BONNET D. and Y. JAFFRÉ, eds, 2003, Les maladies de passage. Transmissions, préventions et hygiènes en Afrique de l'Ouest. Paris: Karthala.

BOURDIEU P., 1987, Choses dites. Le sens commun. Paris: Éditions de Minuit, Coll.

CALVEZ M., 1989, Composer avec un danger. Approche des réponses sociales à l'infection au VIH et au sida. Rennes: IRTS de Bretagne.

——, 2001, Le risque comme ressource culturelle dans la prévention du sida. *In* Critique de la santé publique: Une approche anthropologique. J. P. Dozon and D. Fassin, eds. Pp. 127–144. Paris: Balland.

COOK J., 1996, La prise en charge d'enfants orphelins du sida: transfert et soutien social. *In* Anthropologie et sida. Bilan et perspectives. J. Benoist and A. Desclaux, eds. Pp. 239–262. Paris: Karthala.

DESCLAUX A., 1996, La recherche anthropologique peut-elle contribuer à la lutte contre la discrimination envers les personnes atteintes par le VIH? *In* Anthropologie et sida. Bilan et perspectives. J. Benoist and A. Desclaux, eds. Pp. 267–281. Paris: Karthala.

DESCLAUX A. and C. RAYNAUT, eds, 1997, Urgence, Précarité et lutte contre le VIH/Sida en Afrique. Paris: L'Harmattan.

DESCLAUX A. and B. TAVERNE, eds, 2000, Allaitement et VIH en Afrique de l'Ouest. Paris: Karthala.

DOZON J. P., 1996, Quelques réflexions sur les médecines traditionnelles et le sida en Afrique. *In* Anthropologie et sida. Bilan et perspectives. J. Benoist and A. Desclaux, eds. Pp. 231–235. Paris: Karthala.

——, 1997, Postface. *In* Le sida en Afrique, Recherches en sciences de l'homme et de la société. Pp. 169–172. Paris: ANRS/Orstom.

DOZON J. P. and D. FASSIN, eds, 2001, Critique de la santé publique, Une approche anthropologique. Paris: Balland.

DOZON J. P. and L. VIDAL, eds, 1993, Les sciences sociales face au sida. Paris: Éditions de l'Orstom.

DRESSLER W., 2001, Medical Anthropology: Toward a Third Moment in Social Science? MAQ 15(4):455–465.

FAINZANG S., 1986, L'intérieur des choses. Maladie, divination et reproduction sociale chez les Bisa du Burkina. Paris: L'Harmattan.

——, 1989, Pour une anthropologie de la maladie en France. Un regard africaniste. Paris: Éditions de l'École des hautes études en sciences sociales.

——, 1990, De l'anthropologie médicale à l'anthropologie de la maladie, Encyclopædia Universalis, new edition: 853–860.

——, 1996, Ethnologie des anciens alcooliques. La liberté ou la mort. Paris: Presses universitaires de France.

——, 1997, Les stratégies paradoxales. Réflexions sur la question de l'incohérence des conduites de malades. Sciences Sociales et Santé 15(3):5–23.

——, 2001, Médicaments et société. Le patient, le médecin et l'ordonnance. Paris: Presses universitaires de France.

——, 2002, Lying, Secrecy and Power within the Doctor–patient Relationship. Anthropology and Medicine 9(2):117–133.

FASSIN D., 1996, L'espace politique de la santé. Essai de généalogie. Paris: PUF.

——, 1999, Les enjeux politiques de la santé: études sénégalaises, équatoriennes et françaises. Paris: Karthala.

——, 2000a, Les politiques de l'ethnopsychiatrie. La psyché africaine, des colonies africaines aux banlieues parisiennes. L'Homme 153:231–250.

——, 2000b, Entre politiques du vivant et politiques de la ville. Pour une anthropologie de la santé, Anthropologie et Sociétés 24(1):95–116.

GRUÉNAIS M. E., 1993, Dire ou ne pas dire. Enjeux de l'annonce de la séropositivité à Brazzaville (Congo). In Les sciences sociales face au sida. Cas africains autour de l'exemple ivoirien. J. P. Dozon and L. Vidal, eds. Pp. 207–220. Centre Orstom de Petit-Bassam, GIDIS-CI/Orstom. Paris: Orstom.

GRUÉNAIS M. E., M. BOUMPOTO, G. BOUNGOU et al., 1997, Enjeux sociaux et politiques de la prise en charge des malades du sida au Congo, Attitudes contradictoires. In Le sida en Afrique, Recherches en sciences de l'homme et de la société. Pp. 117–123. Paris: ANRS/Orstom. Paris: Orstom.

HASSOUN J., 1997, Femmes d'Abidjan face au sida. Paris: Karthala.

HAXAIRE C., 2002, Calmer les nerfs: automédication, observance et dépendance à l'égard des médicaments psychotropes. Sciences Sociales et Santé 20(1):63–88.

HUBERT-BARÉ A. and G. DE THÉ, 1988, Modes de vie et cancers. Paris: R. Laffont.

JAFFRÉ Y. and J. P. OLIVIER DE SARDAN, eds, 1999, La construction sociale des maladies. Les entités nosologiques populaires en Afrique de l'Ouest. Paris: PUF.

——, 2003, Une médecine inhospitalière. Les difficiles relations entre soignants et soignés dans cinq capitales d'Afrique de l'Ouest. Paris: Karthala.

MASSÉ R., 2002, La santé publique en France, Sciences sociales et santé 20(4):141–149.

MUHONGAYIRE F., 1997, Les femmes et le sida à Kigali avant avril 1994: impacts socio-économiques et stratégies de réponse. In Le sida en Afrique, Recherches en sciences de l'Homme et de la société. Pp. 129–139. ANRS/Orstom. Paris: Orstom.

OLIVIER DE SARDAN J. P., ed., 1999, Anthropologie de la santé. Bulletin de l'APAD 17.

——, 2001, Populisme méthodologique et populisme idéologique en anthropologie. In Le goût de l'enquête. Pour Jean-Claude Passeron. J-L. Fabiani, ed. Pp. 195–246. Paris: L'Harmattan.

RAYNAUT C., 1996, Quelles questions pour la discipline? Quelle collaboration avec la médecine? In Anthropologie et sida. Bilan et perspectives. J. Benoist and A. Desclaux, eds. Pp. 31–56. Paris: Karthala.

RAYNAUT C. and F. MUHONGAYIRE, 1993, Chronique d'une mort annoncée: problèmes d'éthique et de méthode posés par l'application de la démarche anthropologique au suivi de familles touchées par le sida (à partir du cas rwandais). *In* Les sciences sociales face au sida. Cas africains autour de l'exemple ivoirien. Pp. 299–322. Centre Orstom de Petit-Bassam, GIDIS-CI/Orstom. Paris: Orstom.

RECHTMAN R., 1995, De l'ethnopsychiatrie à l'a-psychiatrie culturelle, L'évolution psychiatrique, 60, 3:125–126.

ROSMAN S., 1999, Sida et précarité. Une double vulnérabilité. Paris: L'Harmattan.

SCHEPER-HUGUES N. and M. LOCK, 1987, The Mindful Body: A Prolegomenon to Future Work in Medical Anthropology. Medical Anthropology Quarterly 1(1):6–41.

SINDZINGRE A. and A. ZEMPLÉNI, 1982, Anthropologie de la maladie. *In* Les sciences de l'homme et de la société en France, analyse et proposition pour une politique nouvelle. M. Godelier, ed. Pp. 161–173. Paris: La documentation française.

SINDZINGRE N., 1984, La nécessité du sens: l'explication de l'infortune chez les Senufo. *In* Le sens du mal. Anthropologie, histoire, sociologie de la maladie. M. Augé and C. Herzlich, eds. Pp. 93–122. Paris: Éditions des archives contemporaines.

TEISSIER S., 1996, Épidémie à VIH et institutions socio-sanitaires: quelle réorganisation de l'espace médical. *In* Anthropologie et sida. Bilan et perspectives. J. Benoist and A. Desclaux, eds. Pp. 287–298. Paris: Karthala.

VAN DER GEEST S. and S. R. WHYTE, eds, 1988, The Context of Medicines in Developing Countries: Studies in Pharmaceutical Anthropology. Dordrecht: Kluwer Academic Publishers.

VAN DONGEN E. and S. FAINZANG, eds, 1998, Medical Anthropology at Home. Anthropology and Medicine, special issue 5(3):245–250.

VIDAL L., 1996, Le silence et le sens. Essai d'anthropologie du sida en Afrique. Paris: Anthropos-Economica.

——, 1999, La transmission. Le sida et ses savoirs. L'Homme 150:59–84.

VIDAL L., A. D. BLOBOLO and B. T. N'GUESSAN, 1997, Structures sanitaires et malades confrontés à la prise en charge du sida à Abidjan (CI). *In* Le sida en Afrique, Recherches en sciences de l'homme et de la société. Pp. 153–159. Paris: ANRS/Orstom.

ZEMPLÉNI A., 1982, Anciens et nouveaux usages sociaux de la maladie en Afrique. Archives des sciences sociales des religions 54(1):5–19.

——, 1985, La maladie et ses causes. Special issue 2–3. L'Ethnographie 96/97:13–44.

ZIMMERMANN F., 1995, Généalogie des médecines douces. Paris: Presses universitaires de France.

ZONABEND F., 1989, La presqu'île au nucléaire. Paris: Odile Jacob.

Chapter 6

SPAIN

Topographies, Folklore, and Medical Anthropology in Spain

Josep M. Comelles, Enrique Perdiguero, and Angel Martínez-Hernáez

The Field of Medical Anthropology

The subdiscipline medical anthropology is so recent in the field of anthropology that it has hardly received any attention from science historians. Its origins are generally considered to date back to Rivers or Forrest Clements, but Black, Pitrè, Seppilli, De Martino, Fanon, the French Africanists, Latin American authors, and foundational works from Great Britain, France, and Spain are forgotten. In a certain sense, presenting the current state of research in the field gives it both legitimacy and visibility. Spanish anthropology, like most anthropology written in languages other than English, is not well known. However, the reverse is less true: anthropologists who speak Latin languages are used to reading in English, whereas those who write in English tend to read only works in the language of Shakespeare. We have the advantage of having a broader, more cosmopolitan outlook than our colleagues who are confined to their linguistic and cultural ghetto.

To speak of medical anthropology in Spain and in Europe generally raises a methodological issue: we cannot compare the discipline to medical anthropology in North America, because it has not developed along the same lines. Moreover, neither its presence nor its social uses are evident in Spain. The relations between anthropology and medicine are quite different in Europe and in North or South America. In Europe, the creation of welfare states has given hegemony to quantitative and epidemiological analyses to the detriment of qualitative and cultural analyses. European anthropologists have often been indifferent, even hostile, to applied anthropology, following Augé (1986) who condemned the "venality," or mercenary nature, of the US medical anthropology project.

Over the course of the 20th century in Europe, ethnographic writing on health, medicine, and illness was a secondary methodology in medicine and other academic fields. In the United States, Kleinman (1995) located medical anthropology on the margins of both medicine *and* anthropology. In the European context prior to 1980–90, "medical" ethnography was considered by medicine as merely folklore with a medical bent to it, often written by physicians. Anthropology did not take much interest in medical matters, except as peripheral topics in studies of magic, religion, and shamanism.

In general, since the development of professional anthropology in the United States and of modern medical practice throughout the world, anthropology has lost its interest in health and illness that was present to some extent in general anthropology projects, *à la* Broca, while medicine has lost interest in the social and cultural realms. The identity of professional anthropology was based on a naturalist empiricism and a refusal to focus on the biological analysis of individuals, concentrating instead on collective behavior; by contrast, medicine was increasingly based on experimental medicine, setting aside the social and cultural dimensions of illness.

The epistemological divide between anthropologists and physicians in Europe, and the breach within the overall anthropology project between ethnology and a biologically focused medicine, points to two parallel processes: anthropology's subordination of medical issues, and medicine's subordination of anthropological practices and ethnographic techniques (this has been less true for psychiatry). In the former, the "medical" realm is limited to examples used only to empirically verify anthropological hypotheses, while in the latter, research on care practices that lie beyond the cultural boundaries of biomedicine is delegated to anthropology. This is why in Europe it has been difficult to delineate a relatively specific medical anthropology, as it has also been for empirical sociology or applied anthropology. On the other hand, there are many examples in Europe of approaches connected to our current fields of interest, be they social sciences, folklore, medicine, psychiatry, public health, or the history of medicine: medical topographies, medical folklore, social medicine reports on living conditions among the underprivileged, or philosophical writings on the conditions of patients or on the doctor–patient relationship. In what follows, we will distinguish between these two areas.

Anthropology and Medicine in Spain

It is impossible to cover the entire body of ethnographic descriptions carried out in the New World, many of which dealt with issues related to illness, remedies, or therapeutic practices (Pardo 2002). Such writings became increasingly rare in 19th century Spain despite continued scientific expeditions, as we can see by the gray literature on health in the Moroccan protectorate and in Guinea (Medina and Molero 2002). Among the most interesting metropolitan sources are those that convey an interest in the material living and working conditions of people from the perspective of physicians. Most of these studies were developed by ethnological societies (Bouza 2002; Ronzón 1991), or folklorists (Aguilar-Criado 1990). The folklorists had an appreciation of the medical value of caregiving knowledge, and in 1883 one of the groups, *El folklore castellano*, sent a *Cuestionario* to priests, teachers, and doctors of the region. The doctors were asked to answer questions on subjects as diverse as "home care and superstitions," "childbirth," "the moon," "color and numbers in medicine," and "songs and popular names" for illnesses.

The only Spanish article on medical folklore was written by Eugenio Olivarria y Huarte, secretary of *El folklore Castellano*, which was published in 1885 in the journal *Archivio per lo studio delle Tradizioni Popolari*, edited by Pitrè and Salomone Marino. The most ambitious study was a questionnaire survey sent by the *Ateneo de Madrid* to its correspondents in the provinces, which aimed to characterize the "Spanish people" and their *Volksgeist*, a rather vague concept made all the more obscure by the enormous cultural and linguistic diversity of the Iberian Peninsula. That survey led, amongst other things, to research on the Catalonian, Basque, Galician, and Andalusian *Volksgeist*. The work of Xosemiel de Barandiarán (1889–1991), who piloted a regional ethnography project entitled *Atlas Etnográfico de Vasconia* (1995, 1998), was also part of that line of research.

In the south of Europe, the notion of "folk medicine" appeared towards the end of the 19th century (Comelles 1996; Charuty 1997; Diasio 1999). Before that, physicians spoke of superstitions or common errors, and folklorists of superstitions or beliefs. This new concept came from doctors involved in the medical acculturation of the peasants, and constituted a professional strategy for defining the cultural boundaries of medical practice. The epistemological and methodological break came with Pitrè's book (1896), *Medicina Popolare Siciliana*, wherein he proposed a specific methodology for field studies on folk medicine and a model for *cultural* monographs inspired by Tylor and by the *Kulturkreise*. The radicalism of that book was in sharp contrast with the rest of his vast body of folklore studies. In spite of the admiration that European folklorists had for him, they did not follow in his path. Not being doctors, they did not feel entitled to use his methodology. Only physician folklorists like Lis-Quibèn (1980), in Galicia, or Erkoreka (1985), in the Basque country, followed his lead.

The Origins of Professional Medical Anthropology in Spain

In 1949, George Foster traveled across Spain with his wife and Julio Caro Baroja. Foster was interested in the relation between Spanish medicine of the Golden Age and medical knowledge in New Spain (Foster 1994). In their wake, a small group of American and English anthropologists conducted fieldwork in Spain over the next 20 years. Julio Caro Baroja wrote masterpieces on witchcraft and the Inquisition.

Professional anthropology in Spain got its kick-off when Esteva Fabregat created the Escuela de Estudios Antropológicos in Madrid, around 1960, and began teaching at the University of Barcelona, in 1969. Upon return from Mexico, he made a proposal to the Faculty of Arts for an anthropology program with four sections, but his attempt failed. In the context of Francoism, his students rejected US culturalism and the culture and personality school with which he identified (Esteva 1973), instead adopting the British social anthropology approach introduced by Carmelo Lisón, or Marxist anthropology from France.

The founder of medical anthropology in Spain is without a doubt the Catalan, Lluis Mallart, who taught in Paris for many years. His work on the Beti of Cameroon (Mallart 1978, 2003) propelled medical anthropology forward in Spain. The lack of African research in Spain has limited its immediate influence, although the recent but still timid development of fieldwork in Latin America and in Africa has given it a broader recognition. The first anthropologists working "at home" produced little work on medical issues, with a few rare exceptions: some books on the links between social history and anthropology, research that used the objects of medical studies to test anthropological hypotheses, and a grab-bag of autodidactic and exploratory research which opened the way for medical anthropology.

Historians

The first to take an interest in the field were historians of medicine, who had a good knowledge of the international development of relations between history and the social sciences. The main authors were Luis Gil (1969) on folk medicine in the Classical world, Agustín Albarracín (1972) in his article on pluralism in medical care, and García-Ballester (1977) with his book on Moorish medicine in Granada, re-edited in 1984. In the beginning none of these works, including the work of Caro Baroja, had any influence on young Spanish anthropologists, in spite of the fact that they used notions such as *marginal groups* and *subcultures* and were influenced by Ackerknecht (1985).

García Ballester considered medicine to be a cultural form. He compared Moorish medicine and Galenic medicine to show how, in spite of their shared roots, Moorish medicine had been marginalized and had declined under the Kingdom of Granada's Christianization policies prior to 1610. He presented it as a subaltern medicine, along the lines of De Martino in Italy and Menéndez (1981) in Mexico. The difference was that Menéndez and De Martino were influenced by Gramscian Marxism, whereas García Ballester remained within the framework of cultural history and Ackerknecht's culturalism. However, his interest in the "actors' viewpoints" in his work on historical documentation was a novelty in Spain. Although he remained a medical historian, he never gave up his personal dialogue with anthropology. The only comparable research prior to 1980 was Contreras' still unpublished 1971 master's thesis on the relation between medical knowledge and lay knowledge in the 18th century. Later on, Comelles' work on public mental health policies (1991), and Larrea's work on miasmatic theory (1997), were part of the same field of interest.

Anthropologists

During the period when Mallart was conducting research in Cameroon, Carmelo Lisón, who was studying with Evans-Pritchard in Oxford, did fieldwork in Galicia in connection with an ambitious regional ethnology project in which he made frequent reference to health, illness, lay medicine and, more specifically, to the connections between witchcraft and illness (1971, 1979). Later, he published a study on therapeutic possession rituals at the Galician sanctuary of Corpiño. Although he had opened the door onto the study of medical pluralism in 1971, there is no mention of it in his last volume. His work is closer to Evans-Pritchard's study of the Azande than to medical anthropology, because Lisón's intention was to write an ethnography of ritual, and his only theoretical reference in medical anthropology seems to have been Ackerknecht (1985) and, more indirectly, Victor Turner (1972) on rituals.

Maria Cátedra (1976), who was his student, did her fieldwork in Asturias. Her book on the *Vaqueiros* of Alzada is a masterpiece on death, suicide, and illness told from the viewpoint of the actors (1988). An excellent writer with great sensitivity, she focused mainly on analyzing the identity of a marginal rural group. She almost completely ignored the presence and influence of medicine in the configuration of lay knowledge and, true to Anglo-Saxon culturalism, did not directly observe the subalternity of the *Vaqueiros'* conditions of life and death.

Like professional anthropologists from before 1980, Lisón and Cátedra participated in the first project specifically aimed at creating an internationally connected "school" that made it possible to define an "anthropological identity" in Spain distinct from the identity of historians and sociologists. Like the work of Mallart, their research could have led to a culturalist anthropology of illness, but the debate over the reform of the Spanish health system, which began around the time that Francoism declined and most people gained access to social security (85% in 1975), counteracted any more or less ethnic or local model of "lay medicine."

Sociologists and Anthropologists

In Spain, medical anthropology as a specific field of social or cultural anthropology emerged out of a Catalonian anthropology that had no specific leaders (such as Lisón in Madrid), and a flourishing of interests in an extremely broad range of subjects. In the context of this lively intellectual atmosphere, Joan Prat analyzed the role of *ex-voto* offerings in Catalonia for terminal patients for whom medicine had nothing more to offer; this suggested the possibility of analyzing the connections between medicine and religion. Pau Comes (1972) wrote an ethnography of the therapeutic itineraries of disease and death in rural Catalonia, and Comelles (1972) attempted to reinterpret the material of folklorists using concepts from ethnomedicine. Later, in collaboration with psychiatrists, Comelles tested the use of social networks for analyzing the relations between society and psychopathology with a psychotic Gypsy woman (Comelles et al. 1975).

These experiments speak of a desire to shape a profession that has anthropological tools for understanding health and illness, and yet is not medical folklore. The authors faced the problem of how to link together medicine and anthropology. When Lisón or Cátedra were taken as models, anthropology was the only reference, while García Ballester's model lay on the border between anthropology and history; and if one chose to follow the phenomenology of the physician and philosopher, Laín Entralgo, the rhetoric of medical humanism (1964) took over. An anthropology of illness could of course be developed following Cátedra and Laín Entralgo, but their example fostered an ethnomedicine of marginal groups. The Catalonian anthropologists, who had few theoretical references, searched for them among sociologists such as Goffman (1968) or Freidson (1978) who favored the notions of a "moral career" or "lay referral system" that seemed better suited to analyze practices than discourse. Around 1975, there was a break with Ackerknetch and with medical folklore. Thereafter, research tended to obliterate the boundaries between biomedicine and everyday care practices in which historicity could not be ignored.

The formal point of departure for medical anthropology in Spain was a book by the sociologist Jesús de Miguel and the anthropologist Michael Kenny, *La Antropología médica en España* (Kenny and de Miguel 1980), which brought together about twenty texts, half of which were by Spanish authors. There are three seminal texts in the book: an introduction by de Miguel (1980), who saw no difference between medical sociology and medical anthropology; a bibliography on the history of fieldwork with 700 references; and a text by Pujadas et al. (1980) criticizing the distinction between lay medicine and scholarly medicine, which opened the way to an applied anthropology in clinical settings and discussed the limits to the concept of symbolic efficacy. The book was widely circulated in Spain and Latin America. It opened an entirely new field as it was released right in the middle of the debate over the reform of the Spanish health-care system, and around the same time as a number of books on the subject. Meanwhile, Oriol Romaní (1982) was focusing on the cultural aspects and social context of marijuana use in Barcelona's counter-culture at the end of Franco's era and the beginning of the transition regime. His dissertation was an engaged ethnography with autobiographical connotations, his main influences being symbolic interactionism and the sociology of deviance. Comelles (1986) studied the de-institutionalization process in a psychiatric asylum, during which he was able to observe the influences of old ethnographies of asylums, of symbolic interactionism, and of political anthropology. Part of his work was related to Foucault, Castel, and Freidson, in particular, the connection between the meaning of the institution and changes in medical discourse (1980).

Marta Allué's master's thesis (1980) and her article presenting a comparative perspective on death management (1982) played a similar role. She analyzed death based on a critical review of funerary folklore that led to an analysis of the itineraries of death and suffering based on Turner's notions of ritual and rites of passage. However, she was closer to the health-seeking models found among sociologists.

The collective article by Comelles, Andreu, Ferrus, and Paris (1982) also had a programmatic character. To deconstruct the folk/scholarly dualism, they suggested approaching therapeutic itineraries and the pluralism of resources based on the social construction of the right to assistance – perceived as a historical process – and which was not without connection to the emergence of the right to health recognized in the 1978 Constitution. The value of sociological concepts and historical research is apparent here, and Foucault (1979), Goffman (1968), Freidson (1978), and Castel (1976) suggested new ways for looking at medical practice, health policies, and their cultural impacts.

Several years later, Martinez-Hernáez (1993) attempted a critical review of the field. In spite of the diversity of subjects, he believed that there was a sort of medical anthropology project defined by the objects of study, by certain methodological advances, and by an institutionalization open to multidisciplinary discussion.

However, there was no real methodological debate, which made the authors appear as more or less skilful *bricoleurs*, hampered by having had to make it up as they went along and by the lack of discussion on what it means to do anthropology close to home.

The Development of Medical Anthropology (1982–2002)

Unlike other European countries, which had more solid university structures for anthropology (or ethnology), social anthropology did not gain a stable university position in Spain until around 1990–95. The first course in medical anthropology offered in Spain was in 1981 in Tarragona, followed, in 1982, by the first international symposium (Comelles, 1984; *Primeres Jornades d'Antropologia de la Medicina*, 1982). This helps to explain the thematic and geographic dispersal of academic writing, the persistence of medical folklore, and the fact that there were fewer guidelines for applied research. Perdiguero et al. (2000) have reviewed the entire body of Spanish work, summarized in Table 6.1.

Slightly over one-third of the 1,500 publications were written by some thirty researchers who are considered specialists, and one-quarter are studies on sexuality or eating habits from the beginnings of medical anthropology. One-fifth of the publications were written by health professionals with an anthropological sensibility, and the rest are studies in medical folklore. Many authors are cited only once or twice. This shows the limits of a modest academic community, as well as the fact that research has depended to a great extent on individual research interests. Nonetheless, certain themes are recurrent and theoretical influences can be identified.

Drugs

The most significant line of research in medical anthropology from the standpoint of its social impacts and its influence over public policies in Spain, and even in Latin America, has been *studies on drugs* and *addictive behavior*. It has developed out of studies on life paths among heroin users (Funes and Romani 1985; Gamella 1990; Pallarès 1995; Romaní 1982), studies on therapeutic communities and young

Table 6.1   Research Output in Contemporary Medical Anthropology in Spain.

	Books, articles and chapters (no.)	M.A. and B.A. dissertations (no.)	Ph.D. theses (no.)
1970–79	88	2	2
1980–89	502	12	4
1990–99	875	–	30
Total	1465	14	36

people during the 1980s (Comas 1985, 1988; Comas et al. 1992), and more recently, studies on cocaine (Díaz et al. 1992) and on synthetic drugs (Gamella and Alvarez-Roldán 1997) that are transdisciplinary and closer to the medical model. Overall, there seems to be a growing tension between critical theoretical approaches associated with the sociology of deviance and with Marxism, and neopositivist approaches more in keeping with the dominant discourse in international literature.

Cultural Psychiatry and Ethnopsychiatry

To the extent that psychoanalysis has had a modest influence in Spain, and that the issue of cultural diversity has only been truly acknowledged since the country began receiving international migrants, the interest in cultural or transcultural psychiatry has been rather limited (González and Comelles 2000; Obiols 1981), with a few exceptions. The only long-term experience was set up in Galicia by the anthropologist Marcial Gondar and the psychiatrist Emilio González who developed a cultural psychiatry program before the term existed (Gondar and González 1992). It aimed to compare psychiatric practice in rural and urban Galicia and to reflect on the complexity of the role of professionals, torn between traditional conceptions of distress and the problems posed by the CIE-10 and the DSM-IV taxonomies. On the basis of a very thorough ethnographic exploration, their deconstruction of psychiatric practice in rural and urban settings led them to the conclusion that psychiatrists play the role of cultural brokers, a role that involves a long-term relationship with doctors and residents (González 2000).

In Madrid, the hospital psychiatrist Caballero (1997) has supported a more classical cultural psychiatry, in which he has a very solid background. Caballero has taken a particular interest in problems diagnosing culture-bound syndromes and in communication problems in clinical settings. As he is not directly involved in any projects outside the hospital, his work does not have the same impact as that of González, but hospital psychiatric services have been receptive to his approach as they deal with the need for diagnostic protocols. The third experience is that of the psychiatrist Joseba Atxotegui (see Atxotegui 2000; Tizón et al. 1993) who has set up one of the first specialized care services for migrants, in Barcelona.

Generally speaking, there are considerable differences between the position of psychiatrists (with the exception of González) and anthropologists. Recently, a large number of psychiatrists have taken an interest in the subject, but all too often they have very little background in anthropology and are not particularly interested in interdisciplinary dialogue, under the pretext of drawing a boundary between the anthropological approach and the clinical approach. They hide behind the creation of diagnostic protocols for "culture-bound syndromes," avoiding having to learn to use other qualitative methodologies for dealing with cultural diversity. They are incapable of contextualizing psychiatric practice or prevention in the field of mental health, because their training has prepared them only to apply the growing number of clinical, diagnostic, and treatment protocols. The danger of this trend is that it could encourage a generalization of ethnically specialized services, or that culture-bound syndromes could be reduced to symptomatologies of anxiety and depression to which psycho-pharmacological treatments are then applied. As for anthropologists, the trend is to analyze social and cultural logics associated with distress (Martínez-Hernáez 1998, 2000a), considered to be a necessary intermediary step toward interdisciplinary debate. Indisputably, González's position is a good compromise between the two and, more importantly, has practical solutions for everyday practice.

Illness and Handicap

In 1984, Serra París defended a master's thesis on the therapeutic itineraries of a dozen young women with scoliosis. Using methodological approaches developed by American sociologists around "health-seeking behavior," she combined her own life history, observations on health services, and the life histories of other people with scoliosis. This thesis instigated a series of studies concerning chronic illness and disability, many of which were based on autobiographical experiences. Marcial Gondar (1990), for instance, explored accounts of bereavement and death among Galician women, with particular attention to the work on mourning, though little work has been done on this subject since then. Some time later, a hospital rheumatology service hired three anthropologists for a field survey on rheumatoid arthritis (Devillard et al. 1991). They combined participant observation in hospitals and life histories. Along the same lines, Roser Colom (1996) studied rehabilitation processes among paraplegics in hospital services, and Capitán (1999) studied the physically disabled. Villamil (2001) has recently done work on the itineraries of AIDS patients.

Marta Allué's autobiographical account (1996), which describes the painful itinerary of a woman who is handicapped as well as a severe burn victim, witnesses a shift in academic research. It is the account of an anthropologist who is also a patient, and combines an emotional itinerary and a Goffmanian ethnography of various hospital environments. In Spain, the book has become a reference for nursing students and an example of a radical ethnography. Her reputation has only been reinforced with the publication of her second book, an ethnography of disability (2003) in which she takes her work as an engaged anthropologist writing an ethnography of "normal people's" attitudes towards the disabled to discuss disabled people's rights to equality and difference.

The Ethnography of Professionals and Institutions

Following in the footsteps of Freidson, Spanish anthropologists (and some sociologists) have conducted ethnographies of *professionals*. The sociologist De Miguel published two monographs on pediatric (1984) and obstetric (De Miguel and Domínguez-Alcón 1979) rhetoric, while Comelles (1988b) explored the role of psychiatrists in contemporary Spain. Several authors have also written ethnographies of institutions: Uribe (1996) on a front-line health-care center, Xavier Allué (1999) on hospital emergency rooms, Fernández-Rufete (1997) on an internal medicine service specializing in AIDS, Villamil (2001) on AIDS prevention methods among homosexuals and the discourse of epidemiologists, and Marta Allué (1996), Comelles (2000b), and Pallares (2003) on intensive care units. In addition, family planning services (which are a recent phenomenon in Spain following the political transition) have been the object of three Ph.D. dissertations (Bodoque 1996; Castillo 2000; Esteban 1996, 2001).

Pluralism in Health Care

"Medical" pluralism is a medicocentric term that should be banished from our vocabulary, but that in everyday usage covers research on home-care practices and the relations between users and health services. Pluralism is defined by a multitude of complex transactions between individuals and institutions. Thus, social subjects learn from personal experience how to manage the environment and make decisions. The issue of pluralism owes much to many of the contributions described above. In fact, most of the popularized writings of the 1980s aimed to present its main concepts (Balaguer 1988; Comelles 1985; Perdiguero 1992). One of the most interesting books on the topic by an anthropologist was a book by Roca (1996) on the role of popular literature in health and family life under Franco. Also interesting were studies on healers (Gómez 1997), on culture-bound syndromes (Erkoreka 1995), and on lay practices (Fresquet 1995), as well as two collective publications, one by González Alcantud and Rodríguez Becerra (1996) and the other by González-Reboredo (1997), which are a blend of strictly medical anthropology texts and writings that keep the folklore fire burning. Lasala (2003) has written on the transactions between healers and the current health system in Spain, and Canals (2002) has written a very significant book on the development of self-help groups in the context of Spain's crisis in the welfare state.

Among historians of medicine there has been a slow but sure adoption of anthropological concepts on the health/illness/care complex (Perdiguero 1997; Zarzoso 2001). This is one of the most explored subjects in the academic literature and the subject on which anthropologists and historians converge most convincingly, as can be seen for example in the dossier on medical pluralism in the journal *Dynamis* (Ballester et al. 2002).

The Body, Gender, and Emotions

Martínez-Hernáez's dissertation (2000b) attempted to bridge the epistemological gap between an anthropology of illness and an anthropology of practice. The author explored the possibility for a more culturalist approach to illness based on an analysis of how symptoms are interpreted by psychiatry and anthropology; however the project also involved an anthropology of practices and of biomedicine's production of discourse. Likewise, José M. Uribe's 1996 dissertation on the transformation of the health-care system in the Basque country stepped back from the dominant approaches of the previous years, which were closer to political economy, and incorporated the culturalist discourse of clinically applied anthro-pology. Mari Luz Esteban, an anthropologist with a medical background and a daughter of the feminist movement, introduced contemporary reflections on gender and the body (1993) into Spanish medical anthropology, issues which have been widely developed in the last few years (Miqueo and Cruz 2001).

Migrations and Health

In Spain, studies on migrations and health have stemmed mainly from an excellent report by the psychiatrist Cabaleiro in 1997. More recently, an article (Obiols 1987) and a collective publication by several psychiatrists (Tizón et al. 1993) assessed the clinical implications of cultural diversity in our society. Later, Esteban and Diaz (1997) published a field study on health issues among migrants, an issue that has risen to the forefront because of its impact on the health-care system and the problems facing professionals who had always neglected the cultural aspects of health.

It is always tempting to reify the social and the cultural as an identifying vari-able to be placed in a decision protocol. However, for anthropologists, psychologi-cal distress is increasingly considered to be a way of approaching and expressing cultural hybridization in cases where ethnic groups have been de-territorialized, of examining the interface between people and the health system, and of describing experiences of suffering and affliction.

Theoretical Positions

We have restricted our choice to a modest portion of the 1,500 references in medical anthropology in Spain since 1960 (Perdiguero et al. 2000). It is not easy to try to draw out the theoretical foundations and influences behind these studies. On the one hand, a large number of them were based on participant observation, life histories, therapeutic itineraries and network analyses, as well as on a reality that was often close to the authors and with which they were often quite personally involved. Since a huge portion of the research was not funded and was carried out by research groups, most of the researchers had university positions or had received pre-doctoral fellowships (which were granted individually for a long time) or else they funded the research out of their salaries. The choice of subjects, for the most part, has been based on personal or autobiographical interests, which has led to self-teaching and eclecticism.

As most of the studies are focused on an anthropology of practice, inevitably they have certain points in common: to begin with, they share influences from symbolic interactionism ethnographies, and narrative styles from ethnographies by sociologists of deviance. The good side to this is that the researchers have been interested in ethnography and have developed techniques for systematic observa-tion. The negative side, however, is a dependency on the authors' narrative skills. Second, the authors tend to feel that life histories somehow answer all of the ques-tions posed by research and that only the actor's point of view is valid. Finally, the fact that the researchers have often been close to the subjects and objects of their studies has led to an engaged anthropology.

From a theoretical viewpoint, for generational reasons, the dominant lines of thinking over the past twenty years have been from the constructivist schools. This has led to a rich dialogue with the history of medicine. Two parallel texts, by Perdiguero (1993) and by Martínez-Hernáez (1993), are representative of this trend. The former concluded that the paths of medical history and medical anthropology are converging, while the latter felt that what was needed was an openness to the culturalist and phenomenological schools, and that the hegemony of practice-oriented research had meant that illness had been ignored as an object of study.

This diagnosis reflected the broad-reaching influence of the Argentinean anthropologist now living in Mexico, Eduardo Menéndez, and his theoretical position on the health/illness/care complex (1990). His position, which was influenced by De Martino and Gramsci, made it possible in Spain to move beyond the sociological models of health-seeking behavior. He shared the same concerns as Young and the future "critically applied anthropology." In addition, his positions echoed those of the Italian anthropologists at the Centro Sperimentale di Educazione Sanitaria in Perugia (Italy), a Mecca for Spanish public health doctors during the 1980s. The relationship with authors such as Bartoli (1989) and Seppilli (1983, 1989) was consolidated by the regular presence of Italians and of Menéndez in Tarragona.

Whereas Perdiguero advocated a historical anthropology for historians, Martínez-Hernáez took up Needham's distinction (1969) between the *cultural* and the *social* as well as between *emotion* and *structure* to advocate that Spanish medical anthropology focus on cultural phenomena. Ten years later, both paths are apparent. A good overview can be found in a recent collective publication edited by Perdiguero and Comelles (2000).

Future Imperfect

The adoption of the Declaration of Bologna, which is aimed to normalize European diplomas, and the generalization of a European research space whose priorities have created a period of uncertainty among most of the older university disciplines such as anthropology, have resulted in some fundamental changes. Today, the goal is to work as groups, not individuals, to create interdisciplinary organizations, and to develop relations with international interlocutors. Within the European Union, the health sciences are in a much weaker position than they are in the United States, and health authorities are not so willing to recognize their role.

This new scenario will have impacts in four areas, the first of which is specialized education. Second, researchers will have to adapt to subjects that have been decided in advance by international bodies. Third, the discipline's role in lifelong learning and coaching for professionals in the field will be recognized, particularly in the case of medical anthropology. And lastly, this new scenario will establish medical anthropology's position in health education and promotion, with the attendant flood of issues: the role of user agency, health promotion policies, strategies for patient groups, etc. All of these areas force a debate on the position of medical anthropology within anthropology, and a debate on its social and cultural significance.

A review is always a somewhat nostalgic view of the past. But that is not what we want. Now we look to the future under conditions that ten or twenty years ago would have seemed like a dream. Today, Spanish medical anthropology is an academic community that sends researchers out into the world on a fairly regular basis, that has a relatively significant international presence, and that is helping to build a space for communication in Latin languages. Our active presence in the *Medical Anthropology at Home* network, which is promoting a European medical anthropology community, finds us at a stimulating turn in the dialogue between Europe and the other continents. And the European Union's research funding policy is forcing us, thankfully, to collaborate with our continental colleagues. For a field of anthropology with modest resources in Europe (nothing like the *Society of Medical Anthropology*), this starting point is encouraging more personal relationships based on mutual trust, and is helping us to envision the future together. We are strengthening ties with our historian and sociologist colleagues, and with nurses and doctors. The context of the future is no longer the nation-state, but the diversity of issues related to European social policies, or those raised by international cooperation. This diversity is the basis for our continental citizenship, with all its problems and contradictions, and that citizenship is beginning to be perceived as an issue for the future in Latin America and elsewhere.

Medical anthropologists are very poorly acquainted with the European context characterized by the construction and deconstruction of the welfare state. It is amazing how easily we import research objects tailored for multicultural countries, but without the health systems that are able to make the universal right to medical assistance a reality. These mechanisms have created specific business cultures, different professional cultures (such as government-salaried physicians, the majority in Spain), as well as very different ways of creating lay knowledge, different attitudes towards the body, and different cultures of illness embodied in that citizenship. Today they all are facing the reality of migration, a fascinating *métissage*, and the development of new forms of transactions with health services. These are important issues, both for anthropologists and for health professionals who had long ago forgotten how to deal with diversity, *métissage*, and cultural hybridization. Clearly, an adequate response to these issues would be a compelling demonstration of the validity of European citizenship. The days are gone when the goal of public health specialists was to do away with epidemics by drawing up statistical records. Nowadays, the welfare state needs qualitative evaluation and research techniques to put forward its vision, as these are the only methods for situating the local in a global context, and for explaining the hierarchical dynamics present in consensus between classes, the only methods that can help us to *understand* what is often so difficult to grasp: that which is not us, but which, by right of citizenship, is also us. For the engaged anthropologists that we are, it is no longer the "outsider's perspective" but the "close-up" view that is essential for preserving the right to our wonderful social, cultural and linguistic diversity within this shared citizenship, a product of secular cross-fertilizations that are constructed and deconstructed, in order to preserve for future generations the nuances in our ways of living, loving, feeling and expressing our suffering, our joy and our desire for peace.

References

ACKERKNETCH E. H., 1985, Medicina y Antropología Social. Madrid: Akal.

AGUILAR-CRIADO E., 1990, Cultura popular y folklore en Andalucía (los orígenes de la antropología). Seville: Diputación Provincial.

ALBARRACÍN A., 1972, Intrusos, charlatanes, secretistas y curanderos. Aproximación sociológica al estudio de la asistencia médica extracientífica en la España del siglo XIX. Asclepio 24:323–366.

ALLUÉ M., 1980, Siemprevivas e inmortales. Rituales e instituciones funerarias en las comarcas de Tarragona. Mémoire de licence. Tarragone: Universitat de Barcelona.

——, 1982, La Gestión del Morir: Para una Antropología del enfermo terminal en la sociedad Occidental. Jornades d'Antropologia de la Medicina. Comunicacions 2(1):4–34.

——, 1996, Sauver sa peau. Paris: Seli Arslan.

——, 2003, DisCapacitados. La reivindicación de la igualdad en la diferencia. Barcelona: Bellaterra.

ALLUÉ X., 1999, Urgencias. Abierto de 0 a 24 horas. Factores socioculturales en la oferta y la demanda de las urgencias pediátricas. Saragossa: Mira Editorial.

ATLAS ETNOGRÁFICO DE VASCONIA, 1995, Ritos Funerarios en Vasconia. Bilbao: Eusko Jaurlaritza–Gobierno de Navarra–Etniker Euskalerria. La quitaría.

——, 1998, Ritos del nacimiento al matrimonio en Vasconia. Bilbao: Eusko Jaurlaritza–Gobierno de Navarra–Etniker Euskalerria. La quitaría.

ATXOTEGUI J., 2000, Los duelos de la migración: una aproximación psicopatológica y psicosocial. In E. Perdiguero and J. M. Comelles, eds. Medicina y cultura. Estudios entre la antropología y la medicina. Pp. 83–100. Barcelona: Bellaterra.

AUGÉ M., 1986, L'Anthropologie de la maladie. L'Homme 97/98:81–89.

BALAGUER E., 1988, El conocimiento popular de la salud y de la enfermedad, Canelobre 11:5–10.

BALLESTER R., M. L. LOPEZ-TERRADA and A. MARTINEZ-VIDAL, eds, 2002, La realidad de la práctica médica: el pluralismo asistencial en la Monarquía Hispánica (ss. XVI–XVIII), Dynamis, vol. 22. Granada: Universidad de Granada.

BARTOLI P., 1989, Antropología de la Educación Sanitaria. Arxiu d'Etnografia de Catalunya 7:17–25.

BODOQUE Y., 1996, Discursos y praticas sobre sexualidad y reproducción: los centros de planificaciión familiar. Ph.D. thesis, Tarragona: Universidat Rovira i Virgili.

BOUZA J., 2002, El hombre com problema. Filosofia, ciencia y subversión en la Antropología del Siglo XIX. Barcelona: Ediciones del Serbal.

CABALEIRO M., 1997 [1967], Sindromes psicopatoloxicas pola immigração e emigração. Saint Jacques de Compostelles: Xunta de Galicia.

CABALLERO L., 1997, Psiquiatria clinica y buénas metáforas, Psiquiaria. Cultural para Clínicos 1:1–12.

CANALS J., 2002, El regreso de la reciprocidad. Grupos de ayuda mutua y asociaciones de personas afectadas en el estado del bienestar. Ph.D. Thesis. Tarragona: Universitat Rovira i Virgili.

CAPITAN A., 1999, Angeles Rotos. Las imágenes culturales de los amputados y su gestión social. Ph.D. thesis. Barcelona: Universitat de Barcelona.

CASTEL R., 1976, L'Ordre Psychiatrique. L'Âge d'or de l'aliénisme. Paris: Les Éditions de Minuit.

CASTILLO A., 2000, Factores Socioculturales en la práctica de la planificación familiar: el caso de la contracepción hormonal oral. Ph.D. thesis. Tarragona: Universitat Rovira i Virgili.

CÁTEDRA M., 1976, Notas sobre la envidia:los ojos malos entre los Vaqueiros de Alzada. *In* Temas de Antropología Española. C. Lisón, ed. Pp. 9–48. Madrid: Akal.

——, 1988, La muerte y otros mundos. Enfermedad, suicidio, muerte y más allá entre los vaqueiros de Alzada. Madrid: Júcar Universidad.

CHARUTY G., 1997, L' invention de la médecine populaire, Gradhiva, 22:45–57.

COLOM R., 1996, Aprender a vivir. La construcción de la identidad de la persona con discapacidad física. Ph.D. thesis. Barcelona: Universitat de Barcelona.

COMAS D., 1985, El uso de las drogas en la juventud. Madrid: Instituto de la Juventud.

——, 1988, El tratamiento de la drogodependencia y las comunidades terapéuticas. Madrid: Ministerio de Sanidad y Consumo.

COMAS D., M. ESPIN and E. RAMIREZ, eds., 1992, Fundamentos Teóricos en Prevención. Madrid: Grupo Interdisciplinar sobre Drogas.

COMELLES J. M., 1972, Terapéutica y sociedad. Un caso gallego. Ethnica 4:49–88.

——, 1980, Ideología asistencial y práctica económica. *In* Actas del I Congreso Español de Antropología, vol.1. Pp. 337–400. Barcelona: Universitat de Barcelona.

——, 1984, L'Antropologia de la Medicina a l'Estat espanyol. *In* Antropologia i Salut. J. M. Comelles ed. Pp. 137–157. Barcelona: Fundació Caixa de Pensions.

——, 1985, Sociedad, salud y enfermedad: los procesos asistenciales. Jano 655:71–83.

——, 1986, La crisis de la psiquiatría española durante el Tardofranquismo y la Transición. El caso del Institut Mental de la Santa Creu (1971–1986), RAEN. Revista de la Asociación Española de Neuropsiquiatría 6(19):619–636.

——, 1988a, La importancia creciente de los no profesionales en los procesos asistenciales. Canelobre 11:11–19.

——, 1988b, La razón y la sinrazón. Asistencia psiquiátrica y desarrollo del Estado en la España Contemporánea. Barcelona: PPU.

——, 1991, Psychiatric Care in Relation to the Development of the Contemporary State: The Case of Catalonia. Culture, Medicine and Psychiatry 15(2):193–217.

——, 1996, Da superstizioni a medicina popolare: La transizione da un concetto religioso a un concetto médico. Rivista della Società italiana di antropologia médica 1/2:57–89.

——, 2000a, The Role of Local Knowledge in Medical Practice: A Trans-Historical Perspective. Culture, Medicine and Psychiatry 24:41–75.

——, 2000b, Tecnología, cultura y sociabilidad. Los límites culturales del hospital contemporáneo. *In* Medicina y cultura. Estudios entre la antropología y la medicina. E. Perdiguero and J. M. Comelles, eds. Barcelona: Bellaterra.

COMELLES J. M., M. CASAS, U. UDINA and E. ALVAREZ, 1975, Oposición estructural en el medio urbano: Asociaciones informales de parentesco y trastorno psiquiátrico en una enferma gitana. Ethnica 10:29–46.

COMELLES J. M., A. ADREU, J. FERRUS and S. PARIS, 1982, Aproximación a un modelo sobre antropología de la Asistencia. Arxiu d'Etnografia de Catalunya. 1:13–31.

COMES P., 1972, Enfermedad y muerte en el familismo rural. Ethnica 3:29–52.

DE MIGUEL J., 1980, Introducción al campo de la antropología médica. *In* La Antropología Médica en España. M. Kenny and J. De Miguel, eds. Pp. 11–40. Barcelona: Anagrama.

——, 1984, La amorosa dictadura. Barcelona: Anagrama.

DE MIGUEL J. and C. DOMÍNGUEZ-ALCÓN, 1979, El mito de la Inmaculada Concepción. Barcelona: Anagrama.

DEVILLARD M. J., R. OTEGUI and P. GARCIA, 1991, La voz callada. Aproximación antropológico-social al enfermo de artitris reumatoide. Madrid: Comunidad de Madrid.

DIASIO N., 1999, La science impure. Anthropologie et médecine en France, Grande-Bretagne, Italie, Pays-Bas. Paris: Presses universitaires de France.

DIAZ A., M. BARRUTI and C. DONCEL, 1992, Les linies de l'èxit? Naturalesa i extensió del consum de cocaïna a Barcelone. Barcelona: ICESB/Ajuntament de Barcelona.

ERKOREKA A., 1985, Análisis de la medicina popular vasca. Bilbao: Instituto Labayru-CAV.

——, 1995, Begizkoa. El mal de ojo entre los vascos. Bilbao: Ekain.

ESTEBAN M., 1993, La salud de las Mujeres:nuevas preguntas para nuevas respuestas. *In* Sistemas de Género y Construcción (Deconstrucción) de la desigualdad. M. Díez and V. Maquieira, eds. Pp. 243–257. La Laguna: Asociación Canaria de Antropólogos-FAAEE.

——, 1996, Relaciones entre feminismo y Sistema Médico-Científico. Mujeres de Ciencia. Mujer, Feminismo y Ciencias Naturales, Experimentales y Tecnológicas. Pp. 143–184. Granada: Instituto de Estudios de la Mujer de la Universidad de Granada.

——, 2001, El género como categoría analítica. Revisiones y aplicaciones a la salud. *In* Perspectivas de género en salud. Fundamentos científicos y socioprofesionales de diferencias sexuales no previstas. C. Miqueo, C. Tomás and M. Cruz, eds. Pp. 25–52. Madrid: Minerva Ediciones.

ESTEBAN M. and B. DIAZ, 1997, La salud de los inmigrantes extranjeros en el barrio de San Francisco (Bilbao). Bilbao: Fundación EDE.

ESTEVA C., 1973, Cultura y Personalidad. Barcelona: A. Redondo.

FERNÁNDEZ-RUFETE J., 1997, Sanar o Redimir. Los procesos asistenciales en VIH-SIDA en el medio hospitalario. Ph.D. thesis. Tarragona: Universitat Rovira i Virgili.

FOSTER G. M., 1994, Hippocrates' Latin American Legacy. Humoral Medicine in the New World. Amsterdam: Gordon and Breach.

FOUCAULT M., 1979, Les machines à guérir. Aux origines de l'hôpital moderne. Bruxelles: Atelier Pierre Madarga.

FREIDSON E., 1978 [1970], La profesión médica. Barcelona: Península.

FRESQUET J. L., ed., 1995, Salud, enfermedad y terapéutica popular en la Ribera Alta. València: Universitat de València.

FUNES J. and O. ROMANI, 1985, Dejar la heroína. Madrid: Cruz Roja.

GAMELLA J., 1990, La Historia de Julián. Memorias de heroína y delincuencia. Madrid: Editorial Popular.

GAMELLA J. and A. ALVAREZ-ROLDAN, 1997, Drogas de síntesis en España. Patrones y tendencias de adquisición. Plan Nacional sobre drogas. Madrid: Ministerio del Interior.

GARCÍA-BALLESTER L., 1984 [1977], Los moriscos y la medicina. Un capítulo de la medicina y la ciencia marginadas de la España del siglo XVI. Barcelona: Labor.

GIL L., 1969, Therapeia: la medicina popular en el mundo clásico. Madrid: Guadarrama.

GOFFMAN E., 1968 [1961], Asiles. Études sur la condition sociale des malades mentaux. Paris: Éditions de Minuit.

GOMEZ P., ed., 1997, El curanderismo entre nosotros. Granada: Universidad de Granada.

GONDAR M., 1990, Mulleres de Mortos. Cara a unha antropoloxía da muller galega. Vigo: Xerais.

GONDAR M. and E. GONZÁLEZ, eds, 1992, Espiritados. Ensaios de Etnopsiquiatria Galega. Saint-Jacques-de-Compostelle: Laiovento.

GONZÁLEZ E., 2000, A unidade de Saúde Mental como broker cultural: alternativas a xestión da locura nun municipio rural galego. Ph.D. thesis. Saint-Jacques-de-Compostelle: Universidade de Santiago.

GONZÁLEZ E. and J. M. COMELLES, eds, 2000, Psiquiatría Transcultural. Madrid: Asociación Española de Neuropsiquiatría.

GONZÁLEZ-ALCANTUD J. A. and S. RODRIQUEZ-BECERRA, eds, 1996, Creer y Curar: La Medicina Popular. Granada: Diputación Provincial.

GONZÁLEZ-REBOREDO X. M., ed., 1997, Medicina popular e Antropoloxía da Saúde, In Actas do Simposio internacional en homenaxe a D. Antonio Fraguas. Saint-Jacques-de-Compostelle: Consello da Cultura Galega.

KENNY M. and J. DE MIGUEL, eds, 1980, La Antropología Médica en España. Barcelona: Anagrama.

KLEINMAN A., 1995, Writing at the Margin. Discourse between Anthropology and Medicine. Berkeley: University of California Press.

LÁIN ENTRALGO P., 1964, La relación médico-enfermo. Historia y Teoría. Madrid: Revista de Occidente.

LARREA C., 1997, La cultura de los olores. Una aproximación a la antropología de los sentidos. Quito: Abya-Yala.

LASALA A., 2003, Curarse en salud. Las medicinas como sistemas de transacciones. Ph.D. thesis. Tarragona: Universitat Rovira i Virgili.

LIS-QUIBEN V., 1980 [1949], La medicina popular en Galicia. Madrid: Akal.

LISÓN C., 1971, Antropología Social en España. Madrid: Siglo Veintiuno.

——, 1979, Brujería, estructura social y simbolismo en Galicia. Antropología cultural en Galicia. Madrid: Akal.

——, 1990, En de Moniados en Galicia hoy. La España Mental 11. Madrid: Akal.

MALLART L., 1978, Witchcraft Illness in the Evuzok Nosological System. Culture, Medicine and Psychiatry 2(4):373–396.

——, 2003, La Forêt de nos ancêtres. Tervuren: Musée Royal de l'Afrique Centrale.

MARTÍNEZ-HERNÁEZ A., 1993, Veinte Años de Antropologia de la Medicina en España. In Antropología de la salud y de la medicina. O. Romaní and J. M. Comelles, eds. Pp. 13–34. La Laguna: Asociación Canaria de Antropólogos-FAAEE.

——, 1998, Has visto como llora un cerezo? Pasos hacia una antropología de la esquizofrenia. Barcelona: Universitat de Barcelona.

——, 2000a, What's Behind the Symptom? On Psychiatric Observation and Anthropological Understanding. Amsterdam: Harwood Academic Publishers.

——, 2000b, Has visto como llora un cerezo? Pasos hacia una antropologia de la esquizofrenia. Barcelona: Barcelona University Press.

MEDINA R. and J. MOLERO, 2002, Medicina y poder colonial en el África Española. Un acercamiento preliminar a la perspectiva de género desde el marco legislativo colonial.

In Las Mujeres en el África Subsahariana. Antropología, literatura, arte y medicina. A. Martín, C. Velasco and F. García, eds. Pp. 312–330. Madrid: Ediciones del Bronce, Yo la quitaría.

MENÉNDEZ E., 1981, Poder, estratificación y salud. Análisis de las condiciones sociales y económicas de la enfermedad en Yucatán. México, DF: La Casa Chata.

——, 1990, Antropología Médica. Orientaciones, desigualdades y transacciones. México, DF: CIESAS.

MIQUEO C. T. and M. CRUZ, eds, 2001, Perspectivas de género en salud. Fundamentos científicos socioprofesionales de diferencias sexuales no previstas. Madrid: Minerva.

NEEDHAM R., 1969, Structure and Sentiment. A Test Case in Social Anthropology. Chicago: The University of Chicago Press.

OBIOLS J., 1981, Factores étnico-culturales en psicopatología. Revista del Departamento de Psiquiatria de la Facultad de Medicina de Barcelone 8:96–103.

OBIOLS J. and J. V. BELLOCH, 1987, El paciente extranjero en las salas de psiquiatría. Patología del choque intercultural. Revista del Departamento de Psiquiatría de la Facultad de Medicina de Barcelona 14:170–172.

OLAVARRIA E., 1982 [1885], Supersticiones españolas de medicina popular. *In* Medicina Popular. W. G. Black, ed. Pp. 326–355. Barcelona: Alta-Fulla, Yo la quitaría.

PALLARES A., 2003, El mundo de las unidades de cuidados intensivos. La última frontera. Ph.D. thesis. Tarragona: Universitat Rovira i Virgili.

PALLARÈS J., 1995, La dolça punxada de l'escorpi. Antropologia dels ionquis i de la heroina a Catalunya. Lleida: Pagès Editors.

PARDO J., 2002, Oviedo, Monardes, Hernandez el tesoro natural de América colonialismo y ciencia en el siglo XVI. Madrid: Nivela.

PERDIGUERO E., 1992, The Popularization of Medicine during the Spanish Enlightenment. *In* The Popularization of Medicine, 1650–1850. R. Porter, ed. Pp. 160–193. London: Routledge.

——, 1993, Historia de la medicina y antropología de la medicina. *In* Antropología de la salud y de la medicina. O. Romaní and J. M. Comelles, eds. Pp. 35–36. La Laguna: Asociación Canaria de Antropólogos-FAAEE.

——, 1997, Healing Alternatives in Alicante, Spain, in the Late Nineteenth and Late Twentieth Centuries. *In* Illness and Healing Alternatives in Western Europe. M. Gijswijt-Höfstrat, H. Marland and H. de Waardt, eds. Pp. 205–223. London: Routledge.

PERDIGUERO E. and J. M. COMELLES, eds, 2000, Medicina y cultura. Estudios entre la antropología y la medicina. Barcelona: Bellaterra.

PERDIGUERO E., A. ERKOREKA and J. M. COMELLES, 2000, Cuarenta años de antropología de la medicina en España (1960–2000). *In* Medicina y cultura. Estudios entre la antropología y la medicina. E. Perdiguero and J. M. Comelles, eds. Pp. 353–446. Barcelona: Bellaterra.

PITRÈ G., 1896, Medicina Popolare Siciliana. Turín: Carlo Clausen.

PRAT CARÓS J., 1972, El ex-voto: un modelo de religiosidad popular en une comarca de Catalunya. Ethnica 4:137–171.

PRIMERES JORNADES D'ANTROPOLOGIA DE LA MEDICINA, 1982, II Colloqui de l'ICA. Comunicacions 1. Tarragone: Arxiu d'Etnografia de Catalunya.

PUJADAS J. J., J. M. COMELLES and J. PRAT, 1980, Una bibliografía comentada sobre antropología médica. *In* La Antropología Médica en España. M. Kenny and J. De Miguel, eds. Pp. 323–353. Barcelona: Anagrama.

ROCA J., 1996, De la Pureza a la Maternidad. La construcción del género femenino en la postguerra española. Madrid: Ministerio de Educación y Cultura.

ROMANÍ O., 1982, Droga i Subcultura:una historia cultural del haix a Barcelone (1960–1980). Ph.D. thesis. Barcelona: Universitat de Barcelona.

——, 1999, Las drogas. Sueños y razones. Barcelona: Ariel.

RONZÓN E., 1991, Antropología y Antropologías. Ideas para una historia crítica de la Antropología española. El siglo XIX. Oviedo: Pentalfa.

SEPPILLI T., ed., 1983, La medicina popolare in Italia. Dossier. La Ricerca Folclorica, vol. 8. Brescia: Grafo Edizioni.

——, (comp.), 1989, Le Tradizioni Popolari in Italia. Medicine e Magie. Milan: Electa.

TÍZON J. L., M. SALAMERO, N. PELEGRO, F. SAINZ and J. ATXOTEGUI, 1993, Migraciones y salud mental. Un análisis psicopatológico tomando como punto de partida la inmigración asalariada en Catalunya. Barcelona: PPU.

TURNER V. W., 1972, Les tambours d'affliction. Analyse des rituels chez les Ndembu de Zambie. Paris: Gallimard.

URIBE J. M., 1996, Educar y cuidar. El diálogo cultural en atención primaria. Madrid: Ministerio de Cultura.

URTEAGA L., 1980, Miseria, miasmas y microbios. Las Topografías Médicas y el estudio del medio ambiente en el siglo XIX. Barcelona: Geocrítica, Universidad de Barcelone.

VILLAMIL F., 2001, Homosexualidad y sida. Ph.D. thesis. Madrid: Universidad Complutense de Madrid.

ZARZOSO A., 2001, El pluralismo médico a través de la correspondencia privada en la Cataluña del siglo XVIII. Dynamis 21:141–159.

Chapter 7

ITALY

Suffering, Politics, Nation: A Cartography of Italian Medical Anthropology
Mariella Pandolfi and Gilles Bibeau

The unique character of Italian medical anthropology can be traced to the country's vast regional diversity, which, until the 1980s, gave Italian anthropology a strong regionalist tone. Medical anthropology in Italy has historically been more deeply rooted in theories of cultural anthropology and *demologia*[1] than the medical anthropology practiced in other countries, notably the United States. The theoretical frameworks that have inspired Italian medical anthropology over the course of its history have drawn liberally from major philosophical schools such as Benedetto Croce's historicism (1866–1952)[2] and Antonio Gramsci's Marxist theories (1891–1937). These approaches have provided Italian intellectual debates with strong political overtones and have produced within the discipline a strong inclination toward sociopolitical involvement. Italian intellectuals, especially those who define themselves as "organic intellectuals," have also integrated various critical theories from the Frankfurt School to Michel Foucault, and from phenomenology to psychoanalysis. In this chapter we will make frequent reference to the philosophical landscape of Italy and we will demonstrate that medical anthropology is related to both cultural anthropology and *demologia*, as well as to debates about the nation and the conditions under which the Italian State was formed.

Political and Historical Markers in the Genesis of Italian Anthropology

It is important to remember that Italy only became a unified political entity in the 1860s, following Cavour's diplomatic action. Anthropologists have clearly demonstrated that one can speak of several "Italies," for the national unity that emerged out of the risorgimento was primarily political and administrative in nature. Despite the promotion of natural consciousness and the binding networks of public institutions such as schools, the media, and the administration, multiple regional cultures continue to survive within the constructed national space and have served to make Italian anthropology an especially rich tradition. Homogenization has not played as significant a role in the Italian national dynamic as it has in other countries such as France, where Paris' administrative centralism was forcefully imposed on the entire country, or Germany, where Bismarck's Prussian-based federalism promoted the notion that all Germans belonged to a single community based on linguistic and blood ties.

The deep regional variations that political power has attempted to reduce within the unified Italian State can be traced back several millennia to the period of the Magna Grecia. This period gave the Italian Mezzogiorno its basic cultural configuration that has remained primarily intact, distinguishing the rural south from regional cultures in the north and those in the center. The "issue of national identity" has long taken center stage in Italian cultural and political debates, predating Benedetto Croce and Antonio Gramsci. In *La Scienza Nuova* (1725), Giambattista Vico (1668–1744) was already pondering the universal pattern of nations (Vico 1986).[3] The historical tension between the north and south of Italy constantly resurfaces in the strategies of political parties and in debates over the Italian nation, with *Lega Nord* as its most recent manifestation.

The *"Questione Meridionale"* as an issue of national identity constantly resurfaces in Italian political, social, and cultural debates.[4] For example, during the general strike of 1920 when the factories in northern Italy were closed, the fascist leaders appealed to the peasants of the south to replace striking workers. Gramsci, a model militant in the Italian communist party, puzzled over why Italian peasants agreed to replace striking workers, because that action marked a break in the workers' solidarity with the social and economic revolution initiated in the north. Gramsci's reflections on the failure of Italy's revolutionary movement, and more specifically his exploration of the role of peasant culture in Italian society and the *Questione Meridionale* (1975), serve as important background for examining the internal contradictions in Italian society. Gramsci's prison writings (1975), which analyze with extraordinary clairvoyance the role of proletarian power, "organic intellectuals," and the relationship between hegemony and subalternity, lay at the heart of various approaches in medical anthropology, such as those inspired by Ernest De Martino.

Gramsci died in a Roman clinic in 1937 before completing his prison sentence. At that time, Il Duce's fascist government was preparing to adopt the racial laws (1938)[5] that mystified rural life, canonized a particular type of Italian, and excluded foreigners. This marked the peak of the xenophobic nationalizing view that fascists attempted to impose on all Italians as of 1922; opposing that view cost Gramsci his life. During the fascist period, biological anthropology in the tradition of Cesare Lombroso (1835–1909) was used to establish the biological foundation of race, legitimizing racial hierarchy and justifying the fascist policy of "defending the race." It was also during that period that the Italian social sciences adopted a neopositivist stance that suppressed creative and innovative scholarship, particularly in anthropology.

Italy's relatively weak position as a colonial power also had a strong impact on the practice of anthropology in the peninsula. Italian anthropologists have tended to work in Italy, whereas other European anthropologists primarily performed research in their former colonial empires. Some Italian ethnologists performed research in Mexico and Africa, particularly in Ethiopia where Mussolini administered a colony during the fascist period. However, the field research carried out in colonized territories has been much less significant in the development of Italian anthropology than research carried out in the different regions of Italy, notably the Mezzogiorno. Italian anthropologists have found the "other," the primitive savage, "at home." As a result, "alterity" in this tradition was reflected upon through the inferior, "othered" peasant that would become its symbol.

Italy has developed regional anthropologies "at home" rather than a truly national anthropology. This seems to represent the first of the two main paths toward national anthropologies: (1) a rarer form of anthropology (found in Italy, Spain, Brazil, and other countries where strong regionalisms have remained strong) that tends to highlight regional differences within a mainly imagined nation (Anderson 1991); and (2) the more common form of national anthropology that emphasizes a country's collective national identity.[6]

From Zanetti to Basaglia: A Shared Concern for Politics and a Passion for Reform

Italian intellectuals have a long tradition of critical vigilance with regard to public institutions. This tradition is best represented by the psychiatrist Franco Basaglia, but can be traced back in many ways to the health service reform movement instituted by Italian public health physicians in the 19th century. In this section, we will illustrate this commitment to reform by describing Zeno Zanetti and other 19th-century medical practitioners, as well as Franco Basaglia, a revolutionary author whose work a century later greatly influenced the development of medical anthropology and cultural and social psychiatry within Italy.

Zeno Zanetti was a physician (1978) who practiced in Perugia and throughout Umbria in the 19th century. Zanetti's political consciousness was mirrored by his contemporaries in other areas of Italy, such as Giuseppe Pitré (1896) who practiced in Sicily.[7] Zanetti and other physicians in the hygienist movement brought medicine to the forefront of political and social discourse, especially following the unification of Italy. The unified Italy of the 19th century was viewed as a diseased nation. Efforts were undertaken to clean up areas with high rates of "malaria," a typically Italian expression found in pathology treatises.[8] Public hygiene campaigns were aimed at infectious diseases such as tuberculosis, cholera, diphtheria, and syphilis. Syphilis was introduced in the 16th century by Spanish troops in the south of Italy and infections remained primarily in military populations.[9] A modernization strategy for the Mezzogiorno was also set up to fight poverty-related illnesses prevalent at the time in the villages of the south. The physicians who had been gathering information on folk-care practices became hygiene educators and reformers who sought to change the living conditions of the poor. The unification of medicine, education, and politics created a truly social medicine that established direct links between the presence of infectious agents, poor living conditions among the peasantry, and folk systems used for interpreting and treating illness.

We believe that there are three reasons for the powerful politicization seen in the work of folklorists like Zanetti and Pitré: (1) it was believed that folk systems which dealt with illness spread superstitions and magical ideas, which physicians attempted to eradicate through health education activities; (2) it was believed that the rift between the industrialized north and the peasant south with its large latifundia landholdings could only be bridged by the modernization and industrialization of the Mezzogiorno; (3) it was believed that the entwined nature of folk medicines and ancient religious beliefs deepened the gap between scientific medical systems and healer-related folk practices. Zanetti, Pitré, and colleagues transformed health from an issue viewed solely in medical terms, to one that was understood to have deeply political roots.

Nearly a century later another critical social examination of illness was developed by a psychiatrist known as Franco Basaglia (1924–1981). Basaglia's reform of Italian psychiatry, radical critique of public institutions, and renewed vision of Italian society made him a leading figure of the second half of the 20th century and one of Italy's greatest, most progressive intellectuals. Basaglia promoted the deinstitutionalization movement known as *"Psichiatria Democratica"* in Trieste, where he began working in 1971. He was influential in shaping several countries' decisions to adopt a new model for dealing with the mentally ill, and he helped foster a sense of social responsibility for psychological suffering. Following his reform of psychiatric hospitals, Basaglia proposed a new institutional model that was intended to stem the destruction of the lives of those living on the fringes of capitalism, the free market, and postwar consumer society. He thus paved the way for a new understanding of public institutions as a whole (1971, 1974, 1981–82). Throughout his life, Basaglia reconciled psychopathology and phenomenology within the realm of psychiatry, and succeeded in politicizing the field of mental illness, formulating one of the most radical critiques of public institutions. In collaboration with his colleagues, Basaglia accomplished the miraculous feat of ensuring the passing of Law 180, which approved a radical reform of Italian psychiatric institutions. The law has had worldwide impact as the Italian model was widely taken up by other nations. From Michel Foucault to Robert Castel, from Brazil and Mozambique to the United States, Basaglia's reforms mobilized a vast intellectual and political shift.

Basaglia's young, progressive colleagues recognized in his vision an ethical and universal dimension that served as a foundation for their social and political commitments (Colucci and Di Vittorio 2001). In the years that followed, social and democratic psychiatry found a clear path with a "strong" political epistemology that led from social psychiatry to transcultural and cultural psychiatry, and finally to ethnopsychiatry. Physicians, psychiatrists, and psychoanalysts transformed their theories and practice to promote an increasingly "politicized" medicine that first focused on people of Italian origin who had emigrated from villages in the Mezzogiorno. The movement would later focus increasingly on foreign immigrants who arrived in Italy after the 1980s.

Within Italy, Basaglia's ideas had a major impact on the work of the central figures in medical anthropology and ethnopsychiatry. During what is known as his philosophico-scientific period, Basaglia promoted a phenomenological psychiatry that was unique in its ability to reinstate dignity to the fractured life of the sufferer through an ethically oriented treatment plan. While Basaglia's ideas were central to the phenomenological movement within psychiatry, researchers and practitioners from other schools of thought have also been drawn to this movement. Phenomenological approaches to psychiatry are widely popular in Italy, especially in comparison with the philosophical and psychological approaches that are more predominant in Germany. Central figures in this phenomenological movement include Alberto Gaston (1987) who promoted a dialogue between psychoanalysis and phenomenology, Bruno Callieri (Callieri and Faranda 2001), and Sergio Mellina (1997). Luigi Frighi (1992) and Goffredo Bartocci (1994) helped develop a transcultural approach to mental health. Giuseppe Cardamone (Cardamone and Pini 1996; Cardamone and Schirripa 1990; Cardamone and Zorzetto 2000), Salvatore Inglese (Inglese 1993, 2003; Ingelese and Madia 1989; Ingelese and Peccarisi 1997), and Nino Losi (2000) reinterpreted Basaglia in light of De Martino, Tobie Nathan and the Dakar School, among others.

The other fundamental turning point in Basaglia's work is what Mario Colucci and Pierangelo di Vittorio (2001) have defined as a practico-political shift in which Basaglia addressed the destructive mechanisms that the mentally ill develop upon diagnosis, which are furthered by internment in institutions (Basaglia 1981–82:286). According to Basaglia, psychiatric patients' subjectivities can only be restored by combining two processes: the destruction of the institution that has locked up the patient, and the mobilization of the "force of madness." Basaglia viewed insanity as an enabling force that permitted the individual to reconstruct the fragments of his or her history. Thus, the category "mental illness" is called into question as the mentally ill can regain their liberty through their release from the psychiatric hospital.

Frantz Fanon's "Wretched of the Earth" (1961) and Franco Basaglia's wretched of the "*istituzione negata*" (1974) share the same radicalism that reasserts the rights of the subject and denounces the violence of the destructive authority that is hidden in all institutions. Basaglia foresaw the danger that his visionary position could induce (Colucci and Di Vittorio 2001:215). Indeed, in many places the "*istituzione negata*" was transformed into a new ideology, a bureaucratic formula emptied of its radicalism, perhaps precisely because of the strength of its creator. Following Basaglia's death in 1981, his anti-institution philosophy and its implementation in Trieste enabled younger generations to build upon his foundational work and create an expressly political space for their clinical work. Notable research in this area includes the work of Roberto Beneduce and others working among immigrants and refugees living in Italy.

Within the Italian landscape of psychiatry and medical anthropology, three other major figures can be identified that indirectly occupy independent and original positions within the discipline. The first of these figures is Giovanni Jervis (1994, 2003), a psychiatrist and psychoanalyst who collaborated with De Martino (1961). Jervis was associated with the Psichiatria Democratica movement founded by Basaglia. The second figure is Umberto Galimberti (1983), a philosopher and psychoanalyst who opened up new perspectives on critical trends in medical anthropology and ethnopsychiatry with his studies of the body. In Galimberti, a student of Jaspers, the anthropology of the body found a theoretician who advanced thinking in the field. Such contributions to the anthropology of the body have been developed alternatively by anthropologists such as Laura Faranda (Faranda 1996; Faranda and Callieri 2002), Claudia Mattalucci (2003), and Ivo Quaranta (2003). The third person is Michele Risso (Risso and Böker 1992), a psychoanalyst who has developed a psychopathology of immigration within a cross-cultural perspective.

Ernesto De Martino: A Founding Source for Italian Medical Anthropology

Ernesto De Martino (1908–65) was a foundational figure in an innovative and controversial school of anthropology in Italy. His historico-political reconsideration of village practices in the Mezzogiorno was the basis for a large body of writings that opened Italian anthropology to new interpretative perspectives. De Martino emphasized the need for the ethnographer to become politically engaged. He had strength of conviction that, while different in content, was similar to the Jesuits' zeal in their mission to spread the Gospel in the "Italian Indies."[10] The Italian tradition of anthropology "at home" inaugurated a period that was rich in ethnographic research, theoretical creativity, and political involvement. This specifically Italian tradition took root several decades before Europe was considered worthy of anthropological analysis. Moreover, it demonstrated that certain magico-religious rituals or traditional therapeutic itineraries were profoundly connected to logics of hegemony and subalternity, power relations, and class relations. It was not until the 1980s that gender relations and struggles between the sexes were integrated into these analyses. De Martino's analysis focused on possession rituals and highlighted the meaning that the rituals held for the individual and for subaltern culture (1959, 1961, 1973). He located them in a rural south that he portrayed as fragmented and heterogeneous. Using Gramsci, he interpreted the rituals as attempts to legitimize all expressions of folklore as the primarily implicit response of an oppressed class to the risk of losing itself in the field of the "everyday."

At first glance, the Italian literature appears circumscribed by the work of Demartinian exegetes and philologists whose work is incomprehensible to anyone who did not participate directly in their debates. There are, however, a few notable essays produced during this period (Lombardi Satriani 1979, Ginzburg 1978 Rossi, 1975). Like Devereux, De Martino had a penchant for posing questions rather than providing answers, and he was drawn to elaborating general theories replete with dazzling intuitions. In De Martino's view, Italy could no longer be defined geographically, only politically and socially (1959). The task of ethnography was therefore to give the south a new interpretative dimension by reconstructing its religious history in a sociopolitical perspective. De Martino's work was simultaneously ethnological and political and established a particular type of ethnologist, promoting a position not far from what is now known as hermeneutics (1941).

De Martino was inspired by Gramsci's observations on folklore and established a research program on the tarantula ritual (1961). His "critical ethnocentrism," and later "ethnographic humanism," outlined a new subjectivity for the ethnologist that revealed the constant tension between historicism and phenomenology. He placed the critical examination of Western history at the heart of ethnographic research. For De Martino, recognizing the historical dimensions of cultural categories did not necessitate lapsing into a relativism that would prevent the West from critical self-examination.

One of De Martino's most suggestive, and criticized, ideas is the notion of "the crisis of presence." De Martino maintained that an awareness of the temporality and rhythm of life is asserted when people experience critical life events. The feeling of needing to "be there" during such turning points generates "the crisis of presence," because each event that requires being present simultaneously reveals the risk of not "being there" (De Martino 1956, 1959). De Martino believed that this "the crisis of presence" led to the mechanism of magic. All magic rituals pivot around two problematical nodes: a release of any accumulated tensions that could set off episodes of violence towards oneself or others (possession rituals); and the alternative representation of a favorable existential reality to replace the reality at the origin of the frustrations (propitiatory rituals). De Martino presented the existential category of distress as a possible anthropological object. This is an important theme whose implications opened the Demartinian crisis of presence to other interpretative possibilities and led to broader reflections on the historicity of humankind. The theme of cultural apocalypses is developed as an example in his unfinished book *La fine del mondo . . .* (1977). His intention was first and foremost to redraw the uncertain boundaries between the pathological and the cultural in cases where the "end of the world" becomes a global daily experience.

For the first time in anthropological theory, an author was trying to work at a level of absolute reciprocity between the macroscopic or cultural apocalypse, and the microscopic or the impact of a catastrophe on subjectivity and pathology. He directly juxtaposed: (1) the historicity of the event, (2) the social resonance in the group, and (3) the risk of catastrophe for the individual. De Martino believed that the anthropological challenge was to elaborate a general theory of cultural apocalypses based on an analysis of psychopathological apocalypses. A person's subjectivity can be lost as the result of an exterior catastrophic event, but that subjectivity can also be recreated or restored through ways of living that are as of yet unimaginable. However, the dimension of risk, which is both an ontological and a historical dimension, always remains (1964, 1977).

The first generation of Italian anthropologists to reformulate De Martino's heritage in the field of medical anthropology are Clara Gallini (1977, 1988), Vittorio Lanternari (1992, 1995), Luigi Lombardi Satriani (1968a, 1968b, 1979), and Tullio Seppilli. Gallini, who was De Martino's student and later his assistant, proposed an original analysis of folk medicine and of the phenomena of contamination between medicine and magic. Her work is a convincing combination of the

Italian tradition and French symbolic anthropology (Gallini 1988). Lombardi Satriani attempted to demonstrate the connections between magico-religious practices and customary law in a framework that draws attention to the close relationship between violence and resistance among subaltern classes (1968a, 1968b, 1979). Other notable work includes the research of Alfonso M. di Nola (1993), Vittorio Lanternari (1992, 1995), and Elsa Guggino (1983, 1993). In the next section, we will further examine the work of Tullio Seppilli who worked as an assistant to De Martino during the 1950s.

It is important to note that other anthropologists, such as Amalia Signorelli (1986), have continued De Martino's legacy although their work is not formally in the field of medical anthropology. For example, the perspective promoted by Matilde Callari-Galli (1996, 1999) is an interesting parallel to De Martino's legacy. After training in the United States, Callari Galli returned to Italy where she introduced Italian anthropology to an original synthesis of the reflections taking place outside of Italy on complex societies, globalization and, with Gualtiero Harrison (2001), human rights. Other anthropologists have drawn on the Demartinian tradition while remaining open to a variety of schools of thought, notably Paolo Apolito (2002) and Silvia Mancini (1991). The next generation of anthropologists introduced a variety of concepts, theories, and methods to Italian medical anthropology from different approaches within medical anthropology and ethnopsychiatry. The main influences are the Dakar School, the French anthropology of illness (*anthropologie de la maladie*, in particular Marc Augé, Didier Fassin, and Andràs Zempléni), Devereux's and Nathan's ethnopsychiatry, the Harvard and McGill schools, and medical anthropology at the Université de Montréal. These authors include Roberto Beneduce, Andrea Caprara, Piero Coppo, Salvatore Inglese, Pino Schirripa, and many others who have developed original perspectives by combining different traditions of thought in medical anthropology and cultural psychiatry.

We wish to emphasize that there are theoretical approaches in Italian medical anthropology other than those engendered by De Martino's work. Examples include the ethnomedical research carried out by Italo Signorini (1996) and Alessandro Lupo (1999) with the Huavès of Mexico, and Bernardo Bernardi's work (1990) on spiritual healing practices among Kenyan prophets, which was inspired by the British anthropological tradition.[11] Finally, Tullio Tentori (1979) is a figurehead for the specific version of the "culture and personality" school in Italy.

Three Figures in Italian Medical Anthropology

In this section we will examine Italian medical anthropology and ethnopsychiatry by focusing on three figures whose contributions established unique forms of dialogue between national and international "political" perspectives. We realize that this narrow focus cannot do justice to the broad range of scientific contributions made by Italian medical anthropologists. This approach runs the risk of neglecting some very interesting work, particularly the research being performed by the new generation of medical anthropologists. We have chosen to focus on these colleagues because we believe that their contributions represent some of the original approaches that have developed within the broader, unified discipline of Italian medical anthropology. As we discuss each of the three authors, Tullio Seppilli (1956, 1959, 1990, 1994a, 1994b, 1995, 1996, 2001), Mariella Pandolfi (1986, 1989, 1990, 1991, 1996, 2002, 2003), and Piero Coppo (Coppo 1985, 1990, 1993, 1994, 1996; Coppo and Keita 1990), we will present other medical anthropologists whose work is closely related to the perspectives of the selected authors.

Tullio Seppilli: Founder of the Perugia School

Tullio Seppilli is highlighted here because he exemplifies a typically Italian style of anthropology. As soon as he was hired at Perugia in late 1955, Tullio Seppilli began to create the Istituto di etnologia e antropologia, the first true institute of cultural anthropology in Italy. The institute broke with *demologia* which focused on the study of folk traditions, and with the institutions inspired by biological anthropology that were founded during the fascist period, notably by Giovanni Sergi and Paolo Mantegazza. Seppilli directed the Perugia institute until he retired in 2000. For nearly half a century Professor Seppilli also worked in close collaboration with the Centro sperimentale per l'educazione sanitaria, a center where medical anthropologists contributed to health education campaigns, the cultural adaptation of clinical practices, and health service reform.

Seppilli's early writings dealt with the relations between anthropology and public health (1956, 1959), the cultural aspects of behavior, and the cultural relevance of health education messages. Seppilli's medical anthropology practice was applied, and one of his ongoing concerns was how to demonstrate that anthropology could help public health services better adapt to the social and cultural characteristics of local communities. At the end of the 1950s Seppilli carried out research on the peasant cultures of Umbria, and central Italy in general, taking an interest in the processes of sociocultural change and rural–urban migration. He worked with a team directed by De Martino with healers in Lucania. During the same period, he began his own research on folk medicine in Rome and in the region of Perugia, studying folk practices and healers. Seppilli helped to consolidate Italian medical anthropology through his teaching and his commitment to achieving recognition for medical anthropology within the health sciences and within anthropology itself (1994b, 1995, 2001).

Seppilli is credited with having drawn together the divided heirs of De Martino in a logic of medical anthropology, and having stimulated dialogue between the Italian tradition and other national medical anthropology traditions, particularly that of Spain. This movement towards synthesis and cross-fertilization began in 1983 with a national conference in Pesaro that resulted in the proceedings entitled *La Medicina popolare in Italia* (Seppilli 1983) (see also *Medecine e magie. Le Tradizioni popolari in Italia*, 1990). In 1988, the Italian medical anthropology society was founded, and in 1996 AM (Rivista della Societa italiana di antropologia medica) was created. Through the Italian Society of Medical Anthropology (SIAM), which he helped to found, Seppilli was the tireless leader of an ever-expanding group of medical anthropologists.[12] Seppilli can indisputably be considered the main disciple of Ernesto De Martino within Italian medical anthropology.

Mariella Pandolfi: A Biopolitics of Distress and Disease

Mariella Pandolfi's work is central to italian medical anthropology because her contributions rest at the border between the Demartinian tradition and other intellectual traditions, particularly North American medical anthropology, French anthropology of illness, ethnopsychoanalysis, and the politicization of the body. Mariella Pandolfi has transformed the "land of remorse," that Ernesto De Martino had said was haunted by the continual return of "a bad past," into a "land of resistance," marked by women who speak through their bodies of their own distress as well as that of their country. In a south Italy traditionally dominated by male values, Pandolfi demonstrates that women emerged from an imposed silence to act out their resistance through a powerful language of emotions and a new use of the body. In the melancholic behavior of the women of Samnium, Pandolfi uncovers the same suffering that was once expressed in rituals of tarantism. The aspects of female identity that were relegated to the ambiguous zone between illness and emotion, a realm of disease, are conveyed through a form of suffering that is foundational to female identity (1989, 1990, 1991). Pandolfi demonstrates that women's emotions are inscribed in the body as a kind of corporeal memorial, and are interpreted as an intermediary space where the south's regional history, sociocultural context, and women's daily lives are linked together.

In *Itinerari delle emozioni . . .* (1991), Pandolfi focused on an analysis of three main trajectories among the women of Samnium: the manifestation of emotions through an event-related temporality, the itinerary of "unveiled emotions," and the itinerary of "embodied emotions." Pandolfi uses three main concepts to place the different levels of emotion in resonance with one another. The most powerful concept is that of "trace," which extends Demartinian thought without reproducing its determinist leanings with regards to the theory of the reflection between the subjective and the social. The second concept is women's "body-emotion," which evokes the disturbing nature of the female body as well as women's pain as it is rooted in a regional history of suffering, and women's potential for corroding the social order. The third concept, which gives coherence to her approach, is that of "event," where the event is understood to lift the veil on the contradictions inherent in daily life. Pandolfi takes as her starting point De Martino's conceptualizations of the interpenetration of cultural apocalypse and subjectivity in crisis. She outlines a theory of rite and narrative as acts of liberation and echoes between personal and collective histories.

Pandolfi's approach extends and breathes new life into De Martino's program: it adds complexity to studies that examine the relationship between hegemonic and subaltern cultures; explores the perspectives opened by Merleau-Ponty's phenomenology; and places medical anthropology and French ethnopsychiatry tradition (of Marc Augé, Jeanne Favret-Saada, Tobie Nathan, and Andràs Zempléni) in conversation with research in American anthropology (as practiced by Lila Abu-Lughod, Ellen Corin, Vincent Crapanzano, Michael Herzfeld, and Paul Rabinow). Pandolfi's studies have opened a radical political space in the Italian Mezzogiorno, anticipating her more recent work on "Le arene politiche del corpo" (1996, 2003a) in which she borrows the notion of "biopower" from Michel Foucault and "bare life" from Giorgio Agamben to extend the political dimensions of her research. In traumatized territories, such as the postcommunist Balkans, the need for a critical analysis of humanitarian interventions is imperative. Humanitarian invention is steeped in power relations, and under the pressure of temporality and the politics of emergencies, anthropologists have had to shift the terrain of their political involvement (Pandolfi 2002, 2003b). As anthropologists begin to address the heterogeneous experiences of refugees, illegal aliens, and trauma victims, they are compelled to engage in new research terrains that are increasingly shifting and mobile. As the field shifts away from localized experiences of the body, anthropologists must create innovative methods and approaches to capture the experiences of contemporary forms of domination.

Piero Coppo: Insanity among the Dogon of Mali

Piero Coppo's research among the Dogon of Mali (Coppo 1985, 1990, 1993; Coppo and Keita 1990) is representative of a medical anthropology practiced beyond Italian borders, and his research focuses on ethnopsychiatry (Coppo 1994, 1996), a dynamic field of study in Italy. Coppo began his work among the Bandiagara of Mali in 1977, and spent the better part of fifteen years working in Dogon country. Between 1977 and 1983, Coppo carried out his first ethnopsychiatric research with Leila Pisani in Dogon villages; and from 1984 to 1990 he directed an interdisciplinary team of researchers from Italy and Mali at the "Center de recherche sur la medicine traditionnelle de Bandiagara." Through this large-scale Italian – Malian project, funded by "Cooperazione Sviluppo" of Italy's Foreign Affairs department, Coppo's team studied the anthropological, psychological, epidemiological, and medico-psychiatric dimensions of mental health problems among the Dogon (1985). After 1990, Coppo worked primarily in Italy. In collaboration with Cardamone, Inglese, Pisani, and others, Coppo founded ORISS[13] which functions as a support group for research in medical anthropology, ethnopsychiatry, and ethnopharmacology. On the basis of his experience among African healers, Coppo laid the foundation for an original ethnopsychiatry that is gaining favor among psychiatrists, anthropologists, and other specialists through the "Gruppo di autoformazione sul curare."[14]

After completing an ethnography of rural Dogon society that focused on modernization processes, Coppo studied the sociocultural bases of psychopathology among Dogon villagers. Coppo's work on social change outlined the limits of the more folkloric ethnographies of the Dogon written by French anthropologists (Dierterlen, Griaule, Rouch). Coppo's position at the crossroads between anthropology, ethnopsychology, cultural psychiatry, and social epidemiology, enabled him to describe the local configurations of psychopathological disorders in Dogon country (1993). Coppo and his colleagues, such as Barbara Fiore (2001) and Roberto Lionetti (1992), shed light on therapeutic knowledge and the sociocultural bases of Dogon psychopathology in a context of modernization. Coppo's collaborative research team included ethnopsychologists, most notably Leila Pisani (Losi and Pisani 1992), as well as other professionals, such as epidemiologists. An ambulatory ethnopsychiatric consultation service founded by Coppo and colleagues helped to familiarize clinicians with local forms of illness interpretation and contemporary forms of psychiatric problems among the Dogon.

Coppo maintains that shifts in individual and collective rites, and resultant changes in identity construction, have led to a collapse in the symbolic order that has had serious consequences for the social life of the group and the mental health of individuals (1994). Deeply influenced by sociology, Coppo refused to employ the "overculturization" popular in North American transcultural psychiatry, and he challenged the perfectly ordered, mythological, and ritualized world prevalent in French ethnology. He focused instead on elucidating the changes and contradictions that shape how modern African subjects live, highlighting how contemporary economic hardship and political power shape individual lives. Coppo's short treatise entitled *Etnopsichiatria* (1996) affirms that he is both firmly rooted in the great Italian tradition of De Martino and Basaglia, and willing to integrate several innovative references including the clinical-anthropological approaches of Dr Henri Collomb and the Dakar school, Dr Lambo in Abeokuta in Nigeria, Devereux's ethnopsychiatric tradition, and the McGill School, especially Dr Henry B. M. Murphy. Coppo integrated these influences into an ethnopsychiatry that is part of the Italian tradition, yet his integration of other schools of cultural psychiatry makes him a central figure in Italian ethnopsychiatry.

Conclusions: Current Challenges in Italian Medical Anthropology

To conclude we will illustrate contemporary trends in Italian anthropology by describing some of the work of the new generation of anthropologists. It is difficult to predict exactly which direction Italian anthropology will take, yet under the influence of medical anthropology, it is likely that Italian anthropology will become increasingly international in scope through the integration of new theories, heuristic concepts, and methods. However, there is no doubt that it will remain rooted in the powerful Demartinian intellectual tradition, which is becoming increasingly recognized outside of Italy.

1   The first challenge facing Italian anthropologists today is creating a dialogue between the legacy of Italian anthropological thought and other great anthropological traditions. The new generation appears to be torn between the tradition of Italian thought and imported ideas that have been increasingly sweeping through Italian universities. The challenge for young anthropologists is to

maintain the identity and originality of the vigorous Italian intellectual tradition while remaining open to other ways of thinking. Many young anthropologists are interested in internationalizing debates by stimulating dialogue with colleagues from abroad. For example, Andrea Caprara (1996, 2001) combines North American and French approaches in his study of contagion among the Alladian of the Ivory Coast. Likewise, Pino Schirripa (2000, 2002) draws on Lanternari's work in his analysis of Ghana's prophetic churches. Antonella Crudo (2004) takes a similar position, drawing mainly on the Harvard School's interpretive approaches (Kleinman, Good, and Del Vecchio-Good). Today's medical anthropologists are much more eclectic than their predecessors, and are more engaged in transatlantic dialogue. It is too soon to predict whether they will be willing or able to remain rooted in the great traditions that have historically nourished Italian anthropology.

2   The second challenge is that the integration of new approaches could run the risk of displacing some of the best of Italy's intellectual heritage. An increasing number of Italian anthropologists from this new generation have studied or performed fieldwork outside of Italy, and are encouraging cross-border dialogue within Italian anthropology. The relationship between Italian anthropology "at home" and so-called "exotic" field sites is changing as more immigrants and refugees settle in Italy. For example, Rosalba Terranova Cecchini (1990), a pioneer in cross-cultural awareness, founded a group known as the Gruppo per le relazioni transculturali in Milan, which was later incorporated under the Cecchini Pace Foundation. The group was established in collaboration with the prominent transcultural psychologist Paolo Inghilleri (1999), as well as other psychiatrists, psychologists, and sociologists. The group has developed a training center for international development workers and government employees working in public health services, and it publishes the journal *Rivista di Scienze Transculturali*.[15] Another recent and interesting example of the discipline's development is the postgraduate training in medical anthropology offered at the Universita degli Studi di Milano Bicocca. This program provides an essential introduction to the discipline of medical anthropology. This training program analyzes the relationship between different medical systems, and highlights the complex articulations that occur among different cultural communities in the contemporary world. The program's director, Roberto Malighetti, has united scholars from throughout Italy and the world to take part in this innovative program.

Having spent time abroad, this contemporary generation of anthropologists has introduced alternative approaches into Italian universities and research centers. These influences are evident in the recent issue of *Antropologia* coordinated by Claudia Mattalucci (edited by Ugo Fabietti) that focuses on the body (Mattalucci 2003). Some anthropologists have also participated in international development projects. For example, Fiore and Lionetti have participated in projects directed by Coppo in Mali. Other anthropologists work on humanitarian interventions, such as Nino Losi (Losi 1992; Losi and Pisani 2000), who has worked in Mali and in Kosovo on projects with ambitious, even visionary, approaches. Whatever the topic, it is clear that Italian medical anthropology is drawing inspiration from a wide variety of sources. However, this diverse work has not coalesced into a unified vision.

3   The third challenge is applying medical anthropology and ethnopsychiatry to clinical practice. Authors such as Beneduce, Cardamone, Coppo, and Inglese have undertaken work in this arena, but more work needs to be done. Inglese[16] has shown exceptional originality and sensitivity in combining the perspectives of De Martino, Basaglia, and Nathan in his academic work and psychiatric practice, while Beneduce has experimented with new models for integrating and treating patients at psychiatric institutions in post-Basaglian Italy and in Africa. These authors, and others like them, have incorporated the contributions of other contemporary schools of medical anthropology and cultural psychiatry, grafting them onto Basaglia's radical critique of the institution with an attention to ethical considerations. Basaglia's thinking no doubt already contained elements of illness narratives, the distinction between illness and sickness, and the idea of broadening the therapeutic stage to include a range of therapies. It is up to the new generation of anthropologists to expand upon these ideas and link them to theories and categories developed elsewhere. The new generations of medical anthropologists and cultural psychiatrists (De Micco and Martelli 1993; Donatella Cozzi 1996; Pizza 1998; Ranisio 1996) are working to transform psychiatric and medical institutions by inventing meaningful clinical practices in the pluralistic context of contemporary Italy.

Thanks to Gramsci, De Martino, Basaglia, and the encounter with Foucault's critical theories, Italian anthropologists have taken seriously the experiences of others. Yet even a disciplinary field such as anthropology that is viewed as a "global political act" maintains its Italian specificity. This unique character should not be disavowed but, in our view, deserves greater international recognition. The authors of this chapter are in perfect agreement that, unfortunately, the majority of academic writing published in Italian remains unknown because it is not translated and is rarely published in international journals. Many of the themes being studied in contemporary academic medical anthropology have already been amply developed within Italy's geographical and political borders. It is up to new generations of post-Demartinian, post-Gramscian and post-Basaglian anthropologists to meet today's challenges and approach them like their predecessors: as political duties. Before this generation lies the responsibility and opportunity to export the complex, contradictory, and visionary Italian intellectual tradition.

Notes

1.   A clear distinction is made in Italian anthropology between ethnology, as practiced by ethnographers working with foreign ethnic groups, and *demologia* (literally "people's science" often known elsewhere as folklore), which is practiced "at home" usually among rural groups. A tradition of demological research developed in Italy

to include journals, conferences, and chairs, and only died out after bitter methodological debates distinguishing anthropology, ethnology, demology, and folklore.

2. The philosopher Benedetto Croce (1938) made history the keystone of a system that reconciled politics, economics, aesthetics, and ethics, a system he defined as "absolute historicism" where social actors are viewed as having a large measure of freedom. With his colleague Giovanni Gentile (1875–1944), Croce continually opposed the thinking of Hegel, Marx, and Vico to the dominant philosophy in Italy of the 1920s and 1930s, that is, scholastic thought, neopositivism, and critical rationalism. B. Croce took the ideas of Giambattista Vico (1986) further, correcting the philosophy of history, and paving the way for the work of Antonio Gramsci.

3. Vico's "New Science" recognized the role of myth and imagination in the construction of human societies. In his book published in 1725, this Neapolitan philosopher presented a comparative study of human societies, giving Italy what can be considered its first work of anthropology.

4. A parallel could no doubt be made with the "National Question" in Québec.

5. On July 14, 1938, the government of Dictator Benito Mussolini passed the "Manifesto della razza," which, similar to Nazi Germany, authorized the persecution of Jews and Blacks (called Hamites or Chamites).

6. In France, priority has been given to national institutions (e.g., the work of Marc Abélès 2001 on the National Assembly) and the study of republican institutions (schools, army, etc.); regional cultures have been relegated to folklore rather than anthropology.

7. Other postunification physicians who worked on folk medicine include: G. Battista Bastanzi in the Venitian Alps, D. G. Bernoni in Venise, C. Coronedi Berti in Bologna, Antonio de Nino in Molise and Abruzzo, C. Pigorini in the Marches, and P. Riccardi in the Modena region.

8. The name "malaria" ("bad air") makes sense in the context of the miasmatic theory of contagion, according to which particles of corrupted air, called miasmas, carried disease.

9. It was not until the Italian Renaissance that physicians, most notably Girolamo Fracastoro (1546), explicitly interpreted the central mechanism of contagion as the result of different forms of contact between individuals. The so-called theory of "con-tagium," which prefigured the microbes of germ theory, was developed in the context of debates around syphilis, the French disease as the Italians called it, or the disease of Naples, as the Spanish insisted. Fracastoro, like other Italian physicians, thought that syphilis, which affected many Spanish soldiers who participated in the siege of Naples, was introduced into Europe by sailors who went to America with Christopher Columbus. Fracastoro was the first to apply the theory of "contagium" to syphilis, asserting that the disease was transmitted via body fluids, primarily through sexual contact.

10. During the period when the Italian Jesuits were penetrating and evangelizing the rural south of Italy, they considered it to be a particularly demanding world that was not very open to a more urban form of Christianity. They spoke of the region as "*las Indias de por acà*," a metaphor still used today to refer to the peasant world of the south of Italy.

11. In his autobiography (1990), Bernardi himself acknowledged that he was one of the few Italian anthropologists to have placed social functionalism at the heart of his anthropological reflections.

12. These include: Alessandro Alimenti, Giancarlo Baronti, Carlotta Bagaglia, Paolo Bartoli (1997), Andrea Caprara, Paola Falteri (1997), Sabrina Flamini, Graziella Guaitini, Lara Iannotti, Laura Lepore, Cristiano Martello, Massimiliano Minelli, Cristina Papa (1988), Caterina Pasquini, Maya Pellicciari, Enrico Petrangeli, Giovanni Pizza, Chiara Polcri, Roberta Pompili, Riccardo Romizi, Pino Schirripa (2000, 2002), César Zuniga Valle. (This list has been copied from: Seppilli T., 2001, Medical anthropology "At Home": A Conceptual Framework and the Italian Experience. *AM Rivista della Società italiana di antropologia medica* 11–12:23–36.)

13. ORISS is the acronym for "*Organizzazione Interdisciplinare Sviluppo e Salute*".

14. For an in-depth study of the research done by Piero Coppo and his team, see Bibeau and Charland (1994).

15. Today there are three journals in medical anthropology in Italy: *I Fogli dei ORISS, A.M.,* and *Rivista di Scienze Transculturali*.

16. The concept of community ethnopsychiatry is drawn from a comparative study between groups' psychodynamic and cultural therapeutic models. This method is dedicated to refugees by the Transcultural and Community Unit of the public Mental Health Service – Catanzaro (Calabria).

References

ABÉLÈS M., 2001, Un ethnologue à l'Assemblée. Paris: Odile Jacob.

ANDERSON B., 1991, Imagined Communities: Reflections on the Origin and Spread of Nationalism. London: Verso.

APOLITO P., 2002, Internet e la Madonna. Milano: Feltrinelli.

BARTOCCI G., 1994, Psicopatologia, cultura e dimensione del sacro. Roma: Edizioni Universitarie Romane.

BARTOLI P., P. FALTERI, F. LOUX and F. SAILLANT, 1997, Non fissare il cielo stellato. Le verruche nella medicina popolare in Italia, in Francia e Québec. AM Rivista della Società italiana di antropologia medica: 103–144.

BASAGLIA F., 1971, La maggioranza deviante. Nuovo Politecnico, vol. 43. Torino: Einaudi.

——, 1974, L'istituzione negata: rapporto da un ospedale psichiatrico. Torino: Einaudi (Coll. Nuovo Politecnico).

——, 1981–82, Potere e istituzionalizatione. De la vita istituzionale a la vita de comunità, Scritti, 2 vol. Torino: Einaudi.

BERNARDI B., 1990, An Anthropological Odyssey. Annual Review of Anthropology 19:1–15.

BIBEAU G. and C. CHARLAND, 1994, Sur la piste des errances du Renard pâle. Les recherches d'une équipe italo-malienne sur le haut-plateau dogon, Psychopathologie africaine 16(3):341–385.

CALLARI-GALLI M., 1996, Lo spazio dell'incontro. Percorsi nella complessità. Roma: Meltemi.

——, 1999, Diritti umani e antropologia della contemporaneità. Pluriverso 4(30):55–59.

CALLIERI B. and L. FARANDA, 2001, Medusa allo specchio. Maschere fra antropologia e psicopatologia. Roma: Edizioni Univ. Romane.

CAPRARA A., 1996, Similitudine e contiguità. Elementi di antropologia del contagio. AM Rivista della Società italiana di antropologia medica 1/2:89–110.

——, 2001, Interpretare il contagio. Una indagine storico-etmografica sulle pratiche mediche presso gli Alladian della Costa d'Avorio (prefaced by Gilles Bibeau). Perugia: Argo/Fondazione Angelo Celli per una Cultura della Salute (Coll. Biblioteca di Anthropologica Medica).

CARDAMONE G. and P. PINI, 1996, Risorse communitarie e salute mentale. I Foglie di ORISS 5:57–78.

CARDAMONE G. and P. SCHIRRIPA, 1990, Lo scolio e la salvezza: un culto terapeutico in Calabria. Daedalus 4:127–145.

CARDAMONE G. and S. ZORZETTO, 2000, Salute mentale di comunità. Elementi di teoria e pratica. Milano: Franco Angeli.

COLUCCI M. and P. DI VITTORIO, 2001, Franco Basaglia. Milano: Bruno Mondadori.

COPPO P., 1985, Une enquête épidémiologique psychiatrique auprès d'une communauté rurale africaine: quelques questions méthodologiques. Santé, Culture, Health 3(3):3–9.

——, 1990, Problèmes et limites méthodologiques des études épidémiologiques en situation transculturelle. Psychopathologie africaine 23(3):279–285.

——, 1993, Essai de psychopathologie Dogon. Perugia/Bandiagara: Éditions CRMT/PSMTM.

——, 1994, Guaritori di foglia; storie dell'Altopiano Dogon. Torino: Bollati Borhinghieri editore.

——, 1996, Etnopsichiatria. Milano: Il Saggiatore.

COPPO P. and A. KEITA (dir.), 1990, Médecine traditionnelle: acteurs, itinéraires thérapeutiques. Roma: Edizioni E.

COZZI D., 1996, Narrazioni corporee. Le donne, il corpo, la depressione: una ricerca in Carnia (Friuli, Italia), AM Rivista della Società italiana di antropologia medica 1/2:215–244.

CROCE B., 1938, La storia some pensiero e come azione. Bari: Laterza.

CRUDO A., 2004, Ripensare la malattia, Dall'etnomedicina all'antropologia medica e alla psichiatria culturale della Harvard medical school (prefaced by Mariella Pandolfi). Lecce: Argo.

DE MARTINO E., 1941, Naturalismo e Storicismo in Etnologia. Bari: Laterza.

——, 1956, Crisi della presenza e integrazione religiosa. Aut-Aut 31:17–38.

——, 1959, Sud e Magia. Milano: Feltrinelli [1999, Italie du Sud et magie. Paris: Les Empêcheurs de penser en rond].

——, 1961, La terra del rimorso. Milano: Il Saggiatore [1999, La terre du remords (postfaced by Tobie Nathan). Paris: Les Empêcheurs de penser en rond].

——, 1964, Apocalissi culturali e apocalassi psicopatologiche. Nuovi Argomenti 69/71:105–141.

——, 1973 [1948], Il mondo magico. Torino: Boringhieri [1999, Le monde magique (introduction by Sylvia Mancini). Paris: Les Empêcheurs de penser en rond].

——, 1977, La fine del mondo, contributo all'analisi delle apocalissi culturali. C. Gallini, ed. Torino: Einaudi.

DE MICCO V. and P. MARTELLI, 1993, Passaggi di confine. Napoli: Liguori.

DI NOLA A., 1993, Lo specchio e l'olio. Le superstizioni degli italiani. Bari: Laterza.

FANON F., 1961, Les damnés de la terre. Paris: François Maspero.

FARANDA L., 1996, Dimore del corpo: Profili dell'identità femminile nella Grecia classica. Roma: Meltemi.

FARANDA L. and B. CALLIERI, 2002, Medusa allo specchio. Maschere fra antropologia e psicopatologia. Roma: Edizioni Universitarie Romane.

FIORE B., 2001, Il Bosco del guaritore. Torino: Bollati Boringhieri (Coll. Variantine).

FRACASTORO G., 1546, De contagionibus et contagiosis morbis et eorum curatione. Venezia: Luego.

FRIGHI L., 1992, Le problematiche trans-culturali in Psichiatria e in Igiene Mentale. *In* Cultura malattia migrazioni. La salute degli immigrati extracomunitari in Italia ed in Campania: aspetti sociali, medici e psicologici. A. Dama, T. Esposito and T. Arcella, eds. Pomigliano D'Arco: Regione Campania USL 27: Dipartimento di Salute Mentale.

GALIMBERTI U., 1983, Il corpo. Antropologia, psicoanalisi, fenomenologia. Milano: Giangiacomo Feltrinelli Editore.

GALLINI C., 1977, Introduzione. *In* La fine del mondo. E. De Martino, ed. Pp. 9–93. Turino; Einaudi.

——, 1988, La ballerina variopinta. Napoli: Liguori [1988, La danse de l'argia. Lagrasse: Verdier].

GASTON A., 1987, Genealogia dell'alienazione. Milano: Giangiacomo Feltrinelli editore.

GINZBURG C., 1978, La fine del mondo di Ernesto De Martino, Studi Storici 40:238–242.

GRAMSCI A., 1975, *In* Quaderni dal carcere (4 vol.). V. Gerratana, ed. Torino: Einaudi. [1978, Cahiers de prison (5 vol.). Paris: Gallimard (Coll. Bibliothèque de Philosophie)].

GUGGINO E., 1983, La magia in Sicilia. Palermo: Sellerio.

——, 1993, Il corpo è fatto di sillabe. Figure di maghi in Sicilia. Palermo, Sellerio.

HARRISON G., 2001, Fondamenti antropologici dei diritti umani. Roma: Meltemi.

INGHILLERI P., 1999, From Subjective Experience to Culural Change. Cambridge: Cambridge University Press.

INGLESE S., 1993, L'inquieta alleanza tra psicopatologia e antropologia. San Giovanni in Fiore: Edizioni Pubblisfera.

——, 2003, La follia perfetta: variazioni etnopsichiatriche sulla schizofrenia. *In* Ripensare le schizofrenie. Un dibattito italiano. G. Tagliavini and G. Cardamone, eds. Pp. 169–201. Paderno Dugnano: Edizioni Colibrì.

INGLESE S. and B. MADIA, 1989, Ideologia della morte, tecniche rituali e immaginario collettivo a San Giovanni in Fiore: un'osservazione sul campo. Daedalus 2:108–150.

INGLESE S. and C. PECCARISI, 1997, Psichiatria oltre frontiera. Viaggio intorno alle sindromi culturalmente ordinate. Milano: UTET Periodici.

JERVIS G., 1994, La psicoanalisi come esercizio critico. Milano: Garzanti.

——, 2003, La depressione. Un vuoto oscuro e maligno che possiamo colmare. Roma: Il Mulino.

LANTERNARI V., 1995, Medicina, Magia, Religione, Valori. Napoli: Liguori.

LANTERNARI V., V. DE MICCO and G. CARDAMONE, 1992, Psicopatologia dell'emigrazione in prospettiva transculturale. Napoli: Liguori.

LIONETTI R., 1992, Éthique et dialectique de l'évaluation de l'efficacité. *In* Les rapports techniques des consultants auprès du programme spécial Médecine traditionnelle au Mali. Pp. 111–125. Pregia/Bandiagara: Centro Sperimentale per l'Educazione sanitaria interuniversitario/CRMT.

LOMBARDI SATRIANI L. M., 1968a, Analisi marxista e folklore come cultura di contestazione. Critica marxista 6:64–88.

——, 1968b, Antropologia culturale e analisi della cultura subalterna. Messina: Peloritana.

——, 1979, Il Silenzio, La Memoria, Lo Sguardo. Palermo: Sellerio.

LOSI N., 2000, Vite altrove. Migrazione e disagio psichico. Milano: Giangiacomo Feltri-nelli Editore (Coll. Campi del sapere).

LOSI N. and L. PISANI, 1992, Coopération et santé au Mali. Roma: Instituto Italo-Africano (Coll. Studi e ricerche, 4).

LUPO A., 1999, Capire è un pò guarire: il rapporto paziente-terapeuta fra dialogo e azione. Antropologia Medica 7/8:53–92.

MANCINI S., 1991, Le monde magique selon De Martino. Gradhiva 10:71–83.

MATTALUCCI C., ed., 2003, Special issue, "Corpo." Antropologia 3.

MELLINA S., 1997, Medici e Sciamani fratelli separati. Roma: Lombardo Editore.

PANDOLFI M., 1986, Medical Anthropology in Europe: The State of the Art. Italy. Medical Anthropology Quarterly 17(4):90–91.

——, 1989, La femme est une gitane à vie. Santé Culture Health 6(1):5–23.

——, 1990, Boundaries Inside the Body: Women's Suffering in Southern Peasant Italy. Culture, Medicine, and Psychiatry 14(2):253–271.

——, 1991, Itinerari delle emozioni: Corpo e identita femminile nel Sannio Campano. Milano: Franco Angeli.

——, 1996, Perché il corpo. Utopia, sofferanza, desiderio. Roma: Meltemi.

——, 2002, Moral Entrepreneurs, souverainetés mouvantes et barbelé: le bio politique dans les Balkans post-communistes. Pandolfi M. and M. Abélès, eds. Special issue, "Politiques et jeux d'espaces." Anthropologie et Sociétés 26(1):1–24.

——, 2003a, Le arene politiche del corpo. C. Mattalucci, ed. Special issue, "Corpo." Antropologia 3:35–48.

——, 2003b, Contract of Mutual (In)difference: Governance and the Humanitarian Appa-ratus in Contemporary Albania and Kosovo. Indiana Journal of Global Legal Studies 10(1):369–389.

PAPA C., 1988, Les Fantaisies de la grossesse. Entre médecine officielle et médecine popu-laire en Ombrie, Les femmes et la modernité. Peuples méditérranéens 44:175–191.

PITRÉ G., 1896, Usi e costumi, credenze e pregiudizi del popolo siciliano. Palermo: Clausen.

PIZZA G., 1998, Figure della corporeità in Europa. Roma: CISU.

QUARANTA I., 2003, AIDS, sofferenza e incorporazione della storia a Nso' (provincia del Nord-Ouest del Camerun). Antropologia 3(3):43–74.

RANISIO G., 1996, Venire al mondo. Credenze, pratiche, rituali del parto. Roma: Meltemi.

RISSO M. and W. BÖKER, 1992, Sortilegio e delirio. Psicopatologia dell'emigrazione in prospettiva transculturale. Napoli: Liguori Editore.

ROSSI P., 1975, Sul relativismo culturale De Martino e l'introduzione di cases a Il Mondo magico. Rivista di filosofia 67:165–176.

SCHIRRIPA P., 2000, L'ambulatorio del guaritore. Forme e pratiche del confronto tra bio-medicina e medicine tradizionali in Africa e nelle Americhe. Perugia: Argo/Fondazione Angelo Celli pet una Cultura della Salute (Coll. Biblioteca di Antropologia medica).

——, 2002, Health, Charismatic Cults and Contemporary Folk Culture. AM Rivista della Società italiana di antropologia medica 13/14:191–204.

SEPPILLI T., 1956, Contributo alla formulazione dei rapporti tra prassi igienico-sanitaria ed etnologia, in Società italiana per il Progresso delle Scienze, Atti della XLV Riunione (Napoli: 16–20 ottobre 1954). Pp. 295–312. Roma: S.i.p.s.

——, 1959, Il contributo dell'antropologia culturale all'educazione sanitaria. L'Educazione Sanitaria Periodico ufficiale del Centro sperimentale di educazione sanitaria delle popo-lazioni 4(3–4):325–340.

——, ed., 1983, La medicina popolare in Italia. Special issue. La Ricerca Folklorica 8.

——, 1990, Medicine e Magie. Le tradizioni popolari in Italia. Milano: Electa.

——, 1994a, Per un'antropologia dell'alimentazione. Determinazioni, funzioni e significati psico-culturali della risposta sociale a un bisogno biologico. La Ricerca Folklorica 30:7–14.

——, 1994b, Le biologique et le social. Un parcours anthropologique. Ethnologie Française 24(3):514–530.

——, 1995, Ernesto de Martino e la nascita dell'etnopsichiatria italiana. Storia, Antropologia e Scienza del Linguaggio 10(3):147–156.

——, 1996, Antropologia Medica: fondamenti per une strategia. AM Rivista della Società italiana di antropologia medica 1/2:7–22.

——, 2001, Medical Anthropology At Home: A Conceptual Framework and the Italian Experience. AM Rivista della Società italiana di antropologia medica 11/12:23–36.

SIGNORELLI A., 1986, Lo storico etnografo. La ricerca folklorica 13:5–14.

SIGNORINI I., 1996, Influenze cognitive sulla scelta terapeutica. Il caso dei Huave dell'istmo di Tehuantepec (Oaxaca, Messico). AM Rivista della Società italiana de antropologia medica 1/2:141–154.

TENTORI T., 1979, Note e memorie per una discussione sulla impostazione della antropologia culturale in Italia negli anni' 50. Problemi del socialismo 16:95–122.

TERRANOVA CECCHINI R. and P. INGHILLERI, 1990, Nuove frontiere della psicologia transculturale. Milano: Franco Angeli.

VICO G., 1986 [1725], Principes d'une science nouvelle relative à la nature commune des nations. Paris: Les Éditions Nagel.

ZANETTI Z., 1978 [1892], La medicina delle nostre donne, M. R. Trabalza and M. R. Città di Catello, eds. Milano: Edizioni Clio.

Chapter 8

GERMANY

Medical Anthropology(ies) in Germany
Angelika Wolf, Stefan Ecks, and Johannes Sommerfeld

Introduction

Germany can look back on some 150 years of knowledge elucidating the relationship between society, culture, health, healing, and medicine. As early as 1848, the physician Rudolf Virchow called medicine "a social science, and politics nothing else than medicine at large" (Virchow 1848:125).[1] Ever since, fields as diverse as social medicine (*Sozialmedizin*), medical sociology (*Medizinsoziologie*), and a philosophically inclined medical anthropology (*medizinische Anthropologie*) have become established in the German university system, mainly in faculties of medicine and those of social science. At a much slower pace, the more culturally comparative perspective of ethnomedicine (*Ethnomedizin*) has been taken up within the field of cultural anthropology (*Ethnologie, Kulturanthropologie,* or *Völkerkunde*), which is traditionally part of faculties of humanities or cultural studies. While there is a longstanding tradition of ethnomedical research in Germany, there is still no clear institutional or scientific equivalent to what in the Anglo-American context is called "medical anthropology" (Tuschinsky 1999). However, there are also many reasons to rejoice. For example, in 2003, the Association for Ethnomedicine (Arbeitsgemeinschaft für Ethnomedizin[2]) celebrated the 25th birthday of its flagship journal *Curare*. And a working group of the German Society for Cultural Anthropology (Deutsche Gesellschaft für Völkerkunde), the Arbeitsgemeinschaft Medical Anthropology,[3] was founded in 1997 to unite the scattered medical anthropologists within their professional organization. Moreover, medical anthropology is increasingly being taught at German universities.

Our overview of medical anthropologies in Germany attempts to illustrate the wide range of scientific activities at the interface of anthropology and medicine, representing academic as well as nonacademic, and disciplinary as well as cross-disciplinary scholarly traditions. Instead of focusing exclusively on German-speaking *Ethnomedizin* as a central component of medical anthropology, we will also present trends and schools of thought and scientific practice in other fields of (medical) knowledge. Two main criteria guide our description of these fields: in the historical section, we focus on knowledge that is in continuity with present approaches; in the sections on current trends and future developments, we discuss studies that are based on original ethnographic field research. As this review can only attempt to sketch the broad trends, it will not be able to do full justice to individual scholarly contributions. We have chosen to talk about the medical anthropolog*ies* of Germany in the plural to bring out the diversity of approaches to the study of the linkages between health, medicine, and culture.

Precursory Developments at the Interface of Anthropology and Medicine

Historical Background

Two prominent figures of the 19th century can be credited with laying the ground-work for medical anthropology in Germany: Adolf Bastian (1826–1905) and Rudolf Virchow (1821–1902). Bastian was one of the founding fathers of cultural anthropology. He had traveled widely as a ship's doctor and had conducted fieldwork in East Asia before holding the first position as professor in the newly emerging field of cultural anthropology. He was the founder of the Berlin Museum of Ethnology, which became the leading institution of its kind during that period. Bastian and Virchow founded the Berlin Society for Anthropology, Ethnology and Prehistory (Berliner Gesellschaft für Anthropologie, Ethnologie und Urgeschichte) in 1869 and co-edited the *Journal of Ethnology* (*Zeitschrift für Ethnologie*). One of Bastian's students at Berlin, Franz Boas (1858–1942), later left for the United States and became one of the pioneers of the emerging field of cultural anthropology. In his theoretical work, Bastian gave a first formulation to the principal ideas of cultural anthropology. He believed that the basic patterns of cultural ideas, practices, and traditions are shared by all humanity.

Although Bastian was both a medical doctor and a cultural anthropologist, he did not make health and healing a focus of his scholarly work, in contrast to his colleague Rudolf Virchow. During the second half of the 19th century, Virchow not only dominated German medical research, but also pioneered critical approaches in medical anthropology. He was appointed by the Prussian government to examine the causes of an epidemic of typhus in Upper Silesia. Much to the government's dismay, his report laid most of the blame for the typhus outbreak on poverty, hunger, lack of education, and political oppression. Virchow held that sociopolitical reforms were more effective measures against epidemics than medical interventions. Consequently, he became engaged in politics: he served on the Berlin City Council, focusing on the improvement of public health and the building of hospitals, and was later a member of the German parliament for many years. Given that Virchow was first and foremost a laboratory researcher and is regarded as the founder of cellular pathology, his vision of medicine as a *social* science is highly remarkable.

Virchow and his colleagues not only helped to found modern biomedicine but also social medicine and public health. When epidemic diseases were seen as a manifestation of social and cultural maladjustment, compulsory meat inspections and appropriate sewage disposal systems were put forward as examples that required political rather than medical action. In the 19th century, medical doctors saw the health of the people as a matter of direct social concern and initiated public provision of medical care for "paupers," prohibition of child labor, protection of pregnant women, and removal of toxic substances. Nowadays, as "health is disappearing from health policy" in the context of cost-effectiveness considerations, contemporary scholars are often reminiscent of what Virchow taught, namely "that the goal of medicine is not scientific understanding for its own sake but knowledge applied to the promotion of health through social means" (Eisenberg 1984:530).

One of Virchow's students, Georg Groddeck (1866–1934), made seminal contributions to psychosomatic medicine. Long before medical anthropologists distinguished disease from illness and sickness, Groddeck posited a difference between "disease" (*Krankheit*) and "falling ill" (*Erkrankung*). In his 1893 essay "*Krankheit*," he stated that "In reality there are no such things as diseases, there are only sick human beings" (Groddeck 1990:24).[4] This was a courageous statement in an era dominated by the idea of cells being the locus of disease. According to Groddeck's definition, health and ill-health are not opposite conditions, but are to be conceived as gradual differences in human life. For him, there were no monocausal explanations for why, if, and when someone got sick. His thoughts about the phenomena of a patient who does not *have a disease*, but *feels sick* (Groddeck 1990:31) comes close to the definition of sickness as "a process for socializing disease and illness" (Young 1982:270). This thinking brought Groddeck to develop the idea of *IT* (*ES*), defined as the unconscious mind that enables the interaction between the lived body (*Leib*) and mind/soul (*Seele*).[5]

Groddeck's ideas inspired clinicians and psychotherapists such as the neurologist Viktor von Weizsäcker (1886–1957), another influential proponent of psychosomatic medicine. In the psychosomatic model, mind and body are seen as mutually dependent entities. The concept of the organism as an integrated whole includes a view of the human individual as subject. In his critical and philosophical approach to clinical medicine, von Weizsäcker tried to broaden the reductionistic biomedical view, criticizing it for focusing on the human body (*Körper*) without considering the lived body (*Leib*).[6] Von Weizsäcker called for a link between medicine and philosophy based on three principles: an anthropological orientation, a more rigorous observation of methodological questions, and an interdisciplinary approach (Hahn 1991). This "philosophical nucleus" was characteristic of German medical anthropology of that time and seems to be a major point of divergence from the Anglo-Saxon tradition of medical anthropology (Schröder 1978:474).

Although medicine and cultural anthropology were intertwined through their main protagonists from the beginning, early cultural anthropologists tended to neglect medical aspects in their studies. As Ackerknecht perceptively points out, the medical background of many early anthropologists might have hindered an anthropological approach to healing rather than facilitating it:

> The recording of primitive medicine probably reached its lowest ebb towards the end of the 19th century, paradoxically enough just when the emerging scientific ethnography was to a very large extent in the hands of trained medical men . . . However

it is quite possible that it was precisely because of their professional preparation that these men were more prejudiced against the medical customs of primitives than against any other field of their activities (Ackerknecht 1971:114).

If they paid attention to medicine at all, they altogether overlooked rational healing measures and emphasized magical practices (Drobec 1955). In the 19th and well into the 20th century, the mainstream view of the time was that there was a clear demarcation line between "rational biomedicine" on the one hand, and folk medicine and the medicine of "primitive people" on the other (Lux 2003). If research was conducted by medical historians (Buschan 1942), it lacked possibilities for empirical comparisons.

The early rather diverse development of medical anthropological thinking, both in medicine and in ethnology, reflects academic divides in the German university system: contrary to the North American tradition, in Germany cultural anthropology, physical anthropology, archaeology, and linguistics are taught in separate departments. Moreover, German academics distinguish between *Volkskunde* and *Völkerkunde*. *Volkskunde* (folklore) as the science of one's "own" people is concerned with the study of local cultures within Germany and to some extent within Europe. *Völkerkunde* – or nowadays *Ethnologie* – is usually but not exclusively dedicated to research on non-European societies. However, the work of early scholars has led to great diversity in the German university system: although Groddeck's and Weizsäcker's work is very little known outside German-speaking countries, it contributed a great deal to the establishment of psychosomatic medicine as a discipline. Virchow's early ideas are still present in disease prevention measures and often guide political decision-making in health policy. As these scholars viewed medicine as a social as much as a biological science, they urged closer attention to the patient's perspective and reflection on social issues of disease.

The institutional context reflects German history, notably during the Nazi dictatorship. The Nazi regime's racist policies had an impact not only on the academic field per se, but also on the lives of many scientists who where forced to leave their posts and to flee the country. Other anthropologists at that time held themselves to "silence in the darkness" (Dostal 1994). Some even gave support to the ideologies of the "Nordic race"; physical anthropologists in particular were involved in Nazi politics. Their "scientific studies" related physical measures to mental and social behavior and thereby contributed a great deal to the formulation of racist theories. Because of the fascist period, German anthropology became cut off from international developments, and struggled to re-engage itself for several decades after the war.

Establishing the Field

German medical anthropology started growing and expanding its scope in the 1970s. Two major trends dominated the field in the early years: traditional ethnomedicine and health policy implications in primary health care. One of the founding figures of modern medical anthropology was Joachim Sterly (1926–2001), whose doctoral dissertation at the University of Cologne examined sacred healers in Melanesia. In 1969, he laid the groundwork for a research unit for medical anthropology at the University of Hamburg. In the following year, Sterly was one of the co-founders of the Working Society on Ethnomedicine (Arbeitsgemeinschaft Ethnomedizin), which was also based in Hamburg until its move to Heidelberg in 1975. In 1971, Sterly started to publish *Ethnomedicine: Journal for Interdisciplinary Research*, the first German journal devoted to transcultural approaches to healing. In 1976–77, the journal published a landmark article on the ideational history of German ethnomedicine (Hauschild 1976–77). Among his many other activities, Sterly helped to organize a number of international conferences (Sterly 1983). He brought a deeply philosophical sensitivity to the subject, and much of his work was steeped in the phenomenology of Edmund Husserl and Martin Heidegger (Sterly 1974). Taking the phenomenology of *Lebenswelt* ("life world") as the foundation of his work, Sterly stressed that healing cannot be studied in a positivistic manner. Whatever the subject of one's study, it had to be examined in relation to human *Dasein* ("being-there"). His *chef d'œuvre* is the three-volume ethnobotany on *Simbu Plant-Lore* (Sterly 1997). During his five years of fieldwork in the Highlands of Papua New Guinea, Sterly collected more than 1,900 botanical specimens and documented in detail the local lore around them.

In 1978, the German Association for Ethnomedicine (Arbeitsgemeinschaft für Ethnomedizin) started publishing *Curare*, a "Journal for Ethnomedicine and Transcultural Psychiatry." Partly in response to the national and international success of *Curare*, Sterly discontinued his journal *Ethnomedicine* in 1982.[7] *Curare* set out to provide "a regular communicative forum for people interested in problems associated with health for all by the year 2000" (Schuler 1998). Now in its 25th year, *Curare* has published close to four hundred original research articles, as well as book reviews, commentaries, and conference reports. The journal views itself as "a forum for exchange and discussion between all those who are interested in traditional medical systems, medical aid programs, health planning, and related issues" (Schuler 1998). While many of the published articles are in German, *Curare* has attracted many international medical anthropologists and published articles in English and French. Since 1994, the journal has been published twice a year, each with a focus topic.[8]

During the early 1980s, medical anthropology in Germany received a major boost through the publishing of a number of monographs and edited volumes (Hinderling 1981; Rudnitzki 1977). Academic centers emerged at the Universities of Cologne, Heidelberg, and Hamburg. In Cologne and Heidelberg, research and teaching in medical anthropology increased significantly. At the Department of Ethnology at Hamburg University, under the leadership of Beatrix Pfleiderer, medical anthropology became a major focus of teaching and research. A first edited volume (Ludwig and Pfleiderer-Becker 1981), followed by the first German-speaking textbook on medical anthropology (Pfleiderer and Bichmann 1985), now in its third edition (Greifeld 2003), were published. Numerous master's theses and at least 15 doctoral theses dealt with medical anthropological topics. A number of the doctoral theses were later published in a series entitled "Medical Cultures in Comparison" (*Medizinkulturen im Vergleich*),[9] now encompassing more than 20 issues. In 1988, Pfleiderer organized a major conference on West European and North American Perspectives, bringing together well-known North American and European medical anthropologists (Pfleiderer and Bibeau 1991).

Heidelberg University has, for a long time, been hosting activities in medical anthropology. The Department of Tropical Medicine and Public Health of the University's Medical School, under the leadership of Hans Jochen Diesfeld (Diesfeld 1974), started activities in this area in the early 1970s with the creation of a first medical anthropology position. The ethnomedical approach, still largely prevalent in Germany in the 1970s, was re-conceptualized and systematized as a *kulturvergleichende medizinische Anthropologie* ("medical anthropology in cross-cultural comparison"), situating medical anthropology at the interface of anthropology, philosophy, and medicine (Sich et al. 1993). Medical anthropology became an integral component of the department's teaching activities, aiming at sensitizing medical doctors and development workers to work in non-Western medical pluralistic settings. A number of medical dissertations and master's theses were produced in applied medical anthropology. Research carried out by staff and students of the department have dealt with a broad range of topics, ranging from concepts of illness and health in various settings to the social and cultural ramifications of health-care delivery. In the late 1990s in particular, the Department of Tropical Hygiene maintained a number of medical anthropological research projects related to international public health. It also hosted a university-wide work group "Medical Anthropology and Public Health," promoting the interaction of both fields through interdisciplinary research, teaching and scientific exchange (now organized by the Department of Anthropology). Studies carried out by the department covered risk research related to community-based insurance and to antenatal care, the anthropology of reproductive disease as well as medical anthropological research on cardiovascular disease prevention. Research on the anthropology of infectious diseases and their control focused on the behavioral, cultural and social factors as they relate to strategies dealing with transmission dynamics and the perception of and ability to cope with infectious diseases. A special focus was on the social and cultural aspects of newly emerging infectious disease and of infectious disease epidemics (Sommerfeld 1994). In addition, the cross-disciplinary collaboration of medical anthropology and epidemiology (Trostle and Sommerfeld 1996) constituted a major area of research. A series of lectures and seminars in medical anthropology and its application to public health were set up. The health social sciences in general, and medical anthropology in particular, are still regular components of the curriculum of the department's Master of Science Program, "Community Health and Health Management in Developing Countries." In 1997, an international symposium entitled "The Role of Medical Anthropology in Infectious Disease Control" brought together medical anthropologists and epidemiologists from a variety of countries (Sommerfeld 1998).

Current Trends

The following section will review academically based networks, research and teaching activities in medical anthropology in Germany, discussing trends starting in the late 1990s.

Professional Networks

Within the German Society for Cultural Anthropology (Deutsche Gesellschaft für Völkerkunde) a medical anthropology working group was founded in 1997. The group unites medical anthropologists from Germany, Austria, and Switzerland; moreover, members from neighboring disciplines such as medicine, psychology, or pharmacology form part of this section. Similar to other groups, such as the Society for Medical Anthropology (SMA) within the American Anthropological Association, the aim of the working group is to promote the field of medical anthropology and to encourage the establishment of medical anthropology in German universities. The group contributes to the biannual conferences of its society by organizing panels dedicated to specific points of interest in the field.[10] It defines itself as a forum for discussion, where its members are able to reflect on the methodological, theoretical and practical issues of medical anthropology independent of their institutional affiliation. A closely related group exists for anthropologists working on German and European cultures. Scholars who explore issues of medicine and culture within European ethnology, often employing a strongly historical perspective, have joined together in the network "Health and Culture within Folklore Studies" (Netzwerk Gesundheit und Kultur in der volkskundlichen Forschung).[11]

Teaching and Research

Currently, a number of universities in Germany regularly offer courses in medical anthropology as part of general or regional anthropological studies. Institutes at the universities of Heidelberg, Berlin, and Göttingen have been combining their teaching activities with recent research topics in medical anthropology.

As mentioned above, the University of Heidelberg has a strong tradition of medical anthropology: roughly twenty years ago, members of the Department of Tropical Hygiene and Public Health started to offer introductory courses and encouraged interdisciplinary research and applications in health sciences. Since the early 1990s, members of the Department of Anthropology in the South Asia Institute in Heidelberg have also been working on medical anthropology. With the arrival of its new chair, William Sax, the department has made medical anthropology its priority in research and teaching since 2000. Among other steps, a position exclusively dedicated to medical anthropology with a regional focus was created. The department now offers three to four courses each semester, combining theoretical and methodological issues in medical anthropology with an ethnographic interest in the cultures of South Asia. The department also runs the cross-disciplinary Heidelberg Medical Anthropology Working Group, providing a forum for students, staff, and researchers to present current or planned projects on issues in the field. The group aims to promote the subject in dialogue with public health, history of medicine, medical sociology, and other related disciplines.[12] The Medical Anthropology Working Group cooperates closely with the German Society for Cultural Anthropology.

The Institute for Social and Cultural Anthropology at the Freie University of Berlin usually provides one course in medical anthropology per year for advanced students in social anthropology.[13] The regions where medical anthropology research is conducted are Orissa/India, under the direction of Georg Pfeffer, and Eastern and Southern Africa, led by Ute Luig. A group conducting research on AIDS in Africa is examining the overall consequences of the epidemic, which in addition to being a health problem, is creating social, economic, and political problems. The rising number of infected people in sub-Saharan Africa points to an obvious gap between knowledge and behavior and raises doubts about the efficiency of AIDS campaigns. The research projects consequently concentrate on ". . . conceptions of sexuality, gender and childhood, kinship and solidarity, moral and religious values and norms, cultural ideas of illness and healing, as well as conceptions of risk, death and life in general . . ." (Dilger 2001a).

In the Department of European Ethnology at the Humboldt University in Berlin, the impact of the life sciences on everyday concepts of body and health has recently become a focus of research and teaching. Holding one of German anthropology's first "Junior Professorships," Stefan Beck conducts research on how popular views of health and relatedness are being transformed by human genome technologies (Beck 2004). Another research project looks at the role of medical technologies in Germany, with a special focus on abortion (Knecht 1996). The department is very active in establishing medical anthropology in relation to science and technology studies (STS) in Germany. In 2003, the first of a series of international conferences on emergent anthropological research on the life sciences was held near Berlin.

Göttingen University also has a long tradition in teaching medical anthropology.[14] A research project in emerging medical technologies, particularly in reproductive medicine and organ transplantation, was led by Brigitta Hauser-Schäublin and funded by the German Research Foundation (DFG). The project examined not only the way in which professionals – medical personal, patients, and their relatives – deal with new technologies, but also how these technologies influence social relationships. The research is embedded in reflections on the meaning of the individual person, identity, and society (Hauser-Schäublin et al. 2001).

Other institutes for cultural anthropology at the Universities of Halle, Leipzig, Munich, and Münster offer courses in or lectures on medical anthropology on a more or less regular basis, though they currently have no ongoing research projects in the field. In a guide to anthropology in German-speaking countries (Krickau et al. 1999), these institutes mentioned no particular focus in medical anthropology. Given that there are approximately 25 institutes for cultural and social anthropology in Germany and a great number of students interested in medical anthropology, it is indeed remarkable that medical anthropology has not yet reached any considerable degree of institutionalization. To date, there are still no specialized departments, research centers, or formal degree programs for medical anthropology.

During the 1990s, German medical anthropologists made significant inroads into applied work. Typically, this work is not labeled "medical anthropology," but rather "intercultural health care studies" or "intercultural competence for health-care providers." Two developments may be highlighted here. In 1998, the medical anthropologist Monika Habermann became Professor of Nursing Sciences (*Pflegewissenschaften*) at the Hochschule Bremen. The Bremen program combines teaching of the cultural aspects of health with an education in nursing management, and aims to train students for executive positions in hospitals, retirement homes, and facilities for the disabled. In Freiburg, AMIKO (Arbeitsgruppe Medizinethnologie und Interkulturelle Kommunikation) established a teaching program for health-care professions. They offer courses to nurses, midwives, and social workers on issues of migrants' health and cultural aspects of healing (Adam and Stülb 2001).

Affiliated Research Projects in Medical Anthropology

A great deal of research in the field of medical anthropology is undertaken by graduate students, with wide-ranging regional and thematic topics. Most of these studies have an actor-centered approach, but narrative-, historiographic-, and structure-centered descriptions are also used. Much research is done outside of Europe, but an increasing number of studies are being carried out in Europe and Germany. These studies have focused on, for example, organ donation, globalizing practices around birth, and the introduction of Ayurveda and acupuncture into German biomedical practice. Research on new medical technologies has opened up new horizons for medical anthropology. For instance, the aim of a recent study was to examine how people experience and live with organ transplants (Kalitzkus 2003). Medical technology not only gives new meaning to death, it also generates the paradox of a (biologically) living corpse, and hence transgresses the boundaries of the embodied self. Other research related to organ donation is carried out on topics such as the commodification of body parts or how concepts of the immune system create the "modern body" and how this body is presented through the media and perceived in public (Obrecht 2000). Likewise, colleagues in Austria working in close cooperation with German anthropologists are investigating techniques of reproductive medicine.

Increasing attention is being paid to perceptions of birth within our own culture. During the last 20 years, more and more pregnant women in Germany have embraced birth practices from far-away cultures as being preferable to their own habits (Kneuper 2003). Very often they proclaim birth to be a "natural" event; this is then compared with practices in other ethnic groups that are portrayed as being more in contact with nature than are people in industrialized countries. Other research focuses on migrant women and their habits surrounding birth

(Delius 2003). When migrant women are separated from their extended family, they sometimes miss guidance or advice by their mothers or other elderly women. This lack of support sometimes leads to postpartum mood disturbances or even perinatal depression. Postpartum studies consequently consider questions that are relevant to medical anthropology.

Biomedical practitioners' motivation to use homeopathy or the introduction of Ayurveda and acupuncture into biomedical practice are other interesting fields to investigate within our own culture (Frank 2002; Frank and Stollberg 2002). Likewise, Asian concepts of medicine are rapidly spreading all over the world. However, these concepts do not remain unchanged once they are introduced at the local level; doctors hybridize them with biomedical modes of treatment and explanations. By adopting a comparative perspective, it is possible to describe the specific nature of pluralistic health care in Germany as well as in India and to observe how modes of explanations for differing concepts influence each other in local settings.

Using a global perspective to investigate medical issues – and thereby contribute to the debate about globalization and medicine – is characteristic of recent studies in the classical regions of anthropology. How *medicoscapes* as a dimension of global landscapes are interrelated at local as well as at global levels as shown in a recent book that covers issues of globalization in the medical sectors of Africa, Asia, (South) America, and Europe (Wolf and Hörbst 2003). In reference to Appadurai's concept of global cultural flows (Appadurai 1990:6), the authors define *medicoscapes* as:

> globally scattered landscapes of people and organizations in the wider medical sector, which thicken in given localities but at the same time connect places, human beings, and institutions in the medical sector. These landscapes are formed by internationally therapy-offering as well as therapy-searching people, by the world-wide pharmaceutical industry, by the WHO as the global guardian of biomedicine, by organizations of so called traditional healers, by regionally disseminated healing-practices and their perception from distant places, by world-wide known therapies, and by organizations in international aid and development with a medical focus. They are part of heterogeneous medical flows that transgress cultural and national borders, and trigger change at local levels, which then may have global repercussions. (Hörbst and Wolf 2003:4)

Various global medical phenomena are investigated in fields such as HIV/AIDS in Africa, gender and health, or issues of modernization. In some countries of southern Africa, nearly one-third of the sexually active population is infected with HIV, despite the widespread knowledge about the causes and effects of HIV/AIDS. A possible reason for the lack of success might be inappropriate messages in prevention programs (Offe 2001). Such programs are grounded in notions of time and future that stem from European concepts of the Enlightenment and the independent role of the individual that are not necessarily attuned to local ideals. On the other hand, the "lures of modernity" render new concepts of gender and sexuality, and hence have a strong impact on the practices of young people (Dilger 2003).

However, a globalized concept such as "Living PositHIVely," which is applied worldwide in AIDS programs by and for the infected, shows that the conditions and values which give meaning to such a model may differ according to its context (Dilger 2001b). Nonbiomedical healing institutions carry out cleansing rituals and bring communities together, yet their importance is very often overlooked (Rakelmann 2001). The mediating position of indigenous healers is also underestimated. In many African countries, HIV/AIDS is often interpreted in reference to indigenous concepts of sexually transmitted diseases (Wolf 2001). As a historiographic study in Tanzania shows (Bruchhausen and Roelcke 2002), the role of healers in Africa was strongly shaped by colonialism. The authors demonstrate how the introduction of biomedicine created niches for traditional healers, for example, herbalism that served the desire for "natural healing," and "spirit possession" and "witchcraft detection" that addressed the relationship needs of human beings. Thus, biomedicine already had global effects during the time of colonialism (Hörbst and Wolf 2003).

Processes of globalization and modernization also constitute recent anthropological perspectives on popular and professional concepts of the body. A study conducted in Kolkata (West Bengal, India) addresses these issues, with special reference to ideas about the belly and digestive system (Ecks 2003, 2004). By altering the routines and practices of daily life, changes brought about by urban modernity are often associated with a decline in mental and physical well-being. Research focused on how people in Kolkata perceive their bodies, how these perceptions are negotiated in three different medical settings (biomedicine, homeopathy, Ayurveda), and how this discourse reflects anxieties about the consequences of modernity.

Another study carried out in western Mexico shows how responsibility for causing illness is ascribed to places outside the human body (Hörbst 2002). These places, situated in the local landscape, are called upon for treatment and prevention on an individual, family-based and social level, and as the author argues, places thus may form agents of healing. Healing traditions in northern Ecuador are under constant interchange with other practices of curing from inside as well as outside of the country (Wörrle 2002). Thus, patients in modern Ecuador can still choose from among a variety of treatment possibilities and do so actively. In a similar vein, for people migrating from the Caribbean to New York, religion provides a resort for healing, although cults take on new meaning in the context of migration (Schmidt 2003).

As classical topics still may provide new insights, research on indigenous concepts of disease, patient behaviors, and the question of what determines a patient's choice of healers are also prominent themes in German medical anthropology. A study from the Amazon region of Ecuador calls into question the long used distinction between "traditional" and "modern" medical practice (Knipper 2004). It takes the indigenous disease category "*mal aire*" as the starting point to investigate intercultural communication within the medical praxis. The behavior of patients and what determines their choice of healers is the focus of a study in the Urumbu valley of Peru (Montag 2001). A study from Orissa in India analyzes how central concepts of society are reflected in how people deal with distress (Otten 2003). Not only healers but also sickness is distinguished by social status, and healers among the Rona in Orissa are only allowed to perform healing rituals for illnesses that meet their status (Otten 2004).

Research on children and the role they play in the process of negotiating about and giving meaning to illness is still rare. A study about a Yupno child in Papua New Guinea shows how this society charts the onset and course of sickness in relation to imbalances in bodily humors caused by disturbed social relations (Keck 2003). An international multidisciplinary group of scientists conducted a Concerted Action Research Project in several European countries and in one location in the United States which looked at healthy seven-year-old children's perceptions of illness and medicine (Wirsing 1996a). They asked children to draw a picture of their last illness episode and to talk about their corresponding experiences (Wirsing 1996b). The German team also took part in a follow-up project involving children with asthma and their parents which examined their illness perception and coping strategies.[15]

An important point can be observed about current research and teaching: in seminars at universities in Germany, it has become common to read articles and books of medical anthropology written in English. Nonetheless, most German medical anthropologists still publish in German. Thus, whereas the "input" is in an international idiom, the "output" remains "local." As a consequence of this language gap, developments in the field and the results of research often remain unnoticed abroad in the international scientific community.

Future Trends

The aim of this section is to provide an overview of medical anthropology projects that are currently underway or about to begin in 2004. In order to go beyond published results, material for this part of our article is largely based on interviews and personal encounters with researchers. Needless to say, the sample chosen here only provides a glimpse of the variety of ongoing projects, and foretelling the future is always a rather risky business.

Medical Anthropology Within Cultural Anthropology

Medical anthropology is likely to grow in importance in the research and teaching of several departments and institutes across Germany. Building on current trends both in Germany and internationally, it is also likely that there will be increased research on the use of new medical technologies, and their influence on popular perceptions of body and society. Another field of research is the social consequences of HIV/AIDS, especially in Africa.

Given that there are still no professorships dedicated exclusively to medical anthropology, the field will most likely expand through research arising from the established theoretical and/or regional interest of institutes of anthropology, for example in Heidelberg or in Berlin. In addition to these institutes which already have a focus on medical anthropology, it is likely that more "traditional" themes in anthropology, such as religion and ritual, will be increasingly reconsidered in terms of their healing potentials as well.

In Heidelberg, the Ritualdynamik (Dynamics of Ritual) project was inaugurated in 2002 and is set to run for up to ten years. The aim of this project is to study the sociocultural contexts in which rituals emerge, transform, and vanish. A number of anthropological field studies are linked to Ritualdynamik (Merz 2002; Sax 2002; Schömbucher-Küsterer 2004). All these studies combine their interests in health and healing with a strong focus on religion, ritual, and performance theory. A range of other projects is also linked to Ritualdynamik, such as a study that sets out to describe how Sufi shrines of the Moroccan Isawiyya brotherhood provide a space for healing both physical and psychological ills. Researchers from the Department of Clinical Psychology, who adopt an ethnoclinical approach to the role of ritualization among adolescent drug users in Germany, are also participating in this interdisciplinary study of ritual dynamics. There are two projects currently in progress at the Freie University of Berlin that are dedicated to this theme. The first describes the Bali Yatra "earth pilgrimage" in the Indian state of Orissa. The Bali Yatra is a ritual performed largely by women every three years in order to secure the prosperity and fertility of humans, animals, and plants. Another research project in Berlin looks at how the biomedically trained staff of a psychiatric clinic in Ghana combines drug treatment with Christian faith healing.

Apart from the study of ritual healing, much of the ongoing work is centered on specific diseases and cultural responses to them. A team of Berlin anthropologists examines how people in different African settings deal with the impact of AIDS on the community. Going beyond an earlier emphasis on social perceptions of the spread of AIDS infections, they look at AIDS in a wider cultural context. One study tries to capture different notions of being "male" among three groups in Cape Town, South Africa. Two other projects will focus on survival options and strategies of widows in Zambia and orphans in Malawi who live in child-headed households. Rather than seeing AIDS as an isolated disease, the members of the Berlin team see it as a problem with strong repercussions on notions of gender, the family, political change, and globalization. Such an approach to AIDS entails a dialogue with researchers from other fields, notably with sociologists and epidemiologists and public health specialists. Another Heidelberg-based project is currently being planned that will study how AIDS is being conceptualized and treated by healers of the informal health sector in urban South Asia. Among current projects that focus on particular disease entities, a study of neurological disorders in the Mariana Islands (Western Pacific) occupies a unique position. The initial aim was to find out if there might be specific cultural risk factors that contribute to these disorders. In the course of the work, however, the anthropologist started to turn a critical gaze on the impact that the intense biomedical investigations were having on the local community. The dynamics of traditional medicine in the context of globalization are the topic of a study conducted on the professionalization of Tibetan medicine in the Spiti Valley of the Indian Himalayas.

Medical Anthropology Outside of Anthropology Departments

All of the projects mentioned thus far are conducted in settings outside of Germany, especially in South Asia and sub-Saharan Africa. However, there is a great deal of research being conducted outside of these cultural anthropology departments. Whenever this is the case, the projects tend to have an applied perspective, and are likely to be part of interdisciplinary teams. A good example of this trend is the pilot project ProBenefit that aims to develop a bilateral legal framework for the uses of medicinal plants in the Amazon area of Ecuador. Based on the United Nations' Convention for Biodiversity (CBD) of 1992, the venture is funded by the German Ministry for Education and Science (BMBF) and brings together a team of biologists, biochemists, lawyers, sociologists, and anthropologists in both Ecuador and in Germany. Anthropological involvement in such a project is one example of the growing demand among German policy-makers for the expertise of medical anthropologists. Another example of ongoing applied medical anthropology, which incidentally is also set in Ecuador, is a study of medical pluralism and intercultural cooperation in primary health care. The study builds on several years of clinical practice in a health station in Amazonian Ecuador. In terms of institutional affiliation, the researchers are based in the medical school of the University of Gießen, instead of an anthropology department.

Although most German medical anthropologists will continue to do work in other countries, there is a growing trend towards doing research in German settings. Due to longstanding academic traditions, German medical cultures have so far been studied mostly by sociologists, folklorists, and historians of medicine. The fact that medical anthropologists are making inroads into this field is mostly due to a blurring of disciplinary boundaries. To identify oneself as a "medical anthropologist" is to identify oneself with a set of theoretical interests and ethnographic methods of fieldwork.

Studies of doctor–patient relationships in biomedical settings are being carried out in different regions. In cooperation with a group of biomedical physicians and psychologists, one Göttingen-based anthropologist has started documenting and analyzing interactions between GPs and chronically ill patients. There is a plan to videotape all consultations that take place in one week in each of the offices of the sixteen participating GPs, as well to conduct in-depth interviews with selected patients. From this material, one salient case will be selected and presented to the other participating GPs each week. The practical goal of this applied research is to work out a framework with the health-care professionals for understanding the dynamics of interaction, and thus to improve medical care for the chronically ill.

A Bonn-based researcher is planning to study doctor–patient interactions from the point of view of medical ethics. The field site will be a doctor's chamber in a rural area in Western Germany. Based on previous explorations, the project examines to what extent the patients' explanatory models of illness are informed by folk-medical and humoral ideas. The research is particularly interested in how doctors and patients might have a different concept of bodily integrity and disability, and what ethical implications these differences might have for treatment.

Bodily integrity is also the theme of an exploration of voluntary cesarean sections at the University Clinic in Munich. This project is carried out by a physician and a medical anthropologist, with a grant provided by the University of Munich for interdisciplinary gender studies. While there are a growing number of medical publications discussing the rise of voluntary cesarean sections, women's motivations are still largely unknown. How gender concepts are transformed in biomedical consultations is a question for medical anthropologists in the future. Two projects that look specifically at the impact of high-tech diagnostic techniques are in progress. A study has just been completed on how patients in a Berlin clinic experience breast cancer, with a particular interest in changes of perception that occur through the diagnostic and therapeutic process. The long-term goal of this work is to develop an understanding of how "life" and "risk" are being defined and redefined in exchanges between physicians and patients. Another medical anthropologist is undertaking fieldwork in Ghana and Tanzania on ultrasound screenings. The study aims to show how ultrasound technology translates pregnant bodies into images, and how these images change the women's perceptions of both their own bodies and the bodies of the fetuses. This is one of the first studies that looks at patients' experiences of high-tech medicine in non-Western countries. Given that cultural studies of medical technologies are on top of the international research agenda, it is likely that projects of this kind will take a firmer hold in German medical anthropology in the future.

In anthropology departments across the country (even those which do not explicitly focus on medical anthropology), there are a large number of M.A. theses that look at medical anthropology topics in Germany. Most of these theses are based on original fieldwork of up to six months. However, it remains a more or less explicit rule that Ph.D. or post-doc research should be carried out outside of Germany to qualify as "truly anthropological." It remains to be seen if the preference for non-German settings will continue to be a characteristic feature of German medical anthropology in the future. Given the quality of studies carried out in Germany, a broadening of perspectives would be most welcome.

Conclusion

Many diverse trends shape the field of medical anthropology in Germany, bringing us to speak in the plural of medical anthropolog*ies*. We have traced some historic roots and presented recent trends and schools of thought and scientific practice. Partly due to the rather low level of institutionalization of the subject in German universities, much of the research is at least as oriented toward an audience of general cultural anthropologists as toward a specific audience of medical anthropologists. Nevertheless, there is an increasing tendency in these studies to refer to the theoretical and methodological trends of Anglo-American medical anthropology. As in international circles, medical anthropology in Germany is losing its reputation as a niche specialty and is becoming an important point of reference even in discussions in mainstream cultural anthropology. Despite its lack of continuity at universities, there is an extraordinary involvement of scholars in work-groups, professional associations, and societies.

Academic institutionalization is crucial for the future of German medical anthropology. The German system of higher education is currently undergoing tremendous changes and new opportunities for the further development of medical anthropology in Germany may emerge. In our view, German-speaking medical anthropology is set to grow significantly over the next decade. By calling medicine "a social science, and politics nothing else than medicine at large," Rudolf Virchow (1848) set a research agenda for medical anthropology, both in Germany and world-wide, that is as significant and challenging for the future as it was in the past.

Acknowledgments

The authors would like to thank Hansjörg Dilger, Karina Kielmann, and Rolf Wirsing for their detailed comments on an early draft of this article, as well as Thomas Hauschild for his insights on the past and present of the field. As always, mistakes or omissions are the sole responsibility of the authors.

Notes

1. "Die Medicin ist eine sociale Wissenschaft, und die Politik ist weiter nichts, als Medicin im Grossen"
2. http://www.agem-ethnomedizin.de, accessed April 20, 2004.
3. http://www.medicalanthropology.de, accessed April 20, 2004.
4. In Wirklichkeit gibt es gar *keine Krankheiten*, es gibt nur *kranke Menschen*.
5. This *IT* was later adopted by Freud and transformed to *id*.
6. For a critique of this model see Ots (1991).
7. The journal had seven volumes with a total of 145 scientific articles on a wide range of ethnomedical and related topics, both in German and English.
8. A detailed directory for 20 years of *Curare* (1978–97), indexed by content, authors, and keywords, was published in 1998 (Volume 21, Issue 1), both in German and English. The *Curare* Special Topics series includes issues on birth from a cross-cultural perspective (1/1983), a Festschrift for George Devereux (2/1984), ethnobotany (3/1985), death and dying (4/1985), traditional healers (5/1986), pain (6/1989), West European and North American anthropologies of medicine (7/1991), birth (8/1995), transcultural care (10/1997), women and health (11/1997), the medical anthropologies of Brazil (12/1997), shamanship (13/1998), and ethnotherapies (14/1998).
9. http://www.lit-verlag.de/reihe/MIV, accessed April 20, 2004.
10. Panel topics included "Medicine and Globalization," "Reflections on the Relationship between Religion and Medicine," "Contributions of Medical Anthropology to other

Fields of Social and Cultural Anthropology," "Transgressing Borders between Anthropology and Medicine," "Professional Perspectives of Medical Anthropology in Germany," and recently, "Methods and Methodologies in Medical Anthropology" (www.medicalanthropology.de, accessed April 20, 2004).

11. The groups' yearly meetings focus on topics about the relationship between the human body and society that are published in a series (Alsheimer 2000, 2001).
12. www.sai.uni-heidelberg.de/abt/ETHNO/index.htm, accessed April 20, 2004.
13. Courses cover topics as diverse as "Theories of medical anthropology," "Ethnography of AIDS in Africa," "Indian medical systems," "Gender and Health," and "Religion and medicine."
14. Courses offered covered topics such as "death and dying," "perceptions of the body," "AIDS," and "bio-politics."
15. http://www.hs-zigr.de/+wirsing/chronic.html, http://www.hs-zigr.de/+wirsing/asthmKid.html, accessed April 20, 2004.

References

ACKERKNECHT E., 1971, Medicine and Ethnology: Selected Essays. Baltimore: The Johns Hopkins Press.

ADAM Y. and M. STÜLB, 2001, Zwischen Multikulturalismus und Individualität, Culture shopping von Hebammenschülerinnen und Migrantinnen in einem medizinethnologischen Unterrichtsprojekt. Körperlichkeit und Kultur. In Dokumentation des 4. Arbeitstreffens des Netzwerk Gesundheit und Kultur in der volkskundlichen Forschung. R. Alsheimer, ed. Pp. 11–25. Bremen: Universität Bremen.

ALSHEIMER, R., ed., 2000, Körperlichkeit und Kultur. Dokumentation des 3. Arbeitstreffens des Netzwerk Gesundheit und Kultur in der volkskundlichen Forschung. Bremen: Universität Bremen.

——, 2001, Körperlichkeit und Kultur. Dokumentation des 4. Arbeitstreffens des Netzwerk Gesundheit und Kultur in der volkskundlichen Forschung. Bremen: Universität Bremen.

APPADURAI A., 1990, Disjuncture and Difference in the Global Cultural Economy. Public Culture 2(2):1–24.

BECK S., 2004, Reflexible Körper. In Anmerkungen zur Transformation von Gesundheitsverständnissen und Verwandtschaftsverhältnissen durch humangenetisches. R. W. Wissen and U. A. Brednich, eds. Münster: Natur–Kultur.

BRUCHHAUSEN W. and V. ROELCKE, 2002, Categorising African Medicine. In The German Discourse on East African Healing Practices, 1885–1918. W. Ernst, ed. Pp. 76–94. Plural Medicine. London: Routledge.

BUSCHAN G., 1942, Über Medizin, Zauber und Heilkunst im Leben der Völker. Leipzig.

DELIUS M., 2003, Befindlichkeit im Wochenbett – globaler Körper und sozialer Kontext. In Medizin und Globalisierung: universelle Ansprüche – lokale Antworten. A. Wolf and V. Hörbst, eds. Pp. 129–151. Münster: Lit-Verlag.

DIESFELD H. J., 1974, The Prospect of Utilization of Existing Traditional Health Care Systems as a Complement to the Delivery of Modern Primary Health Care. In Community Health and Health Motivation in South East Asia. Proceedings of an international seminar organized by the German Foundation for International Development and the Institute of Tropical Hygiene and Public Health, South Asia Institute, University of Heidelberg. Wiesbaden, Steiner. Pp. 81–89.

DILGER H., 2001a, AIDS in Africa: Broadening the Perspectives on Research and Policy-Making. Afrika Spectrum 36(1):5–16.

——, 2001b, Living positHIVely in Tanzania: The Global Dynamics of AIDS and the Meaning of Religion for International and Local AIDS Work. Africa Spectrum 36(1):73–90.

——, 2003, Sexuality, AIDS, and the Lures of Modernity: Reflexivity and Morality among Young People in Rural Tanzania. Medical Anthropology 22(1):23–52.

DOSTAL W., 1994, Silence in the Darkness: German Ethnology during the National Socialist Period. Social Anthropology 2(3):251–262.

DROBEC E., 1955, Zur Geschichte der Ethnomedizin. Anthropos 50:950–957.

ECKS S., 2003, Digesting Modernity: Body, Illness and Medicine in Kolkata (Calcutta). Ph.D. thesis, Department of Anthropology, London School of Economics, University of London.

——, 2004, Bodily Sovereignty as Political Sovereignty: "Self Care" in Kolkata (India). Anthropology and Medicine 11(1):75–89.

EISENBERG L., 1984, Rudolf Ludwig Karl Virchow, Where are You Now That We Need You? American Journal of Medicine 77(3):524–532.

FRANK R. 2002, Integrating Homeopathy and Biomedicine. Medical Practice and Knowledge Production among German Homeopathic Physicians. Sociology of Health & Illness 24:796–819.

FRANK R. and G. STOLLBERG, 2002, Ayurveda Patients in Germany. Anthropology and Medicine 9(3):223–244.

GREIFELD K., ed., 2003, Ritual und Heilung. Eine Einführung in die Medizinethnologie. Berlin: Reimer Verlag.

GRODDECK G., 1990, Krankheit als Symbol. Schriften zur Psychosomatik. Frankfurt: Fischer [org. 1893, re-published and commented by H. Siefert in 1966, Wiesbaden: Limes].

HAHN P., 1991, The Medical Anthropology of Viktor von Weizsäcker in the Present Clinical Context in Heidelberg. In Anthropologies of Medicine. A Colloquium on West European and North American Perspectives. B. Pfleiderer and G. Bibeau, eds. Pp. 23–35. Braunschweig, Vieweg.

HAUSCHILD T., 1976/77, Zur Ideengeschichte der Ethnomedizin. Ethnomedizin 4:357–368.

HAUSER-SCHÄUBLIN B., V. KALITZKUS, I. PETERSEN and I. SCHRÖDER, 2001, Der geteilte Leib. Die kulturelle Dimension von Organtransplantation und Reproduktionsmedizin in Deutschland. Frankfurt: Campus.

HINDERLING P., 1981, Kranksein in primitiven und traditionalen Kulturen. Norderstedt: Verlag für Ethnologie.

HÖRBST V., 2002, Heilungslandschaften. Umgangsweisen mit Erkrankung und Heilung bei den Cora in Jesus Maria, Mexiko. Unpublished dissertation, University of Freiburg.

HÖRBST V. and A. WOLF, 2003, Globalisierung der Heilkunde. Eine Einführung. In Medizin und Globalisierung: universelle Ansprüche – lokale Antworten. A. Wolf and V. Hörbst, eds. Pp. 3–30. Münster: Lit-Verlag.

KALITZKUS V., 2003, Leben durch den Tod. Die zwei Seiten der Organtransplantation. Eine medizinethnologische Studie. Frankfurt: Campus.

KECK V., 2003, Social Discord and Bodily Disorders: Healing among the Yupno of Papua New Guinea. Durham: Carolina Academic Press.

KNECHT M., 1996, Ethnologische Forschung in öffentlich umstrittenen Bereichen: Das Beispiel Abtreibungsdebatte und Lebensschutzbewegung in Deutschland. *In* Ethnologie Europas. Grenzen, Konflikte, Identitäten. W. Kokot and D. Dracklé, eds. Pp. 225–240. Berlin.

KNEUPER E., 2003, Die natürliche Geburt – eine globale Errungenschaft? *In* Medizin und Globalisierung: universelle Ansprüche – lokale Antworten. A. Wolf and V. Hörbst, eds. Pp. 107–109. Münster and London, Lit-Verlag

KNIPPER M., 2004, Mal Aire und die medizinische Praxis der Naporuna. Eine medizinisch-ethnologische Feldstudie im Amazonastiefland von Equador. Münster: Lit-Verlag.

KRICKAU O. and ARBEITSKREIS FÜR INTERNATIONALE WISSENSCHAFTSKOMMUNIKATION, eds, 1999, Studienführer. Guide to German-speaking Anthropology. Göttingen: Association for Scientific Communication (Ethnologie im deutschsprachigen Raum Band 2).

LUDWIG B. and B. PFLEIDERER-BECKER, 1981, Materialien zur Ethnomedizin. Bensheim: Kèbel-Stiftung.

LUX T., 2003, Krankheit und ihre kulturellen Dimensionen: Ein ideengeschichtlicher Abriss. *In* T. Lux, ed. Kulturelle Dimensionen der Medizin. Pp. 145–176. Berlin: Reimer.

MERZ B., 2002, Bhakti and Shakti: Göttliche und menschliche Agency im Kontext des Heilkults der Göttin Horati in Nepal. Ph. D. thesis, Department of Anthropology, University of Heidelberg.

MONTAG D., 2001, Gesundheit und Krankheit im Urumbu-Tal/ Peru. Münster: Lit.

OBRECHT S., 2000, Grenzgänge. Das immunologische Selbst und die ersten Herztransplantationen Ende der 1960er Jahre. *In* Körperlichkeit und Kultur. Dokumentation des 3. Arbeitstreffens des Netzwerk Gesundheit und Kultur in der volkskundlichen Forschung. R. Alsheimer, ed. Pp. 57–75. Bremen: Universität Bremen.

OFFE J., 2001, Smart Guys Plan for the Future! Cultural Concepts of Time and the Prevention of AIDS in Africa. Afrika Spectrum 36(1):53–72.

OTTEN T., 2003, People of the Hills: How Rona deal with Social Change. *In* People of the Jangal: Reformulating Identities and Adaptations in Crisis. M. Carri. Tambs-Lyche, eds. Kopenhagen: Curzon Press, in press.

——, 2004, Healing Through Rituals: Concepts of Illness among the Rona of Highland Orissa. Ph.D. thesis.

OTS T., 1991, Phenomenology of the Body: The Subject-Object Problem in Psychosomatic Medicine and the Role of Traditional Medical Systems herein. *In* Anthropologies of Medicine. A Colloquium on West European and North American Perspectives. B. Pfleider and G. Bibeau, eds. Pp. 43–58. Braunschweig: Vieweg.

PFLEIDERER B. and G. BIBEAU, eds, 1991, Anthropologies of Medicine: A Colloquium on West European and North American Perspectives. Braunschweig: Vieweg.

PFLEIDERER B. and BICHMANN W., 1985, Krankheit und Kultur. Berlin: Reimer.

RAKELMANN G., 2001, We Sat there Half the Day Asking Questions, but They Were Unable to Tell where AIDS Comes from . . . Local Interpretations of AIDS in Botswana. Afrika Spectrum 36(1):35–52.

RUDNITZKI G., ed., 1977, Ethnomedizin: Beiträge zu einem Dialog zwischen Heilkunst und Völkerkunde. Barmstedt: Kurth.

SAX W., 2002, Dancing the Self – Personhood and Performance in the Pandav Lila of Garhwal. New York: Oxford University Press.

SCHMIDT B., 2003, El significado de la religión de la santería para migrantes del Caribe en Nueva York. *In* Emigración Latinoamericana: Comperación Interregional entre América del Norte, Europa y Japon (JCAS Symposium Series, 19). Y. Matsuo, ed. Pp. 95–112. Osaka: Japan Center for Area Studies.

SCHÖMBUCHER-KÜSTERER E., 2004, Wo Götter durch Menschen sprechen. Besessenheit in Indien. Habilitationsschrift, Department of Anthropology, South Asia Institute, University of Heidelberg.

SCHRÖDER E., 1978, Ethnomedicine and Medical Anthropology. Reviews in Anthropology 5(4):473–485.

SCHULER J., 1998, Editorial. Curare 21(1):4.

SICH P., H. J. DIESFELD, A. DEIGNER and M. HABERMANN, eds, 1993, Medizin und Kultur. Frankfurt/Main: Peter Lang.

SOMMERFELD J., 1994, Emerging Epidemic Diseases: Anthropological Perspectives. Annals of the New York Academy of Sciences 740:276–284.

——, 1998, Medical Anthropology and Infectious Disease Control. Tropical Medicine and International Health 3:993–995.

STERLY J., 1974, Zur Wissenschaftstheorie der Ethnomedizin. Anthropos 69:608–615.

——, ed., 1983, Ethnomedizin und Medizingeschichte. Symposium 2–4 May, 1980 Berlin.

——, 1997, Simbu Plant-lore: Plants Used by the People in the Central Highlands of New Guinea. Berlin: Reimer.

TROSTLE J. and J. SOMMERFELD, 1996, Medical Anthropology and Epidemiology. Annual Review of Anthropology 25:253–274.

TUSCHINKSY C., 1999, Vom ewigen Anfang: Die Medizinethnologie in Deutschland. *In* W. Kokot and D. Dracklé, eds. Festschrift für Hans Fischer. Pp. 291–313. Berlin: Reimer.

VIRCHOW R., 1848, Der Armenarzt [The Poverty Physician]. Die medicinische Reform 18(3 November 1848):125–127.

YOUNG A., 1982, The Anthropologies of Illness and Sickness. Annual Review of Anthropology 11:257–285.

WIRSING R., 1996a, The Use of Conventional and Unconventional Medicine in the Treatment of Children's Diseases. The Role of Parents. *In* Children, Medicines and Cultures. P. Bush, ed. Pp. 229–254. Binghampton, NY: Haworth Press.

——, 1996b, Perceptions of German Children and Their Parents on Health, Illness and Medicine Use. *In* Childhood and Medicine Use in Cross-cultural Perspective. D. Trakas and E. Sanz, eds. Pp. 123–147. Luxembourg: Office for Official Publications of the European Communities.

WOLF A., 2001, AIDS, Morality and Indigenous Concepts of Sexually Transmitted Diseases. Afrika Spectrum 36(1):97–107.

WOLF A. and V. HÖRBST, eds, 2003, Medizin und Globalisierung: universelle Ansprüche – lokale Antworten. Hamburg: Lit-Verlag.

WÖRRLE B., 2002, Heiler, Rituale und Patienten. Schamanismus in den Anden Ecuadors. Berlin: Reimer.

Chapter 9

THE NETHERLANDS

A Cultural Fascination with Medicine: Medical Anthropology in the Netherlands
Sjaak Van der Geest

It is said that the Netherlands has the highest density of anthropologists in the world. It could well be true and seems to dovetail with two other "records," equally based on impression. During the heydays of missionary activity, the country produced an incredibly large number of Christian missionaries who could be found all over the world, particularly in Africa and in Indonesia, previously a Dutch colony. In the wake – and forefront – of the preaching missionaries were large numbers of doctors and nurses who spent a few – and some, many – years of their life in what later came to be called developing countries. Some of these medical "development workers" worked on government contracts but many of them were attached to a missionary organization. The origins of medical anthropology in the Netherlands are thus closely linked to the activities of missionaries and medical workers in developing countries.

The most elaborate discussion of past and present Dutch medical anthropology is – perhaps not surprisingly – from an outsider: the Italian anthropologist Diasio (1999, 2003), who studied medical anthropological traditions in four European societies, namely France, Great Britain, Italy, and the Netherlands. She writes that Dutch anthropologists are over-modest, and downplay their own anthropological merit. They do not seem to think that they have made a significant contribution to the discipline and see themselves as a mixed breed of foreign and interdisciplinary influences. I agree with her thesis on the mixed provenance of Dutch medical anthropology, but I do not downplay its contribution to the development of this subdiscipline.

"Alien" Origins

The first Dutch study that explicitly referred to "medical anthropology" appeared in 1964. It was a dissertation by a medical doctor, Vincent van Amelsvoort, on the introduction of "Western" health care in the former Dutch colony of New Guinea (now an uneasy province of Indonesia). It was only one year after Scotch had delineated medical anthropology as a formal field of research and teaching and as a subdiscipline of cultural anthropology.[1] Van Amelsvoort's study focused on the clash between two entirely different (medical) cultures (Van Amelsvoort 1964a). In that same year he (Van Amelsvoort 1964b) published a short note on the new field of medical anthropology in a Dutch medical journal. Discussing the origins of the new subdiscipline, Van Amelsvoort referred mainly to social scientists and health professionals who had worked in the field of health development (as he had done himself) and had analyzed the relationship between culture, health, and health practices, such as Erasmus, Wellin, McDermott, and Carstairs. Seeing medicine as a part of culture, he wrote:

> Medicine consists of a vast complex of knowledge, beliefs, techniques, roles, norms, values, ideologies, attitudes, customs, rituals and symbols, that interlock to form a mutually reinforcing and supporting system. . . . In its totality this system is functioning to solve a universal major problem of every society: disease. (Van Amelsvoort 1964a:13)

Van Amelsvoort was a "tropical doctor" with a keen interest in culture. That interest was thrown upon him during his work as a colonial doctor in New Guinea. Later on he became professor of health care in developing countries in the Medical Faculty of the University of Nijmegen.[2] The biographical background of his work in medical anthropology typifies the "alien" origins of the discipline in the Netherlands. "Alien" refers to both disciplinary and geographical territories. Medical anthropology in the Netherlands started far from home, in tropical areas, and those who initiated it were not anthropologists but medical doctors.

Medical Initiatives

I can think of mainly two reasons why physicians and not anthropologists took up the issue of culture and medicine. The social and cultural character of health problems manifests itself much more prominently in medical practice than in anthropological research. In their attempts to improve health conditions, tropical doctors continuously encountered "cultural barriers." It forced them to think about the nature of these barriers and to reflect on their own mission. Whatever opinion they developed about the practical implications of cultural barriers, many of them at least realized that it was crucial to learn more about them. There was a need for knowledge about local cultures, particularly medical cultures.

This awakening of cultural interest among Dutch tropical doctors can be observed in the work of some early physicians in the Dutch colony of the Dutch Indies. J. P. Kleiweg de Zwaan (1910) published a study about indigenous medicine among the Menangkabau people in North Sumatra, J. M. Elshout (1923) did the same for the Dayak people in Borneo, and J. A. Verdoorn (1941) wrote a study about indigenous midwifery in various ethnic groups of the colony. Another colonial precursor of medical anthropology was F. D. E. van Ossenbruggen, a lawyer who studied general aspects of local Indonesian cultures and was particularly interested in how illness and health practices were embedded in the general culture. His work includes a comparative study of rituals against smallpox among different populations (Van Ossenbruggen 1916; see also Diasio 2003; Niehof 2003). Van Amelsvoort's dissertation in 1964 followed the tradition of colonial doctors, as did a study by G. Jansen (1973) on doctor–patient relationships in Bomvanaland (South Africa). Jansen had spent 11 years as a missionary doctor in Bomvana society. It was around that period, in the 1970s, that Dutch anthropologists became interested in the cultural identity of health and medicine and "took over" the job of medical anthropology from their medical colleagues.

The medical (applied) purpose of medical anthropology remained strong after anthropologists became involved in the work. Many of the first *anthropological* medical anthropologists in the Netherlands worked in close cooperation with – or in the service of – medical projects. The anthropologist Douwe Jongmans, for example, moved from the University of Amsterdam to the health section of the Royal Tropical Institute and did research among North African immigrants. His main contribution lies in cultural perceptions and practices around fertility and birth regulation (Jongmans 1974, 1977).[3] Several other anthropologists continued – in varying degrees – to practice "anthropology *in* medicine," abroad, but also increasingly in the Netherlands among migrants (Van Dijk 1981, 1987).

A second explanation for the "failure" of anthropologists to grasp the opportunity of medical anthropology at an early stage might have been their weariness of applied anthropology, which dominated the postcolonial era of anthropology. In the 1950s and 1960s, most anthropologists fostered the principle of – as much as possible – nonintervention. "Proper" anthropologists, it was believed, should not get their hands dirty on government- or mission-initiated development projects. Problems of illness and death were first of all to be studied as occasions for social conflict and religious ceremony. Illness and death as a subject did not really interest them. Only when they occurred in their immediate environment and touched them personally were they likely to become more actively involved. Many anthropologists, for example, distributed medicines to members of "their family" and to neighbors and helped them in other ways. Some anthropologists were known to "play doctor" and even held "consulting hours." Such activities remained however entirely separated from their scientific work and did not lead them to anthropological reflection. They were not only activities that fell outside the scope of their research, they were even in conflict with the "rules" of proper anthropological fieldwork: nonintervention and participant *observation*, with the emphasis on the last word.

The "classic" anthropological allergy to biology probably contributed to anthropologists' reluctance to get involved in medical issues. It was only in the 1970s that anthropologists "discovered" body and biology as cultural phenomena and became fascinated by medical topics. It was at this moment that medical anthropology in the Netherlands – as in many other countries – became a recognized and popular field of study within cultural and social anthropology.[4]

Xenophilia

The other type of alienage during the first years of medical anthropology in the Netherlands was geographical. The research that was recognized as "medical anthropology" had always taken place far away, on foreign territory. This is no surprise, since at the time anthropology was seen as the study of "other cultures," as Beattie (1964) confirmed in the title of his handbook on anthropology. With some exaggeration one could say that it was not the topic but rather the topos that made a study "anthropological." Studies on social and cultural aspects of health, body, mind, emotion, and well-being that would now be considered as typically anthropological but which took place in Dutch society were automatically excluded from the anthropological library (to be more precise, not only were they never considered for inclusion or reference, they were never even noticed). Conversely, work done under the tropical sun was embraced as anthropology or anthropologically relevant, even if it was rather far removed from anthropology in theoretical and methodological respects.

The following two examples illustrate my point.[5] The first concerns the pioneering studies of the physician, biologist, psychologist, and philosopher F. J. J. Buytendijk (1887–1974), who is hardly ever referred to in the publications of the early Dutch medical anthropologists. Buytendijk's main concern can be characterized as a consistent attempt to overcome the body/mind dichotomy, a theme which some thirty years later became the inspiration for one of the most influential publications in medical anthropology (Scheper-Hughes and Lock 1987). Using data from physiology and ethology, Buytendijk tried to render the French philosopher Merleau-Ponty's (1908–61) ideas about the body-subject plausible and acceptable to a forum of hard scientists. He argued for an "anthropological physiology": a physiology that – as Merleau-Ponty suggested – reacted meaningfully to human experiences. He applied his views to bodily reactions such as sleeping and being awake, pain, being thirsty, blushing, sweating, and fainting. Buytendijk felt closely affiliated to the Heidelberg group in Germany where Viktor von Weizsäcker, Herbert Plügge, Thure van Uexküll, and others worked for a nondualistic brand of medicine.[6] Buytendijk, whose work has been translated into English, shows that there is subjectivity and meaningful reaction in physiological processes. Just as the body is a cultural product, bodily dysfunction is a meaningful and cultural act, a form of being human (Buytendijk 1974). As I said before, Buytendijk's publications were not thought to be relevant to cultural anthropologists. The negligence was indeed mutual. Buytendijk took his inspiration and data from biology and psychology, from humans as well as from animals, but never referred to studies of people in other cultures. It is doubtful that he read anthropological work, an amazing omission in hindsight.

A similar story could be told about the Dutch psychiatrist Van den Berg. Outside the Netherlands Van den Berg is best known for a brief treatise on the psychology of the sick-bed, which has been translated in many languages. Within his own country he drew considerable attention through his book "*Metabletica . . .*" (1956), a study of societal changes in a historical perspective. Some years later he published his monumental study of the human body from a "metabletic" perspective (Van den Berg 1959, 1961). His main thesis was that the human body has changed through the ages (his study takes the reader back to the 13th century). He does not only argue that the *meaning* of the body has been changing all the time but that the body itself, "in its materiality," has changed. Van den Berg's style of reasoning does not fit in any conventional discipline and one could characterize him best as a "postmodernist *avant la lettre*." His argument follows unpredictable associations, from paintings by Brueghel, Rubens, and Picasso, to a mystic's vision, a book of devotion, a scientific study of the heart, a paper clipping about the rescue of a drowning person, a collection of lyrics, an X-ray photograph, and a building by Le Corbusier. The body, Van den Berg writes, reflects the ideas and politics of its period. As with Buytendijk, this viewpoint is busily discussed by anthropologists today, but unnoticed by them at the time. Conversely, again, it should be noted that Van den Berg showed no interest in anthropologists' descriptions of human bodies in other cultures. The xenophilia of the anthropologists paralleled the "xenophobia" of the other disciplines that occupied themselves with body, culture, and society.[7]

I have pointed out the divergent origins of Dutch medical anthropology. The subdiscipline's mixed historic and cultural identity is the result of a unique interplay of inclusion and exclusion of outside influences. Using hygienic, almost medical, language, Diasio (1999) speaks of an "impure science," a purposely unfortunate adjective, as no cultural phenomenon can remain "pure." Continuing her medical metaphor, "purity" would indeed imply sterility. One could also propose the anthropological metaphor of exogamy for the geographical and disciplinary vagaries of Dutch medical anthropology.[8]

Current Affairs

Describing the present situation of "medical anthropology" in the Netherlands is not much different from writing about multicultural society. People switch identity according to situational needs and interests. Sociologists and psychologists may decide to call themselves (medical) anthropologists if they regard this as being advantageous in their work or academic situation. Conversely anthropologists may call themselves something else for the same reason. A growing number of people with training in a (para)medical profession decide to study medical anthropology, then return to their original profession, without professing their anthropological identity. I estimate that at present about fifty medical anthropologists work in different areas of health care, social work, and health policy, though they are hardly identified as such. This elastic character of "medical anthropology" should be taken into account while reading the remainder of this article.

Chairs in Medical Anthropology

By now, medical anthropology is a well-established academic discipline in the Netherlands. And though it is taught at various universities, the center of medical anthropological teaching and research is no doubt the Medical Anthropology Unit at the University of Amsterdam. Over the past decade the University of Amsterdam has appointed five professors to chairs in medical anthropology or closely related fields.

In 1990 Pieter Streefland was appointed as professor of applied development sociology, in particular with regard to health. In 1994 the University of Amsterdam established the first "proper" chair in medical anthropology in the Netherlands with Van der Geest as its occupant (Van der Geest 1995a). In 1995 Corlien Varkevisser became professor of interdisciplinary research in health and development,[9] and in 2000 Stuart Blume, professor of science and technology dynamics, joined the Medical Anthropology Unit. In 2002 Anita Hardon was appointed professor of the anthropology of care and health.

At the University of Leiden, Annemiek Richters holds a chair in culture, health and illness in the Medical Faculty. She has degrees in medicine, anthropology, sociology, and philosophy and has specialized in gender issues, trauma, and human rights. At the Free University of Amsterdam, Ivan Wolffers holds a professorship on health care and culture in the Medical Faculty and Joop de Jong is professor of transcultural psychiatry in the same faculty. In Utrecht David Ingleby is professor of intercultural psychology. At the University of Nijmegen, Frank Kortmann is professor of transcultural psychiatry (his favorite adage being "All psychiatry is transcultural").

Teaching[10]

Since 1978 an introduction into medical anthropology has been offered – initially by Klaas van der Veen and Sjaak van der Geest – at the University of Amsterdam to both anthropology students and students from other disciplines. Later on others joined in: Anita Hardon, Anja Krumeich, Cor Jonker, Els van Dongen, Ria Reis, Maud Radstake, Marian Tankink, and Diana Gibson. Over the years other courses were added to the introduction, such as Health and Development (Corlien Varkevisser, Trudie Gerrits, Winny Koster), Anthropology and Psychiatry (Els van Dongen, Han ten Brummelhuis), Gender and Reproductive Health (Anita Hardon, Jeanet van de Korput, Trudie Gerrits, Lia Sciortina), Medicine and Science Dynamics (Stuart Blume, Anja Hiddinga, Olga Amsterdamska), Anthropology of Aging (Sjaak van der Geest, Els van Dongen), Anthropology of Infectious Disease (Pieter Streefland), Anthropology and Epidemiology (Anita Hardon and Walter Devillé), Anthropology and Children (Ria Reis, Anita Hardon), and three courses on the regional aspects of Ethnographies of Health and Health Care in Africa (Sjaak van der Geest, Ria Reis), Asia (Han ten Brummelhuis, Pieter Streefland, Leontine Visser, Maarten Bode), and Europe (Els van Dongen).

In 1997 the Amsterdam Unit started an international master's in medical anthropology, the "AMMA."[11] The course attracts between 15 and 20 students yearly from all over the world. From 2003 onwards the unit offers a Dutch master's in medical anthropology and sociology.

In addition to the University of Amsterdam, courses in (or closely related to) medical anthropology are taught at three universities. At the Free University of Amsterdam two courses are offered to medical students: Culture and Health, and Health and Development.[12] Anja Krumeich, at the University of Maastricht, teaches an Introduction in Medical Anthropology.[13] Several courses are taught at the

University of Leiden, one of them being Medical Sociology for Developing Countries. This course started as early as 1971. The first organizer was Willem Buschkens,[14] one of whose concerns was to bridge the gap between medical professors and sociologists/anthropologists in the context of health development. After his death the course was continued by Hans Speckman[15] and Jan Slikkerveer. Other courses at the University of Leiden fall under the responsibility of Annemiek Richters. They are taught in the Medical School and focus on health and human rights and multicultural medicine.[16] At the University of Utrecht David Ingleby organizes courses in the field of intercultural and cultural psychology.[17]

Research[18]

It is not possible to do justice to all medical anthropological research activities in the Netherlands and I apologize beforehand for the many omissions in this brief overview. Most research which can be characterized as "medical anthropological" has been carried out by the research group at the University of Amsterdam. Over the past 25 years an estimated 20 doctoral dissertations and a hundred master theses have been produced by and under the supervision of members of the Amsterdam Unit. Together with other research projects they cover almost any imaginable topic, but six main themes may be distinguished among all of this diversity.

The first theme covers perceptions and practices concerning health and illness. Seeing health and illness and people's responses to them as social phenomena embedded in cultural conventions has been the starting point of a wide variety of explorations in medical anthropology. This perspective of health and illness has inspired research in the Unit, which deals with cultural variations in the conception and treatment of specific diseases such as malaria, tuberculosis, HIV/AIDS, nutritional disorders, and chronic diseases such as epilepsy and diabetes. Other projects focus on therapeutic traditions, and concepts of sanitation and prevention.[19]

The next theme is medical knowledge and technology, including pharmaceuticals and immunization. For more than twenty years, the Unit has played a pioneering role in the anthropological study of pharmaceuticals. Another facet of medical technology that has been studied by the Unit is the social, cultural, and historical context of immunization. This comparative research project has been carried out in seven different countries. Most recently the history of the production of medical science and technology has been added to the Unit's research program.[20]

A third theme relates to gender, reproductive health, and population policy. Projects on this theme aim to gain an understanding of the way in which men and women regulate their fertility and how they experience their reproductive health. The projects hope to contribute to gender-aware and culturally acceptable reproductive health interventions. Particular attention is paid to the influence of population policy on the quality of family planning services. Although much has been written on the violation of reproductive rights of women in developing countries, until now little research has been directed towards how women and men themselves could be given a voice on this issue. One study, which was carried out in seven countries, centered on the development and functioning of family planning programs as well as the advances in fertility regulating technologies.[21]

A fourth theme covers chronic illness and aging, including long-term care and the "unending work" of the afflicted themselves. The anthropological and socio-logical study of chronic illness, the life of the elderly, and long-term care arrange-ments reflect both changing trends in morbidity and mortality and a current concern in health-care policy at large. Care for the chronically ill and the aged, which often takes place in the home, requires a growing amount of effort and financial investment. The Unit explores the social and cultural variations of this type of care but also focuses on how older, chronically ill, and disabled people "care" for and present themselves in public life. The "public appearance" of older and chronically ill people is another research theme of the Unit. The research aims to formulate suggestions for adequate policy in this field.[22]

As a fifth theme, the Unit conducts research on mental health. The burden of mental health problems is likely to become heavier in the coming decades and will raise obstacles to global development and human emancipation. Important issues in this area are migration and mental health, violence and trauma, the "graying" of society, substance abuse, oppression, poverty, identity formation, and social memory. Medical anthropology explores the social and cultural variations of dealing with mental health problems and tries to formulate suggestions for action. It also contrib-utes to the development of theories that can enable cross-cultural comparison.[23]

Finally, the Unit focuses on health-care policy and management. Community-based health care holds a special attraction, as it is a consistent attempt to put health care into the hands of those to whom it matters most. With its focus on the layperson's perspective, anthropology has a logical interest in how health care functions at the community level as well as at other levels of the sociomedical organization. Special attention is given to the way it endures the pressures of structural adjustment. The social implications of policies of health reform, for example through cost-sharing, are also a matter of interest.[24]

Of all these themes, the anthropology of medicines has probably attracted the most international attention. In 1991 the Amsterdam Unit organized an interna-tional conference on this topic in cooperation with the University of Copenhagen. In addition it published several books and articles that have become trendsetters in "pharmaceutical anthropology" (Etkin and Tan 1994; Hardon 1989; Senah 1997; Tan 1999; Van der Geest and Whyte 1988; Van der Geest et al. 1996; Whyte et al. 2002). Other themes to which the Amsterdam Unit has made substantial contributions are the study of immunization (Blume and Geesink 2000, Streefland 2001, Streefland et al. 1999) and reproductive health (Hardon 1998; Hardon and Hayes 1997).

The leading research position of the Amsterdam Unit is also reflected in other activities. The Unit is the publisher of a Dutch/English journal *Medische Antrop-ologie* and three book series: *Health, Culture and Society, Current Reproductive Health Matters*, and *Community Drug Use Studies*.

Research activities by Annemiek Richters and colleagues at the *University of Leiden* deal with a variety of topics including: gender violence, trauma, health and healing; the quality of reproductive health care for migrant women in the Netherlands; Western medicine and the body politics of women in the context of globalization; health and human rights; and HIV/AIDS in a cultural perspective. The main focus of the research is the effect of globalization on gender identities and gender violence (Hof and Richters 1999; Richters 1998, 2001). At the same university Jan Slikkerveer has for many years worked on local knowledge systems, including medical knowledge (Slikkerveer et al. 1993; Warren et al. 1995).

In the Medical Faculty of the Free University of Amsterdam, Ivan Wolffers leads a research project on AIDS and migration in a few Asian countries. This program includes several research projects that focus on understanding the factors that lead to vulnerability in migrants. The research is aimed at empowerment and concentrates on interventions and tools for advocacy (Wolffers et al. 2002). A spinoff of this project is research on the health hazards of sex work in several Asian countries. At the same university, Joop de Jong is involved in research on war violence and mental health in Africa, Asia, and Europe, and Arko Oderwald on philosophical and ethical aspects of health and health care. Oderwald has published extensively on issues of health and illness in literary imagination and ego-documents (Oderwald 1994, 2001).

At the University of Maastricht Bernike Pasveer and colleagues are heading a research project on "The Mediated Body." They study the historical and contemporary medical, artistic and philosophical angles arising from the project's conjecture that medical knowledge of the human body as well subjective experience of the body are phenomena affected by the mediating procedures and instruments with which bodies are studied and represented. Rather than assuming that medical instruments of visualization are transparent windows onto a given body, the hypothesis is that what is known of the body, as well as the ways people experience their body, is mediated through/results out of the very instruments used to produce and represent knowledge.

Somewhat in the same vein, Annemarie Mol, medical philosopher at the University of Twente, studies the social and cultural contingencies of biomedical science and practice. Her publications deal with issues of gender, the body, technology, and texts. The ethnography of one of her books (Mol 2002) is situated in a Dutch hospital.

At the University of Nijmegen, Fenneke Reysoo is involved in research on the social processes of sex and reproductive choice. The focus is on socioeconomic determinants (marital status, family structure, housing conditions, rural–urban divide, religion, secularization, exposure to mass-media, and purchasing power), as well as on meaning systems of gender, love, honor and shame, marriage, reputation, power, and property. Part of the research is based on the ethnographic literature of various countries, another part on ongoing data-collection in Morocco.

Administrative Matters

Research projects by Dutch universities are usually registered in large research schools that accommodate both senior and junior researchers, including Ph.D.

candidates. Most of this research is funded by the universities, by Dutch ministries, and by sponsors such as WHO, the European Union, commercial funds and NGOs. The research schools are evaluated by external commissions.

Most of the research mentioned in this overview is part of the Amsterdam School of Social Science Research (ASSR), the Research School for Resource Studies for Development (CERES), and Science, Technology and Modern Culture (WTMC).

Theoretical and Ethical Considerations

The variety of research themes in Dutch medical anthropology equals that of the theoretical concepts and perspectives they explore. If we push things just a little, we may, however, discern a few more or less central foci of theoretical discussion. Six theoretical concepts deserve special mention: the symbolic potential of medical phenomena; the power aspect of medical thinking, acting, and technology; the globalization and localization of medical knowledge and practice; the relationship between biology and culture; the agency of patients; and the applicability of research. They cut across the themes and topics presented above. Ethical considerations are intertwined with all these concepts but particularly with the last two.

Symbols and the Social Experience of Health and Illness

Symbols are the "stuff" of human thinking and acting. Culture is increasingly regarded as a universe of shared symbols. Through symbols people communicate social relations and cultural experiences. If illness and health are at the center of culture and society, it is not surprising that the domains of ill health and wellness and of fortune and misfortune are some of the most important providers of metaphors and metonyms that people use to order their existence, attach meaning to it, and communicate with others. Consequently, the body as primary experience stands out. Thus, the sick body becomes the "topos" of vulnerability in a hostile or indifferent environment, the body afflicted by chronic illness represents the chronic ailments of society and the aging body becomes a metaphor for a world that has lost its appeal. The AIDS epidemic worldwide is perhaps the most defeating example of this symbolism of destructiveness.

The able as well as the sick or disabled body is the intimate point of reference from which and through which people explore the world. The immediacy of the bodily experience infuses bodily symbols with special rhetorical force. These symbols enable people to make contingent situations "self-evident" and to render diffuse experiences concrete. Medicalization and somatization are not only part and parcel of professional medical practices, they are also constituents of the everyday life of ordinary citizens.

The anthropological approach to illness and health illuminates the way people produce culture and society and, in turn, are "products" of social and cultural processes. Medical phenomena as carriers of connotations ("good to think with") constitute a crucial study area for Dutch anthropologists.

Medical Hegemony: Acceptance and Resistance

If medical phenomena occupy such a central place in the production of symbols and the maintenance of social relations, then it is also understandable that they lend themselves easily to the exercise of power. Medical discourses contribute to the construction of others as beings who need help and control; medical services are political means by which that control is achieved. Introducing the concept of "bio-power" (the power to heal instead of the power to kill), Foucault was one of many to draw attention to the political dimension of medical phenomena. Some Dutch anthropologists apply another concept, "naturalization," to this dimension of medicine. In medical practice the social is declared "nature" and presented as self-evident.

Medical knowledge and health care are not only the products of a state authority that takes care of its civilians. They also give that state the right to exist and facilitate the exercise of political power. Tropical medicine, for instance, made an essential contribution to the implementation of colonial regimes, being used to legitimate these regimes. Public health in Dutch society has the same effect. Conversely, failures in the provision of health care bring governments into great political jeopardy.

Power and politics are connected to the "medical" in still many other ways. Epidemiological research shows that social and economic inequalities are the best predictors of health and access to health care. Poverty in an economic sense usually implies a lack of control about one's own body and health. The professionalization of health care and the monopolization of control over medical technology are yet other examples of the interweaving of power and the medical.

Finally, research on the configuration of psychiatric care and power shows that culture is not only a binding force but also a manipulative system that marginalizes, excludes, labels, and punishes people. The marginalization of older people in society demonstrates how closely physical and social "weakness" are related.

Globalization and Localization of Health-care Arrangements

The force of medical symbolism expresses itself vividly in processes of globalization and localization, that is, in the diffusion of bioscientific medicine and in local reinterpretations or resistance against this encroachment. Research on the execution of vaccination campaigns and the distribution, perception, and use of pharmaceutical products, including contraceptives, puts this global development into sharp focus. World-wide processes of expansion and adaptation are also exemplified by research on the social history of the production of medical knowledge and technology.

In the context of an international policy to reduce population growth, contraceptives are disseminated even to the most remote corners of the world. The "life cycle" of contraceptive technologies, from inception through production to application, demonstrates clearly the tension between globalization and localization. Research on contraceptive practices addresses this issue at the global as well as at the local level and shows how consumers and producers of these techniques influence each other.

The ambiguity of globalization vis-à-vis localization presents itself in the uneasy encounter between imported and indigenous medical traditions. In India, for example, the hegemony of Western pharmaceuticals has met with the opposition of Ayurveda. Ayurvedic pharmaceuticals provide Indian cultures with a concrete and evocative symbol for expressing their own identity in contrast with Western images (Bode 2002).

The study of the perception and actual use of pharmaceuticals shows how the globalization effect of the dissemination of pharmaceuticals is mitigated by the cultural reinterpretation that these products undergo. They acquire new local meanings that may deviate drastically from their "global" biomedical definition (Whyte et al. 2002).

Globalization also plays a role in research on perceptions and practices concerning vaccination, for example with respect to prevailing views about the prevention of illness and the protection of health. Studies using a multilevel perspective show how international goals translate into national and local programs and practices. These often substantial shifts in the contents of goals can cause miscommunication between different levels of organization and constitute considerable policy problems.

The Coproduction of Biology and Culture

Anthropology has had a lifelong fascination and feud with biology. It arose partly as a critique against biologism and scientism and was shaped to a considerable degree by this opposition. Unfortunately, the discussions have often led to irreconcilable viewpoints that are both deterministic in nature: cultural against biological reductionism. Anthropologists should avoid these fallacies of exclusive thinking. They should study both the cultural character of biology and the biological features of culture. The repeal of dualistic thinking is one of the main issues and aims of medical anthropology.

The inseparable unity of the "body-subject" (Merleau-Ponty's term) can hardly be observed and described better than in the experience of being ill and becoming well. At the level of the body, the physical implications of meaning-making are undeniable and illness and well-being show themselves as "co-productions" of nature and culture. It is impossible to make sense of the cause, the etiology, the expression, and the experience of health complaints without placing these in a social and cultural perspective.

In anthropology the body is not only seen as the arena where battled is waged over meanings of "nature" and "culture" but also as the place where reconciliation is possible. The human body itself is a convincing demonstration of the untenability of the Cartesian dichotomy.

Agency of Patients

Anthropological studies of health and illness often portray patients as "patient" and "passive" recipients of care designed and executed by others, such as professionals and relatives. Publications discuss institutions and arrangements of care and medical intervention but pay little attention to the "never-ending work" (to paraphrase Strauss) that patients carry out themselves. Health care does not simply exist in institutions and professional expertise, but is a continuous process of "being done" and "being made." Studies of health-care activities focus on their *interactional* (what patients do in reaction to what others do to them, and vice versa) and *transformational* (how do health arrangements and patients change as a result of that interactional process) effects. Dutch anthropologists want to focus more on patients as central actors in and around the provision of health care, but also in and around the production of new biomedical knowledge and new diagnostic and therapeutic tools. Under certain circumstances, patient groups succeed in influencing the development of biomedical science (Blume and Catshoek 2002). Anthropologists promote a greater influence for patients with regard to what and how health research should be conducted.

Applicability

Application of research results is a constant practical and theoretical challenge. How to put anthropological research results to use has indeed proven to be a thorny question. Often the improvement in our understanding of how and why certain phenomena operate paralyzes rather than invites the search for concrete solutions. If everything relates to everything, as anthropologists often claim, then how can one take action? The result is that practically inclined disciplines often do not wish to engage themselves in anthropological research and that anthropologists hardly bother to ask what is or could be done with their research.

This gap between theory and ethnography on one side and practical work on the other needs to be bridged. Anthropological research should also lead to practical conclusions. The application of research is an essential part of the anthropological quest. The practical application of the insights gained implies seriously considering the ideas and interests of "others." Moreover, focusing on applicability implies a victory over academic ethnocentrism and widespread disciplinary encasing (Van der Geest 1995b).

One of the main problems of applied research is that its results are often least accessible to those who are most entitled to it. It is regularly the case that the outcome of research that is carried out as a service to the least privileged is presented to the most privileged, who have a vested interest in everything remaining the same.

The Netherlands   175

The focus on applicability as an objective and theoretical challenge can be traced in many research projects presented in this overview. Studies of "community drug use" try, on the one hand, to formulate recommendations for the improvement of medicine use, and, on the other, to seriously consider the ideas of those who use these medicines "wrongly." A similar task is confronted in the research on various aspects of reproductive health that reveals notions and practices that may be harmful from a biomedical point of view but are of great value in the local culture. The ways in which people deal with diseases such as tuberculosis and HIV/AIDS confront the anthropologist with a similar problem and require a great deal of creativity on her/his part to formulate respectful and culture-sensitive recommendations for change.

Cultural respect is not, however, a blind kind of respect devoid of criticism. In the final instance, respect for culture must be rooted in respect for *people*, the ones who live in that culture. Defending cultural traditions which the members of that culture experience as oppressive would become a new form of cultural imperialism, a reversed ethnocentrism. Taking this into consideration, medical anthropologists should look for respectful solutions that receive the approval and support of those who are immediately affected by them (Van der Geest and Reis 2002).

Prospects

It is hard to predict medical anthropology's future in the Netherlands, but two related developments are likely to take place. The first one leads us back to the opening paragraphs of this article. Medical anthropology will distance itself more and more from its "alien" beginnings and come "home." The Amsterdam Unit actively promotes research in its own society as is shown in its involvement in three international conferences on Medical Anthropology at Home (1998, 2001, 2003).

The home-coming of Dutch medical anthropology is further stimulated by the changing epidemiological scene. Chronic disease and old age are gaining an increasing amount of attention. The emphasis is shifting from active medical intervention to care and social attention. The role of the social and cultural context is becoming more important, as is the study of this context by anthropologists.

The growing number of citizens of foreign origin with different cultural perceptions of health and medicine constitutes a third factor that will increase the need for anthropological research in Dutch society. Anthropologists are drawing attention to the "culturalization" of health problems among migrant citizens (Van Dijk 1998) and to policies of exclusion in health care. A large number of initiatives (both research and training courses) have been taken to address the interculturalization of health and health care.[25]

All three reasons for this "home coming" imply more cooperation between anthropologists, health-care professionals, and patients. Medical anthropologists will be pushed out of their safe haven of "pure" anthropology. The old medical roots of medical anthropology will be revitalized, but the picture will be more complex than before.

Acknowledgments

Writing an overview of such a diverse field as medical anthropology in the Netherlands is a precarious undertaking, especially if one is strongly immersed in it, as is the case for this author. I thank the many colleagues who helped me in collecting the information (especially Annemiek Richters and Rob van Dijk) and apologize for omissions and (Amsterdam) "biases." I quoted liberally from a document, which I wrote for my own research unit at the University of Amsterdam (Medical Anthropology/Sociology Unit (MASU) 2003). Other overviews that I consulted were: Diasio (2003), Richters (1983), and Streefland (1986).

Notes

1. A birth date of medical anthropology does not exist but 1953 was without doubt an important year. In that year, Caudill, by training a psychiatrist, wrote a contribution to Kroeber's *Anthropology Today* about "Applied anthropology in medicine" (Caudill 1953). Ten years later, Scotch published his overview of medical anthropological work, which he started as follows: ". . . In every culture there is built around the major life experiences of health and illness a substantial and integral body of beliefs, knowledge and practices" (Scotch 1963:30). It was one of the first attempts to define the study object of medical anthropology.

2. Vincent van Amelsvoort died in 2001. For brief biographies of his life, see several contributions to the Festschrift for his retirement (Braakman 1986) and his (Dutch) obituary (Van der Geest and Hamel 2001).

3. In 1983 Douwe Jongmans became professor of the "Intercultural Study of Human Fertility" at the University of Utrecht. He retired in 1986. More information on his life and work can be found in a Festschrift made for him at his retirement (Hoogbergen and de Theije 1986).

4. I suspect that medical anthropology developed along similar lines in other countries. The most prominent ancestors of medical anthropology in Britain, for example, were physicians (Rivers, Lewis, Loudon) and the same goes for the United States (Ackerknecht, Paul, and Kleinman). For the medical roots of British medical anthropology, see Diasio (1999:44–122).

5. Another, much earlier, example (not included in my brief overview) would be the work of Dutch Hygienists in the 19th century, in particular that of Pruys van der Hoeven, who emphasized the social and political nature of health and disease. Richters (1983) and Diasio (1999, 2003) discuss the Hygienists' (unrecognized) link with medical anthropology.

6. In Heidelberg the term "medical anthropology" (*medizinische Anthropologie*) was used long before the word was introduced in the Anglophone world, but it had another meaning: the philosophical reflection on illness, health, and healing (Von Weizsäcker 1927). As a consequence, German medical anthropologists were unable to adopt the term, as it already had another destination. They are still struggling to give a decent name to the discipline which their colleagues outside Germany term "medical anthropology."

7. The anthropological predilection for "things from far," exoticism in brief, was of course an inverted type of ethnocentrism. See for example Van der Geest (2002a).

8. One could perhaps say that Dutch medical anthropology is in yet a third way alien-oriented. The literature read in university courses is overwhelmingly foreign, demonstrating an extreme form of nonchauvinism. Dutch authors are hardly mentioned in the most popular handbooks and readers of medical anthropology. The most ambitious study on the foundations of medical anthropology written by a Dutch author is entirely devoted to a debate with the American school of Kleinman and hardly touches on the achievements of the "Dutch school" (Richters 1991). For an English summary and review of this study, see Maretzki (1994).

9. She held her inaugural lecture in 1995 on Health Systems Research (Varkevisser 1996).

10. An elaborate – but now partly outdated – overview of courses in medical anthropology in the Netherlands was published some years ago in *Anthropology and Medicine* (Van Dongen 1997).

11. Extensive information on the AMMA (Amsterdam Master's in Medical Anthropology) can be found on the website (http://www2.fmg.uva.nl/amma/). A brochure can be requested from the secretariat (amma@pscw.uva.nl).

12. Information: Anke van der Kwaak (a.van_der_kwaak.social@med.vu.nl).

13. Information: Anja Krumeich (A.Krumeich@ZW.unimaas.nl).

14. Willem Buschkens, who called himself a "non-Western sociologist," worked in Suriname, Ethiopia, and Somalia. He died in 1991. For a brief biography, see Speckmann (1991).

15. Hans Speckman specialized in the social and cultural aspects of family planning. He did research and taught in Suriname, Indonesia, and other countries. He died in 1997. For a brief biography, see Van der Geest (1997).

16. Information: Annemiek Richters (j.m.richters@lumc.nl).

17. Information: D.Ingleby@fss.uu.nl.

18. Research activities and publications in the field of medical anthropology are too numerous to be mentioned here. For an overview of research and published work by members and affiliated researchers of the Amsterdam Medical Anthropology Unit from 1993 to 2002, see Medical Anthropology Unit (MAU) (1997) and Medical Anthropology/Sociology Unit (MASU) (2003).

19. Publications in this field include: Nijhof (2002), Reis (2001), Van Dongen and Fainzang (2002), Van Duursen et al. (2002).

20. Some of the publications on this topic are: Adome et al. (1996), Amsterdamska and Hiddinga (2000), Blume (1997, 1998, 1999, 2000, 2002), Blume and Geesink (2000), Bode (2002), Gibson (2001), Streefland (1995, 2001), Vermeulen (2000), Whyte et al. (2002), Zaman (2004).

21. Publications related to reproductive health include: Gerrits (2002), Hardon (1998), Hardon and Hayes (1997), Koster (2003), Krumeich (1994).

22. Publications on old age, long-term care, and chronic disease include: Nijhof (2002), Van der Geest (2002b), Van Dongen (2002a) Von Faber (2002), Von Faber et al. (2001).

23. Publications on mental health include: Van Dongen (2000, 2002b, 2002c, 2003), Van Dongen and Van Dijk (2000).

24. Some publications focusing on health policy and intervention are: Arhinful (2003), Streefland (1998), Vulpiani et al. (2000).

25. Dutch medical anthropologists are taking part in a large European study about the exclusion of migrants from national health care in nine European countries (see Vulpiani et al. 2000). Likewise, there is an intercultural mental-health center of

expertise in the field of ethnic and cultural diversity (MIKADO). Its main objective is to improve mental health care by improving the transfer of knowledge, promoting intercultural expertise, and initiating research. For information: n.sonmez@mikado-ggz.nl; website: www.mikado-ggz.nl, accessed June 2004.

References

ADOME R. O., S. R. WHYTE and A. HARDON, 1996, Popular Pills: Community Drug Use in Uganda. Amsterdam: Het Spinhuis.

AMSTERDAMSKA O. and A. HIDDINGA, 2000, The Analysed Body. *In* Medicine in the Twentieth Century. J. Pickstone and R. Cooter, eds. Pp. 33–417. London: Harwood Publishers.

ARHINFUL D. K., 2003, The Solidarity of Self-interest: Social and Cultural Feasibility of Rural Health Insurance in Ghana. Research report 71. Leiden: African Studies Centre.

BEATTIE J., 1964, Other Cultures. Aims, Methods and Achievements in Social Anthropology. London: Routledge.

BLUME S., 1997, The Rhetoric and Counter Rhetoric of a Bionic Technology, Science Technology and Human Values 22:31–56.

——, 1998, From Bench to Bush: Problems of Vaccine Development and their Analysis. *In* Problems and Potential in International Health. P. Streefland, ed. Pp. 82–169. Amsterdam: Het Spinhuis.

——, 1999, Histories of Cochlear Implantation. Social Science and Medicine 49(9):1259–1268.

——, 2000, Medicine, Technology and Industry. *In* Medicine in the Twentieth Century. J. Pickstone and R. Cooter, eds. Pp. 85–171. London: Harwood Academic Publishers.

——, 2002, Testing and Empowerment: On the Boundary Between Hearing and Deafness, Medische Antropologie 14(1):55–69.

BLUME S. and G. CATSHOEK, 2002, Articulating the Patient Perspective: Strategic Options for Research. Utrecht: Stichting Patiënten Praktijk.

BLUME S. and I. GEESINK, 2000, Vaccinology: an Industrial Science? Science as Culture 9:41–72.

BODE M., 2002, Indian Indigenous Pharmaceuticals: Tradition, Modernity and Nature. *In* Plural Medicine, Tradition and Modernity, 1800–2000. W. Ernst, ed. Pp. 184–203. London: Routledge.

BRAAKMAN M., ed. 1986, Gezondheidszorg en kultuur kritisch bekeken. Medisch-antropologische opstellen aangeboden aan Prof. Dr. Vincent F. P. M. van Amelsvoort. Groningen: Konstapel.

BUYTENDJIK F. J. J., 1974, Prolegomena to an Anthropological Physiology. Pittsburgh: Duquesne University Press (Version originale allemande 1965).

CAUDILL W., 1953, Applied Anthropology in Medicine. *In* Anthropology Today. A. L. Kroeber, ed. Pp. 771–806. Chicago: University of Chicago Press.

DIASIO N., 1999, La science impure. Anthropologie et médecine en France, Grande-Bretagne, Italie, Pays-Bas. Paris: Presses Universitaires de France.

——, 2003, Traders, Missionaries and Nurses and Much More. Early Trajectories towards Medical Anthropology in the Netherlands. Medische Antropologie 15(2):263–286.

ELSHOUT J. M., 1923, Over de geneeskunde der Kenja-Dajak in Centraal-Borneo in verband met hun godsdienst. Amsterdam: Johannes Müller.

ETKIN N. L. and M. L. TAN, ed., 1994, Medicines: Meanings and Contexts. Quezon City: Health Action Information Network.

GERRITS T., 2002, Infertility and Matrilineality. The Exceptional Case of the Macua. *In* Infertility around the Globe: New Thinking on Childless, Gender and Reproductive Technology. M. C. Inhorn and F. van Balen, eds. Pp. 46–233. Los Angeles: University of California Press.

GIBSON D., 2001, Negotiating the New Health Care System in Cape Town, South Africa. Medical Anthropology Quarterly 15(4):515–532.

HARDON A. P., 1989, Confronting ill Health: Medicines, Self-Care and the Poor in Manila. Quezon City: Health Action Information Network.

——, ed., 1998, Beyond Rhetoric: Participatory Research on Reproductive Health. Amsterdam: Spinhuis.

HARDON A. P. and L. HAYES, eds, 1997, Reproductive Rights in Practice: A Feminist Report on the Quality of Care. London: Zed Press.

HOF C. and A. RICHTERS, 1999, Exploring Intersections between Teenage Pregnancy and Gender Violence. Lessons from Zimbabwe. African Journal of Reproductive Health 3(1):51–66.

HOOGBERGEN W. and M. DE THEIJE, eds, 1986, Vruchtbaar onderzoek. Essays ter ere van Douwe Jongmans. Utrecht: Instituut voor Culturele Antropologie, ICAU Mededelingen 24.

JANSEN G., 1973, The Doctor–Patient Relationship in an African Tribal Society. Assen: Van Gorcum.

JONGMANS D. G., 1974, Socio-cultural Aspects of Family Planning: An Anthropological Study at the Village Level. *In* The Neglected Factor. Family Planning. Perception and Reaction at the Base. D. G. Jongmans and H. J. M. Claessen, eds. Pp. 33–64. Assen: Van Gorcum.

——, 1977, Gastarbeider en gezondheidszorg. Eer en zelfrespect: De Noord-Afrikaanse boer en de overheid. Medisch Contact 32:509–512.

KLEIWEG DE ZWAAN J. P., 1910, De geneeskunde der Menangkabau-Maleiers. Amsterdam: Meulenhoff.

KOSTER W., 2003, Secret strategies. Women and Induced Abortion in Yoruba Society, Nigeria. Amsterdam: Aksant.

KRUMEICH A., 1994, The Blessings of Motherhood. Health, Pregnancy and Child Care in Dominica. Amsterdam: Het Spinhuis.

MARETZKI T. W., 1994, A Dutch View on Medical Anthropology: Criticisms and Suggestions. Social Science and Medicine 39(11):1579–1584.

MEDICAL ANTHROPOLOGY/SOCIOLOGY UNIT (MASU), 2003, Social Studies of Health and Health Care. An Overview of Projects and Publications (1997–2002). Amsterdam: MASU.

MEDICAL ANTHROPOLOGY UNIT (MAU), 1997, Research by the Medical Anthropology Unit, University of Amsterdam. An Overview of Projects (1993–1997). Amsterdam: MAU.

MOL A., 2002, The Body Multiple. Ontology in Medical Practice. Durham, NC: Duke University Press.

NIEHOF A., 2003, The Indonesian Archipelago as Nursery for Leiden Anthropology. Supplementary Notes to Nicoletta Diasio. Medische Antropologie 15(2):292–295.

NIJHOF G., 2002, Parkinson's Disease as a Problem of Shame in Public Appearance. *In* Sociology of Health and Fitness. S. Nettlreton and U. Gustafson, eds. Pp. 188–198. Cambridge: Polity Press.

ODERWALD A. K., 1994, Lijden tussen de regels. Zoetermeer: NCCZ.

——, 2001, Vertrouwd anders. Medische Antropologie 13(1):36–45.

REIS R., 2001, Epilepsy and Self-Identity Among the Dutch. Medical Anthropology 19(4):355–382.

RICHTERS A. J. M., 1983, De medische antropologie. Een nieuwe discipline? Antropologische Verkenningen 2(3):39–69.

——, 1991, De medisch antropoloog als verteller en vertaler. Met Hermes op reis in het land van de afgoden. Delft: Eburon.

——, 1998, Sexual Violence in Wartime. Psycho-Sociocultural Wounds and Healing Processes: the Example of the Former Yugoslavia. In Rethinking the Trauma of War. P. J. Bracken and C. Petty, eds. Pp. 112–128. London: Free Association Books.

——, 2001, Gender Violence, Trauma and Healing in Situations of Ethno-National Conflicts: The Cases of Former Yugoslavia and Tajikistan. In Hommes armés, femmes aguerries. Rapports de genre en situations de conflict armé. F. Reysoo, ed. Pp. 137–165. Berne: Commission nationale suisse pour l'UNESCO.

SCHEPER-HUGHES N. and M. M. LOCK, 1987, The Mindful Body. A Prolegomenon to Future Work in Medical Anthropology. Medical Anthropology Quarterly NS 1(1):6–41.

SCOTCH N. A., 1963, Medical Anthropology. Biennial Review of Anthropology 1963:30–68.

SENAH K. A., 1997, Money Be Man: The Popularity of Medicines in a Rural Ghanaian Community. Amsterdam: Het Spinhuis.

SPECKMANN J. D., 1991, In Memoriam Willem Frederik Lodewijk Buschkens. Medische Antropologie 3(2):25–322.

SLIKKERVEER L. J. et al., eds. 1993, The Expert Sign. Semiotics of Culture. Towards an Interface of Ethno and Cosmosystems. Leiden: DSWO Press.

STREEFLAND P. H., 1986, Medical Anthropology in Europe. The State of the Art. the Netherlands. Medical Anthropology Quarterly 17(4):91–94.

——, 1995, Enhancing Coverage and Sustainability of Vaccination Programmes. An Explanatory Framework with Special Reference to India. Social Science and Medicine 41(5):647–656.

——, ed., 1998, Problems and Potentials in International Health. Transdisciplinary Perspectives. Amsterdam: Het Spinhuis.

——, 2001, Public Doubts about Vaccination Safety and Resistance against Vaccination. Health Policy 55(3):72–159.

STREEFLAND P. H., A. M. R. CHOWDHURY and P. RAMOS-JIMENEZ, 1999, Patterns of Vaccination Acceptance. Social Science and Medicine 49(12):1705–1716.

TAN M. L., 1999, Good Medicine. Pharmaceuticals and the Construction of Power and Knowledge in the Philippines. Amsterdam: Het Spinhuis.

VAN AMELSVOORT V. F. P. M., 1964a, Early Introduction of Integrated Rural Health into a Primitive Society. A New Guinea Case Study in Medical Anthropology. Assen: Van Gorcum.

——, 1964b, Medische antropologie, een terreinverkenning. Nederlands Tijdschrift voor Geneeskunde, 108:90–128.

VAN DEN BERG J. H., 1956, Metabletica of leer der veranderingen. Nijkerk, Callenbach.

——, 1959, Het menselijk lichaam. Een metabletisch onderzoek. Vol. 1. Het geopende lichaam. Nijkerk: Callenbach.

——, 1961, Het menselijk lichaam. Een metabletisch onderzoek. Vol. 2. Het verlaten lichaam. Nijkerk: Callenbach.

VAN DER GEEST S., 1995a, Hoe gaat 't? Vijf opmerkingen over medische antropologie en etnocentrisme. Inaugural Lecture, Medical Anthropology Unit, University of Amsterdam.

——, 1995b, Editorial. Overcoming Ethnocentrism. How Social Science and Medicine Relate and Should Relate to one Another. Social Science and Medicine 40(7):869–872.

——, 1997, In memoriam Hans Speckman (1928–1997). Medische Antropologie 9(2):430–433.

——, 2002a, Introduction. Ethnocentrism and Medical Anthropology. *In* S. Van der Geest and R. Reis, eds. Ethnocentrism. Reflections on Medical Anthropology. Pp. 1–23. Amsterdam: Aksant.

——, 2002b, Respect and Reciprocity. Care of Elderly People in Rural Ghana. Journal of Cross-Cultural Gerontology 17(1):3–31.

VAN DER GEEST S. and J. HAMEL, 2001, In Memoriam Vincent van Amelsvoort (1931–2001). Medische Antropologie, 13(1):165–167.

VAN DER GEEST S. and R. REIS, eds, 2002, Ethnocentrism: Reflections on Medical Anthropology. Amsterdam: Aksant.

VAN DER GEEST S. and S. R. WHYTE, eds, 1988, The Context of Medicines in Developing Countries. Studies in Pharmaceutical Anthropology. Dordrecht: Kluwer.

VAN DER GEEST S., S. R. WHYTE and A. HARDON, 1996, The Anthropology of Pharmaceuticals. A Biographical Approach. Annual Review of Anthropology 25: 78–153.

VAN DIJK R., 1981, Ziekte en ziektegedrag bij Marokkaanse arbeiders in Nederland. Een terreinverkenning. Hilversum: JAC 't Gooi.

——, 1987, De dokter vertelde dat ik niet meer beter word! Turkse arbeidsongeschikten en somatische fixatie. Amsterdam: OSA.

——, 1998, Culture as Excuse: The Failures of Health Care to Migrants in the Netherlands. *In* The Art of Medical Anthropology. Readings. S. Van der Geest and A. Rienks, eds. Pp. 243–250. Amsterdam: Het Spinhuis.

VAN DONGEN E., 1997, Courses in Medical Anthropology: the Netherlands. Anthropology and Medicine 4(3):26–321.

——, 2000, Anthropology and Psychiatry. Two of a Kind but Where is the Other? *In* Anthropological Approaches to Psychological Medicine. Crossing Bridges. V. Skultans and J. Cox, eds. Pp. 123–456. London: Jessica Kingsley.

——, 2002a, Skeletons of the Past, Flesh and Blood of the Present. Remembrance and Older People in a South African Context. *In* Ageing in Africa. Sociolinguistic and Anthropological Approaches. S. Makoni and K. Stroeken, eds. Pp. 77–257. Aldershot: Ashgate.

——, 2002b, Walking Stories. An Oddnography of Mad People's Lives. Amsterdam: Rozenberg Publishers.

——, 2002c, Contesting Reality: Therapists and Schizophrenic People in a Psychiatric Hospital in the Netherlands. *In* Ethnocentrism. Reflections on Medical Anthropology. S. Van der Geest and R. Reis, eds. Pp. 67–90. Amsterdam: Aksant.

——, 2003, Worlds of Psychotic People. London: Routledge.

VAN DONGEN E. and S. FAINZANG, eds, 2002, Towards a Medical Anthropology of Lying. Special issue. Anthropology and Medicine 9:2.

VAN DONGEN E. and R. VAN DIJK, 2000, Migrants and Health Care in the Netherlands. *In* Health for All, All in Health. P. Vulpiani, J. Comelles and E. van Dongen, eds. Pp. 47–69. Rome: Cides/Alisei.

VAN DUURSEN N., R. REIS and H. TEN BRUMMELHUIS, 2002, Dezelfde zorg voor iedereen? Een explorerende studie naar allochtonen en autochtonen met chronische buikklachten. Amsterdam: Slotervaartziekenhuis, University of Amsterdam.

VAN OSSENBRUGGEN F. D. E., 1916, Het primitieve denken, zoals dat zich uit voor-namelijk in pokkengebruiken op Java en elders. Bijdrage tot de pre-animistische theorie. Bijdragen tot de Taal, -Land- en Volkenkunde van Nederlandsch-Indië 71:1–370.

VARKEVISSER C. M., 1996, Health Systems Research. De knikkers en het spel. Inaugural lecture, University of Amsterdam, Royal Tropical Institute.

VERDOORN J. A., 1941, Verloskundige hulp voor de inheemsche bevolking van Nederlandsch-Indië: Een sociaal medische studie (Obstetric help for the indigenous population of Dutch Indies). Gravenhage: Boekencentrum.

VERMEULEN E., 2000, Een proeve van leven. Praten en beslissen over extreme te vroeg geboren kinderen (A Trial of Life: Discussing and Deciding about Extremely Premature Babies). Amsterdam: Aksant.

VON FABER M., 2002, Maten van succes bij ouderen. Gezondheid, aanpassing en sociaal welbevinden (Measures of Success among Older People: Health, Adjustment and Social Well Being). Rotterdam: Optima.

VON FABER M., A. BOOTSMA-VAN DER WIEL, E. VAN EXEL, J. GUSSEKLOO, G. LAGAAY, E. VAN DONGEN, D. KNOOK, S. VAN DER GEEST and R. WESTENDORP, 2001, Successful Aging in the Oldest Old. Who Can Be Characterized as Successfully Aged? Archives of Internal Medicine 161:2694–2700.

VON WEIZSÄCKER V., 1927, Ueber medizinische Anthropologie. Philosophischer Anzei-ger 2:236.

VULPIANI P., J. COMELLES and E. VAN DONGEN, eds. 2000, Health for All, All in Health. European Experiences on Health Care for Migrants. Rome: Cidis/Alisei.

WARREN D. M., L. J. SLIKKERVEER and D. BROKENSHA, eds, 1995, The Cultural Dimension of Development. Indigenous Knowledge Systems. London: Intermediate Technology Publications.

WHYTE S. R., S. VAN DER GEEST and A. HARDON, 2002, Social Lives of Medicines. Cambridge: Cambridge University Press.

WOLFFERS I., I. HERMANDEZ, S. VERGHIS and M. VINK, 2002, Sexual Behaviour and Vulnerability of Migrant Workers for HIV infection. Culture, Health and Sexuality 4(4):459–473.

ZAMAN S., 2004, Broken Limbs, Broken People. Life in a Hospital Ward in Bangladesh. Amsterdam: Aksant.

Chapter 10

THE UNITED KINGDOM

British Medical Anthropology: Past, Present, and Future[1]

Ronald Frankenberg

The relationship between medicine and anthropology is intense but also tense. Medical anthropology, like other anthropologies, is oriented to past and future: history is never anything but present. (Benjamin Villefranche)

A passenger on a Malumfashi lorry knows where he wants to go, but he does not know (nor want to know) anything about engines, highway codes, maps. And when he walks the final stretch home or uses a donkey to carry his loads, he is not "switching codes." Indeed (to his father's disgust) he may be as ignorant about donkeys as he is about lorries. People do not, in my experience, face intellectual problems in embarking on the appropriate method of treatment (or travel) – there are many more pressing, practical problems to cope with. (Last 1981)

How English is English Medical Anthropology?

Nearly all the founding figures of modern British social anthropology came from outposts of Empire, especially South Africa; from elsewhere abroad, or from the equivalent of Calvin's "monstrous regiment" of women emerging from the purdah of relative academic exclusion. The writer did not, however, at once recognize the adjective "English" as appropriate in this context. Having written the paper nevertheless, the author concedes that there may after all be a distinctly, eclectic but fruitful, agnostic English way of doing medical anthropologies.

In spite of this, most medical anthropologists in Britain, like their general anthropological counterparts, derived their general theory throughout the 20th century from less eclectic, more philosophical, French precursors. To name only the most prominent, they range from Durkheim and Mauss and proceed through Griaule, Saussure and Levi-Strauss, Merleau-Ponty to Foucault (often however second hand by way of California). The more radically inclined turned to German-speaking Virchow, Marx, Freud, and Jung, although these again were often inspired by their French interpreters, Terray, Meillassoux, Godelier, and Bourdieu (see Bloch 1975). More recently Lacan, Derrida, and their feminist commentators have been added. Turning to AIDS/HIV, and other epidemics, they sought shelter from native mathomaniacs in Herzlich and

Pierret (1984, translation 1987), but left or right, East European or Asian, notwith-standing their varied national backgrounds, they "Englished" it.

For example, the current issue of the British (but international) journal *Anthro-pology & Medicine* (11(1)April:2004), edited by University College London medical anthropologist and psychiatrist, Sushrut Jadhav, is mainly devoted to papers influenced by Bourdieu and Foucault and the latters' applicability across the East–West, North–South divides. The guest editors are from Denmark; the writers from Denmark, Sweden, Germany, and Switzerland. The areas in which the research was carried out are Uganda, Burkina Faso, Tanzania, Germany, Kolkata, India, and Cambodia when still under the sway of French colonial rule. There is no overt anglophone insularity, anthropological (or even medical) isolationism or atheoretical empiricism.

One of the many aspects of their formation that British anthropologists have shared in the past with their medical counterparts, however, is a general suspicion of theory and, more recently, an obsession, positive or negative, with methodology. Empiricist individualism has been replaced by the (statistically) evidence-based – these are loosely linked by the translation of social danger into personal risk sometimes made to appear more convincing by an often ill-informed (or too astute?) arithmetical manipulation of probability theory (Prior 2001). Medical students, after a preliminary training in natural science continued into biochemistry, physiology, and anatomy, have until recently been subjected to a liminoid experience of being isolated in their access to time and space by the intensity of their hospital (total institution) training. This parallels, especially for the sensitive, the anthropologist's, until recently obligatory, socialization by simultaneous traumatization and sensitization through the imposed and prolonged exposure to the social and cultural other provided by fieldwork (Frankenberg 1994a, Good and Good 1993, Sinclair 1997).

The Late Prehistory of Modern English Medical Anthropology

Although a few British anthropologists acknowledge "medical" as their only or main professional designation, many more are also deeply involved in other fields as well, within or outwith the field. Peter Worsley (1982), for example, contributed "Non-Western Medical Systems" to the *Annual Review of Anthropology* and supervised the Ph.D. of Pauline Ong who became a professor of health planning and a part-time health service administrator in the English Midlands. Victor Turner (1964) somewhat reluctantly published only one work specifically labeled as medical. In their later detailed studies of healing practices, he and Edith Turner rethought themselves and their family through sharing Ndembu healers' and their patients' existential and emotional space (Turner and Turner 1978, see especially "Appendix A: Notes on Processual Symbolic Analysis" in Turner et al. 1992:243–255). They claimed to *know* from experience as well as *know about* from observation, and this enabled them to develop their general analysis of ritual liminality elsewhere. This and a set of concepts derived and developed from the work of Van

Gennep's *rites de passage* remains influential in British medical anthropology. It does not provide a set of answers but suggests one way of formally posing questions that helps to define the boundaries of the known and the unknown.

In the early days of the cooperation of physicians and social scientists,[2] writers referred to anthropology (or sociology) of, in or for medicine and this distinction remains useful. Anthropology *of* medicine or health-service practice looks at its subject matter as a whole; *in* medicine, health or services, it looks at individual or related parts; *for* medicine, it may be commissioned from within or imposed from without, but has the aim of advancing the activities and aims of practitioners. The last shades into the applied anthropology of medicine, which does not necessarily feel obliged to advance, at the same time, the understanding of general anthropology. However, I feel uneasy about its quality if it does not do so. One has also to distinguish between *grandes oeuvres* based on many years of dedicated immersion and minor fact-finding studies. Both are difficult to achieve and each has its importance. The former, with shared inside vision, defines theoretical questions for the discipline and, paradoxically, the limits of time, place, and situational specificities of knowledge; the latter, by providing a new context for insider knowledge, may make it sufficiently strange to be visible even to those who produce and live it, day by day.[3]

One of the earliest practitioners of medical anthropology in Britain was Derek Allcorn, whose first study, in the early 1950s, was in fact commissioned by Jerry Morris, head of social medicine at the London Hospital and by Professor R. M. Titmuss, who held the chair in social policy at the London School of Economics.[4] Allcorn's first research is innovative both because it is sited in London and uses participant observation. He studied the social network relationships of healthy young men. Peptic ulcer was then the commonest social disease of young men, and the social characteristics of its sufferers were well charted. The epidemiological physicians recognized, however, a need to know how the sick differed from the healthy. Allcorn received his Ph.D. for the work, which was never published (but see Allcorn 1994). Allcorn is also acknowledged as having read and commented on the whole content of *Sociology in Medicine* (initially a textbook for the Manchester Diploma in Public Health, an advanced training for physicians) published by South African physician and epidemiologist Mervyn Susser and Scottish social anthropologist W. Watson in 1962.[5] Chapter 2, "Culture and Health," is centerd on anthropology which also features in other chapters. Sir Douglas Black was influenced by the Manchester Social Medicine Department when he reformed the Manchester Medical School curriculum and he cited it as Chief Medical Officer in his work on inequalities in health.

Crucial Conference and US Influence

The launch-pad for medical anthropology in Britain was the annual meeting of the Association of Social Anthropologists at the University of Kent at Canterbury in the spring of 1972. Most of the papers were revised and published (Loudon 1976) as ASA Monograph 13: *Social Anthropology and Medicine* (note no medical adjective and the use of "and" rather than "of"). Twelve authors, including seven women presented eleven papers. Four came from South Africa, including Harriet Ngubane (Sibisi). Three were physicians, including Loudon. Jeanne Bisilliat presented her fieldwork-based paper on Songhay disease classification in French (translated in print by Loudon 1976:553–593). Two papers were based on fieldwork in Britain; Ruth Sulzberger on cancer in East Anglia and Vieda Skultans on spiritualism and healing in Swansea, West Wales. Murray Last's paper, based on three years' research in Nigeria, was the first of many reports on continuing field-based study there. He also aimed to provide teaching material for medical students at Ahmadu Bello University. He did not look just at the sick but the whole population as potential patients before they chose healers. His co-convenorship of medical anthropology seminars at University College London alongside his editorship of *Africa* and involvement with the IAI as well as his support of younger scholars up to and beyond his retirement in 2003 has made him a central figure in the continuing development of medical and general anthropology (see Littlewood n.d.).[6] South African Mervyn Jaspan's tragically early death meant that his paper was published posthumously (1976). His 1969 inaugural lecture on "Traditional Medical Theory in South-East Asia," given at Hull, was probably the first of its kind in Britain (he also initiated a museum including medical artefacts). Una Maclean, an anthropologically trained physician, reported on her fieldwork: "Some aspects of sickness behavior amongst the Yoruba." She later collaborated with the sociologist of psychiatry George Brown (e.g. see Brown and Harris 1989), in extending and testing his hypotheses on the social origins of mental disorder, in general, to the Scottish Island of South Uist (Brown et al. 1977). She produced a "sociological" textbook for Edinburgh nursing courses (Maclean 1974) that, like the community nursing course in Manchester, had routine lectures in anthropology.[7]

The conference and book resulted from prolonged discussions among senior scholars in anthropology initiated by South African migrant, Meyer Fortes, who had trained as a psychologist and married a practicing psychiatrist. He was, with Gluckman and Evans-Pritchard, considered a follower of Radcliffe-Brown, and seen as structural-functionalist rather than structuralist. They presented an alternative core of theory to more direct followers of functionalist Malinowski against whom they had rebelled. Firth (whose wife and field collaborator, Rosemary Firth, was a medical sociologist) was Malinowski's successor at the London School of Economics. Firth later told me, that with Fortes, Gluckman and perhaps others, as representatives, the ASA had had informal conversations with members of the General Medical Council (as they had had almost as unsuccessfully with school educational authorities) to try to get links for social anthropology into medical teaching and research. Firth felt that the project failed through the claims made by some of the anthropologists that physician educators urgently needed anthropology to correct their mistakes.

The book's extensive introductory matter and its content, the delay in publication, and the general tone suggest uneasiness about possible negative reactions from both anthropologists and physicians. Fortes had, however, put forward the possibility as soon as he became Chairman of the ASA in 1970. He created an advisory committee of three members of the association, two of whom were physicians, J(oe) B. Loudon, by then back at Swansea, and Gilbert A. Lewis who had trained at medical school and the London School of Economics and taught for most of his life at Cambridge. The third, James Woodburn, represented Association members outside the future subdiscipline and doubtful of its legitimacy. Loudon and Lewis, as was not uncommon for British medical doctors trained in the 1950s and before, came from distinguished medical families. Indeed, Loudon devoted critical pages (Loudon 1976:25–30) of his Introduction to the two related problems of recruiting medical students by patrilineal descent and either the total exclusion of women or their confinement to specialties which were thought to be centered on care rather than cure. He argued, unfashionably among medical educators of the time, that this was for unacceptable political and sociocultural rather than genetic reasons. Loudon, after his spare-time anthropological fieldwork on so-called Zulu hysteria as a medical practitioner in Natal, formally trained at the London School of Economics and then became a lecturer in anthropology at Swansea in southwest Wales. He thus lived and studied for most of his life in the Vale of Glamorgan where he had worked as a general practitioner with his father. Before retiring, his medical qualification enabled him to share the life of the Tristan da Cunha Islanders and to produce an account of their unique historical ethnography. Gilbert Lewis retired from Cambridge in 2003 but remains an active inspiration in the field for his original papers (one presented at the 1972 conference) and his books on the Gnau of New Guinea. Especially important is his extended study of the illness and death of one New Guinea man during 1968–69 – *A Failure of Treatment*, published only in 2000. It was based on intense participation in, and sharing of, experience at the time, several revisits, and 25 years of thought and consideration. He provides critical analysis of viewpoints in the field, changing through time, as well as developing methods and theories in Britain, the United States, and elsewhere since. It helps guide the reader to an understanding of past and continuing currents in British medical anthropology, many of which it critically foreshadows.

Fortes' Foreword to the 1976 volume regrets the emphasis on institutional forms and cultural schemata of earlier discussions as well as their succession by studies focused on myth, ritual and cognitive systems and modes of thought. These approaches subordinate the task of understanding human actors to theoretical analysis dominated by concepts and paradigms borrowed from linguistic theory or technical philosophy.[8] He continues, graphically:

> The analogy that comes to mind is that of a science of flight for which it is only the quantitative and physicalist variations between the flight of eagles, barnyard fowls, sparrows and jet liners that are relevant, whereas for the ornithologist there is a world of qualitative diversity to be appreciated and understood here – differences between the respective ecological niches of natural species, the goals and tasks of species maintenance, innate and acquired capacities, and so forth, let alone the more fundamental differences between natural fliers and the artefacts represented by the jet plane. (Fortes 1996:X)

He argues that health and illness appertain peculiarly to individuals and to the human actor and since these are heuristically satisfactory concepts for directing attention to the most critical determinants of human existence, the focus has to be on the actors, their reactions and interpretations. This apparent paradox of paying close attention to personal experience on both sides of the healer/patient divide (and latterly that of the anthropologist) but within the framework of the meticulous study of social process still remains the central feature of most British medical anthropology. Whether this is analyzed qualitatively or quantitatively, it is the objective data on subjectivity which underlie the claim of anthropology practitioners, that they do not to give answers in advance relating to individual instances but make it possible to ask informed, evidence-based questions. One way in which this has been creatively developed has been by a distinguished line of medical anthropologists at the London School of Hygiene and Tropical Medicine,[9] Robert Pool (1984, 2000) argues that, given the merger of cultures that a meeting of minds, actions, and shared time in fieldwork involves, it is the emergence and reemergence of a series of hybrid, temporarily shared, cultures which are the substrate of final analysis:

> This ethnography is the product of the difference resulting from my initial lack of understanding of local interpretations and competence in the vernacular. After all, had I been a native I would probably not have found the terms that are the subject of this ethnography problematic and therefore intriguing in the first place, and I would not have felt the need to spend so much time enquiring about their meanings. My enquiries were fruitful because as I did not initially know what people were talking about I had to construct my own, partially unique understanding. Yet the interpretation is not simply a result of my lack of understanding. It is rather, a product of enquiries, generated on the one hand by my anthropological knowledge and my ignorance of local language and culture, and, on the other, by my informants' interpretations of their culture and their attempts [to] teach me the meanings of vernacular terms.

Proficiency is necessary, but it has to be developed gradually *during* fieldwork and *through* fieldwork. Of course the ethnographer will make mistakes in his translations, of course he will retranslate texts as his competence increases, revise interpretations, change his mind. The natives will also change their minds and revise their interpretations (as a result of the contaminating "paraliterate feedback" of which Owusu is so afraid). But that is what ethnography is all about, and it should therefore be explicitly presented rather than shamefully effaced from the final monograph.

> Fluctuation, fragmentation and indeterminacy are only a problem as long as we continue to assume the pre-existence of an external objective reality or an underlying order capable of being gradually revealed by the application of proper research methodology or analytical techniques and then authentically represented in the final monograph through some form of literary realism. Once we accept that "real" native culture does not exist out there in some pure or pristine form waiting to be discovered

and represented by the ethnographer, but that ethnography is, above all, shared praxis, dialogue, performance and production, in which communication is often not unambiguous and complete but indeterminate and fragmentary, then the problem appears in another light. (Pool 1994:238–239)

Fortes' preface argued that as anthropologists we are entitled and qualified to study non-Western people. It cited as a still useful but surprising outcome of such studies, Rivers's observation that Torres Straits Islanders were "more rational than us" in that their "modes of diagnosis follow more directly from ideas of causation". Nevertheless Fortes felt that Rivers's emphasis is more psychological than it is either physiological or sociocultural and he fails to provide a correlation of "leech-craft" with Western scientifically objective[?] accounts of pathology (xiii–xiv). This would have been one way of testing how strongly a priori beliefs and ideas prevailed in the face of inescapable facts of nature accessible to the observation and understanding of a prescientific culture. Fortes asserts that such an approach to some extent prevails and leads to transcultural psychiatry. He sees this as unfortunate and as having misled Turner and Evans-Pritchard into the adoption of emic categories and thence into reductionist overemphasis on sorcery, magic, and socially readjustive ritual practices. They left, as mere residual categories, rational diagnosis, treatment, and prophylaxis. The book he is introducing ought properly to have put the emphasis on the person and her/his treatment rather than on the nature of illness treatment in general. In so far as it deals with healers it should also deal with the healer in person rather than the healers' craft in abstract terms. In short the aim should be to analyze the lived experiences, pleasant and unpleasant, of individuals, families and communities reflecting complex processes, which crosscut several levels of existence. All types of medicine including our own are based on both providing interpretations and attempting to control the processes underlying lived experience of this kind. Despite the best forecasts based on "actuarial virtuosity," uncertainty of incidence and outcome still remain and Evans-Pritchard's account of the Zande sociocultural questions "Why me? Why now? Whose fault is it?" are still as central as when they were identified in Western medicine by its socialist historian and theorist (Sigerist 1951:157). This is, in Fortes's view:

> perhaps . . . the core of any anthropological study of a system of medicine, viewed as an institutional apparatus of defence against the incursion of pain and the ever looming threat of annihilation that is the human lot. (xix–xx)

Loudon's introduction is even more directive about what should and should not have been included and had more force in having been, at least in part, formally communicated to contributors in advance. The injunctions were not in the event sanctioned by exclusion of the paper from the conference, although offending paper-writers (including Leeson and Frankenberg) were sharply criticized in the oral discussion and unmentioned, rather than rebuked, in the printed introduction. He was most concerned, as a medical practitioner himself, to distinguish the experienced practitioner from the merely trained, even if expert, physician. Despite the eminence of the Torres Straits ethnographers and their later Fellowships of the Royal Society, their anthropology, like their medicine was, notwithstanding their fieldwork experience, obsessed with medical and psychological theories. They overlooked the pragmatic within the then accepted Western tradition of a balanced mix of science, arts and humanities, in theory, fact and practice. At that time, and even very recently, when the General Medical Council called for more attention to patient experience in the training of doctors, it was quick to rename its proposed social science input "behavioral science" and largely to interpret it as psychological or consumer based. This could be presented as less critically threatening than supposedly radical sociologists critical of society at large or anthropologists who seemed at best to be half-hearted enthusiasts for colonial rule, direct or indirect. Loudon had little enthusiasm for either behavioral or social science. He saw vocational knowing and caring about patients as commonsense and fitting social science into the curriculum could be a threat to the time needed to give training in "real" science. This paradoxically, in Loudon's view, opened a space for those whom he styled medically trained dream scientists, exemplified by Oliver Sachs and R. D. Laing ("a pied piper"), with idealist dreams of total health rather than amelioration, cure, or care. The last of these in Loudon's view was already more subordinate than it should be. He did not, then, relate this to the fact that carers were doubly muted as nurses, and for the most part, women.

He presents the homespun ethics of a traditional country doctor as a model of reality for the would-be anthropologist (see Berger and Mohr 1967 whom he cites approvingly), and at the same time perhaps underestimates the possibility of change to a more considered understanding for the practitioner.[10] He concludes this section first by a plea for the practitioner to seek efficacy rather than popularity (later he suggests that in medical emergency, the equivalent to the methods of the plumber may sometimes be more desirable than those associated with a priest) and for the anthropologist to remember the blood and guts, combined with a sense of impending doom, that inhabits the patients' and doctors' common experience of mundane medicine.

Loudon does not mention that between the conference and the book report, he and I together with Roger Jeffery from Edinburgh had serendipitously been invited by Charles Leslie[11] to attend a workshop conference on "Theoretical Foundations for the Comparative Study of Medical Systems" (see Leslie 1978). Arthur Kleinman there presented the ideas, which became central topics of debate in US medical anthropology for several decades. These include the conceptual distinction between illness and disease; folk, popular, and professional. Loudon and Frankenberg, invited too late to write papers in advance, almost inadvertently, in the spirit of necessity for dialogue, adopted views which were both oppositional and diverse; Loudon, by leaving early, and because, perhaps in a characteristically English way, his theoretical astuteness was muted by its interment in empirical example, became general scapegoat and is little mentioned in the discussion summaries (Dunn and Good 1978; Thomas 1978). Both nevertheless later helped to carry Kleinman's concepts of explanatory models; illness, disease, and sickness and folk, popular, and professional (and later still Scheper Hughes and Lock's three bodies) back into British discourse, if only as supplementary to concepts derived from Evans-Pritchard and Victor Turner.

Part of Loudon's introduction to the Kent conference is, in fact, devoted to unpacking and complicating these concepts of Kleinman at the same time as he discusses their differential import to specialists and nonspecialists. Using Willis's initial work on the Fipa (1972), he finds Kleinman useful in understanding similarities as well as differences between relatively undeveloped societies in Africa and those "dominated by scientific" professional medicine. Medicine, like life itself, finds its place and performance sometimes in the private spaces of domesticity, even in the bed, and sometimes in public places. Consultation, the healer's and the patient's central activity, can occur at either site but always includes an element of performance which lends itself to classic anthropological participation, observation, and analysis; all parties involved may play dramatically to the gallery. Loudon's was more directive advance material than that of earlier conferences. He recognized that anthropologist/physician collaboration had been most effective in the fields of public health/epidemiology and psychiatry, but he discouraged papers in these fields and asked contributors to focus on normality and deviation in terms of biological lifecycle[12] rather than lifecourse; on disease experienced as pathological process seen in terms of invader or as internal disorder, exopathic or endogenous, and the distinction between illness and disease.

General Position in the Field

There have been two main learned societies engaged in the encouragement and regulation of anthropology in Britain. The older and more general, the Royal Anthropological Institute (RAI), publisher of, inter alia, *MAN* and the *Journal of the Royal Anthropological Institute*, is open to all those seriously interested, even as comparative amateurs, and is a continuation of bodies founded in the early-19th century. It provides a general umbrella organization for (mainly British) anthropologists. It performs a generalized, supportive, and sometimes a representative role for them. It has played a particularly important role for medical anthropology. The Association of Social Anthropologists very consciously founded in 1946 as a professional, British Commonwealth, academic association of specifically social anthropologists with doctorates and/or substantial publications in the subject. Those initially thought to be acceptable were almost all employed in university positions in Britain or the Commonwealth and had done overseas fieldwork research. Its title is, of course, significant for the adjectives that it omits. These are biological (called physical at the time), cultural, and material-cultural. Anthropologists focusing on these areas were likely to fail the, at first very rigorous, exclusive, in camera, vetting procedure. Many of the established figures involved in medical anthropology have been associated with both organizations, which are now much more closely associated with each other.[13] The RAI was more welcoming towards the more specialist medical anthropologists. It has had many medical fellows since its earliest days and also has a Wellcome-endowed biennial medal award for anthropological contribution to medical research.[14] Its London premises are readily accessible to the main centers of developing medical anthropology at University College and its associated hospitals, the School of Oriental and African Studies, and the London School of Hygiene and Tropical Medicine. One of the pioneers of teaching medical anthropology as such was Richard Burghart at the School of Oriental and African Studies. Jan Savage remembers hearing about his lectures there when she was an undergraduate at the London School of Economics. She was able to cross institutions and take this module, which she describes as inspirational. He later succeeded Karl Jettmar at the South Asia Institute at Heidelberg. He was American by birth and interested mainly in Nepal where he had done most of his fieldwork. The SAI website says that he was very much interested in modern anthropological theories and infused the spirit of British social anthropology into the mainstream of German ethnology which was still wedded to the idea that nonliterate tribes are the proper subject of this discipline. Unfortunately he died of a brain tumor in 1993 at the age of 49 and was unable to complete his mission (Burghart 1988; Reisland and Burghar 1998). When the informally run and structured British Medical Anthropology Society was revived as a formal committee, the RAI was and continued to be its natural home.[15] After much deliberation and consultation, the now official RAI subcommittee produced a general definition of the subject which goes realistically and beneficially far beyond that envisaged by its "social" pioneers:

> *Medical Anthropology* represents the application of anthropological understanding and methods to issues of health, sickness and suffering. Whilst generally a subdiscipline within social and cultural anthropology, medical anthropology in this wide sense extends to the work of biological anthropologists (for example in population genetics and ecology), archaeologists (e.g. paleopathology), ethnologists and psychologists (e.g. cognition in non human primates), and physicians, nurses and other health professionals (conceptualisations of sickness, pathways into professional care). As a body of knowledge, medical anthropology owes a considerable debt to other disciplines which include biomedicine, history and sociology, development and area studies, psychotherapy and psychoanalysis, linguistics and philosophy.[16]

Medical Anthropology and Public Health

English medical anthropology, especially when related to epidemiology and public health, came suddenly of age with the AIDS/HIV epidemic in 1981. There was initially medical and political panic. This led to the wider recognition of social science as responsible and perhaps even useful (Frankenberg 1995). Medical anthropologists and sociologists found themselves summoned to high-level policy meetings. Phil Strong, an ethnographic sociologist, was first director and then, for a period, codirector with Virginia Berridge of the research program in the department of Public Health and Policy at the London School of Hygiene and Tropical Medicine. The account of the history of AIDS policy in the UK (Berridge 1996) says little about the anthropological contribution and still less about its reflexive effect on anthropology.[17] Phil Strong died suddenly and the gap was partially filled by Rosaline Barbour and Guro Huby (1998), in a book dedicated to his memory. The last chapter (14) is a posthumously published article of his, introduced and presented by his long term companion in both domestic and professional activity, anthropologist Anne Murcott (Strong 1998).[18] The book is also valuable in that it draws attention to two unique features of British medical anthropology. The first is its continuous close association with both the Medical Research Council and Social Science Research Council and its research units, which were already at that time predominantly operating in Scotland. Second, it recognized the value of social anthropological and sociological (and other) contributions to health studies in general and encouraged synergies. This continues and is supplemented by the MRC Health Services collaboration formed in 1998, and centering on, but not confined to, the Bristol Department of Social Medicine. A leading figure in this is Stephen Frankel, a collaborator with Gilbert Lewis in Papua New Guinea. This radiates through a network extending towards the Northeast.[19]

Another important Scottish research enterprise has been the Public Health Research Unit[20] at the University of Glasgow. Under its auspices, Marina Barnard, a Glasgow University social anthropologist, carried out with Neil McKeganey a series of ethnographic studies of prostitute women and/or drug users who used hypodermic needles in the Glasgow Area (McKeganey and Barnard 1992) which followed analysis with creative policy proposals.

Several anthropologists worked with, attended, helped to organize, contributed to and continue to attend the British Sociological Association's major subgroup, the Medical Sociology Group's annual and local conferences. Some have given plenary addresses to it over the years. The several beneficial consequences of this are spelled out in the introductory matter to Barbour and Huby (1998). One of these, which is worth noting in the light of current controversy about what is significant and what is trivial, is the reference (1998:4) to Michael Herzfeld:

> sensitivity to immediate context . . . helps shift the focus away from perspectives that are already, to some extent, determined by the structures they were set up to examine. (Herzfeld 1992:15)

Another was the early presentation at the same series of conferences of Davey Smith et al. (1993) which reports on field observation of the complicated local ethnoscience of childhood diarrhea classification and its impact on the effectiveness of health reform in Nicaragua and helps the understanding of the urban/rural divide's role in undermining the support of its then government. A very major contribution to the social anthropological understanding of AIDS over a period of over more than 15 years has been that of Sophie Day of Goldsmith's College in London working closely with Helen Ward, at first a clinician and then an epidemiologist, at Imperial College. They, at first almost alone in the world, sympathetically, objectively, and pragmatically investigated the fourth scapegoat of the famous four H's; Homosexuals, Haitians, Heroin addicts, and Hookers. They offered health services to, and studied the lifestyle in detail of, first London street-walking sex workers, and later those elsewhere, and found that their use of condoms made them least likely to give or receive HIV from their clients. At the time their findings averted blame but were later generalized into an argument to suggest cutting preventive and welfare services for prostitute women, worldwide. Nevertheless, as anthropologists often do, they set an example of the importance of direct and subject cooperative observation as an answer, as against the "informed" but prejudiced guess (Day 2000; Day and Ward 2004; Day et al. 1988).

Mary Douglas's study of *Leviticus* (1999), works on risk and *How Institutions Think* (1987), have all influenced medical anthropologists in Britain as they have elsewhere. AIDS also stimulated her into publishing, in collaboration with Breton, Maurice Calvez, a rare direct contribution showing how her cultural theory could be applied to epidemics (Douglas and Calvez 1990).

Perhaps, however, the most dramatic intervention of anthropology was not in relation to AIDS but in the popular field of cardiac epidemiology in the much[21] studied areas of South Wales (Davison et al. 1991, 1992; Frankenberg 1994b). Charlie Davison and his colleagues[22] encouraged doctors and health promoters to document the process of "lay" epidemiology based on direct observation of cases rather than statistical probabilities. Seeing that expressions of scepticism about health education messages were rational responses based on claims to have an "Uncle Norman" who smoked like a chimney and lived into his eighties; or to know a villager who was the least likely "candidate" for a heart attack who had prematurely succumbed, this provided ways of reexamining the wisdom of current approaches to health education and drawing attention to statistical realities and anomalies. Anthropologists whether medically qualified or not can, as Loudon argued at the first conference, most effectively advance medical anthropology by, through, and in practice (see also Lambert 1998; Lambert and McKevitt 2002).[23] General practitioner Julian Tudor Hart's (1988) long term observations of his South Wales practice and full involvement with most aspects of his patients' lives led him to sharing knowledge with patients in practical *danger* rather than merely at theoretical *risk*. He also, of course, kept quantitative data on each of his patients and had no aversion to counting or calculating when that was necessary or useful. Davison and his medical colleagues began to provide one kind of epidemiology (as the anthropologists of AIDS/HIV are also able to do) which can be created and used by potential patients and self-help and community-based organizations. Multiplying in-depth analyses of repeated single cases by all the social actors involved, especially in chronic and recurring disorders (Strauss et al. 1985), can do more than provide less than generalizable answers, it can provide questions. There remain however a persisting methodological clash between a preferred kind of quantitative methodology of neo-Cochraneism (loosely and misleadingly labeled as if it were the only source of evidence-based medicine) and the particularism of the more conventionally anthropological of anthropologists. This is often too antagonistic to be easily overcome but can sometimes be the stimulus (as just described) to important new ways of seeing not available to either disciplinary approach on its own.

Medical Anthropology and Psychiatry

Epidemiologists and medical anthropologists can fruitfully and in complementary fashion explore and exploit the same habitat (Frankenberg 1984). Psychiatry and anthropology, at least in the person of some not entirely rare scholars, often unite in one physical body or several institutional bodies to show truly hybrid vigor. A recent collection of 12 conference papers, all but three written by scholars and/or practitioners working within Britain, helps to demonstrate the above assertion (Skultans and Cox 2000; see also Skultans 2003a, 2003b;[24] Littlewood and Dein 2000) This collection was edited by an experienced social anthropologist, present at the 1972 conference, and a president of the Royal College of Psychiatrists. In it, Roland Littlewood[25] even turns his ethnographic skills on to "Psychiatry's Culture." This, he argues, is necessary because Western medicine seeks to be a naturalistic science and to play down its cultural values both relating to the social relation between patient and doctor as well as to the local understandings through which suffering is experienced. He continues:

> It objectifies experience as if our experience was constructed out of natural entities and, ascribing to them the conditions of our clinical observation, it reifies our personal contingencies as biological necessity. As the French anthropologist, Pierre Bourdieu (1977:96) has put it in Marxist style, "the observer transfers into the object the principles of his relation to the object"; as indeed we do when we talk of "psychiatry" as some entity rather than as actions of certain individuals in their particular moral and political world. (Littlewood 2000:66)

By his endorsement of Bourdieu's antifetishist approach in the style of Marx, he also endorses the important difference between the meaning ascribed to culture by most British social anthropologists (as against some, US cultural anthropologists), namely that cultural analysis is an analysis of experienced process rather than a description and reification of a thing-like entity. This also, until recently, even more sharply divided the theoretical approach of anthropology, by and of nurses and midwives in Britain from many in the United States.

Littlewood's (2000) recent work based on his prestigeful Wilde Lectures at All Souls College, Oxford, shows how it is possible to pursue a kind of applied medical anthropology which, combined with psychiatry, ethnographic perception, philosophical understanding, and history and above all a sensitivity to the creative cultural healing and other processes of very diverse religious movements (for examples, an Earth Mother in Trinidad, Hassidic Rabbinic Prophets in London and New York[26]), can make a major contribution to anthropology as a whole.

There is another interesting and productive hybridity at a different level of clinical psychological activity, namely systemic or family therapy. This owes its very existence to a now neglected, originally English, genius of applied anthropology, Gregory Bateson (1972 et passim). It comes from the research and practice, first at the Marlborough Clinic, and then at the Tavistock Centre, of Inga-Britt Krause (1998, 2003) which most recently poses the problem of "Learning how to ask in ethnography and psychotherapy."[27]

The specifically anthropological study of psychiatric institutions pioneered by Caudill (1958) in the United States does not seem to have been much followed in the UK. Although one of the editors, Neil Mckeganey, of Michael Bloor et al. (1988) wrote his Ph.D. (1982) about a Camphill, Rudolf Steiner Therapeutic Community (see Bloor et al. passim and bibliography for publications on others). Iain Edgar, who has since concentrated on anthropology in relation to dreams, also did his first fieldwork on a therapeutic community (Edgar 1986, 1990). The only published book seems to be Rapoport (1960).[28]

"Medical" Anthropology with Nursing and Midwifery

If the association with public health produced sparks of enlightenment out of a certain antagonism, while in psychiatry, as I have suggested, offspring arose with hybrid vigor from this combination, anthropology in the British situation was enthusiastically incorporated and embodied into practice and research by those nurses and midwives who came across it. One reason for this may be that until very recently (and often still) nurses have been "muted" if not silenced (they spoke but were not heard) in the context of their work (see Ardener 1975; Hart 1991; Savage 1995). Anthropology supplied a language and a voice through which they could be heard. This was in sharp contrast to the very early US situation where the idea that culture was a thing possessed by ethnic minorities or even "other races and religions" which nurses should be aware of, sometimes led to isolation from the mainstream of medical anthropology (see Leininger 1991 and, by contrast, Alan Harwood's very different approach (1981a, 1981b)). Leininger's work, however good its intentions, often led to overuse of reified concepts; of fixed cultural practices rather than observation of processes involving nurses, other staff, and patients in ward and clinic. In Britain a different approach came from many directions in the late-1980s and early-1990s. Holden and Littlewood's work (1991) has already been mentioned. Two full- and part-time master's courses centrally focused on medical anthropology were established at Brunel (directed by Ian Robinson[29]) and Keele (directed by Alan Prout[30] and later Jeanette Edwards) that warmly welcomed nurses with an appropriate second qualification or experience whether it was a degree or diploma, professional or other. The first annual course at Brunel attracted a former senior paediatric nurse[31] from the Department of Health and the leading infection control nurse as well as other nationally known senior nurses. Before the end of the century, approaching 300 nurses had received master's degrees from these two departments alone. Several amongst these, and others from elsewhere in England, Scotland, and Wales, have moved on to doctorates and to lecturing, research and practice in the university departments of nursing, midwifery and primary care which have now become central to nursing education.

Jan Savage was at about the same time (1992) appointed to the Royal College of Nursing Institute,[32] partly to help support the first master's degree in midwifery. She had earlier published on gender and sexuality in nursing (1987) and carried out a path-breaking ethnographic study of nurse–patient interaction as it emerged from a form of innovative ward organization "widely referred to as 'new nursing' Savage 1990" (Savage 1995:1). She brought to this her experience of a fieldwork-based Ph.D. on English notions of procreation and kinship (1991). In this she had found:

> that a notion of "closeness" that referred to an emotional intimacy was central to understanding family or "blood" relationships. . . . Before this, "closeness" in European and American kinship studies had been largely neglected by anthropologists or was widely assumed to refer to similarity of bodily substance, such as genetic material. I was intrigued to see "closeness" being used by nurses to refer to an occupational relationship and to see that the meaning of the term was still taken for granted. At the beginning of the study, there was little reason to suspect that there was a connection between the two notions of "closeness"; one referred to the discrete domain of kinship and the other to the domain of nursing. However, during the research, kinship relations emerged as potential models for nurse–patient relationships and the giving of care. Moreover, it seems that the cultural construct of "closeness" plays an important part in the structuring of relationships across a number of domains.
>
> In terms of the study's findings, very briefly, these suggest that "closeness" is understood as a form of rapport which allows self disclosure or "openness." (1995:3)[33]

Her general approach gives some indication of the way that mainstream anthropology both informed her courses and those of others, then and since, and how far the anthropological, external and self-understanding of nurses has traveled both from their original characterization as a bureaucratic problem for medical administrators in otherwise useful works like the first edition of Susser and Watson (1962) and even their recent characterization by sociologists of organizations as a problem "tribe" at war with equally "tribal" doctors in official government reports (Frankenberg 2002). The courses were followed up by a conference in 1995 organized under the auspices of the health section of *Anthropology in Action*. One nursing colleague who was particularly active in this last activity, Chris McKevitt at Kings College, is also involved in the Bristol-centered research network described elsewhere in the paper (see most recently Lambert et al. 2002; McKevitt 2000; McKevitt and Wolfe 2002; McKevitt et al. 2003). An Ethnography and Health Group consisting mainly of nurses and midwives currently meets in London under the convenorship of Jan Savage (until recently a full time researcher at the Royal College of Nursing Institute). It has done so for about five years on an informal basis and it has, in addition, organized conferences with keynote speakers including Ian Robinson from Brunel and Paul Atkinson from Cardiff.

Complementary and Alternative Medicines[34]

British social anthropologists, although they, like their counterparts abroad, have been interested in pluralism elsewhere (e.g., Frankenberg 1981; Frankenberg et al. 1976, 1977; Lambert 1996) have (in contrast to those in many other parts of Europe) paid scant attention to the folk traditions when they turned their attention to the culture and social organization of their home lands (see Philpin 2003 for a rare and recent exception of a study in the field). Nor until recently did they concern themselves with the professionally unorthodox as against conventional biomedicine (despite historical and recent Royal and aristocratic patronage of both anthropology and unconventional healing). Jean Comaroff from the United States mentions it in her early papers (1976a, 1976b) on general practice written when she was at Swansea and Manchester in 1971/72; the American Hans Baer did extensive studies of osteopathy and other therapies in Britain in the 1970s. Comaroff centered her discussion of it around the idea of placebo effects, which Ursula Sharma (1992), in the book that pioneered the serious long term anthropological study of *complementary and alternative medicine* in Britain, gently and modestly (but nevertheless firmly) reproaches as a methodological device.

> I am not very enthusiastic about the use of the term "placebo effect" as an explanatory concept since I believe it conflates all those symbolic aspects of the healing process which medical sociologists and medical anthropologists (and many holistic) practitioners regard as important. The problem for both orthodox and nonorthodox medicine is to identify precisely which factors in the treatment process contribute to the placebo effect in any particular kind of case – is it the fact of having been given something to take or do? Is it the confidence inspired by the practitioner's manner or personality. These may be very difficult to disentangle from the more concrete aspects of the treatment (the substances administered, the manipulation or massage, the insertion of the needles, the dietary changes recommended). (1992:74)

This advice alone, to all anthropologists studying healing practices, who often accept the explanations of Western biomedicine unquestioningly and those of others with scepticism, underlines the value of adding alternative medicine to the anthropologists' stock-in trade. By and large British medical anthropologists of *complementary and alternative medicine* have not followed up, in their research, either the political economy approach of Baer (1984) or the classification of folk, popular, and professional suggested by Kleinman. They have however contributed to the theoretical arguments about pluralism, often from the inside, as practitioners themselves. They have been particularly concerned recently with the problems that arise out of the dynamics of change in practice, not so much out of mechanical contact of cultures, as out of the conflicting expectations of patients and healers in polycultural rather than merely multicultural contexts. The focus has been on holistic, rather than Cartesian, embodied experience and the meanings to which the former gives rise to. Sharma suggests (personal communication, 2004) that a common interest in complementary medicine more readily overrides undue emphasis on the differences between sociological and anthropological approaches than do conventional interests.

Recent and Current Developments[35]

The organization of the British National Health Service is currently undergoing a measure of rethinking, not least in the revision and continuing standardization of medical education as well as education and training of other professionals within it. This is being accompanied by a reorganization also of the university system that in some universities is opening up opportunities for medical anthropology to contribute in new as well as established ways.

The University of Bristol does not have an anthropology department as such, but as we have already seen houses a number of leading anthropologists mainly in alliance with epidemiology but also with psychiatry and sociology. It is the organizing center for interuniversity workshops in most of the fields of collaboration we have discussed.

Brunel University has consolidated its custombuilt M.Sc. in medical anthropology (now directed by Melissa Parker, the Oxford human sciences graduate crossing the social/biological/anthropology divide, who also directs its extensive international medical anthropology program) in association and sharing courses with master's programs on the cultures of children and on psychoanalysis. One innovative course given by Eric Hirsch, called the Anthropology of Human Kinds, draws on the work among others of Ian Hacking, Allan Young, Geoff Bowker, and Susan Leigh Star, to show how amongst other experiences human beings shape and are shaped specifically by their bodily sufferings. Cecil Helman, a pioneer in the field of teaching anthropology first to general practitioners of which he is one, and later to nurses and other clinical professionals, has an appointment there, although he also teaches at the University College London, Cambridge and elsewhere (see Helman 2001). Medical anthropology also encouraged the development, and feeds directly into, the university's increasingly important focus on international public health.

Cambridge is one of the first (perhaps historically because of the tripos system) of the several departments that now offer intercalated bachelor's degrees in anthropology to its medical students. Others are Durham (which also offers them to students from other medical schools), Goldsmith's London, Kent (in association with King's College Hospital in London), and Oxford. Cambridge also produces large numbers of doctorates and medical anthropology has been for many years a specialization in its undergraduate degrees. A new development in 2003 was the initiation of comparative studies in biotechnology and accountability (CBA) by Marilyn Strathern (chair) and Maryon McDonald (director). Its fifteen or so associates provide links with institutions in London as well as to Cambridge Genetics.

Its first publication, edited by McDonald (forthcoming), is *Languages of Account-ability* (see also Konrad 2003).

Durham's approach to medical anthropology emphasizes the shared contributions of social and biological anthropology. The latter has been strongly present in the work and teaching of Catherine Panter-Brick for some years and reinforced by the recent recruitment of Tessa Pollard. Although students choose a compulsory module in either medical or biological anthropology, in the optional courses they are presented with the possibility of interesting combinations of social, cultural, and biological approaches often related to individual medical and public health issues.

The work of Sophie Day at Goldsmith's College in the University of London has already been mentioned. Brian Morris, now emeritus, introduced medical anthropology there some years ago and Pat Caplan, ex head of department is still extremely active. She has researched food use in southwest Wales and edited published sets of papers related to concepts of risk (2000) and to food especially in relation to health (1997), both of which are central to the teaching of medical anthropology. Simon Cohn's recent research has been concerned with the social anthropological study of knowledge creation from the use of imaging techniques in brain research in particular and in medicine in general. He also has many doctoral students and has now introduced dedicated masters' degrees.

The University of Kent at Canterbury is, under the leadership of its head of department, Roy Ellen (significantly styled professor of anthropology and human ecology), developing a medical anthropology program on public medicine in a unique and exciting way based not merely, as has been done in the past, on public health, but also on environmental medicine and related specialisms. Although a full medical anthropology degree is a recent innovation, as Roy Ellen's title suggests, the department has very long experience unparalleled in Britain of social scientists in general and social anthropologists in particular working in close cooperation with so-called "hard" scientists. There are plans to provide medical education in Kent and in London. They also plan to introduce a medical anthropology B.Sc. as an intercalated year for medics, as well as an M.Sc. on general offer. They have recruited extra staff and intend to teach not only social anthropology but also bioanthropology approaches, including epidemiology, nutrition, and human ecology. They will also develop medical ethnobotany and ethnopharmacology as part of their ethnobotany program, making use of their existing links with the Joderell Laboratory at Kew Gardens and the School of Pharmacy in London.

The Institute of Social and Cultural Anthropology (ISCA) at Oxford University has, through Professor David Parkin, long been a center of medical anthropology and research. As has been noted above, Oxford's Human Sciences undergraduate degree has been a major supply of combined social science and human biology graduates to other medical anthropology centers. ISCA has also intended for some time to develop a specifically focused master's degree in medical anthropology. The appointment of Elizabeth Hsu has made this possible, and it had a temporary uniqueness in its approach until the course at Kent got under way. The courses are in their general aims similar, although Kent is perhaps more adapted to practical ecological intervention overseas, while Oxford shares this interest but leans beneficially towards studying and learning from the past. Hsu has used her fieldwork and scholarly knowledge of Chinese culture to illuminate and analyze the dynamic aspects of developments of medicine in China itself (1999) as well as its changing impact in other parts of the modern world including, especially, her empirical research area, Tanzania.

The University of Sussex instituted an M.A. in Medical Anthropology during the academic year 1903/4 under the leadership of Maya Unnithan, importantly offering a unique link with their Institute of Development Studies.

Like the four-field pattern (archaeology, biology, culture, linguistics) of the United States as against social anthropology in Britain, there will continue to be the two extremes, their combination and the various compromises. What is beyond argument is that medical anthropology in all its diversity has an important role to play not only in the development of its parent fields but also in the various fields of shared interest discussed here. In addition, there are probably other fields that the author is not yet aware of, but that may well already exist in the minds and as yet unpublished writings of others.[36]

Notes

1. The reader should know that this chapter is written by a person who absentmindedly drifted into emerging medical anthropology, as it was beginning to be titled, 30 years ago. This followed 20 years after his purposeful but unresentful abandonment, after the first undergraduate degree stage, of an intended medical career for that of social anthropology in general. His return to interest in health and disease he owes largely to Dr Joyce Leeson, with whom he was privileged to live and work in the UK and in Zambia, as well as to other members and associates of the then Department of Social Medicine in Manchester in the 1960s.

2. Holden and Littlewood (1991), in their book on anthropology and nursing, adopt a similar strategy. See also the excellent review of this by Kathryn Hopkins Kavanagh (1993).

3. Davis (2000) is a brilliant exemplar of the former and Hart (1991) of the latter.

4. Titmuss was innocent of even school-leaving certificates, or indeed formal training, let alone a degree of any kind (see the subtly nuanced discussion of the relationships of eugenics, social medicine, and medical sociology in Oakley 1997).

5. Watson's research for his original Ph.D., a study of, *inter alia*, health, in a Scottish mining village was rejected at Cambridge as anthropology because it was based in Scotland and as sociology because Cambridge did not recognize the subject. He was eventually awarded the consolation prize of an M.Sc. His Ph.D. was a study of the Mambwe in what is now Zambia. He worked with Allcorn and others on mental and other health problems in Leigh, Lancashire.

6. This is based on the tribute seminar held to mark his official retirement in 2003 and includes papers from Finland, Belgium, Italy and Holland (two), even so a considerable understatement of his international influence and standing. The use of the plural "anthropologies" in the title points to the wide range of theoretical and empirical

topics covered, and "on knowing and not knowing" is borrowed from an earlier paper of Last himself (1981), and a recognition of his scholarship which acknowledges and encourages awareness of knowing what one does not know.

7. One of the nurses who suffered this from Watson, the present writer, and Max Gluckman himself (all in retrospect monumentally uninformed about the realities of nursing), Judith Monks found the experience less than enlightening at the time, but later gained a research master's in medical anthropology at Keele, worked in Latin America and taught on medical anthropology master's courses both at Keele and Brunel. Her Ph.D. used phenomenological anthropological theory to analyze the situation of people with multiple sclerosis in the UK (see Monks and Frankenberg 1995).

8. Out of charity or certainty that his audience would understand, he fails to preface the adjectives with the implied modifiers "continental," Leachian, or even "sociological."

9. MacCormack, Kris Heggenhougen, Ann Murcott. and Helen Lambert. Others, including Gillian Hundt , Jessica Ogden, and Karina Kilman, have worked on specific projects. Paul Wenzel Geissler, a convert from epidemiology and biology, is currently a fellow senior lecturer to Robert Pool. Geissler, with a Ph.D. from Copenhagen and a Ph.D. from Cambridge, has conducted long term fieldwork amongst the Luo in Western Kenya and is currently preparing a comparative study on aging, memory, and death in East Africa and the UK. Amongst all these, Carol MacCormack, who taught there for ten years, exercised a profound influence from there and earlier from Cambridge on both feminist and medical anthropology in Britain (see Heggenhougen's obituary 1997).

10. General practice has had little attention from medical anthropologists in Britain to this day with the notable exceptions of Jean Comaroff and textbook author, anthropologist, artist, writer, and general practitioner, Cecil Helman (1978, 1987a, 1987b, 2001), also originally from South Africa.

11. Leslie had invited Jeffery as a fellow Indianist, but had been urged by his NSF and Wenner Gren sponsors to add, at the last minute, nonspecialists on Asia, and to seek a wider international representation. He had already as Asian specialists Francis Zimmerman from CNRS Paris and Paul Inschuld from Marburg in Germany. Michael Banton, former editor of the series of ASA monographs was staying with Leslie in Rochester at the time and recommended Frankenberg and Loudon. The fact that the representatives of the UK came from Scotland, England, and Wales respectively was a happy chance.

12. Conception, growth, maturation, senescence, and death including comparison with animals and its place in organic systems.

13. Many were also members of the American Anthropological Association and its section, the Society for Medical Anthropology, or at least attended its meetings. At least two were Malinowski Lecturers of the US Society for applied anthropology (Sfaa).

14. 2003 Kit Davies, 1998 Allan Young, 1996 Margaret Lock, 1994 Nancy Scheper-Hughes, 1992 Paul Farmer & Roland Littlewood, 1990 Zachary Gussow, 1988 no award, 1986 Francis Zimmermann, 1984 Janice Reid, 1982 Alan Harwood, 1980 Arthur Kleinman (highly commended Shirley Lindenbaum), 1978 John Janzen and Gilbert Lewis.

15. That is not to say, however, that the subject disappeared from the purview of the now much more tolerant and universalizing ASA. At its Fifth Decennial meeting in Manchester in 2003 there was a plenary on neuroscience organized by Ronnie Frankenberg

and led by the anthropologically experienced neuroscientist Professor Turner (son of Victor and Edie Turner) and in total five panels out of 40 were centrally based in medical anthropology; in order of appearance, Roland Littlewood convened one on anthropology and psychiatry (seven papers); Guro Huby and Liz Hart (six papers) on health services research (seen mainly from the outlook nf Nurses); Bob Simpson and Martin Sexton (three papers) posed the question of what an anthropology of contemporary medical ethics might look like caught between microrealities and macroethics; Helen Lambert (eight papers) on notions of evidence in law and medicine (this included an important paper on evidence in alternative medicine by Christine Barry); James Fairhead and Melissa Leach (five papers) on science, policy and struggles over African health and environment; David Parkin and Elizabeth Hsu (seven papers) on mutual influences of medical practices and religious epistemologies; Rachel Gooberman Hill (five papers) on the science of functioning bodies; and Maggie Bolton and Karen Sykes (four papers) on anthropological perspectives on anatomy and dissection. It is estimated that another 28 papers in various panels would have been considered as legitimate submissions to journals devoted to medical anthropology, making a possible total of 73 papers.

16. For the benefit of potential employers the committee even more courageously added a definition of what might legitimately be considered a professional medical anthropologist:

    A Medical Anthropologist, by contrast, for research appointments and job descriptions etc., is someone (i) trained in one or more of the major divisions of anthropology – most commonly social/cultural anthropology – and (ii) whose major areas of research and publication include medical anthropology. In the overwhelming majority of instances this would necessitate a research degree awarded by a university department that is based on original research. Possession of a master's degree in medical anthropology does not in itself constitute a professional qualification as a "medical anthropologist" any more than a master's degree in any other specialization within anthropology.

    Only those who have not beneficially been enlightened by the study, even at second hand, of the desert ecology of the Bedawin would think inappropriate, the application of the English saying; "A camel is a horse created by a committee" to this definition. The apparent superiority of horses is perhaps an artefact of the Western Société du Spectacle analyzed by Guy Debord.(1968).

17. This it is not a criticism of Berridge, writing a history of, or even collecting material on, social science contributions was not part of her remit. Strong died before he could transform his notes into a report let alone a publishable volume. Berridge also generously acknowledges the hospitality and help of the Wenner Gren Foundation and its Director, Sydel Silverman, as well as the conference participants at Estes Park, Colorado, United States organized by American anthropologists Shirley Lindenbaum and Gilbert Herdt (Berridge 1996:ix; Herdt and Lindenbaum 1992). See also Silverman (2002:86–93) and Frankenberg (1994b).

18. Anne Murcott later became Director of a national ESRC five-year program of the social science study of food. Not least of its achievements was the extension of her own earlier anthropological considerations of the relationship of food culture and health which is, at the time of writing, a major British political issue. See also Caplan 1997.

19. It follows the Great Western Railway to Wales, has a stop in London and continues on the LNER, to York, Newcastle, St Andrews, Dundee, and Aberdeen. Aberdeen was,

contemporary with London, the early Scottish center of medically oriented social science including medical anthropology under the influence of Professor Sir Dugald Baird who, having noted the impact of the trawling fishing industry on the life histories of its women, invented "Social Obstetrics." Like his London contemporaries his "progressive" activities were as much eugenically as sociologically focused. His activities related to abortion and sterilization would now not be seen as ethical, and although only civil offences in Scotland might have been considered as illegal elsewhere, if fully known even at the time. He was a leading influence on the reform of abortion legislation in Britain as a whole.

20. Funded by the Chief Scientist Office of the Scottish Home and Health Department and the Greater Glasgow Health Board.

21. Cochrane himself was not above "insightful" intuition as in his belief/hypothesis that Welsh miners got more serious symptoms from less biopathology because the many migrants from the coalfield had creamed off not only the most enterprising but the most healthy. The physicists who worked under him had a different view, as did the miners' union by whom the present writer was, at the time, employed.

22. Frankel, as has been remarked already, had worked in New Guinea and Davy Smith, a leading epidemiologist had as we have seen done brief but revealing, anthropological-style, fieldwork in Nicaragua.

23. I am grateful to Helen Lambert whose advice has greatly clarified this section and who also reminded me that this notion of lay epidemiology, based on "naturally" observed patterning of health and disease, is distinct from lay or so-called "popular" epidemiology which is participatory in nature. In this quantitative data is collected by lay people or community organizations, sometimes encouraged by professionals. Tudor Hart during his practice years in South Wales used both these methods and more!

24. The reader will notice in Skultans's editorial (2003b) and in Littlewood 2003 how different is the use of narrative here to that in Kleinman's work. Four additional papers in this series have appeared in Volume 11 of the Journal.

25. Former president of the Royal Anthropological Institute, Wellcome Medal winner and well-known both as a practicing psychiatrist and for his theoretical and philosophical abilities (Littlewood 2001) as well as ethnographic, singleton, and collaborative fieldwork achievements in areas as diverse as Trinidad, Haiti, Brooklyn Heights, NY, and Stamford Hill, London.

26. For an earlier and necessarily less nuanced approach to the relationship of perception of psychiatric illness and religion see Loudon (1962). The empirical study is not dated but seems to be around 1960. Frankenberg (1957) records the unwillingness of North Wales villagers in 1953 to accept their respected practitioner's account of a mental disorder until the patient's diagnosed paranoia was directed against themselves, individually, and not merely other villagers at large. Heald's 1994 collection of empirical studies has a different approach tending to be based on the application, by anthropologists, of psychoanalytical approaches to understanding culture. This is, of course, much more common in the United States than in British anthropology. Despite his close friendship with Margaret Mead and many practicing psychoanalysts, and his admiration for Wulf Sachs (1937), Gluckman delayed publishing the full version of his psychoanalytically influenced study of Shaka Zulu (1974; see especially pp. 140–141) for many years.

27. See also an article in a very early issue of *BMAR* (1994), the photocopied predecessor of *Anthropology and Medicine* 1994 and two books (1998 and 2003).

28. The celebrated Three Hospital Study (Brown et al. 1966) was conducted by examining the statistics of outcomes for patients and relating them to different styles of patient management and hospital internal and external environment gained by inspection of the stuation.

29. A pioneer in multiple sclerosis and motor neuron disease research, and organizer and editor of the pioneer Fulbright Symposium on Life and Death under High Technology Medicine (Robinson 1994). This was a sequel to and development of the conference held in McGill in 1988 (Weisz 1990). There was a useful overlap of participants and the two publications together helped to establish medical ethics as a central concern of British medical anthropology.

30. Alan Prout had previously pioneered the anthropological study of sickness in school children while working at Hughes Hall in Cambridge and later became director of a national ESRC program on childhood. While at Keele, with Katie Deverell he evaluated a project on a scheme for providing services to men who had sex with other men without identifying as gay (Prout Deverell 1995). He was also amongst the first medical anthropologists seriously to engage with social studies of science and technology.

31. A definition of "medical anthropology" was added to *Baillière and Tindall's Nursing Dictionary* as a result!

32. The Royal College of Nursing is a characteristically British institution (despite its current general secretary being an American), which, like other Royal colleges in the field of medicine and surgery and the British Medical Association, manages to combine trades union, professional, regulatory, research, and educational functions. The last two in this case are carried out by the Royal College of Nursing Institute.

33. Readers who wish to follow up the implications of this argument both for anthropology in general and for the cognate field to medical anthropology of new reproductive technologies should see Bouquet (1993), Edwards et al. (1999) and Edwards (2000) and the many references in the latter to Strathern, especially Strathern (1992).

34. This section owes a great deal, both for information and analysis, to past close association with, and recent correspondence from, Dr Ursula Sharma and Dr Christine Barry, which the author gratefully acknowledges. He, of course, takes full responsibility for the use he has made of what they (and others during the writing of this chapter) have generously shared with him.

35. The activities of some university departments have already been noted. The attentive reader will note that this section is arranged in alphabetical order of university names. It is based on general research, on correspondence with the principals concerned, and reference to websites where updated information can be found. There is considerable cooperation, seminar attendance, and interchange amongst the staff and graduate students of universities in or within easy reach of London.

36. The writer expects, for example, that in the near future the tendency of US anthropology in general and that part of it concerned with health to cooperate with and learn profitably from studies in science and technology, which is already developing in UK, will be much more marked than it is at present. It has developed already in and from Europe, see especially Annemarie Mol (2002:subtext 18–23, 78–82, 147–148) who in turn acknowledges it having been good some times to come across Sarah Franklin (1997:xi) and to have found Marilyn Strathern, among anthropologists, a potent source. See also Law and Singleton (2005).

References

ALLCORN D., 1954, Social Life of Young Men in a London Suburb. Ph.D. Dissertation, University of Manchester.

——, 1994, *In* Questions in Sociology and Social Anthropology, A Collection of Papers Published Posthumously. CSAC Monographs 7. D. Goss, ed. Kent: Center for Social Anthropology and Computing, The University of Kent at Canterbury.

ARDENER S., ed., 1975, Perceiving Women. London: J. M. Dent.

BAER H., 2004, Towards an Integrative Medicine; Merging Alternative Therapies with Biomedicine. Walnut Creek, CA: AltaMira Press.

BARBOUR R. S. and G. HUBY. eds, 1998, Meddling with Mythology: AIDS and the Social Construction of Knowledge. London: Routledge.

BATESON G., 1972, Steps to an Ecology of Mind. New York: Chandler.

BERGER J. and J. MOHR, 1976 (1967), A Fortunate Man: The Story of a Country Doctor. London: Writers and Readers Co-operative.

BERRIDGE V., 1996, AIDS in the UK: The Making of Policy 1981–1994. Oxford, Oxford University Press.

BERRIDGE V. and P. STRONG, eds, 1993, AIDS and Contemporary History. Cambridge History of Medicine. Cambridge: Cambridge University Press.

BLOCH M., ed., 1975, Marxist Analyses and Social Anthropology. ASA Studies 2. London: Malaby Press.

BLOOR M., N. MCKEGANEY and D. FONKERT, 1988, One Foot in Eden: A Sociological Study of the Range of Therapeutic Community Practice. London: Routledge.

BOUQUET M., 1993, Reclaiming English Kinship. Manchester: Manchester University Press.

BOURDIEU P., 1977, Outline of a Theory of Practice. Cambridge: Cambridge University Press.

BROWN G. W. and T. O. Harris, eds, 1989, Life Events and Illness. London: Unwin Hyman.

BROWN G. W., M. BONE, B. DALISON and J. K. WING, 1966, Schizophrenia and Social Care. Institute Of Psychiatry, Maudsley Monographs 17. Oxford: Oxford University Press [the three hospital study].

BROWN G. W., S. DAVIDSON, T. HARRIS and U. MACLEAN, 1977, Psychiatric Disorders in London and South Uist. Social Science and Medicine 11:367–377.

BURGHART R., 1988, Penicillin: An Ancient Ayurvedic Medicine. *In* The Context of Medicines in Developing Countries: Studies in Pharmaceutical Anthropology. S. van der Geest and S. Reynolds Whyte, eds. Pp. 289–298. Dordrecht: Kluwer Academic Publishers.

CAPLAN P., ed., 1997, Food, Health and Identity. London: Routledge.

——, ed., 2000, Risk Revisited. London: Pluto Press.

CAUDILL W., 1958, The Psychiatric Hospital as a Small Society. Cambridge, MA: Harvard University Press (for the Commonwealth Fund).

COMAROFF J., 1976a, A Bitter Pill to Swallow: Placebo Therapy in General Practice. Sociological Review 72(1):79–96.

——, 1976b, Communicating Information about Non-fatal Illness: The Strategies of a Group of Practitioners. Sociological Review 72(3):269–290.

DAVIS C. O., 2000, Death in Abeyance: Illness and Therapy among the Tabwa of Central Africa. International African Library no. 23. Edinburgh: Edinburgh University Press for International African Institute, London.

DAVISON C., S. FRANKEL and G. DAVEY SMITH, 1992, The Limits of Lifestyle: Re-assessing "Fatalism" in the Popular Culture of Illness Prevention. Social Science and Medicine 34:675–685.

DAVEY SMITH G., A. GORTER, J. HOPPENBROUWER, R. M. P. SWEEP, C. GONZA-LEZ, P. MORALES, J. PAUW and P. SANDIFORD, 1993, The Cultural Construction of Childhood Diarrhoea in Rural Nicaragua: Relevance for Epidemiology and Health Promotion. Social Science and Medicine 36:1613–1624.

DAY S., 2000, The Politics of Risk Among London Prostitutes. In Risk Revisited. P. Caplan, ed. Pp. 29–581. London: Pluto Press.

DAY S. and H. WARD, 1998, Prostitute Women and AIDS; anthropology. AIDS 2:421–428.

——, 2004, Sex Work, Mobility and Health in Europe. London: Kegan Paul.

DAY S., H. WARD and J. R. W. HARRIS, 1988, Prostitute Women and Public Health. British Medical Journal 297:1585.

DEBORD G., 1995, Society of the Spectacle. Cambridge, MA: Zone Books, MIT Press (issued 1968, French edition 1996).

DOUGLAS M., 1987, How Institutions Think. London: Routledge and Kegan Paul.

——, 1999, Leviticus as Literature. Oxford: Oxford University Press.

DOUGLAS M. and M. CALVEZ, 1990, The Self as Risk Taker: A Cultural Theory of Contagion in Relation to AIDS. Sociological Review 38(3):445–464.

DUNN F. L. and B. J. GOOD, 1978, Priorities for Research to Advance the Comparative Study of Medical Systems: Summary of the Discussion at the Final Session of the Conference. Medical Anthropology, Special Issue, "Theoretical Foundations for the Comparative Study of Medical Systems." C. Leslie, ed. Social Science and Medicine 18(2b):135.

EDGAR I., 1986, An Anthropological Analysis of Peper Harow Therapeutic Community with particular reference to the use of myth, ritual and symbol. M.Phil. Thesis, University of Durham.

——, 1990, The Social Process of Adolescence in a Therapeutic Community. In Anthropology and the Riddle of the Sphinx: Paradoxes of Change in the Life Course. ASA Monographs, 28. P. Spencer, ed. Pp. 45–57. London: Routledge.

EDWARDS J., 2000, Born and Bred: Idioms of Kinship and New Reproductive Technologies in England. Oxford: Oxford University Press.

EDWARDS J., E. HIRSCH, S. FRANKLIN, F. PRICE and M. STRATHERN, 1999 (1993), Technologies of Procreation: Kinship in the Age of Assisted Conception. London: Routledge.

FORTES M., 1996, Foreword. In Social Anthropology and Medicine. ASA Monograph, 13. J. B. Loudon, ed. Pp. ix–xx. London: Academic Press.

FRANKENBERG R. J., 1957, Village on the Border. London: Cohen and West (2nd edition with additional material, Illinois: Waveland Press, 1990).

——, 1981, Allopathic Medicine, Profession and Capitalist Ideology in India. Social Science and Medicine 15A:115–125.

——, 1984, Incidence or Incidents: Political and Methodological Underpinnings of a Health Research Process in a Small Italian Town. In Social Researching: Politics, Problems, Practice. C. Bell and H. Roberts, eds. Pp. 88–103. London: Routledge and Kegan Paul.

——, 1994a, Divided by a Common Language: The Body in Narrative Anthropology and Scientific Medicine. British Medical Anthropology Review (n.s.) 2(2, Winter): 5–17.

——, 1994b, The Impact of HIV/AIDS on Concepts Relating to Risk and Culture within British Community Epidemiology: Candidates or Targets for Prevention. Social Science and Medicine 38(10):1325–1335.

——, 1995, Learning from AIDS: The Future of Anthropology. *In* The Future of Anthropology: Its Relevance to the Contemporary World. A. Ahmed and C. Shore, eds. Pp. 110–133. London: The Athlone Press.

FRANKENBERG R. J. and J. LEESON, 1976, Disease, Illness and Sickness: Social Aspects of the Choice of Healer in a Lusaka Suburb. *In* Social Anthropology and Medicine. ASA Monograph, 13. J. Loudon, ed. Pp. 223–258. London: Academic Press.

——, 1977, The Patients of Traditional Doctors in Lusaka. African Social Research 23:217–234.

FRANKLIN S., 1997, Embodied Progress: A Cultural Account of Assisted Conception. London: Routledge.

GLUCKMAN M., 1974, The Individual in a Social Framework: The Rise of King Shaka of Zululand. Journal of African Studies 1(2):113–144.

GOOD B. J. and M-J. DELVECCHIO GOOD, 1993, "Learning Medicine": The Constructing of Medical Knowledge at Harvard Medical School. *In* Knowledge, Power and Practice. S. Lindenbaum and M. Lock, eds. Pp. 81–107. Berkeley: University of California Press.

HART L., 1991, A Ward of My Own: Social Organization and Identity Among Hospital Domestics. *In* Anthropology and Nursing. P. Holden and J. Littlewood, eds. Pp. 84–109. London: Routledge.

HARWOOD A., ed., 1981a, Ethnicity and Medical Care. Cambridge, MA: Harvard University Press.

——, 1981b, Guidelines for Culturally Appropriate Health Care. *In* Ethnicity and Medical Care. A. Harwood, ed. Pp. 482–587. Cambridge MA: Harvard University Press.

HEALD S. and A. DELUZ, eds, 1994, Anthropology and Psychoanalysis: An Encounter Through Culture. London: Routledge.

HEGGENHOUGEN K., 1997, Obituary: Carol Pulley MacCormack. Anthropology and Medicine 4(3):327–328.

HELMAN C. G., 1978, Feed a Cold, Starve a Fever: Folk Models of Infection in an English Suburban Community, and their Relation to Medical Treatment. Culture, Medicine and Psychiatry 2:107–137.

——, 1987a, Heart Disease and the Cultural Construction of Time: The Type A Behavior Pattern as a Western Culture-bound Syndrome. Social Science and Medicine 25:969–979.

——, 1987b, General Practice and the Hidden Health Care System (1987 Albert Wander Lecture). Journal of the Royal Society of Medicine 80:738–740.

——, 2001 (1988), Culture, Health and Illness: An Introduction for Health Professionals, 4th Edition. Oxford, Butterworth Heinemann.

HERDT G. and S. LINDENBAUM, eds, 1992, The Time of AIDS: Social Analysis, Theory and Method. London: Sage Publications.

HERZFELD M., 1992, The Social Production of Indifference: Exploring the Symbolic Roots of Western Bureaucracy. Chicago: University of Chicago Press/Berg.

HERZLICH C. and J. PIERRET, 1987 (1984), Illness and Self in Society. Baltimore: The Johns Hopkins Press.

HOLDEN P. and J. LITTLEWOOD, eds, 1991, Anthropology and Nursing. London: Routledge.

HSU E., 1999, The Transmission of Chinese Medicine. Cambridge Studies in Medical Anthropology 7. Cambridge: Cambridge University Press.

JASPAN M., 1976, Traditional Medical Theory in South-East Asia, inaugural lecture delivered in The University of Hull on 10 March 1969. In J. B. Loudon,, ed., Social Anthropology and Medicine. ASA Monograph, 13. Pp. 259–284. London: Academic Press.

KAVANAGH K. H., 1993, Review of Holden P. and J. Littlewood, eds, 1991, Anthropology and Nursing. London: Routledge. Medical Anthropology Quarterly 7(4):405–407.

KIEV A., ed., 1974 (1964), Magic, Faith and Healing: Studies in Primitive Psychiatry Today. New York: The Free Press of Glencoe.

KLEINMAN A., 1988, The Illness Narratives: Suffering, Healing and the Human Condition. New York: Basic Books.

KONRAD M., 2003, From Secrets of Life to the Life of Secrets: Tracing Genetic Knowledge as Genealogical Ethics in Biomedical Britain. Journal of the Royal Anthropological Institute 9(2):339–358.

KRAUSE I-B., 1998, Therapy Across Culture. Perspectives on Psychotherapy. London: Sage Publications.

——, 2003, Learning How to Ask in Ethnography and Psychotherapy. Anthropology and Medicine 10(1):3–22.

LAMBERT H., 1996, Popular Therapeutics and Medical Preferences in Rural North India. Lancet 348:1706–1709.

——, 1998, Methods and Meanings in Anthropological, Epidemiological and Clinical Encounters: The Case of Sexually Transmitted Disease and HIV Control and Prevention in India. Tropical Medicine and International Health 3(12):1002–1010.

LAMBERT H. and C. McKEVITT, 2002, Anthropology in Health Research. From Qualitative Methods to Multidisciplinarity. British Medical Journal 325:210–213.

LAST M., 1981, The Importance of Knowing about Not-knowing. Social Science and Medicine 15B:387–392.

LAW J. and SINGLETON V., 2005, Object lessons. Organization 12(3):331–355.

LEININGER M., 1991, Transcultural Nursing: The Study and Practice Field. Imprint 38(2):55–66.

LESLIE C., ed., 1978, Medical Anthropology, Special Issue, "Theoretical Foundations for the Comparative Study of Medical Systems." Social Science and Medicine 18(2b).

LEWIS G., 2000, A Failure of Treatment. Oxford Studies in Social and Cultural Anthropology. Oxford: Oxford University Press.

LITTLEWOOD R., 2000, Psychiatry's Culture. In Anthropological Approaches to Psychological Medicine: Crossing Bridges. V. Skultans and J. Cox, eds. Pp. 66–93. London: Jessica Kingsley.

——, 2001, Religion, Agency, Restitution. The Wilde Lectures in Natural Religion 1999. Oxford: Oxford University Press.

——, 2003, Why Narrative? Why Now? V. Skultans, ed. Special issue, "Psychiatry and the Uses of Narrative." Anthropology and Medicine 10(2):255–261.

——, (forthcoming), On Knowing and Not Knowing in the Anthropologies of Medicine. London: Athlone Press.

LITTLEWOOD R. and S. DEIN, eds, 2000, Cultural Psychiatry; Medical Anthropology: an Introduction and Reader. London: Athlone Press.

LOUDON J. B, 1962, Religious Order and Mental Disorder: A Study in a South Wales Rural Community. In The Social Anthropology of Complex Societies. ASA Monograph, 4. M. Banton ed. Pp. 69–96. London: Tavistock Publications.

LOUDON J. B., ed., 1976, Social Anthropology and Medicine. ASA Monograph, 13. London: Academic Press.

McDONALD M., ed., (forthcoming), Languages of Accountability. Cambridge: Cambridge University Press.

McKEGANEY N. and M. BARNARD, 1992, AIDS, Drugs and Sexual Risks: Lives in the Balance. Buckingham: Open University Press.

McKEVITT C., 2000, Short Stories about Stroke: Interviews and Narrative Production. Anthropology and Medicine 7:79–96.

McKEVITT C. and C. WOLFE, 2002, What Does Quality of Life Mean? The Views of Health Care Professionals. Quality in Ageing 3:12–19.

McKEVITT C., A. LUSE and C. WOLFE, 2003, The Unfortunate Generation: Stroke Survivors in Riga, Latvia. Social Science and Medicine 56:2097–2108.

MACLEAN U., 1974, Nursing in Contemporary Society. London: Routledge and Kegan Paul.

MOL A., 2002, The Body Multiple: Ontology in Medical Practice. Durham NC: Duke University Press

MONKS J. and R. FRANKENBERG, 1995, Being Ill and Being Me: Self, Body, and Time in Multiple Sclerosis Narratives. *In* B. Ingstad and S. Reynolds Whyte, eds, Disability and Culture. Pp. 107–134. Berkeley: California University Press.

OAKLEY A., 1997, Making Medicine Social: The Case of the Two Dogs with Bent Legs. *In* Social Medicine and Medical Sociology in the Twentieth Century. Rodopi Wellcome Institute Series In the History of Medicine. D. Porter, ed. Pp. 81–96. Amsterdam: Atlanta GA.

PHILPIN S., 2003, Wool Measurement: Community and Healing in Rural Wales. *In* Welsh Communities: New Ethnographic Perspectives. C. A. Davies and S. Jones, eds. Pp. 117–134. Cardiff: University of Wales Press.

POOL R., 1994, Dialogue and the Interpretation of Illness: Conversations in a Cameroon Village. Explorations in Anthropology. Oxford: Berg.

——, 2000, Negotiating a Good Death: Euthanasia in the Netherlands. New York: The Haworth Press.

PRIOR L., 2001, Rationing Through Risk Assessment in Clinical Genetics: All Categories Have Wheels. Special issue, "Health Care Rationing." Sociology of Health and Illness 23(5):570–593.

PROUT A. and K. DEVERELL, 1995, Working with Diversity: Evaluating the MESMAC Project. London: Health Education Authority.

RAPOPORT R. N., 1960, Community as Doctor: New Perspectives on a Therapeutic Community. London: Tavistock Publications.

REISLAND N. and R. BURGHART, 1998, The Quality of a Mother's Milk and the Health of Her Child: Beliefs and Practices of the Women of Mithila. Social Science and Medicine 27(5):461–469.

ROBINSON I., ed., 1994, Life and Death under High Technology Medicine, Fulbright Papers 15. Manchester: Manchester University Press (in association with the Fulbright Commission).

SACHS W., 1937, Black Hamlet, The Mind of an African Negro revealed by Psychoanalysis. London: Geoffrey Bles.

SAVAGE J., 1987, Nurses, Gender and Sexuality. London: Heinemann.

——, 1991, Flesh and Blood: Notions of Relatedness among some Urban English Women. Ph.D. Dissertation, University of London.

——, 1995, Nursing Intimacy: An Ethnographic Approach to Nurse–Patient Interaction. London: Scutari Press.

SHARMA U., 1992, Complementary Medicine Today: Practitioners and Patients. London: Routledge.

SIGERIST H. E., 1951, A History of Medicine, vol. 1. Primitive and Archaic Medicine. New York: Oxford University Press.

SILVERMAN S., 2002, The Beast on the Table. Walnut Creek, CA: Altamira Press.

SINCLAIR S., 1997, Making Doctors: An Institutional Apprenticeship. Oxford: Berg.

SKULTANS V., ed., 2003a, Special issue, "Psychiatry and the Uses of Narrative." Anthropology and Medicine 10(2).

———, 2003b, Editorial. Culture and Dialogue in Medical Psychiatric Narratives. Special issue, "Psychiatry and the Uses of Narrative." Anthropology and Medicine 10(2):155–166.

SKULTANS V. and J. COX, eds, 2000, Anthropological Approaches to Psychological Medicine: Crossing Bridges. London: Jessica Kingsley.

STRATHERN M., 1992, Reproducing the Future: Anthropology, Kinship and the New Reproductive Technologies. Manchester: Manchester University Press

STRAUSS A., S. FAGERHAUGH, B. SUCZEK and C. WEINER, 1985, Social Organization of Medical Work. Chicago: University of Chicago Press.

STRONG P., 1998, The Pestilential Apocalypse: Modern, Postmodern and Early Modern Observations. In Meddling with Mythology: AIDS and the Social Construction of Knowledge. R. S. Barbour and G. Huby, eds. Pp. 244–258. London: Routledge (posthumous, introduction and presentation by Ann Murcott).

SUSSER M. and W. WATSON, 1962, Sociology in Medicine. Oxford: Oxford University Press (2nd edition 1971, 3rd edition with Kim Hopper 1985 New York: Oxford University Press).

THOMAS A., 1978, Discussion on Arthur Kleinman's Paper. C. Leslie, ed., Medical Anthropology, Special Issue, "Theoretical Foundations for the Comparative Study of Medical Systems." Social Science and Medicine 18(2b):95.

TUDOR HART J., 1988, A New Kind of Doctor: The General Practioner's Part in the Health of the Community. London: Merlin Press.

TURNER E., W. BLODGETT, S. KAHONA and F. BENWA, 1992, Experiencing Ritual. Philadelphia: University of Pennsylvania Press.

TURNER V., 1964, Lunda Medicine and the Treatment of Disease. Livingstone, Northern Rhodesia: Rhodes-Livingstone Museum.

TURNER V. and E. TURNER, 1978, Image and Pilgrimage in Christian Culture. Oxford: Basil Blackwell.

WEISZ G., ed., 1990, Social Science Perspectives on Medical Ethics. Culture Illness and Healing, 16. Dordrecht: Kluwer Academic Publishers.

WILLIS R. G., 1972, Pollutions and Paradigms. MAN (n.s.) 7:369–378.

WORSLEY P., 1982, Non-Western Medical Systems. In Annual Review of Anthropology, vol. 11. B. J. Siegel, ed. Pp. 315–348. Palo Alto: Annual Reviews.

Chapter 11

SWITZERLAND

Anthropology between Medicine and Society: Swiss Health Interfaces

Ilario Rossi

As a multilingual and multicultural country, Switzerland has a plurality of anthropological knowledge and practices, as is evident in its academic sources in French, German, and Italian, with the additional shared Anglo-Saxon reference. Until the beginning of the 21st century, local autonomies[1] were favored to the detriment of planned and structured State policies, without however preventing national-level exchange and collaboration. This is the context in which medical anthropology (now referred to as the anthropology of health) came to be known as a field of academics and research during the 1980s and particularly the 1990s, mainly under the initiative of a few researchers.

The Reference: The Commission Interdisciplinaire d'Anthropologie Médicale suisse/Medical Anthropology of Switzerland (CIAM/MAS)

In the early 1990s, the Société Suisse d'Ethnologie[2] (SSE), which is affiliated with the Académie Suisse des Sciences Humaines, wanted to reinforce the visibility of medical anthropology and clarify its position. It therefore helped to create what would become a reference for Swiss medical anthropology: the Commission Interdisciplinaire d'Anthropologie Médicale (CIAM),[3] or in English, Medical Anthropology of Switzerland (MAS). Created under the initiative of B. Obrist van Euwijk from Basel, M. Verwey from Zürich, and H-R. Wicker from Bern, the CIAM brought together mainly anthropologists, ethnologists, physicians, and psychiatrists, as well as other health practitioners from all regions of Switzerland.[4] The CIAM is currently one of the most active commissions of the SSE and aims to provide a shared platform for representatives of different disciplines interested in the social, cultural, biomedical, psychological, or psychiatric aspects of health.

By creating a network of associated members and by encouraging publications in the field, the CIAM helped to produce the first collective reference book, published by the SSE (Gonseth 1994). The topics reflect international trends in an extremely dynamic discipline, but one which also remains highly diverse, focusing on the multifold realities of the body, health and illness in time and space, as well as the deconstruction of social and cultural logics underlying new relations to health and illness. The book's contents, which explore and analyze social practices in Europe, Africa, Asia, and Latin America, show that regardless of how one may view its effectiveness, medical pluralism constitutes a practical response to misfortune and a search for meaning, the expressions of which are constantly redefined and actualized. The many different health-care methods, both here and elsewhere, reshape the world of both supply and demand. Their use is a spontaneous social response and a self-regulation mechanism for users in the face of clinical standards of "scientific" rationality, and they explicitly raise the issues of recognition and complementarity in the world of health care. The methodological options chosen in the field are openly qualitative, leading to analyses inspired by a wide variety of approaches and authors: the anthropology of illness and the search for meaning dear to Augé and Herzlich (1983) in France; the approach to suffering developed at the School of Medical Anthropology of the Harvard Medical School (Del Vecchio et al. 1992; Good 1994; Kleinmann 1988, 1995); and the anthropology of the body, where the body is interpreted both as a representation of the social arena and a means for analyzing it, following Scheper-Hughes and Lock (1987) and Lock and Scheper-Hughes (1990) in the United States, Le Breton (1990) in France, as well as Kleinmann and Good (1985) (United States) and Helmann (1992) (UK) respectively for approaches to mental health and for issues of health and migration.

The main objective of the CIAM is to foster exchange, reflection, and analysis by organizing seminars, symposiums and other regional, national and international meetings. From the outset, it has created a forum for discussing new knowledge and for sharing research findings, with a particular attention to the epistemological and methodological issues inherent in this specific anthropological approach. A glance at the content of the activities organized by the commission reveals how diverse and rich they have been, witness not only to the development of the themes and their interrelations, but also to the national convergences or the specificities of each university.[5]

Building bridges between medicine and anthropology, as well as between nursing and anthropology, has been a constant concern,[6] whether to help coordinate specific knowledge and practices, or to foster a constructive critical perspective. The methodological choices made by researchers for examining health issues have also been a priority: while it is important to understand specific issues related to fieldwork, it is also critical not to lose sight of the limits of research instruments often used in "rapid" assessment procedures, particularly in the South.[7]

The relationship between migration and health is becoming particularly popular among Swiss researchers.[8] This theme was proposed and elaborated jointly in all of the country's universities with approaches that are often complementary. The topic of migration and health has played a very strong role in promoting a national medical anthropology by creating synergies with institutional government bodies (the Federal Office of Public Health), and with academic circles (the faculties of social sciences and medicine). Anthropologists working in Switzerland have chosen research projects that are firmly rooted in the context of the rapidly changing contemporary world. Indeed, the roles and statuses of health professionals are being renewed as the world's societies undergo major social and cultural transformations. Medical and care-giving skills, characterized by rigorous relational and clinical work, are gradually broadening to include the dynamics of social change in intervention strategies. Increased attention is being paid to the causes and effects of the process of globalization: generalized migration, economic globalization, and technological innovations. These three factors, which form a system, cannot be viewed separately. They are changing medical practice in many ways: an openness to intercultural and transcultural relations and their management has become critical; collaborative work with community interpreters has to be developed; diseases are becoming internationalized; there are new epidemiological problems, including an explosion in chronic illness and the resurgence of infectious diseases; patient care, particularly chronic care, is encountering new difficulties; and the relational and communications aspects of medical practice are more and more complex. In addition to this broadening of the medical horizon, there have been significant changes related to diagnostic, clinical and treatment technology, and it is important to bear in mind that these innovations are part of the context of a structured search for efficiency in which medical rationality and economic rationality converge. Therefore, in an effort to examine the issue of health and migration, the CIAM has organized interdisciplinary debates over the years, making health a window with a view onto changes in society. The CIAM has accompanied and supported the theoretical and practical development of a discipline whose goal is to grasp the complexity of medicine and of contemporary health practices through a systemic outlook, and in light of current health policies and systems. It has encouraged researchers to analyze the interactions governing those health policies and systems, the often uncontrolled interferences between them, and the way in which one element can begin changing rapidly under the effect of the others. The anthropology promoted by the CIAM has helped researchers learn to reflect on these areas as a whole, constantly connecting them more closely with the political, where they converge and are expressed, the political being understood as the ability to act collectively on the course of events.

Over the years, the work of the Commission has given legitimacy to a national movement, while giving meaning to a variety of different expressions and regional specificities. At the same time it has revealed the relationship between short-term logic (the exploration of the interface between medicine and the social sciences and humanities) and long-term logic (going from what is due to circumstances to what is structural within academic institutions).

Pathways in a Dynamic Field: Knowledge Development

The first studies dealing with health-care systems and practices were carried out in the South (Africa, Latin America and Asia) in the absence of a colonial legacy and any tradition of specific fieldwork sites. In the context of their master's or Ph.D. studies, young Swiss researchers have analyzed the logics of a society and a culture through the examination of distress, illness, and the body. The experience of "exotic" fieldwork and the anthropological practice derived from it, as well as the academic knowledge of other cultural worlds, has been the foundation on which an interest in "endogenous" ethnomedical approaches has gradually developed. Thus, the geographical detour via an increasing interest in ethnomedicine elsewhere has led back to a medical anthropology "at home," but with the advantage of a perspective that has undergone a certain decentering.[9]

These "new" research objects have gradually become more visible and have enjoyed greater legitimacy both through academic mandates and activities (particularly in Bern where Wicker and Schoch (1988) and Wicker (1989a, 1989b, 1993) have done ground-breaking work on medical anthropology and the anthropology of migrations), and through work with community organizations and foundations,[10] particularly in French Switzerland in the latter case. While these many initiatives use different strategies and place the researcher in different positions (as we will discuss further in the next section), they share many themes in common: plural societies and cultural pluralism around the relationship between health and migration; supply and demand within Western medical pluralism, specifically the Swiss variety; and therapeutic itineraries and logics underlying health practices. Swiss medical anthropology therefore offers a response to the issues raised by the social and cultural upheavals of contemporary Western societies through a reflection on changes in health as globalization becomes more and more all-encompassing. Both in the South and in the North, changes in mentalities have also led to changes in the perception of health and illness, locally and globally. The implications of this new situation are at the heart of the issues examined by Swiss anthropology.

Thus, it is within the perspective of a changing society and a reconfigured field of health care that both health professionals and researchers in the social sciences and humanities have taken such an interest in the concepts of culture (and cultural pluralism), and complementary medicine (and medical pluralism). By adopting qualitative methodologies, these two groups have developed a complementarity in their approaches to health and illness and in their use of research tools. In no way has the discipline been built on an opposition between diverse conceptions of reality and of the body – the conceptions of scientists, clinicians, patients, and health services users – in which one is considered more real than the others. Instead, the discipline has advocated openness to the ambivalences that the body contains, and to the care-giving practices of each culture.

This theoretical framework of analysis has found many different sources of support. They include funds from the Confederation (including the FNRS[11]) which, in addition to grants for specific projects, also makes calls for papers on specific themes with support from public funds (the National AIDS Research Program[12] and the OFSP,[13] in particular through its health and migration, AIDS, and addictions services), county research funds (particularly through public health services), and institutional, public, and private funds. Swiss medical anthropology has set its course partly on the basis of the research market, according to the funding possibilities available, and it seeks to take responsibility for what comes of these constraints.[14] The overview below will present some of the major trends in recent and current research.[15] During the 1990s, four main fields of research emerged within the discipline, parallel to developments on the international stage, and they have had a strong influence over the direction of analyses and collaboration with health-care workers. The four fields are: migration, pluralism in medicine and health-care practices, AIDS, and North–South relations.

Descriptions of work carried out on these questions illustrate the impact of anthropological contributions. North–South relations have an important position, particularly at the Universities of Basel and Geneva. Specifically, in the fields of international health, medical pluralism, and North–South cooperation, health is being studied as a field for exploring new issues and new priorities. In the context of a renewed paradigm (it has become economically "profitable" to invest in health, as the WHO has said), the strategies designed and promoted for improving the overall health of the world's population have to deal with more and more critical situations: growing social and health inequalities, the explosion of urban areas, and the rapid increase in the number of deaths related to AIDS, tuberculosis, malaria, and smoking. Reflections therefore concern issues connected to the widening gap in health-care access and its economic, social and ethical consequences. Anthropological responses for dealing with the crisis in health-care systems include analyzing political reactions, shedding light on social logics and trends, and recognizing the value of nonscientifically based care-giving knowledge and practices (Droz 1998, 1999; Obrist Van Eeuwijk 1992, 2002a,b; Obrist Van Eeuwijk and Mdungi 1994; Rossi et al. 1997a; Van Eeuwijk 1999, 2000, 2001, 2002).

Anthropology has helped to develop responses to the AIDS epidemic (both in the preventive and curative spheres) within the context of public health strategies by analyzing the sociocultural implications of the epidemiological and medical changes that have gone hand in hand with the development of the syndrome (Kopp Sutter 2002; Rossi et al. 1998). By actively participating in HIV prevention strategies, like other representatives of the social sciences and humanities, anthropologists have found an opportunity to design practical intervention tools for health professionals. In a society in which community-based organizations that are active in defining and defending the rights and obligations of citizens affected by AIDS wish to foster structured collaborations between medicine and society, there are interstices where anthropologists can find a niche.

The question of culture is therefore not about folklore, but rather the capacity and right that humans in society have to give meaning to their individual and collective lives. To reduce that meaning to a single model of measurement, and a medical one at that, is to run the risk of impoverishing the complexity of human societies considerably. In keeping with international research, Swiss researchers point to the hiatus between the practices of medical rationality and patients' health-seeking practices, both here and elsewhere. The therapeutic choices made by the ill are based on their interpretative logic. For health-care users the illness episode most often involves multiple forms of knowledge and practices, resulting in a fragmented and plural identity with respect to health and illness. The latter are in fact often contradictory and ambivalent: if we are to examine social practices that lie outside of the field of medicine, if we are to take into account all the actions that people consider to be curative, then how do we define "therapeutic"? Medical pluralism is a field of social life in which a new culture of care is being invented. Yet the heterogeneity of representations and practices leads to a complete dissociation between the body, health and illness, and their respective cultural contexts (Gonseth 1994; Ossipow 1997; Rossi 1995, 1996, 1997b).

Considerable private and public investments and access to local communities have played a significant role in the development of studies on health and migration. In Switzerland, researchers in the area emulate earlier studies, but often from different fieldwork sites, and with contradictory findings. However, one thing is certain: we live in a multicultural society with many different meanings and values, marked by blatant inequalities. The migratory paths that converge in the country, temporarily or definitively, reveal widely diverse strategies for adapting to and living with the limitations and possibilities of the host country. There are major paradoxes in the individual and community, cultural and social, professional and institutional, and economic and political realities that the various studies explore, as there also are in migrants' reasons, motivations, and plans (Wicker et al. 2003). The dynamics of self-construction, deconstruction, and reconstruction related to these realities, both among migration professionals, including anthropologists, and among immigrants themselves, are often the sign of a mobile, hybrid identity that can create suffering and adaptation difficulties, but also opportunities and openings. However, many people do experience a distancing due to social and cultural difference at some point along the way. Like all states in the Western world, Switzerland has considerable power over the fate of exiles and migrants. The institutions of the host society define them as having certain rights, but mostly as the bearers of responsibilities and specific limitations. Through its policies, the state defines the field of possibilities. Several Swiss studies have shown how decisions that are made echo moral considerations and value judgments, most notably in the field of mental health (Salis Gross 2002) and the organization of health-care systems (Rossi 2002, 2003). The distinction made between the cultural politics of health and the political culture of health is very revealing in that regard. It implies that the "integration" of persons of foreign nationality is less a problem related to specific social groups with their characteristics than a problem of society as a whole, making it an endogenous, not an exogenous, problem. The political management of migration makes immigrants very vulnerable, with the inevitable impacts on their state of health. Health professionals are in a position to observe this empirically in their day-to-day clinical and therapeutic activities. Confronted with the multiplication of human trajectories in space, they find they have to manage intercultural relations in time. Thus, the interactions between individuals, civil society, and care practices become the subject of constant adjustments. These relationships are often influenced by lines of social differentiation, they may be part of the sometimes brutal dynamics of acculturation, or they may reveal incompatible existential meanings and values (Weiss 2003).

This is particularly true of the life paths of people who are suffering, as the logics of their personal trajectories can be understood only by reconstructing their biographical itineraries, their social webs, the painful events they have experienced, and the connections they have created through personal networks and therapeutic itineraries. Care-seeking must therefore be understood as an essentially polysemic phenomenon, making it important to examine all the factors that either threaten or protect people's health and which, beyond strictly individual conditions, affect collective or community problems influenced by politics.

Research in the field as a whole helps to contextualize the problems and to create intervention strategies, while also working to deconstruct institutional and professional logics and the practices of migrants. Studies include work on treating refugee trauma and its consequences (Moser et al. 2001; Obrist and Hirsch 1992; Rossi 1994; Wicker and Schoch 1988; Wicker et al. 1998), on teaching transcultural skills in health-care institutions (Domenig 2001a), on addiction among immigrant populations (Domenig 2001b), on communication and the relationship between care-giver and receiver (Moser 1997; Salis Gross 2001; Salis Gross et al. 1997), on interpreting and cultural mediation (Rossi 1999; Weiss and Stuker 1998), on transnational health strategies among immigrants (Salis Gross and Loncarevic 1999), and on more specific approaches to providing health care (Salis Gross et al. 2002). These studies have all helped to implement national policies (Maggi and Cattacin 2003), specifically in the context of OFSP's "Health and Migration" project for 2002–06.[16]

Interdisciplinary approaches, in particular contributions by medical and clinical anthropology (Hudelson 2002; Rossi 1997b), are helping health professionals to better manage health-care demands. They can also help health workers to understand their professional context and the meaning of their professional activities. This has become a crucial issue for the institutionalization of anthropology, but it is not the only one.

Economics has become an integral part of health care. The search for therapeutic effectiveness now includes efficiency in medical practice, by which every intervention strategy has its price tag. Thus, medical practice becomes tied to the results it must produce. Although this may be justified, it is not without contradictions. Globalization has let the genie (the market) out of the bottle (democracy) in which it had been locked away and tamed. Globalization is "pregnant" with both indisputable promises and very real threats, the most obvious of which is the gradual erosion of the political arena. The best proof lies in the crisis in health-care systems; in the Swiss situation, the obligation of managing resources globally, as established by the federal law on obligatory health insurance (*Loi fédérale sur l'assurance maladie obligatoire*, or LAMal), is evidence of that crisis.

The reform is based on a complex arrangement that attempts to reconcile efficiency, freedom, and solidarity, which means that choices must be made not only to deal with health-care costs, but also to decide what values are worth preserving. The control over financial resources therefore has to comply with a certain number of conditions that society sets out (meeting needs, accessibility, solidarity, equity, ethical rules) without which the combination of medicine, care, economics, and politics would be unthinkable (Rossi 2002, 2003).

One of the most recent national publications (published by the SSE) focuses on health systems and policies and on reinforcing an interpretative anthropology built around the concept of suffering (Salis Gross and Del Vecchio Good 2002). It confirms the interest in locating medical anthropology within the broader field of the anthropology of health via health policies. While the publication deals with the sociocultural aspects of the conditions under which medicine and health policies are produced, it focuses specifically on the moral issues and pragmatic aspects. This constructive and critical approach establishes anthropology's position in the debate over health care in civil society during a period when systems and resources are in crisis and innovations are a permanent feature of the landscape. As a result, anthropology cannot disregard the sociocultural and social-health realities that are both the source and the object of its discourse. Anthropology is increasingly called on to examine health policies and systems at home and abroad, highlighting the relations between health practices, knowledge production, and civil society.

There are many forms of knowledge and diverse paths within Swiss medical anthropology, depending on the type of research being done and on researchers' institutional affiliations (directly with institutes of ethnology or anthropology and/or with institutes in faculties of medicine, public health services or professional associations or schools). As a result, the practice of medical anthropology in Switzerland is very fragmented, a galaxy that is forming as time goes by.

Pathways in a Dynamic Field: Issues Raised by Anthropological Practice

Knowledge development is often linked to research practices that are defined less by institutional and academic strategies to promote them than by random opportunities in the market in medical and public health research. The field of practical medical anthropology is therefore shaped by the interaction between a demand by the relevant bodies and the intellectual supply of ethnological, sociological and anthropological theories. While illness may be an individual experience, health is collective; it is rooted in both the public and private arenas and is a social issue at the heart of anthropological inquiry. It has become a reference value, and defines itself as an elaborate social and political construction whose boundaries are constantly in question. Paradoxical and ambivalent in both its theories and its practices, health is linked to major issues in all societies. Health is therefore an independent object, which makes it possible for anthropologists to analyze its development; this development in turn changes the logic of supply and demand in the field of health-care organization and distribution, and witnesses the appearance of new actors who justify and control those changes. By exploring illness and its representations, and by examining individual and collective health-seeking behavior as a phenomenon of civilization, anthropology is becoming increasingly invested in constructive cooperation between the life sciences and the social sciences and humanities. We are therefore moving from a care-based medicine to a medicine in constant connection with health policies. As a result, Swiss researchers share a conviction that fundamental anthropology (dealing with issues of the body, health, and society) needs to be tied to a reflection on what is at stake when it is applied to medical and health-care knowledge and practices (Rossi 1997b). Whether the researchers have short-term collaborations (where the anthropologist is asked to respond to a medical question), or more medium- or long-term commitments (with a more structured collaboration[17]), many of them come face-to-face with the paradox that medical and health-care institutional environments are at once the object of their socioanthropological studies and their place of work. In other words, the research context influences anthropological practice, and a certain involvement is now part and parcel of observation. The survival, perhaps even the legitimacy, of the "discipline" is connected to the delicate management of its position in academic networks (faculties of medicine and schools of nursing), in the cultural politics of health (public health and community health), and in the political culture of health, civil networks, and public health issues. At the same time it must fulfill the demands of pluridisciplinarity or interdisciplinarity, maintain relations with all health professionals, and manage the cooperation and coordination that this implies.

Swiss medical anthropology has been shaped by academic collaborations on the border between two sciences, two fields of knowledge devoted to humans and their differences. Like medicine, but differently, medical anthropology refers to the ideal of mankind's unified logos and is open to multiplicity. However, it functions as a geometric space where the arrogance of truths can be revealed and dispelled, putting it in a rather awkward position.

Nonetheless, the context calls increasingly for codisciplinarity, which involves managing the different disciplines and how they will cooperate with one another; pluridisciplinarity, interdisciplinarity, and transdisciplinarity must therefore be understood as means for regulating fields of knowledge, and as a social practice of cooperation and coordination. As such, they pursue a specific objective: developing a cognitive and operational platform where the findings of the social sciences and humanities can be jointly integrated into a coherent and organic whole with research conducted in the life and health sciences.

In this overview, we must also consider the critical role given to anthropology and to anthropologists. Twenty-first-century medicine can no longer afford to refuse an alliance with the social sciences and humanities. They will become as necessary to medicine as was anatomy in the late 18th century, biology in the 19th century, and molecular biology, genetics, and epidemiology in the 20th century.

New objects, which do not belong to anyone *a priori*, are often created through codisciplinary work. We must recognize that the field has drawn on, and continues to draw on, contributions from representatives of the social sciences and humanities, as well as the needs expressed by physicians and care-givers for new tools for fostering understanding and openness (Sabbioni et al. 1999; Weiss 2003; Weiss and Stucker 1998). That being said, medical anthropology has several "lineages" at the service of medicine and public health, which are coordinated with them and study them, creating a need for mediations between many different anthropologies and a plural medicine, perhaps even many different medicines. Every time a connection is made between these different poles, a boundary is drawn, and new interrelations and confrontations must be negotiated regarding how the work and the fieldwork are done. The anthropological position and discourse regarding medical knowledge and practices (front-line medicine, medical specializations, from endocrinology to genetics, from PMA to abortion, social and preventive medicine, psychosocial medicine, different psychiatric approaches, or other areas that are independent but strongly linked to these fields, such as psychology and nursing) raise the old issue of the hierarchical relationship between the natural and the social sciences. It is because of this persistent precariousness and the fact that its approach is always secondary and derivative that anthropology is suspicious of the dream of a global approach to health and illness. Although anthropology is increasingly present in medicine and public health, anthropological fieldwork is part of a field of health defined by the diversity of sociocultural contents. Today, it benefits from an openness to codisciplinarity and an exploration of the connections between culturally acquired and genetically innate conditions, which point to new perspectives for research.

This cooperation between different professions depends largely on a shared understanding of notions such as culture and representation, health and illness, without which dialogue is not possible. The interaction between theory and practice and the predisposition to codisciplinary work appears as the basis for a shared identity in the border zone that is medical anthropology, characterized as it is by the value placed on pragmatism and hybrid references, which may seem somewhat unorthodox to proponents of a rigorous academism. While medical anthropology finds meaning in the practices that have created it, it can find legitimacy in the eyes of both anthropologists and medical and health-care professionals only through the accumulation of knowledge and experiences. In spite of its paradoxical situation, medical anthropology has made it relevant for anthropologists to become involved in issues of health.

Training and Research Sites in Medical Anthropology and the Anthropology of Health

Alongside the rapid expansion of the CIAM and the research conducted, teaching has gradually made a place for itself in social sciences and humanities faculties[18] as well as in medical,[19] care-giving, social,[20] and public health training or in community-based networks. However, on many levels the training is differentiated. First, the development of the field has not been encouraged by the same institutions: in the universities of German Switzerland and at the University of Neuchâtel, institutes of ethnology offer courses in ethnomedicine and/or health and illness within the faculties of arts. However, courses are offered more as a matter of circumstance than structure, and only for a given semester or year. Elsewhere, the initiatives come from the faculties of medicine. In Lausanne, for instance, the

Institut Universitaire Romand d'Histoire de la Médecine et de la Santé[21] was the first to formally set up a seminar in medical anthropology. Over the years, this institute has helped the social sciences and humanities to expand within the Faculty of Medicine by encouraging teaching not only in history and anthropology, but also in the philosophy of medicine, medical epistemology, and the sociology of sciences and techniques. It was also at the University of Lausanne that an educational commission for introducing the humanities into medicine (made up of professors from the Faculty of Medicine and from the social sciences, political science, and the arts) was set up to introduce the social sciences and humanities into the course requirements of medical undergraduates in 2004–5. Another medical institution that has openly encouraged collaboration between anthropologists and physicians is the world-famous Swiss Tropical Institute of the University of Basel.[22] It focuses on interdisciplinary approaches to health in a North–South perspective (Obrist van Eeuwijk and Minja 1997; Obrist van Eeuwijk 2002a, 2002b) and migration issues (Salis Gross 2001, 2002). However, the courses may be part of one faculty or another. In Lausanne, for example, the Institute of Anthropology and Sociology of the Faculty of Social and Political Sciences used the momentum to set up courses in the anthropology of health in 2000.[23] At the University of Geneva, seminars are offered by the Institut Universitaire d'Études du Développement (IUED).[24] In French Switzerland, courses have become more regular in recent years, and in German Switzerland the University of Bern, and to a lesser extent, those in Basel and Zürich, have also placed greater importance on such courses in their undergraduate[25] and graduate[26] programs. Although they may have different names (ethnomedicine in German Switzerland, the anthropology of health, medicine, and illness in French-speaking universities, medical anthropology in the faculties of medicine, or the sociology of medicine, transcultural psychiatry, ethnopsychiatry, ethnopsychoanalysis), the theoretical and scientific interest in such questions makes them valid subjects to include in the program, especially considering how fragile current health policies have become.

Other institutions have also contributed to the development of the field. It is worth mentioning the collaborations between anthropologists and health professionals in university medical clinics in Lausanne and Geneva, particularly in the field of migrations (Hudelson 2002; Rossi 2000), at the Forum Suisse pour l'Étude des Migrations et des Populations (FSEMP)[27] in Neufchâtel, the OFSP[28] in Bern, the Institut interuniversitaire suisse pour de la santé publique[29] in Bern, Basel, and Zürich, and the Swiss institute for health promotion.[30]

In both research and education, the legitimacy of the anthropology of health and medicine is to be found in the balance it strikes between fundamental approaches and interdisciplinary work. While necessary, this convergence is insufficient if it does not go hand in hand with the definition of an epistemological horizon within an ethical framework that makes it possible to analyze institutions, knowledge, and social practice in moral and political terms. The efforts made thus far to ensure scientific and ethical rigor in dealing with the complexity of these changes are on the right track; they aim to place the many different forms of knowledge and viewpoints in dialogue in an effort to understand social complexity, to develop structured health strategies, and to put together theories and practices in order to plan, regulate, and assess actions taken in the field of health care. And this goes along with a desire to foster a humanist health-care culture.

The context is changing rapidly. The new European policies defined under the "Bologna Declaration"[31] profoundly reorganize the strategies of each university and radically modify the mandates, objectives, and programs of the anthropology of health. Local autonomy loses meaning with the creation of *"pôles d'excellence"* (specialized centers), which require a more rigorous and structured organization and the creation of interfaculty and interuniversity networks to ensure the survival and development of the discipline. What was collaboration yesterday has become imposed competition and complementarity today.

Restructuring has already begun. I will briefly outline what I see as the likely issues of tomorrow as concerns education and research. First, there is the creation of the National Doctoral School, partnered by the SSE, and structured around the theme "Globalized Fields: New Methods, New Concepts, New Issues" to be offered in all the country's languages plus English. In French-speaking Switzerland, the center for new biotechnologies at the Lausanne École polytechnique fédérale, created by the Swiss Confederation, has been the starting point for these changes, which has forced a reorganization of the entire academic structure of the lemanic basin. The so-called "Triangular Project"[32] links the universities of Lausanne and Geneva where a social sciences master's program in health studies and sciences has been created, bringing together the anthropology of health, psychology and health, the sociology of sciences and techniques, the sociology of gender, the sociology of the body, political sciences of health, the economics of health, and the history of medicine. Transversality and permeability between disciplines will be necessary elements and research projects will be divided into units. In German Switzerland, anthropologists tend to work more in public health settings, while in French- and Italian-speaking Switzerland, professionals have shown an interest in the arrival of "Medical Humanities"[33] with the introduction of the social sciences and humanities in undergraduate and graduate programs in medicine. These approaches are perceived as an instrument for analyzing the causes and consequences of the crisis in modern medicine, and could be defined as an integration of humanist knowledge capable of analyzing the large and small problems created by modern biomedicine. At the same time, they can provide answers and thus help to find better adapted ways for preserving people's health and for improving the health system in terms of the quality of services and maintaining respect for people's quality of life and for the environment.

Changes in university policies and the creation of Hautes Écoles Spécialisées de la santé et du social (HES2) will also focus the anthropological gaze on changes in social and health organizations, and on new knowledge and professional practices, and the issues that they raise. As Swiss anthropology increasingly will have to deal with an aging population, environmental and economic changes, technological developments, generalized migrations and intercultural relations, as well as changes in the workplace, it will take on an important position as a guardrail along the slippery slope the health sector is on, with the growing inequalities it is creating and the way in which it is being instrumentalized. By examining illness and the representations it engenders, and by approaching the individual and public search for health as a phenomenon of civilization, Swiss anthropology is increasingly moving towards considerations and collaborations that will be constructive for the health sciences, located between the life sciences and the social sciences and humanities.

Notes

1. Under the Swiss policy for university training, the counties (Cantons) are responsible for organizing and managing universities. However, the Confederation is responsible for the two *Écoles Polytechniques* in Lausanne and in Zürich. Over the past few years, the context has changed significantly, and the Confederation has taken a greater role in structuring university-level teaching and research (see the section "Training and research sites in medical anthropology and the anthropology of health").
2. Société Suisse d'Ethnologie (www.seg-sse.ch/fr, accessed January 15, 2004).
3. Commission Interdisciplinaire d'Anthropologie Médicale (CIAM), Medical Anthropology of Switzerland (MAS) (www.seg-sse.ch/fr/commissions/ciam.shtml).
4. The Commission's presidency is ensured in turn by one of its members. Since it was created, its presidents have been B. Obrist van Euwijk, from the University of Basel (1992–95), I. Rossi from the University of Lausanne (1995–98), C. Salis Gross, from the University of Bern (1998–2001), and beginning in 2001, P. van Euwijk from the Universities of Basel and Zürich.
5. In regional colloquiums the following themes have been discussed: AIDS prevention, aging and culture, medicine and ecology, medical pluralism here and elsewhere, connections between cultures, ethics, and health experiences. See the MAS website (www.seg-sse.ch/fr/commissions/ciam.shtml, accessed January 15, 2004) under the headings "Colloques" and "Symposium."
6. Notably the meetings organized by the University of Basel with C. Helman 1993: "Building Bridges. Dialogues between Anthropology and Medicine" and A. Kleinmann 1999, "Discourse between Anthropology, Medicine and Psychiatry," "Cultural Perspectives in Clinical Practice: New Relationships between Anthropology and Medicine," "Rethinking Psychiatry. A Critique of DSM4 and ICD 10 from a Cross-cultural Perspective," "Social Suffering and the Transformation of Social Experience in the New World Disorder"; or in Bern, "Culture, Ethics, and Experience: An Anthropological Approach to Moral Theory based on the Ethnography of Social Experience", "Psychosomatics and Local Biologies: How Mind, Brain and Society Interact to Create New Questions for Anthropology and Medicine." The same concern but a different context was evident in the symposiums organized by the University of Lausanne in 1996: "L'anthropologie médicale appliqué" (proceedings published in 1997 (Rossi 1997c); in 1998, "Médecine et pouvoirs" (forthcoming); and in 2003, "La santé en débat. Politiques de la co-disciplinarité."
7. Two national symposiums, organized by B. Obrist and P. van Euwijk (University of Basel), have dealt with the theme, for the first time in 1995, "Rapid Assessment Procedures in Health Intervention Research: Opportunities and Limitations," and for the second time in 2002, "Medizinethnologie im Spannungsfeld von Theorie und Praxis."

8. See, "Migration und Gesundheit" (1994), "Gewalterfahrungen bei Immigrantinnen und Immigranten" (1997), "Médiation culturelle et communication interculturelle" (1998), "Traumatization in the Context of Migration: Mechanisms of Marginalization and Perspectives for Empowerment" (2000), and "Gender, Gesundheit und Menschenrecht" (2001), organized by the Universities of Bern, Lausanne, and Zürich.

9. The findings of those studies were published in several articles and books over the years, including Droz (1999), Obrist van Eeuwijk (1992), Obrist van Eeuwijk and Mdungi (1994), Rossi (1997a).

10. For example, in Lausanne, the Association Appartenances (which does therapeutic work with immigrants and encourages research and training on intercultural relations (www.appartenances.ch)) and the Fondation Ling (which is openly pluridisciplinary and supports medical pluralism (www.ling.ch, accessed January 15, 2004)). In German Switzerland, interdisciplinary cooperation on issues of migration has been made possible through cooperation with associative networks such as the Red Cross and Caritas. Associative movements often work in face-to-face relationships with socially constituted groups, whom they accompany and support.

11. FNRS: Fonds National Suisse de la recherche (http://www.snf.ch/).

12. http://www.aids.ch/d/index.php, accessed January 15, 2004).

13. Office Fédéral de la Santé Publique (http://www.bag.admin.ch/f/index.htm, accessed January 15, 2004).

14. The situation in Switzerland has always been, and is still, quite critical. For a good example, read the debate on clean and dirty money: "Argent propre, argent sale. La SSE et le sponsoring," *Tsantsa* 2002;5:94–109, with contributions by S. Knecht, E. Hertz, P. Znoj, and M. Zürcher.

15. This overview can only indicate some of the main trends in Swiss research and does not claim to cover all of it. Many authors, studies, and articles that have been important in building knowledge in the field are not mentioned here.

16. http://www.bag.admin.ch/themen/migration/index.html?language=fr&dir2=&schriftgrad=, accessed January 15, 2004.

17. For example, B. Obrist is affiliated with the Institute of Ethnology and the Tropen Institute at the University of Basel, C. Salis Gross with the Bern Institute of Ethnology and the Tropen Institut at the University of Basel, C. Kopp with the Bern Institute of Ethnology and the OFSP, I. Rossi with the Institute of Sociology and Anthropology and the Department of Medicine and Community Health at the University of Lausanne.

18. The Swiss universities and institutes of anthropology or sociology offering courses in medical anthropology are as follows:

    Basel (http://www.unibas-ethno.ch/index2.php, accessed January 15, 2004);
    Bern (http://www.cx.unibe.ch/ethno/, accessed January 15, 2004);
    Zürich (http://www.ethno.unizh.ch/);
    Lausanne (http://www-ssp.unil.ch/IAS/iaswelcomesml.html, accessed January 15, 2004);
    Neuchâtel (http://www.unine.ch/ethno/welcome.html);
    Geneva (http://www.unige.ch/iued/new/, accessed January 15, 2004).

19. This field is particularly well covered in continuing education and postgraduate studies. Beginning next year, social sciences and humanities will be an integral part of undergraduate training in the Faculty of Medicine.

20. All of the Hautes Écoles Spécialisées (HES Santé-Social) have courses in medical anthropology or the anthropology of health.
21. Institut Universitaire Romand d'Histoire de la Médecine et de la Santé, under the direction of Professor V. Barras: http://www.hospvd.ch/public/instituts/iuhmsp, accessed January 15, 2004).
22. Swiss Tropical Institute (www.sti.ch/). The anthropologist PD Dr. Brigit Obrist van Eeuwijk coordinates an NCCR research pole at the institute called "Vulnerability, Livelihood and Health in Urban West Africa." Funding: Forschungsprogramm im Rahmen des NCCR "Nord–Süd" (Gesamtleitung: Geographisches Institut, Universität Bern), IP 4 "Health and Wellbeing," Leitung: Schweizerisches Tropeninstitut. Homepage des Zentrums für Afrikastudien der Universität Basel (http://www.unibas-zasb.ch/deutsch/index.php, accessed January 15, 2004).
23. In the context of the courses offered by the Institute of Anthropology and Sociology, the course in the anthropology of health "Health in the Face of Globalization" (Prof. I. Rossi) is funded by the IRIS program 8a *Santé et Société*" (Health and Society).
24. Seminar entitled "Santé et développement: nouveaux enjeux, nouvelles priorités" (health and development: new issues, new priorities), under the direction of F. Grange and J-D. Rainhorn.
25. *At the University of Bern:*

    Prof. H-R. Wicker: Einführung in die Medizinethnologie (Vorlesung);
    Dr. C. Salis Gross: Am Rande der Existenz: Medizinethnologie in extremen Arbeitsfeldern. (Übung im Rahmen der AG Medizinethnologie);
    Dr. C. Salis Gross: Laqueurs Kulturgeschichte des Körpers (Übung im Rahmen der Arbeitsgruppe Ethnopsychoanalyse);
    Prof. H-R. Wicker: Vom interkulturellen zum transkulturellen Arbeiten in Institutionen (Übung);
    Prof. H-R. Wicker: Von kollektiver Gewalt. Eskalation und De-Eskalation (Seminar);
    Dr. C. Salis Gross: Kulturelle Repräsentationen des Todes (Übung); Aktivitäten der Arbeitsgruppe Medizinethnologie; Aktivitäten der Arbeitsgruppe Ethnopsychoanalyse.

    At the University of Zürich:
    Peter van Eeuwijk: Medizinethnologie I: Einführung (Vorlesung); Medizinethnologie II: Vertiefung (Proseminar); Medizinethnologie III: Angewandte Medizinethnologie (Übung).

    At the University of Basel:
    Brigit Obrist: Forschungsansätze der Medizinethnologie (Seminar).
26. The "Migration and Public Health" portion of the interuniversity master's in public health is under the direction of C. Salis Gross of the University of Bern (www.public-health-edu.ch, accessed January 15, 2004). The postgraduate study program at Lausanne's Polyclinique Médicale Universitaire, FARMED (health and migration), is also coordinated by an anthropologist, I. Rossi.
27. Forum Suisse pour l'Étude des Migrations et des Populations (Swiss Forum for the Study of Migration and Population) (www.unine.ch/fsm, accessed January 15, 2004).

28. Office de la Santé Publique (Office of Public Health) (www.bag.admin.ch/f/index. htm, accessed January 15, 2004).
29. Institut Interuniversitaire de santé publique (Interuniversity Institute of Public Health) (http://www.public-health-edu.ch, accessed January 15, 2004).
30. Institut Suisse pour la Promotion de la Santé (Swiss Institute for Health Promotion) (http://www.promotiondelasante.ch/fr/fs.aspnav=ser, accessed January 15, 2004).
31. Declaration   (http://www.unige.ch/cre/activities/Bologna20Forum/Bologne1999/ bologna20declaration.htm, accessed January 15, 2004).
32. http://www.unil.ch/central/part/triangulaire.html, accessed January 15, 2004.
33. For example the "Master international in Medical Humanities", organized by the University of Insubria (Varese/Italy), the University of Geneva, and the Fondazione Sasso Corbaro (Tessin/Switzerland).

References

AUGÉ M. and C. HERZLICH, eds, 1983, Le sens du mal. Anthropologie, histoire, sociologie de la maladie. Paris: Éd. des Archives contemporaines.

DEL VECCHIO M.-J., P. E. BROWIN, B. J. GOOD and A. KEINMANN, 1992, Pain as Human Experience: An Anthropological Perspective. Berkeley: University of California Press.

DOMENIG D., 2001a, Professionnelle transkulturelle Pflege. Handbuch für Lehre und Praxis in Pflege und Geburtshilfe. Bern: Verlag Hans Huber.

———, 2001b, Migration, Drogen, transkulturelle Kompetenz. Bern: Verlag Hans Huber.

DROZ Y., 1998, Patterns of Peasant Livelihood Strategies: Local Actors and Sustainable Resource Use. Eastern and Southern African Journal of Geography (Nairobi) 8:55–65 (with the contribution of Erwin Künzi, Urs Wiesmann and Francis Maina).

———, 1999, Migrations kikuyus: des pratiques sociales à l'imaginaire; ethos, réalisation de soi et millénarisme. Recherches et Travaux no. 14. Neuchâtel: Institut d'ethnologie et Maison des sciences de l'Homme.

GONSETH M.-O., ed., 1994, Les frontières du mal. Approches anthropologiques de la santé et de la maladie. Ethnologica Helvetica 17/18.

GOOD B. J., 1994, Medicine, Rationality and Experience. An Anthropological Perspective. Cambridge: University Press.

HELMANN C., 1992, Culture, Health and Illness. 2nd edition. London: B&H.

HUDELSON P., 2002, Que peut apporter l'anthropologie médicale à la pratique de la médecine? Médecine et Hygiène 60:1775–1780.

KLEINMANN A., 1988, The Illness Narratives. Suffering, Healing and the Human Condition. New York: Basic Books.

———, 1995, Writing at the Margin. Discourse between Anthropology and Medicine. Berkeley: University of California Press.

KLEINMANN A. and B. GOOD, eds, 1985, Culture and Depression. Studies in the Anthropology and Cross-Cultural Psychiatry of Affect and Disorder. Berkeley: University of California Press.

KOPP SUTTER C., 2002, The New Era of AIDS. HIV and Medicine in Times of Transition. Dordrecht: Kluwer Academic Publishers.

LE BRETON D., 1990, Anthropologie du corps et modernité. Paris: PUF.

LOCK M. and N. SCHEPER-HUGHES, 1990, A Critical-interpretive Approach in Medical Anthropology: Rituals and Routines of Discipline and Dissent. *In* Medical

Anthropology: A Handbook of Theory and Method. T. M. Johnson and C. F. Sargent, eds. Pp. 47–72. New York: Greenwood Press.

MAGGI J. and S. CATTACIN, 2003, Needed Basic Research in Migration and Public Health 2002–2006 in Switzerland. Neuchâtel: FSEMP.

MOSER C., 1997, Die Geburt des Patienten. Ritualisierungen und Konstruktionen der Arzt-Patienten Interaktion. Köniz: Edition Soziothek.

MOSER C., D. NYFELER and M. VERWEY, 2001, Traumatisierung von Flüchtlingen und Asylsuchenden: Einfluss des politischen, sozialen und medizinischen Kontextes. Zürich: Seismo.

OBRIST VAN EEUWIJK B., 1992, Small but Strong. Cultural Contexts of (Mal)nutrition among the Northern Kwanga (East Sepik Province, Papua New Guinea). Ethnologisches Seminar der Universität Basel und Museum für Völkerkunde/Wepf. Basler Beiträge zur Ethnologie, Basel.

——, 2002a, Gesundheit in Städten der Dritten Welt. Ein Graduiertenprogramm des Schweizerischen Tropeninstitut und des Ethnologischen Seminars der Universität Basel. In Schweizerische Akademie der Geistes- und Sozialwissenschaften, Forschungspartnerschaft mit Entwicklungsländern. Eine Herausforderung für die Geistes- und Sozialwissenschaften. Pp. 49–54. Bern: Schweizerische Akademie der Geistes- und Sozialwissenschaften.

——, 2002b, Ohne Sauberkeit keine Gesundheit. Hygiene im Alltag von Dar es Salaam, Tansania. Tsantsa 7: 66–76.

OBRIST VAN EEUWIJK B. and S. HIRSCH, 1992, Ich möchte mit meiner eigenen Hilfe auskommen, aber es geht nicht. Eine medizinethnologische Studie über Krankheitserfahrungen türkischer und kurdischer Menschen in der Region Zürich. Zürich: Schweizerisches Arbeiter/Innen Hilfswerk.

OBRIST VAN EEUWIJK B. and Z. N. MDUNGI, 1994, To Play upatu for Health: Supporting Health Initiatives in Low-Income Urban Areas of Dar es Salaam, Tanzania. In Überleben im afrikanischen Alltag: Improvisationstechniken im ländlichen und städischen Kontexte. B. Sottas and L. Roost Vischer, eds. Pp. 143–158. Berlin: Lang Verlag.

OBRIST VAN EEUWIJK B. and H. MINJA, 1997, Reconsidering the Concept of Household Headship: Reflections on Woman's Notions and Practices of Headship in Dar es Salaam, Tanzania. Werkschau Afrika-Studien/Le Forum Suisse des Africanistes. In B. Sottas, T. Hanner, L. Roost Vischer and A. Mayor, eds. Pp. 209–222. Münster: Lit Verlag.

OSSIPOW L., 1997, La cuisine du corps et de l'âme: approche ethnologique du végétarisme. Neuchâtel: Éditions de l'Institut d'Ethnologie et Éditions de la Maison des Sciences de l'Homme.

ROSSI I., 1994, La medicalizzazione degli stranieri tra giustificazioni e interrogazioni. In Attraverso i confini. Aspetti psichiatrici del movimento e del mutamento. Meeting of the Swiss Society of Psychiatry, Lugano. Pp. 139–145.

——, 1995, Pluralisme médical: les enjeux des corps possibles. Cahiers médico-sociaux 39:25–31.

——, 1996, Médecine, Médecines. Parallélisme ou complémentarité? Cahiers médico-sociaux 40:17–24.

——, 1997a, Corps et Chamanisme. Essai sur le pluralisme médical. Paris: Armand Colin.

——, 1997b, L'anthropologie médicale entre théorie et pratique. Médecine Psychosomatique et Psychosociale 1–2/26:2–9.

—— ed., 1997c, Dossier Anthropologie médicale. Médecine Psychosomatique et Psychosociale 1–2.

——, 1999, Médiation culturelle et formation des professionnels de santé: de l'interculturalité à la co-disciplinarité. Soziale und Präventive Medizin 44(6):288–294.

——, 2000, Sistemi di cura e relazioni interculturali. *In* Immigrazione e diritto alla salute. Papers collection. Pp. 125–132. Genova: Erga edizioni.

——, 2002, Réseaux de soins, réseaux de santé. Culture prométhéenne ou liberté de l'impuissance. Tsantsa 7:12–21.

——, 2003, Mondialisation et sociétés plurielles ou comment penser la relation entre santé et migration. Médecine et Hygiène 61(2455):2039–2045.

ROSSI I., A. JEANNIN, F. DUBOIS-ARBER, P. GUEX and M. VANNOTTI, 1998, The Clientele of an Anonymous HIV Test Centre and the General Population Tested: Similarities and Differences. AIDS Care 10(1):89–103.

SABBIONI M., C. SALIS GROSS and U. SEILER, 1999, Le traitement de la douleur chez les patients migrants: perspective interdisciplinaire. *In* L'invalidité en souffrance. Défis et enjeux de la crise. D. Roger, ed. Pp. 41–53. Genève: Éditions Médecine et Hygiène.

SALIS GROSS C., 2001, Vorschläge für die Gestaltung der Arzt-Patienten-Interaktion. *In* Flüchtlinge in der Sprechstunde. Ein Ratgeber für Hausärztinnen und Hausärzte zur Betreuung von Asylsuchenden und Flüchtlingen in der Region Basel. M. Kurmann, ed. Pp. 29–42. Basel: Schweizerisches Tropeninstitut.

——, 2002, Trauma und Medikalisierung: Die Flüchtlingserfahrung in der Schweiz. Tsantsa 7:22–30.

SALIS GROSS C. and M. LONCAREVIC, 1999, Gesundheitsstrategien in den türkisch/kurdischen und bosnischen Communities: Zusammenfassung der Ergebnisse aus der Haushaltbegleitung (community study). NFP 39. Bern: Schweizerisches Tropeninstitut Basel/Institut für Ethnologie der Universität.

SALIS GROSS C. and M-J. DEL VECCHIO GOOD, eds, 2002, Experiencing Medical Power and the State. Special issue. Tsantsa 7: 5–92.

SALIS GROSS C., C. BLOCHIGER and C. MOSER, 1997, Die Arzt-Patienten-Interaction in der hausärztlichen Betreuung von Asylsuchenden und Flüchlingen. Basel: Schweizeriches Tropeninstitut Basel and Bundesamt für Gesundheit.

SALIS GROSS C., D. GILGEN, D. MAUSEZAHL, E. BATTEGEAY, P. FLUBACHER, M. TANNER, G. WEISS and C. HATZ, 2002, Klinische cultural Epidemiology von Gesundheitsproblemen ambulant behandelter Migrantinnen und Migranten aus der Türkei und aus Bosnien. *In* Migration und die Schweiz. Ergebnisse des Nationalen Forschungsprogramms Migration und interkulturelle Beziehungen. H-R. Wicker, H. Werner and R. Fibbi, eds. Pp. 507–530. Zürich: Seismo.

SCHEPER-HUGHES N. and M. LOCK, 1987, The Mindful Body: A Prolegomenon to Future Work in Medical Anthropology. Medical Anthropology Quarterly (Boston) 1(1):6–41.

VAN EEUWIJK P., 1999, Diese Krankheit passt nicht zum Doktor. Medizinethnologische Untersuchungen bei den Minahasa (Nord-Sulawesi, Indonesien). Basler Beiträge zur Ethnologie 41. Basel: Wepf.

——, 2000, Health Care from the Perspectives of Minhasa Villagers, Indonesia. *In* Global Health Policy, Local Realities: The Fallacy of the Level Playing Field. L. M. Whiteford and L. Manderson, eds. Pp. 79–10. Boulder, CO: Lynne Rienner Publishing.

——, 2001, Growing Old in the City. Health Transition among the Elderly in North Sulawesi, Indonesia. An Anthropological Approach to Old-Age Research. Poster presented at the Annual Meeting of the Commission for Research Partnerships with Developing Countries (KFPE), Bern.

——, 2002, Ageing and Health in Urban Indonesia, Urban Health and Development Bulletin 5(3/4):25–31.

WEISS R., 2003, Macht Migration krank? Eine transdisziplinäre Analyse der Gesundheit von Migrantinnen und Migranten. Zürich: Seismo.

WEISS R. and R. STUCKER, 1998, Interprétariat et médiation culturelle dans le système de soins. Rapport de recherche No 11. Neuchâtel: FSM.

WICKER H.-R., 1989a, Bemerkungen zu einer ethnozentrierten Sozialpolitik. In Migrationen aus der Dritten Welt. Ursachen und Wirkungen. Kälin W, Moser R, eds. Pp. 173–184. Bern: Verlag Paul Haupt.

——, 1989b, Orality in the Context of Vietnamese Personality and Culture. In Kinship, Social Change, and Evolution. Proceedings of a Symposium held in Honour of Walter Dostal. Wiener Beiträge zur Ethnologie und Anthropologie. A. Ginrich, S. Haas and G. Paleczek, eds. Pp. 173–184. Horn-Wien: Verlag Ferdinand Berger and Söhne.

——, 1993, Die Sprache extremer Gewalt. Studie zur Situation von gefolterten Flüchtlingen in der Schweiz und zur Therapie von Folterfolgen. Arbeitsblätter No. 6. Bern: Institut für Ethnologie, Universität Bern.

WICKER H.-R. and H.-K. SCHOCH, 1988, Refugees and Mental Health. South East Asian Refugees in Switzerland. In Refugees – The Trauma of Exile. D. Miserez, ed. Pp. 153–178. Dordrecht: Martinus Nijhoff Publishers.

WICKER H.-R, C. MOSER and T. GASS, 1998, Evaluation des Rückkehrhilfe- und Wiedereingliederungsprogrammes für bosnische Staatsangehörige. Bern: Institut für Ethnologie der Universität Bern.

WICKER H.-R., W. HAUG and R. FIBBI, eds, 2003, Migration und die Schweiz. Ergebnisse des Nationalen Forschungsprogramms Migration und interkulturelle Beziehungen. Zürich: Seismo.

Part III

Cross-cutting and Thematic Perspectives

Chapter 12

GENDER

Engendering Medical Anthropology
Carole H. Browner and Carolyn Sargent

Our objective in this chapter is to trace the theoretical and political trajectories that have shaped current research on gender in medical anthropology in the United States. In doing so we articulate explicit and implicit linkages between the fields of anthropology and gender studies and health. Here we focus mainly on US scholars – and Canadians to a lesser extent – in that most of this bridging scholarship emerged in this region. While anthropologists were not alone among social scientists in articulating a research agenda intended to reveal the social constructions of health and gender, for the most part we consider anthropological research, although we selectively include works by scholars from other disciplines. Also because most work in this area has looked at women, for the most part our review addresses issues associated with women's health. We consider male gender and health when there is relevant literature; this field is newly emerging and far more work is needed.[1]

Feminist activists of the 1960s contributed profoundly to the emergence of an anthropology of women and ultimately to feminist theories in anthropology by identifying the multiple and mutually reinforcing dimensions of gender inequality and the structures by which they are reproduced. Powerful social movements of that era sparked concerted efforts to revolutionize women's health care. This dialectic between the 20th-century popular health and feminist movements mirrored that seen in the 19th century. At the same time, scholars within the academy looked to the evolutionary and cross-cultural perspectives of anthropology for the light they could cast on understandings about health, sexuality, and the female body.

The Anthropology of Childbirth and the Political Relations Surrounding Reproduction

The feminist project within medical anthropology was inspired by the activist challenge to the enduring male institutional domination over reproduction and the female patient. Reconstructing the processes that led to the radical transformation from female to male controlled healing traditions, feminist medical anthropologists, along with feminist scholars from other disciplines, showed that "the suppression of female healers by the medical establishment was a political struggle . . . part of the history of the sex struggle in general" (Ehrenreich and English 1973:4).

Along with continued feminist activism, the proliferation of gender studies in anthropology in the 1970s revitalized scholarship on reproduction. In a series of richly detailed cross-cultural investigations, earlier ethnographers had introduced the study of reproductive behavior to the parent discipline; their work, however, was highly descriptive and atheoretical (Browner and Sargent 1996). It took the next generation of anthropologists to see the potential that studies on human reproduction held for defining a new research agenda with immediate political implications.

Brigitte Jordan's *Birth in Four Cultures* (1993) focused anthropological attention on the comparative study of birthing systems and in doing so single-handedly moved the nascent field beyond recording individual and isolated "birth practices" which had characterized earlier work on the subject. As Jordan astutely observed, "within any given system, birth practices appear packaged into a relatively uniform, systematic, standardized, ritualized, even morally required routine" (1993:2). A vast and important literature on the biocultural patterning of birth in both non-Western and Western societies quickly followed (Davis-Floyd and Sargent 1997). This literature, characterized by vivid ethnographic detail and careful analyses of how childbirth articulates with gender ideologies, domestic politics, religion and cosmology, occupational hierarchies, local medicine, and the structure of state-sponsored health services. It documented that birth practices within a particular society may be consensually shaped or bitterly contested (Davis-Floyd and Sargent 1997; Sargent 1989).

Studies by Browner (2000) and Ginsburg (1998), among others, illustrated that members of a given culture do not necessarily share reproductive goals regarding such issues as when to become pregnant or whether to continue an unintended pregnancy. Even in small-scale societies, husbands, kin, neighbors, and members of other social groups may have reproductive goals that conflict with one another – and with those of women themselves. This body of research focused attention on how decisions, including reproductive decisions, are actually made, thereby contributing to the central theme of the anthropology of women by studying what women really do as opposed to what ethnographers and male informants say they do. This work also informed newer anthropological recognition that intracultural diversity was as much a feature of pre-industrial as industrial societies.

Reproductive decision-making, however, concerns more than contested goals. Other social processes (e.g. historical relationships, negotiations among plural medical systems, religious traditions, variable conceptions of risk) also shape women's and men's reproductive decisions, as well as other aspects of their reproductive experiences. Allen's new monograph, for example, describes the competing definitions of risk – those drawn from international and national maternal health policies and those derived from local experience – and shows their effects on women's reproductive strategies and decisions in rural Tanzania (Allen 2002).

Within their continued efforts to analyze the broader social forces shaping women's reproductive experiences, medical anthropologists also focused on the ways the ideologies and practices of biomedicine determined women's reproductive options.

Synergism between feminist scholars and activists generated a political approach to women's health that was fundamentally different from the biomedical one and based on providing greater reproductive options and a redistribution of power between doctors and patients (Ginsburg and Rapp 1995; Morgen 2002).

The Medicalization of Reproduction

A consistent theme in this body of research is that the dominant cultural definition of birth in the United States is one in which pregnancy is viewed as a pathological state, requiring specialist attention and hospital delivery. Accordingly, the medicalization of childbirth, characterized by use of technological interventions during birth such as episiotomy (a surgical incision of the vagina to widen the birth outlet), intravenous medication, and the lithotomy (supine) position for delivery have become standard procedures (Davis-Floyd 1992; Jordan 1993), as has cesarean section, or surgical birth, which in many countries has reached 30% or higher (Sargent and Stark 1987). Davis-Floyd has shown that technocratic childbirth has become "an American rite of passage," in that 98 percent of women deliver in hospitals, in many hospitals more than 80 percent of women receive epidural anesthesia, and at least 90 percent are given episiotomies (Davis-Floyd and Sargent 1997:11).

In her now-classic cultural analysis of reproduction, Emily Martin (1987) extends the critique of medicalization to menstruation and menopause as well as childbirth. Analyzing women's narratives about their birth experiences, she describes their sense of alienation and fragmentation produced by reliance on technological interventions and specialist monitoring, revealing the deep ambivalence women feel about biomedical control as reflected in acts of resistance and opposition. At the same time, Margaret Lock and Dona Davis, among others, offer further cross-cultural analysis of the medicalization of menopause (Davis 1983; Lock 1993).

Breathtaking yet at times dizzying developments in reproductive science and technology continue to change values and expectations associated with conception, pregnancy, and childbirth. Since the 1970s, sharply critical feminist writings have questioned the excessive medicalization of women's reproductive processes, including the harmful effects of routinely used pharmaceuticals such as thalidomide and DES and medical procedures including hysterectomies and sterilizations (Morgen 2002:120). In subsequent decades, along with other scholars, anthropologists further documented ways that pregnancy and childbirth had become increasingly mechanized and pathologized. In addition to childbirth technologies, anthropologists questioned the growing use of fetal diagnostic testing and surveillance technologies. Browner and Preloran (2000) find technologies for the monitoring and surveillance of pregnancy have grown so common that many US women insist on having them, even in the absence of any medical indication. This is particularly true for ultrasound but increasingly for amniocentesis as well (Browner and Preloran 2000). These technologies are also rapidly becoming routine not just in the United States but in many other countries as well (Mitchell and Georges 1998; Morgan 1999; Taylor 2000), and used not just for diagnosing birth anomalies but also for sex determination that often leads to the selective abortion of female fetuses (Miller 2001). Rayna Rapp has eloquently reflected on some of the troubling moral issues inherent in the use of prenatal diagnosis. Through their use, she writes, "women are forced to judge the quality of their own fetuses, making concrete and embodied decisions about the standards for entry into the human community" (Rapp 1999:3).

Until the 1990s, work on the medicalization of reproduction focused largely on contraception, pregnancy, and childbirth; by contrast, infertility was almost completely ignored (Inhorn and Van Balen 2002). Since then a growing anthropological literature has looked at the devastating impact of pregnancy loss and infertility on the lives of those affected (Becker 1997; Layne 2002); there has also been a provocative ethnographic study of surrogacy (Ragone 1994). Marcia Inhorn's *Quest for Conception* (1994), the first comprehensive account of non-Western's women's experiences of infertility, depicted the struggles of poor, urban Egyptian women and their attempts to overcome infertility. Since then, other important cross-cultural accounts have appeared (Inhorn and Van Balen 2002). At the same time, feminist anthropologists warned about the disjuncture between the momentum of the technologies and their social and legal concomitants. The physically demanding and experimental nature of the new medical infertility procedures as well as their low success rates prompted alarm that women's bodies were becoming experimental sites. In this regard, Margarete Sandelowski compellingly describes what she characterizes as the "never-enough quality" of conceptive technologies (Sandelowski 1991). One of the newest directions in the anthropological literature on infertility is its personal and interpersonal impact on men.

The Paradigm of Authoritative Knowledge

A related body of important medical anthropological literature documents women's resistance in Western and non-Western societies to biomedical authority. Brigitte Jordan again broke new theoretical ground with the concept of "authoritative knowledge." She writes that "for any particular domain several knowledge systems exist, some of which, by consensus, come to carry more weight than others, either because they explain the state of the world better for the purposes at hand (efficacy) or because they are associated with a stronger power base (structural superiority), and usually both" (Jordan 1993:152).

Her conceptualization of "authoritative knowledge" has proved extremely useful in analyzing the shifting power relations implicated cross-culturally in struggles for control over childbirth, making visible the enormous work involved in imposing a consensual reality across power differences. The authors of the collection *Childbirth and Authoritative Knowledge* extended Jordan's concept to other reproductive domains, including US pregnant women's self-care practices during pregnancy and the maintenance of indigenous knowledge systems in the face of the global exportation of biomedicine (Davis-Floyd and Sargent 1997).

This newly focused anthropological attention to the structure and organization of expert knowledge and their implications for broader power relations in a given society built on a longstanding anthropological interest in healers and the management of illness. However historically anthropologists, who themselves were mostly men, were more interested in the dramatic, colorful, and often supernaturally inspired male healing specialists, such as spirit-mediums, diviners, and priests, and specialists such as bone-setters and herbalists who controlled well-defined bodies of expert knowledge. Carol McClain's *Women as Healers* (1989) broke new ground by, among other things, describing women as unnamed and informal healers, analyzing why women may be reluctant to assume public healing roles, illustrating the ways that female and mother symbols characterize women's healing practices, and showing how global processes are transforming women's healing techniques and practices. This work also spawned a literature on women in nonbiomedical healing roles.

Midwives have long been a principal focus in the work on women healers, beginning with accounts by Lois Paul, Arthur Rubel, and Sheila Cosminsky (Cosminsky 1976; Paul 1975; Rubel et al. 1971). Cosminsky's comprehensive review of the cross-cultural midwifery literature found that most works of that period were mainly descriptions of midwives' practices. Her own contribution was to examine variation in midwives' statuses and roles cross-culturally (Cosminsky 1976). Theories suggest that the social position of midwives derives from the social standing of women in the larger society, the status of healers who are not midwives (McClain 1989), the nature of the technical and ritual skills that midwives possess (Laderman 1983; Sargent 1989), and whether midwives are chosen by divine selection, self selection, inheritance, or in other ways (MacCormack 1982; Paul 1975). Nonetheless, there is no overarching single theory that fully explains variation in the social status of midwives cross culturally.

Political Economy, Health, and Gender

Within medical anthropology throughout the 1980s, a parallel intellectual orientation was developing focusing on political economy and health. Scholars working within this framework conducted macrolevel analyses of the effects of stratified socioeconomic and political relations within the world economic system on the distribution of disease and health services (Baer et al. 1997). However with rare exception (Morsy 1978), the earliest work in this area was oblivious to gender and it took another decade before researchers recognized that "the study of political economy, gender, and the social production of health can overlap and mutually enrich the resultant analyses" (Whiteford 1996:243).

Work by scholars including Ellen Lazarus, Linda Whiteford, Lesley Doyal, and Soheir Morsy illuminated the links between gender, social class, and health. In Morsy's ethnographic study of an Egyptian Nile Delta village, she investigates the extent to which gender and social class are implicated in the condition of spirit possession known as "*uzr.*" She shows that the incidence of illness and perceived stress in the community are related to asymmetrical power relations derived from subservient socioeconomic status within the national economy and deviation from culturally sanctioned sex role behavior (Morsy 1978). Morsy's work was far ahead of her time in that she presaged the feminist emphasis on difference among women with regard to class, age group, and family structure.

Others broadened their analytical gaze to include race as another powerful determinant. Linda Whiteford, for example, offers the case of an impoverished crack cocaine-addicted pregnant woman who is sentenced to prison. She situates the woman's predicament within the social construction of gender, race, and class and concludes that laws that punish pregnant women for addiction are less about protecting the fetus than about punishing women for being poor, pregnant, non-white, and addicted (Whiteford 1996). Ellen Lazarus considers medical choice, control, and social class in her research in an obstetric clinic in the United States. Focusing on what she refers to as the "intermediate" or institutional level of analysis, she shows that the power differentials between physicians and patients echoed the gender, race, and class hierarchies in the larger society, as the lower class patients in her study felt deserted by the very practitioners they thought would help them (Lazarus 1994). The health affects of race–class inequalities are further reflected in the epidemiological patterning of most diseases. For example, in the United States strokes occur far more often in black than white women and while black women are less likely to be diagnosed with breast cancer, they are more likely to die from it.

Lesley Doyal's classic overview from a political economic perspective, *What Makes Women Sick* (Doyal 1995), offers a comprehensive analysis of the global and local obstacles that prevent women from meeting their health needs, including the persistent gap between the poor and rich nations, poverty as a risk factor for HIV and other sexually transmitted diseases, unsafe sex practices, institutionalized violence against women, occupational hazards, the gendered division of labor, and lack of access to reliable means of regulating reproduction.

Women working outside the home typically spend only slightly less time in domestic work than full time housewives. Particularly in developing countries, women work longer hours than men and the poorer the country, the more hours the women work. Most spend from ten to sixteen hours a day preparing food, doing housework, and caring for children. Quantitative data consistently show that regardless of whether they work outside their homes, women work more hours each day than their husbands. The health effects of this "double day" have still not been well researched; Stellman points to some of the potential interactions:

some of the major health hazards for women at work complement and exacerbate hazards at home. Back injuries and backaches are common to workers on the job as well as to the mother of young children and to the housekeeper at home. Skin irritation and disease are widespread among hospital workers, service workers, and industrial workers just as they are among women in the home role. (Stellman 1997:82)

For poor women in particular, the needs to both produce income and care for children may lead them to take jobs that are more poorly paid but allow flexible hours or permit them to bring along their children. And in the event that their economic burdens increase, they generally work longer hours while continuing to engage in their domestic responsibilities. In doing so, they appear not to trade off one activity for another but instead give up recreation and devote less time to sleep, rest, and relaxation. Competing demands on a woman's time for household versus market production may therefore constrain her ability to protect and promote her own and her family's health. For some women the demands of their multiple roles require more energy than their food intake provides, leading to further deteriorating health and malnutrition.

Several in-depth ethnographic accounts closely explicate the links between gender, political economy, and health by looking at the relationship between women's domestic and waged labor and their health. This was an important corrective in that it took the field beyond its initial focus on reproduction and reproductive health.

In this regard, MacCormack (1994) makes the helpful distinction between direct and indirect risks affecting women's health. Women experience direct risk when their work causes them to stand in water where they can be exposed to parasites such as schistosomiasis, onchocerciasis, and malaria. For example, in Sierra Leone, the sexual division of labor requires women to spend far more time than men working in stagnant water transplanting rice, collecting drinking water, washing clothes, and fishing (MacCormack 1994). Transporting heavy loads such as firewood and water is strenuous, demanding, and exhausting leading to physical effects such as fatigue and painful joints. Medical reports also document that carrying heavy loads can cause prolapsed uterus, spinal and pelvic damage, and reproductive problems. There are specific risks associated with the use of open stoves and cooking fires, including burns and smoke pollution. The activities of weeding, transplanting, postharvest production that are involved in cultivation often cause chronic back and leg problems and may expose women to pesticides.

Indirect risks arise from the consequences of the devaluation of girls and women – early age of marriage and family preferences for making social investments, including for food and health care – in men rather than women. Koblinsky and associates describe the myriad factors associated with health infrastructure and service organizations that restrict women's access to health care, including those associated with distance, transportation, and communication (Koblinsky et al. 1993). And although in most societies women are responsible for their family's health-care needs, these logistical difficulties are reinforced by cultural restrictions on women's mobility and their ability to interact with men.

An extreme example of this comes from Hemming's study of refugees living in Afghanistan under the Taliban regime. Women unaccompanied by male relatives were prohibited from leaving their compounds and often could not get needed medical care as a result (Hemming 1997). Hampshire's study of pastoral nomads in Chad reveals others ways that mobility can determine access to health care. As is true elsewhere in the world, most illness episodes were treated at home and women were responsible for home-based treatments; men, however, controlled the resources that would be needed to obtain medical care outside the home. However, the women who had large social networks had better access to health care when the group was not dispersed on seasonal migrations; when it was, women's health-care options become much more limited, often resulting in delayed treatment (Hampshire 1998).

Gender and HIV/AIDS

The HIV/AIDS pandemic highlighted sexuality and sexual practices as major public health issues. It also generated a vast anthropological literature that explicated links between gendered behaviors, gender ideologies, and risk of HIV infection. This anthropological research has revealed how these gender ideologies and practices embody power relations and assign meaning and value to certain sexual relationships and behaviors (Farmer et al. 1996). It also shows that issues surrounding sex, sexuality, and gender are integrally connected to intimate, private, and personal interactions between and among women and men and further reveal the multiplicity of ways that cultural models of heterosexual or homosexual relationships and family structures are conditioned by political economic relations (Sobo 1995). For example, Brooke Schoepf's extensive analysis of the cultural patterning of HIV risk in central Africa concludes that HIV spreads not through exotic sexual practices but through the contingencies of everyday life. Moreover, her observations confirm that many women at risk for HIV infection are not engaged in commercial sex and that most sexual risk is not under the control of women (Schoepf 1998).

Idioms of Distress

Research informed by the political economic orientation has also focused on how stresses produced by interactions between productive and reproductive responsibilities also put women at risk for a wide range of conditions that have been characterized as "idioms of distress" (Nichter 1981). The concept was developed by Nichter during his research in south India to describe how Brahman women with weak social support networks and few socially approved ways to express distress manifest suffering. These external projections of distress include spirit possession, fasting, locally meaningful symptoms such as "overheat" and "hot head." Other examples of work focusing on folk illness and local idioms of distress are found in the large literature on *nervios* (nerves) in Europe, Latin America, and among US Latino groups (Low 1992; Jenkins 1996; Rebhun 1994). Researchers, who describe a very wide range of symptoms associated with the condition including dizziness, fatigue, headache, chest pain, and feelings of anger, anxiety, sadness, and desperation, tend to conclude that "nerves" is more an "idiom of daily life" than a medical complaint *per se*.

Rebhun (1994) illustrates how the suppression of strong emotions is linked with sickness. Working in northeast Brazil, she finds strong prohibitions against openly expressing the powerful negative emotions, especially jealousy, envy, anger, and hatred, that inevitably arise in the course of everyday life. These prohibitions are particularly problematic for women, who are expected to always be compassionate and selfless. Women use the expression "swallowing frogs" to refer to the need to suppress anger and endure unfair treatment such as husband's extramarital love affairs. Their anguish is expressed in several folk ailments including "nerves" *susto* (soul loss sickness), "open chest," and "blood-boiling bruises," small bruises on their thighs and arms that they attribute to their blood boiling in their veins with anger. Oths's analysis of *debilidad*, characterized by symptoms which include headache, dimmed eyesight, loss of appetite, and "aching or agitated heart," is often experienced by older women living in the northern Peruvian highlands after their children are grown. She ties the syndrome to the reproductive and productive stresses generated by the pressures of harsh social and economic conditions (Oths 1999).

Seeking a concept that transcends the particularistic formulations that have characterized much work on idioms of distress, Finkler proposes the concept of "life's lesions" which express through the body the negative conditions of existence such as poverty, malnutrition, and other adverse life events. Adding to these political and economic processes, she points to the importance of moral imperatives concerning proper behavior in social relations. She suggests that when these relationships are contested and remain unresolved they generate "life's lesions." "Under such circumstances, unresolved contradictions and moral indignations become inscribed on the body, ensuring symptomatology in overall discomfort, pain, and suffering" (Finkler 1994:16).

At the same time, both Michel Foucault and a number of major feminist theorists such as Jana Sawicki (1991) have drawn much needed attention to the many ways state politics and policies – and those of other powerful institutions – may be inscribed upon the body. Within this framework, female disorders such as anorexia and agoraphobia are an unconscious form of resistance. But whereas the idioms of distress literature focuses on the subjective experience of the sufferer (although in relation to political economy), feminists informed by Foucault additionally interrogate subjectivities made manifest by political oppression and social inequalities (see Scheper-Hughes 1992). Physical symptoms, then, are not just biological manifestations but also metaphors that reflect and represent political resistance. A parallel literature, derived from phenomenology, uses the concept of "embodiment." Low (1992:159), for example, observed that women suffering symptoms of *nervios*, or "nerves" carry "the communicative force of culturally generated metaphors of distress that provide symbolic expression of personal conflicts, community upheaval, and social control through bodily experience" (see also Allen 2002 on managing and disciplining Tanzanian mothers and Van Hollen 2003:159 on female subjectivities and reproduction as an object of state surveillance in South India).

Violence Against Women

Among the most pervasive yet least recognized consequences of sexism throughout the world are the many forms of institutionalized violence against women. Heise defines gender violence to include "any act of force or coercion that gravely jeopardizes the life, body, psychological integrity or freedom of women, in service of perpetuating male power and control" (Heise 1993:171). It includes rape, battery, homicide, incest, psychological abuse, forced prostitution, trafficking in women, sexual harassment, acid attacks on girls and women involved in dowry disputes and domestic conflicts, dowry-related murder, or "bride-burning," and selective female infanticide and selective female abortion.

Given the global scope of these problems, it is surprising how little anthropological attention has been devoted to analyzing the responsible factors. For instance, it is estimated that at least 30 percent of US women will be beaten by a partner at some point in their lives. In Papua New Guinea, 67 percent of rural women and 56 percent of urban women report having experienced abuse. A survey from Santiago, Chile finds that 80 percent of women reported abuse by a male relative or partner (Heise 1993).

In parts of India, one in four deaths among women aged 15–24 were due to "accidental burns" and female deaths from burns have been increasing for the past 25 years in conjunction with the commercialization of dowry demands. It appears that homicides and suicides are being recorded as "accidents" rather than intentional injuries (Heise 1993). Additional evidence for this comes from a study in Bangladesh of deaths among women aged 15–44 during an eleven-year period. Eighteen percent of the women's deaths were from intentional or unintentional injuries, 52 percent of which occurred during or immediately after pregnancy. The authors conclude that the underlying causes of these violent deaths, primarily complications of induced abortion, suicides, and homicides, are clearly social and may be seen as a consequence of men's strict control over women's sexual and reproductive lives (Fauveau and Blanchet 1989).

In certain parts of the world, these gender ideologies that hyper-value men have produced not just selective neglect of female children but infanticide and the selective abortion of female fetuses. The classic anthropological work on the subject is Miller's demographic and ethnographic analysis of gender, culture, and mortality in north India (Miller 1981). She shows that the dramatic sex ratio imbalances favoring men which historically had been due to outright infanticide continue today in more subtle ways including discrimination in the allocation of food and medical care. Yet even as feminists throughout the world have forcefully spoken out against these discriminatory practices, new forms of gendered violence are emerging, as Miller shows in her highly disturbing analysis of selective female abortion throughout Asia (Miller 2001). Several million female fetuses have been aborted in the last two decades of the 20th century. This is made possible by the growing availability of technologies, mainly ultrasound and amniocentesis that permit prenatal sex determination.

Medical anthropologists have also analyzed the consequences of war, rape, and genital cutting for women's health and well-being. In a series of insightful papers, Jenkins analyzes female Salvadoran refugees' experiences of trauma and political violence and the effects of these experiences on their mental health. Her objective is to expand anthropological discourses on emotions by examining the linkages among state construction of political ethos, personal emotions, and mental health consequences for refugee women. One of her analyses seeks to explain why some women manifest symptoms of post traumatic stress disorder after experiencing the events and conditions of political violence such as warfare, torture, detention, and sexual assault, while others describe them as mundane. She hypothesizes that the extreme and the mundane may be different expressive modalities for the same severe emotional responses (Jenkins 1996:286). Analysis of the life histories of women who experience political and other forms of violence could help explain the observed variation.

While Jenkins has focused on women who experienced the trauma of warfare, Olujic draws links between the violence women experience in war and peacetime in Croatia and Bosnia-Herzegovina. She shows how wartime gender violence draws on preexisting gender-based power relations and ideologies and concludes that war rapes in this region would not have been as effective as weapons of terror and torture against women were it not for the associations between honor, shame, and women's bodies (Olujic 1998).

The incidence or absence of sexual assault against women is shaped by many factors including a society's overall tolerance for violence, the socialization of boys, and values governing relations between the sexes. In a study of US fraternity gang rape, she shows that masculinist values and practices that encourage the use of force against women are seen in a fraternity culture that emphasize toughness, physical force, and an interpersonal style de-emphasizing caring and sensitivity. She describes in graphic detail drinking, coercive sexual behavior, and the degradation of women that form a central part of much fraternity social life (Sanday 1990).

There are other settings where male violence against women is considered inevitable. The institutionalized battering of women in many societies throughout the world is one example. Another is male violence associated with "survival sex." Some poor women in parts of South Africa have sex with men who they meet in taverns in exchange for money but do not consider themselves commercial sex workers. She shows such women are at risk for violence due to pervasive attitudes condoning forced sex and lack of sanctions against battering women. "This type of environment, where it is socially acceptable for a man to demand sex from a woman for whom he buys drinks or gives gifts, and where short skirts are believed to lead naturally to rape, contributes to a sense of inevitability on the part of women who engage in survival sex" (Wojcicki 2002:278).

Feminist Activism and Women's Health

Since the mid-1970s, women's health care has been dramatically transformed as feminist activists created self-help groups, health collectives, clinics, and organizations that advocated for change in the structure and delivery of women's health care and the principles on which they were based (Morgen 2002). Their work was infused with the understanding that politics saturates all aspects of women's health and health care. Feminist activists engaged in important struggles over contraceptives, abortion, HIV, adolescent pregnancy, forced cesarean deliveries, breast cancer, hormone replacement therapy, environmental causes of cancer and other chronic illnesses, premenstrual syndrome (PMS), female genital cutting, and disability which had far ranging consequences.

Feminist anthropologists have become involved in defining the terms of the debates in many of these issues. For example, Martha Ward's cultural analyses of the politics surrounding teenage reproduction critiques US public and educational programming (Ward 1986). Jordan and Irwin challenge the role of the state as ultimate arbiter of how pregnant women give birth by impelling those who resist their doctors' diagnosis of fetal distress to undergo cesarean deliveries (Jordan and Irwin 1989). Scholars including Barroso and Correa have shown that long acting injectable contraceptives such as Depo-Provera and subdermal implants like Norplant which have serious known side effects are more likely to be given to poor women than to others (Barroso and Correa 1995). Such practices allow the medical establishment and the state to control women's fertility, denying a sense of agency to women themselves (Morsy 1998). The political movements around breast cancer and the use of mammography have to date had little impact on the anthropological literature. An important exception is Kaufert who observes that feminist medical anthropologists have focused more on individual women's experiences with their physicians, tending to ignore the broader corporate structure of medicine such as the economic interests that drive the mammography industry (Kaufert 1996).

Patricia Kaufert has also pioneered in focusing anthropological attention on the contentious issue of routine hormone supplementation for perimenopausal women, which like mammography has been challenged by feminist activists and scholars as driven by economic interests. Kaufert notes that the nature of debates on the safety of estrogen supplements are shaped by the fact that estrogen is prescribed only for women. In tracing the history of the controversy she shows how technological developments in the area of women's health may be determined more by ideological and sociopolitical factors than by women's own interests and needs (Kaufert and McKinlay 1985), thus ignoring the fact that such treatments may have negative consequences for women's health (Anglin 1997).

In contrast to the limited attention anthropologists have paid to certain aspects of medicalization and women's health, they have been deeply involved in articulating the political, ethical, and medical dilemmas raised by cultural practices of female genital cutting. The resurgence of international efforts to eradicate this practice during the last part of the 20th century has forced scholars to confront a pivotal question: "Who has the moral authority to condemn this practice?" (Shell-Duncan and Hernlund 2000). In defining research that traced the history of the movement against female genital cutting in the Sudan, Gruenbaum shows that attempts to develop policies outlawing the practice have failed to acknowledge the linkages between genital cutting and the social goal of marrying daughters in strongly patriarchal societies. She argues effective change can only come about in the context of local women's movements oriented toward ameliorating basic social problems affecting women such as economic dependency, lack of education, and obstacles to employment (Gruenbaum 2001). By contrast, Gordon indicts anthropologists for their failure to take a universalistic moral position against female genital cutting despite militant international women's health movements' agenda for its eradication. He further accuses anthropologists of contributing to a cover-up about its medical risks by instead emphasizing local meanings linked to the practice (Gordon 1991; Obermeyer 1999). Janice Boddy (1991) rebuts those who castigate cultural relativism in their critiques of female genital cutting by observing that understanding a practice is not the same as condoning it. Broadening the debate she adds, "clearly, a central question epitomized so horribly by the practice of female 'circumcision' is why female bodies in virtually every society should be subject to alteration, maiming, mutilation, [and?] control" (Boddy 1991:16).

Emerging Issues

"I am reminded of the sheikh invited to a function in the garden of the Governor General's palace in Khartoum at the outset of this century who, upon spying for the first time a wasp-waisted European woman, inquired how the effect was achieved. On being enlightened, he replied, "It is barbaric! Where does she put her food?" (Boddy 1991:16–17).

Despite an exhaustive literature on body image and eating disorders in the social, psychological, and clinical sciences, anthropologists have paid scant attention to this important topic. Mimi Nichter's recent groundbreaking ethnography *Fat Talk*, however, explores body image and eating habits among European American, African American, and Latina female adolescents (Nichter 2000). In her book, we hear girls' voices explaining how they feel about their own bodies and their mothers' bodies and describe the strategies of restrictive eating, excessive exercise, and a rhetoric of "fat talk" in the absence of dieting (see Becker 1994). A similarly important topic that has also received little anthropological attention is the use and meanings of cosmetic surgery for women and men (Kaw 1993). In spite of these excellent works, far more research is needed on how cultural expectations, media representations of the body, and fashion and fitness industries shape women's and men's ideas about their bodies.

Women's experiences with disability are opening up another set of important issues that deserve far greater anthropological attention from a feminist perspective. Research on attitudes toward disability has focused primarily on the populations most directly affected, such as families of children with disabilities or teachers or other professionals who work with disabled individuals (Press et al. 1998). Most of this work has been informed by the discipline of psychology. Recently, however, disability activists and researchers have begun to examine how individuals construct the meaning of particular disabilities in general or in specific contexts, how they come to determine what it means to be "human" or "normal," and the importance of these qualities for social relationships and social interaction (Landsman 1998). Gender constructs also deeply affect the way individuals with disabilities perceive their sense of who they are in the world (Frank 2000) but this remains an understudied area. An agenda that prioritizes research on the intersections between gender ideologies and disability including the construction of sexuality for those with physical and mental impairments and how gender roles may be compromised by disability or transcended in the establishment of gendered relationships is urgently needed.

Conclusion

In this analysis of the most important research trends at the intersection of medical anthropology, the anthropology of women, and gender studies, we sought to show how the second wave of feminism that began in the 1960s helped define key research agendas.

However, gender studies in medical anthropology have done more than contribute to these anthropological subfields. They have provided rich insight and helped build theory in the larger discipline of anthropology in areas including the political relations surrounding human reproduction, the production and transformation of knowledge systems, the social dilemmas that the increasingly ubiquitous reliance of medical technologies produce, the consequences for women's health of institutional forms of sexism that legitimize male violence against women, and how articulations between class, race, gender, and health help shape human experience. We are optimistic that this fruitful dialectical collaboration between feminist activism and research will continue and that it will continue to help define research issues, enrich the discourses surrounding them, and chart future directions for more equitable and more just societies.

Note

1. In the United States, there is no single journal devoted to this area of inquiry. However, the main feminist journals including *Feminist Studies*, *Signs*, and *Gender and Society*, the chief journals that publish medical anthropology such as *Medical Anthropology Quarterly*, *Medical Anthropology*, and *Social Science and Medicine*, and the general anthropology journals including *the American Anthropologist*, *American Ethnologist*, *Cultural Anthropology*, and *Ethnology* run articles and occasional theme issues. Similarly, there are no programs that specialize in gender studies in medical anthropology. However, the University of California at Los Angeles, San Francisco and Berkeley, New York University, Southern Methodist University, Case Western University, and the University of Michigan are among the schools with faculty whose interests lie at the intersection of gender and health and inform student specializations.

References

ALLEN D. R., 2002, Managing Motherhood, Managing Risk: Fertility and Danger in West Central Tanzania. Ann Arbor: University of Michigan Press.

ANGLIN M., 1997, Working from the Inside Out: Implications of Breast Cancer Activism for the Policies and Practices of Biomedicine. Social Science and Medicine 44(9):1403–1415.

BAER H. A., M. SINGER and I. SUSSER, 1997, Medical Anthropology and the World System. A Critical Perspective. Westport: Bergin and Garvey.

BARROSO C. and S. CORREA, 1995, Public Servants, Professionals, and Feminists: The Politics of Contraceptive Research in Brazil. *In* Conceiving the New World Order. F. Ginsburg and R. Rapp, eds. Pp. 292–307. Berkeley: University of California Press.

BECKER A. E., 1994, Nurturing and Negligence. Working on Others' Bodies in Fiji. *In* Embodiment and Experience. The Existential Ground of Culture and Self. T. Csordas, ed. Pp. 100–116. Cambridge: Cambridge University Press.

BECKER G., 1997, Healing the Infertile Family. Strengthening Your Relationship in the Search for Parenthood. Berkeley: University of California Press.

BODDY J., 1991, Body Politics: Continuing the Anti-circumcision Crusade. Medical Anthropology Quarterly 5(1):15–16.

BROWNER C. H., 2000, Situating Women's Reproductive Activities. American Anthropologist 102(4):773–788.

BROWNER C. H. and H. M. PRELORAN, 2000, Para sacarse la espina (To Get Rid of the Doubt). Mexican Immigrant Women's Amniocentesis Decisions. *In* Bodies of Technology: Women's Involvement with Reproductive Medicine. A. R. Saetnan, N. Oudshoorn and M. Kirejczyk, eds. Pp. 368–383. Columbus: Ohio State University Press.

BROWNER C. H. and C. SARGENT, 1996, Anthropology and Studies of Human Reproduction. *In* Medical Anthropology. C. Sargent and T. Johnson, eds. Pp. 219–235. Westport, CT: Praeger Publishers.

COMINSKY S., 1976, Cross-Cultural Perspectives on Midwifery. *In* Medical Anthropology. F. Grolling and H. Haley, eds. Pp. 229–249. Paris: Mouton.

DAVIS D., 1983, Blood and Nerves. An Ethnographic Focus on Menopause. St Johns: Memorial University of Newfoundland and Institute of Social and Economic Research.

248 **C. H. Browner and C. Sargent**

DAVIS-FLOYD E. R., 1992, Birth as an American Rite of Passage. Berkeley: University of California Press.

DAVIS-FLOYD E. R. and C. F. SARGENT, 1997, Childbirth and Authoritative Knowledge: Cross-Cultural Perspectives. Berkeley: University of California Press.

DOYAL L., 1995, What Makes Women Sick. Gender and the Political Economy of Health. New Brunswick: Rutgers University Press.

EHRENREICH B. and D. ENGLISH, 1973, Witches, Midwives, and Nurses. A History of Women Healers. Brooklyn: The Faculty Press.

FARMER P., M. CONNERS and J. SIMMONS, eds, 1996, Women, Poverty, and AIDS: Sex, Drugs, and Structural Violence. Monroe, ME: Common Courage Press.

FAUVEAU V. and T. BLANCHET, 1989, Deaths From Injuries and Induced Abortion Among Rural Bangladeshi Women. Social Science and Medicine 29(9):1121–1127.

FINKLER K., 1994, Women in Pain. Gender and Morbidity in Mexico. Philadelphia: University of Pennsylvania Press.

FRANK G., 2000, Venus on Wheels. Two Decades of Dialogue on Disability, Biography, and Being Female in America. Berkeley: University of California Press.

GINSBURG F., 1998, Contested Lives: The Abortion Debate in an American Community. Berkeley: University of California Press.

GINSBURG F. and R. RAPP, eds, 1994, Conceiving the New World Order. The Global Politics of Reproduction. Berkeley: University of California Press.

GORDON D., 1991, Female Circumcision and Genital Operations in Egypt and the Sudan: A Dilemma for Medical Anthropology. Medical Anthropology Quarterly 5(1):3–14.

GRUENBAUM E., 2001, The Female Circumcision Controversy: An Anthropological Perspective. Philadelphia: University of Pennsylvania Press.

HAMPSHIRE K. R., 1998, Fulani Mobility. Causes, Constraints and Consequences of Population Movements in Northern Burkina Faso. Ph.D. thesis, University College London.

HEISE L., 1993, Violence Against Women. The Missing Agenda. In The Health of Women. A Global Perspective. M. Koblinsky, J. Timyan and J. Gay, eds. Pp. 171–197. Boulder: Westview.

HEMMING I. M. W., 1997, Gender and Islam, Purdah and Power: The Production and Management of Afghan Women's Health and Illness. Ph.D. Dissertation, Department of Anthropology, University of California, Los Angeles.

INHORN M. C., 1994, Quest for Conception: Gender, Infertility, and Egyptian Medical Traditions. Philadelphia: University of Pennsylvania Press.

INHORN M. C. and F. VAN BALEN, eds, 2002, Infertility around the Globe: New Thinking on Childlessness, Gender, and Reproductive Technologies. Berkeley: University of California Press.

JENKINS J. H., 1996, The Impress of Extremity: Women's Experience of Trauma and Political Violence. In Gender and Health. C. Sargent and C. Brettell, eds. Pp. 278–292. Upper Saddle River, Prentice Hall.

JORDAN B., 1993 [1978], Birth in Four Cultures: A Crosscultural Investigation of Childbirth in Yucatan, Holland, Sweden, and the United States. Prospect Heights: Waveland Press.

JORDAN B. and S. L. IRWIN, 1989, The Ultimate Failure: Court-Ordered cesarean Section. In New Approaches to Human Reproduction. Social and Ethical Dimensions. L. Whiteford and M. Poland, eds. Pp. 13–25. Boulder, Westview Press.

KAUFERT P., 1996, Women and the Debate over Mammography: An Economic, Political, and Moral History. In Gender and Health: An International Perspective. C. Sargent and C. Brettell, eds. Pp. 167–187. Upper Saddle River: Prentice Hall.

KAUFERT P. and S. MCKINLAY, 1985, Estrogen-replacement Therapy: the Production of Medical Knowledge and the Emergence of Policy. *In* Women, Health and Healing. E. Lewin and V. Olesen, eds. Pp. 113–139. London: Tavistock.

KAW E., 1993, Medicalization of Racial Features: Asian American Women and Cosmetic Surgery. Medical Anthropology Quarterly 7(1):74–89.

KOBLINSKY M., J. TIMYAN and J. GRAY, eds, 1993, Health of Women: A Global Perspective. San Francisco: Westview.

LADERMAN C., 1983, Wives and Midwives: Children and Nutrition in Rural Malaysia. Berkeley: University of California Press.

LANDSMAN G. H., 1998, Reconstructing Motherhood in the Age of Perfect Babies: Mothers of Infants and Toddlers With Disabilities. Signs 24(11):69–99.

LAYNE L. L., 2002, Motherhood Lost: A Feminist Account of Pregnancy Loss in America. New York: Routledge.

LAZARUS E., 1994, What do Women Want? Issues of Choice, Control, and Class in Pregnancy and Childbirth. Medical Anthropology Quarterly 8(1):25–47.

LOCK M., 1993, Encounters with Aging. Berkeley: University of California Press.

LOW S., 1992, Embodied Metaphors: Nerves as Lived Experience. *In* Embodiment and Experience. T. Csordas, ed. Pp. 139–163. Cambridge: Cambridge University Press.

MACCORMACK, C. P., 1982, Ethnography of Fertility and Birth. 2nd edition. Prospect Heights, IL: Waveland Press.

——, 1994, Risk, Prevention, and International Health Policy. *In* Gender and Health. C. Sargent and C. Brettell, eds. Pp. 326–338. Upper Saddle River, NJ: Prentice-Hall.

McCLAIN C. S., ed., 1989, Women as Healers: Cross-Cultural Perspectives. New Brunswick: Rutgers University Press.

MARTIN E., 1987, The Woman in the Body: A Cultural Analysis of Reproduction. Boston: Beacon Press.

MILLER B. D., 1981, The Endangered Sex: Neglect of Female Children in Rural North India. Ithaca: Cornell University Press.

——, 2001, Female-Selective Abortion in Asia: Patterns, Policies, and Debates. American Anthropologist 103(4):1083–1095.

MITCHELL L. and E. GEORGES, 1998, Baby's First Picture. The Cyborg Fetus of Ultrasound Imaging. *In* Cyborg Babies. R. Davis and J. Dumit, eds. Pp. 105–125. New York, Routledge.

MORGAN L. M., 1999, Ambiguities Lost: Fashioning the Fetus into a Child in Ecuador and the United States. *In* Small Wars. The Cultural Politics of Childhood. N. Scheper-Hughes and C. Sargent, eds. Pp. 58–75. Berkeley: University of California Press.

MORGEN S., 2002, Into Our Own Hands: The Women's Health Movement in the United States, 1969–1990. New Brunswick: Rutgers University Press.

MORSY S., 1978, Sex Roles, Power, and Illness in an Egyptian Village. American Ethnologist 5:137–150.

——, 1998, Not Only Women: Science as Resistance in Open Door Egypt. *In* Pragmatic Women and Body Politics. M. Lock and P. Kaufert, eds. Pp. 77–98. Cambridge: Cambridge University Press.

NICHTER M., 1981, Idioms of Distress: Alternatives in the Expression of Psychosocial Distress: A Case Study From South India. Culture, Medicine and Psychiatry 5:379–408.

——, 2000, Fat Talk: What Girls and Their Parents Say About Dieting. Cambridge: Harvard University Press.

OBERMEYER C. M., 1999, Female Genital Surgeries: The Known, the Unknown, and the Unknowable. Medical Anthropology Quarterly 13(1):79–106.

OLUJIC M. B., 1998, Embodiment of Terror: Gendered Violence in Peacetime and Wartime in Croatia and Bosnia-Herzegovina. Medical Anthropology Quarterly 12(1):31–50.

OTHS K. S., 1999, Debilidad: A Biocultural Assessment of an Embodied Andean Illness. Medical Anthropology Quarterly 13(3):286–315.

PAUL L., 1975, Recruitment to a Ritual Role: The Midwife in a Maya Community. Ethos 3(3):449–467.

PRESS N., C. H. BROWNER, D. TRAN, C. MORTON and B. LEMASTER, 1998, Provisional Normalcy and Perfect Babies: Pregnant Women's Attitudes Toward Disability in the Context of Prenatal Testing. In Reproducing Reproduction: Kinship, Power, and Technological Innovation. S. Franklin and H. Ragone, eds. Pp. 46–65. Philadelphia: University of Pennsylvania Press.

RAGONE H., 1994, Surrogate Motherhood. Conception in the Heart. Boulder, CO: Westview.

RAPP R., 1999, Testing Women, Testing the Fetus: The Social Impact of Amniocentesis in America. New York: Routledge.

REBHUN L. A., 1994, Swallowing Frogs: Anger and Illness in Northeast Brazil. Medical Anthropology Quarterly 8(4):360–382.

RUBEL A. J., W. T. LIU, M. TROSDAL and V. PATO, 1971, The Traditional Birth Attendant in Metropolitan Cebu, the Philippines. In Culture and Population: A Collection of Current Studies. Monograph 9. S. Polgar, ed. Pp. 176–186. Carolina Population Center: UNNC Chapel Hill.

SANDAY P. R., 1990, Fraternity Gang Rape: Sex, Brotherhood, and Privilege on Campus. New York: New York University Press.

SANDELOWSKI M., 1991, Compelled to Try: The Never-Enough Quality of Contraceptive Technology. Medical Anthropology Quarterly 5(1):29–47.

SARGENT C., 1989, Maternity, Medicine and Power. Berkeley: University of California Press.

SARGENT C. and N. STARK, 1987, Surgical Birth: Interpretations of Cesarean Delivery among Private Hospital Patients and Nursing Staff. Social Science and Medicine 25(12):1269–1276.

SAWICKI J, 1991, Disciplining Foucault: Feminism, Power and the Body. New York: Routledge.

SCHEPER-HUGHES N, 1992, Death without Weeping. The Violence of Everyday Life in Brazil. Berkeley: University of California Press.

SCHOEPF B. G., 1998, Inscribing the Body Politic: Women and AIDS in Africa. In Pragmatic Women and Body Politics. M. Lock and P. Kaufer, eds. Cambridge: Cambridge University Press.

SHELL-DUNCAN B. and Y. HERNLUND, eds, 2000, Female Circumcision in Africa: Culture, Controversy, and Change. Boulder: Lynne Reinner Publishers.

SOBO E. J., 1995, Choosing Unsafe Sex: AIDS-Risk Denial Among Disadvantaged Women. Philadelphia: University of Pennsylvania Press.

STELLMAN J., 1997, Work Is Dangerous to your Health: A Handbook of Health Hazards in the Work Place and What You Can Do about Them. 2nd edition. New York: Pantheon.

TAYLOR J. S., 2000, Of Sonograms and Baby Prams: Prenatal Diagnosis, Pregnancy, and Consumption. Feminist Studies 26(2):391–418.

VAN HOLLEN C., 2003, Birth on the Threshold. Childbirth and Modernity in South India. Berkeley: University of California Press.

WARD M., 1986, Poor Women Powerful Men: America's Great Experiment in Family Planning. Boulder: Westview Press.

WHITEFORD L. M., 1996, Political Economy, Gender, and the Social Production of Health and Illness. *In* Gender and Health. C. Sargent and C. Brettell, eds. Pp. 242–260. Upper Saddle River, NJ: Prentice-Hall.

WOJCICKI J. M., 2002, She Drank His Money: Survival Sex and the Problem of Violence in Taverns in Gauteng Province, South Africa. Medical Anthropology Quarterly 16(3):267–293.

Chapter 13

POLITICS

The Politics of Life: Beyond the Anthropology of Health

Didier Fassin

The academic and scientific space that is medical anthropology has moved in two different directions over the past two decades. On the one hand, it has been sub-divided into a number of specific areas, from ethnomedicine and ethnopharmacology to anthropologies of the body, of illness, and of suffering. On the other hand, it has taken up and reformulated the broader questions of anthropology, breaking with the initial tendency to create what was claimed to be an independent subdiscipline that was willingly medicalized. As a result, the landscape it has painted, in France in particular, is remarkably diverse in both its objects and its fields of inquiry, and less and less distinct from the discipline of anthropology as a whole.[1] The territory I will be describing here is the anthropology of health. Although the issues through which it was created deal with novel dimensions of what we continue, for the sake of convenience, to call medical anthropology, they are pursuing and renewing questions that anthropologists who have explored political or moral issues have also addressed.[2] Rather than present an overview of this relatively young field, I will attempt to highlight the main themes as they appear in France, connecting them to developments in other places. Far from being limited to issues of health,[3] this orientation in medical anthropology is fully engaged in an anthropology of the politics of life.

Health, Between Realism and Constructivism

The most common representation of health is as a simple fact of nature whose boundaries have been conceptualized by Georges Canguilhem (1966). As health is inscribed in the body, and is made visible by the body, either through disease, or more debatably through wellness, it appears self-evident, whether its material substrate is considered to be organs or genes. This self-evidence is then reinforced by the development of professions and institutions that, through the twofold strategy of producing knowledge and legitimizing power, have authority in defining its boundaries. If we say that tuberculosis, hepatitis, or bovine spongiform encephalopathy are health problems, what we see at work are bacteria, viruses and prions that are transmitted, infections that are developed, and people who are sick. If we speak in the same terms of drug abuse or alcoholism, of child abuse or post-traumatic stress disorder, no one questions the harmful physical and psychological effects of addiction or violence. The view of health that is usually taken both by health practitioners and by patients, by political decision-makers and by citizens, is therefore fundamentally a naturalistic view (more than simply biomedical as is often believed) which is further objectified by statistics on mortality and morbidity (Dozon and Fassin 2001). The number of ill or deceased persons is taken as evidence that the health problem is real, and that government authorities and often society as a whole must fight it.

But are things really that simple? Political anthropology proposes two ways of approaching the issues that go against generally accepted ideas. The first is constructivist; it shows how what we call health is also the result of individual and collective work by agents through models and images; it involves conflicts and controversies, and requires alliances and strategies. The second is realistic; it analyzes how what appear to be facts of nature are also the product of structures and organizations, processes of differentiation and inequality, government action and private initiatives that can either prevent or worsen disease and suffering. Health is therefore a social construct, in the sense of what agents express through the language of illness, and at the same time, it is a production of society, in the sense of what the world order inscribes on the body. Therefore, on the one hand there is a "sanitarization" of the social, and on the other, a politicization of health (Fassin 1998). Both movements operate dialectically. That point is essential. The social sciences literature on health has often taken exclusively or at least predominantly, one of the two perspectives: either in the tradition of Peter Berger and Thomas Luckman (1966), by describing how the objects of health are constructed, such as child maltreatment or psychological trauma (Hacking 1995, 1999); or else, in keeping with the approach put forward by Merill Singer and Hans Baer (1995), by emphasizing the socioeconomic conditions that produce illness, thus drawing attention to the disparities and violence that show up in the body (Farmer 1992, 1999). In the approach defended here, both processes are intertwined and both interpretations inform each other.

Let us take the example of lead poisoning in France, and consider the following paradox.[4] In 1981, a review of all the cases of lead poisoning among French children revealed ten observations published over the preceding quarter century. The authors of the study, who were pediatricians and toxicologists from Lyon, pointed out that there were not many cases in France, whereas in the United States the problem was quite widespread. In 1999, national experts from the French health and medical research institute (Inserm) estimated that there were 85,000 contaminated children, on the basis of a variety of epidemiological surveys. Specialists worried that the situation in France was much more serious than in the United States. In less than two decades, the situation had gone from a small number of exceptional cases to an epidemic regularly discussed in the media and for which legislation was passed. Is it possible that in such a short time, lead had spread through the bodies of young children to the point of making this previously rare pathology a new public health priority? Obviously not. In fact, two elements played into the shift:

first, the way in which agents mobilized to have the problem recognized, and secondly, the change in the clinical parameters of the disease. The lead poisoning epidemic is therefore a consequence of individual actions and of a change in indicators, in other words, mixing together humans and nonhumans (Latour 1991), which of course could always result from men and women's actions and interactions.

On the first front, in Paris, a young pediatrician diagnosed a case of lead poisoning in a little girl from Mali and reported it to social services, a procedure often neglected at the time. A social worker was informed of the case and decided to go to the family's home to see what their living conditions were like, an exceptional initiative given the hospital habitus. She was so shocked by the deteriorated condition of the building that she reported it to the institutions for protecting mothers and children. One of the physicians at that service, in collaboration with a toxicologist, then two general practitioners working in two different NGOs (one humanitarian and the other focused on immigrant health), and at about the same time, a public health specialist at a university department (plus a few others), each in their own way, took on and defended the cause. The resistance they encountered was so great that the use of the expression "to defend a cause" is not too strong. Some authorities considered lead poisoning a marginal phenomenon, while others opposed changes because the practical consequences in terms of lodging and improving living conditions appeared overwhelming. In the end, it took five years to have the problem acknowledged and to have a national survey conducted in order to gather evidence; it took eight more years to have the law changed so that children could be tested and treated, and preventive building improvement measures could be made compulsory.

On the second front, in just a few years, the level of lead in the blood considered to constitute an intoxication dropped from 250 µg/l to 100 µg/l. With the first threshold, a few hundred cases were detected, whereas using the second, several tens of thousands of children were considered to be poisoned. Between those two numbers was the work of two teams of epidemiologists, one North American and one Australian, who in the 1980s pointed out the toxic effects of lead in lower amounts on learning abilities and academic achievement. As one can imagine, it was not easy to demonstrate because of the multiplicity of nonbiological factors that interfere with cognitive skills, as those affected were from underprivileged backgrounds, in the case of the United States, often African or Hispanic-American. Complex surveys with multivariate analyses were conducted, and scientific controversies that divided academic circles ensued before the new level was accepted by the ultimate authority in the matter, the Atlanta Center for Disease Control, also a reference for European public health.

To say that there was a social construction of child lead poisoning is in no way to deny its clinical or epidemiological reality; it is to remind us of two things. First, that without the agents to bring that reality into existence, it would have remained what it was until the 1980s, that is, a supposedly infrequent ailment or else a pathology buried in the bodies of immigrant children of African descent. Second, that the disease henceforth referred to as an epidemic is no longer quite the same reality as that of the rare cases reported in clinical studies. Indeed, the latter were often serious neurological manifestations accompanied by comas and seizures related to very high levels of lead in the blood, whereas in the former, there were generally no discernible clinical signs, and the problem mainly involved an increased statistical risk of a reduced intelligence quotient. Both aspects are eminently political. On the one hand, the role of social agents in achieving recognition of a health problem is emphasized. On the other, the importance of technical instruments in understanding health phenomena is highlighted. But there remains one question: Where does lead poisoning come from? Or: How can it be explained? That question was asked all the more stridently as 99% of the children severely affected belonged to African families. To analyze the social production of lead poisoning is to explain this statistic.

In the beginning of the 1970s, the French government announced its intention to end what it called labor immigration. Until then, immigration was mostly related to economic needs, and to obtain a permit, it was generally sufficient to present a contract with an employer. Then the oil crisis and industry restructurings rapidly transformed the labor market. Immigrants, especially nonqualified ones, were less and less needed, except in a few specific sectors such as public works, agriculture, and restaurants. However, the new policy left a hole open for cases of family reunification where a spouse and/or children could join a family member already living in the country, what was henceforth called settlement immigration. In the mid-1980s, that procedure was also severely restricted, as were most other legal means of entering France. At the same time, temporary documents were less and less systematically renewed for the unemployed, for workers in certain protected sectors, and for students who failed their exams. The twofold effect of illegal immigrants arriving and fewer permits being renewed led to an increase in the numbers of foreigners without legal status. The largest, or at least the most visible and vulnerable, group was made up of Africans, mainly from West Africa. During this period, the same economic causes led to an increase in the number of people looking for jobs and a general decrease in social and spatial mobility among the entire population living in France. At a time when there was a scarcity of apartments for rent, low-cost housing became less and less available to foreigners on account of hidden quotas. Immigrants who had arrived most recently had to make do with the cheapest, most dilapidated and insalubrious private apartments on the market, particularly illegal immigrants; in other words, they had to take whatever they could get. It is precisely in those apartments that old lead paint, which has been prohibited since 1948, can still be found. That is where children of African descent were becoming poisoned.

The history of French policies on immigration and housing, as briefly described here, offers a consistent interpretation for the reasons behind the high rates of lead poisoning among children living in poor immigrant families. It shows how contamination in the local environment is the product of social inequalities, particularly those affecting the most economically and legally vulnerable foreigners. However, that was not the explanation that prevailed in the 1980s in France. The interpretation for the higher rates of poisoning in African homes referred to specific cultural practices. Blame was first laid on the inks used by Muslim marabouts and on women's make-up products. Then it was suggested that the ingestion of paint by children was due to a supposed appetite for mineral matter, geophagy, that West African mothers had presumably passed on to their children. Lead poisoning activists had to fight against these culturalist readings to have their materialist analysis heard, and then it was only gradually accepted over the 1990s. As we can see, the social construction of lead poisoning (by agents who had to fight to have it exist not only as an epidemiological reality, but also as a social etiology) and its production by society (as a result of economic mechanisms and political choices) must be conceptualized together.

While the case of lead poisoning is exemplary, it is not of course unique. Examples such as hunger in Brazil (Scheper-Hughes 1992), post-traumatic stress disorder in the United States (Young 1995), or African psychopathology (McCulloch 1995) could also be used to illustrate how cognitive models and political logics are simultaneously constructed and produced, yet society tends to obliterate them by making diagnostic categories into a mere reflection of the nature of things, eluding the social processes by which they become inscribed in bodies. But the epidemic of lead poisoning may have something more to teach us about the anthropological foundations of contemporary societies, beyond this constructivist and realist interpretation of health phenomena, whose observations echo many studies in critical medical anthropology.

When the social worker discovered African families living in hovels in the heart of Paris, lead poisoning suddenly appeared to her almost secondary to the state of dilapidation of their apartments with floors caving in and rickety stairways. Yet it was precisely by fighting against the illness and pleading on behalf of the sick children that she and several others forced Parisian officials to do something for the families. And when, somewhat later, a member of a large humanitarian organization, which was in charge of underprivileged groups at the Ministry of Health, decided to work on the presentation of a legislative text, she used the pitiful icon of lead-poisoned children to promote it. The two ministers that she managed to convince of the importance of her cause were both founding members of Médecins sans frontières who already shared her ethos. In other words, when the indignity of foreigners' living conditions was unable to provoke the local and national political reaction it deserved, resorting to arguments on the deterioration of bodies instead did. The legitimacy of the illness counted more than the illegitimacy of the population. This moral appeal to people's physical lives when their social lives do not appear important enough to justify action (in this case, finding better homes for immigrant families) is currently operating in many areas of government action.

Moral Economy and Humanitarian Rationale

In a much-quoted text, Michel Foucault (1976) proposed a theory of biopower that can shed light on this. For centuries, he wrote, politics were organized around a sovereign power, which was the right to kill. Beginning in the 17th century, through a gradual inversion of the principles and values of government, the main focus of politics became the management of life in the form of a power over life. This bio-power involves both the discipline of bodies – which is carried out through a series of institutions, from schools to the army, from prisons to hospitals – and the control of populations, as seen in the invention of tools such as demography, sociology, psychology, or the regulation of reproduction, disease, and migration. At first glance, public health seems to lie perfectly within this framework since, on the one hand, it attempts to impose individual standards for healthy behavior and, on the other, it organizes the epidemiological knowledge and health administration of human communities. However, the example of lead poisoning suggests another interpretation.

Of course, the goal of this policy was to act on bodies and in the population to identify and prevent cases of lead poisoning among children. But twenty years later, in spite of the fact that we have all the elements for describing, analyzing, and measuring the problem, although associations have been mobilized and legislation has been passed, less than one percent of the families considered to be poisoned have been moved to other living quarters or have had their own home rehabilitated. Biopower thus seems very fragile in the face of the economic implications of implementing such measures and the political risk of a rise in xenophobia. Yet the consensus regarding the victims of lead poisoning was sufficiently broad that two ministers from opposing parties in successive parliamentary majorities defended the legislation. Rather than speaking of a power over life, which would imply effective government action, we should be referring to the power of life, meaning that society recognizes the importance of suffering or ill bodies. This politics has more to do with biolegitimacy than biopower (Fassin 2000), considering biolegitimacy as an order of values – not a hierarchy of powers – that prevails in the contemporary world, which has countless tangible manifestations both in local public health spaces and on the world stage of humanitarian action.

Two philosophers can help us in tracing the genealogy of that order and in understanding what it means. First, Hannah Arendt (1967) states that it was born during the Enlightenment under the French Revolution which made life "the supreme good" and "pity" the primary motivating force for action. She believed that this implied a truth of the body that was connected to necessity and need rather than liberty and dignity and which announced the supremacy of human rights over citizen's rights. Second, on the basis of a reading of Aristotle, Giorgio Agamben (1997) distinguishes between the two meanings of the two Greek words for life, *zoe*, meaning bare life or physical existence, the simple fact of living, and *bios*, a qualified life or political existence, the life of a social group. The tension between these two forms of life, specifically the way in which biological life is constantly used to justify and even to found life in a society, is what he believes characterizes contemporary politics. The example of the management of immigration will elucidate this theoretical discussion.[5] Following the major social and economic changes of the 1970s that resulted in increasingly restrictive policies for foreigners to enter and remain in France, the paths for legally gaining access to French territory became more and more narrow. At the same time, a partisan movement began, first with the Communist Party, then with the National Front, around what became "the immigration question," which was a way of constructing foreign presence as a problem for employment, insecurity, and even AIDS. This dual political and ideological development had the effect of generating suspicious representations of aliens and justifying increasingly inhospitable practices. With the consolidation during the 1990s of what is known as the Schengen area, suspicion and incivility spread to the European Union to the detriment of those from "outside the community," most often people from the Third World. In that context two remarkable things took place.

First, to a large extent political asylum lost its legitimacy. Whereas at the beginning of the 1980s it still had symbolic credit as evidenced by a high level of positive assessments for asylum seekers (approximately 80% were granted refugee status), it became more and more discredited over the following decade (to the point where only 12 percent are recognized as refugees by the French Office for the Protection of Refugees and Stateless Persons; that proportion increases to 18 percent after appeals in front of a special commission). In ten years, the number of political refugees thus decreased sixfold, reaching the astonishingly low number of two thousand new refugees per year (not including children who are granted the same status as their parents when they reach the age of majority) at the end of the 1990s. In parallel, a series of measures intended to dissuade future applicants had the effect of further eroding and weakening refugees' conditions: in 1989, they lost housing assistance, which forced them to resort to emergency units, and as of 1991, they were prohibited from working, which made them dependent on government charity. Far from the generous declarations made during the signing of the Geneva Convention in 1951, France and Europe increasingly view asylum seekers as undesirables, most of whom, moreover, are fated to live illegally on account of the very low rates of acceptance.

Second, humanitarian rationale has imposed itself as a new right. It applies essentially to sick foreigners, insofar as they can prove that their condition is sufficiently serious and that they cannot receive proper medical treatment in their home country (two criteria that can only be subjectively assessed, as one can imagine). The new provision was decided under the pressure, first, of a growing number of foreigners suffering from AIDS during a period when antiretrovirals were not available in the Third World, and second, of a collective group of associations for the defense of immigrants' right to health. The institutionalization of this right took place in three phases. In the early 1990s, prefects began, with increasing frequency, to use their discretionary powers to give illegal foreigners legal papers in cases of illness. Shortly thereafter, legislation on immigration, whose overall goal was to make it more difficult to enter France, included a special clause indicating that sick persons could no longer be taken to the border, and as a result, could be neither legalized nor deported. In 1997, new legislation went one step further by declaring that sick persons were entitled to stay and work if an expert's opinion demonstrated that their medical situation met the two criteria of seriousness and inaccessibility to treatment. Over the decade, the number of legalizations made for what the administration called "humanitarian reasons" multiplied by a factor of seven, affecting some two thousand people a year. Among all the routes for obtaining legal status, this is the one that grew most rapidly by far during a period when the other means for obtaining legal status were drying up.

Two ways of defining a politics of the living are thus at work: one through which political asylum loses legitimacy, the other one by which suffering body regains it. Placing the two phenomena side by side is all the more justified given that, in addition to developing over the same period, they operate interactively. For example, some asylum seekers whose application is rejected then try to prove that they have an illness, often encouraged in doing so by lawyers, associations, and even well-intentioned social workers or civil servants. We are therefore in the presence of a true displacement of legitimacy: in the categories of Hannah Arendt, from the rights of a citizen of the world (threatened in his or her country) to strictly defined human rights (of the ill); or in the terms of Giorgio Agamben, from a political life (*bios*) to a biological life (*zoe*). Nowadays, French society is less likely to acknowledge that a person's life is threatened by an authoritarian regime or by war-related violence than it is to be receptive to the illness or suffering of a person with a serious disease. That form of recognition often also plays into the humanitarian management of displaced persons and refugees (Agier 2002). On a more anecdotal but no less significant note, it was General Pinochet's state of health that was referred to in exempting him from being tried in Spain for crimes against humanity; the same justification was given for freeing the prefect Papon who was imprisoned on the same charge. In both cases the defense attorneys used the term "humanitarian."

To speak of moral economy in discussing the politics of the living is to consider the values underlying the choices made by today's societies regarding situations that threaten not only the physical lives of individuals, but their social lives as well. It offers a much-needed complement to political economy whose analysis of the relations of production sheds light from another angle on decisions made with respect to human lives. In the case of immigrants, political economy reveals how their labor force, which was central to the modernization of Europe in the postwar period, has become marginal under the impact of the economic restructuring of the past three decades. However, moral economy helps us to interpret the inversion that takes place when the healthy body becomes illegitimate and the suffering body is granted a new status, when life is no longer justified by the contribution to a country's wealth, but by the creation of a compassionate protocol. The sick person who is granted a visa simply because he or she is sick acquires what Adriana Petryna (2002), who has studied Chernobyl survivors, has called a "biological citizenship" and discovers a novel and radical form of what Paul Rabinow (1996) on the subject of the human genome has called "biosociality." The threat to biological life becomes the political reason for living.

A rigid opposition between the two forms of life however does not completely account for the complex logics at work here. It would be more appropriate to speak of configurations and tensions which trigger the actions of individuals through value issues, in other words leaving room for subjectivities and strategies in confronting norms and powers. When the rejected asylum seeker reapplies for a visa stating that he (or she) is sick, or even has a psychological disorder as a result of the circumstances preceding exile, when he constructs his justification no longer as a militant being hunted down or the victim of a violent order but as a sufferer or the victim of psychological trauma, it can be assumed that this shift in self-representation, which he presents to others and to himself, is not without effect, if not on his status as a psychological subject, which anthropology is ill-equipped to grasp, at least on his status as a political subject worthy of compassion (for his clinical condition) but not claiming any right (to political asylum). Studies show that people are not passive in such processes, that they use tactics and sometimes resistance, and since the ends justify the means, once they have obtained the precious visa, they reconstruct a social life out of hiding and sometimes even out of their former vulnerability. In other words, while their recognition through biological life was a necessary step on their way, they extend it into the realm of political life and, as actors, into the city. In doing so, they demonstrate that concrete lives can partially escape standardization.

Social History and Embodied Inequality

But life cannot be reduced to this distinction between biological phenomenon and political existence. If what makes us human is language, and if language is also where meaning is the hardest to decipher (Wittgenstein 1961), then life is also our memory of it and the way we tell the story of our life. Life politics are therefore not only the politics of the living; they are also the politics of lived experience. Memory and narrative are based on two different logics, but both of them engrave a meaning of lived experience onto the body and into words. Both are at once individual, in the singular biographical experience, and collective, in shared historical experience. From that viewpoint, the life of immigrants is not revealed only in the words they choose to put to their personal itineraries; their lives also surface as traces from a past in which they are rooted and as the signs of a present that they construct with the society where they now live.

Embodiment can be defined as the way in which society's structures and norms, and the ordeals and marks of time, are inscribed on the body. In the social sciences, Marcel Mauss (1980), with his analysis of the techniques of the body, and Pierre Bourdieu (1979), with his theory of habitus, have given us models for examining the imprint of the social in ways of doing and being. Two complementary concepts help us see this imprint by shedding light on our relation with society and time. On the one hand we can speak of social condition to describe the way in which structural realities are inscribed on the body; and on the other, we can speak of historical experience to refer to the ways in which they are experienced, interpreted, and narrated. The former is a more objective aspect of embodiment while the second conveys its intersubjective dimension. Both are simultaneously individual and collective. Although medical anthropology does not necessarily use these categories, it often implicitly favors one or the other. For so-called critical approaches, the issue of structural violence takes priority, but often to the detriment of the meaning that events have for those involved (Kim et al. 2000; Scheper-Hughes 2002). In the case of phenomenological interpretations, the narrative conveys the experience but often does not do justice to the materiality of lives (Good 1994; Kleinman 1988). It is important to take them both into account, most notably with a view to understanding the mechanisms of inequalities.

The AIDS epidemic in South Africa is tragically exemplary in that regard.[6] As it is constructed and told, the narrative of the epidemic blends several storylines. The first is epidemiological. In one decade, the rate of HIV infection went from less than 1 percent to over 25 percent of the adult population and AIDS became the main cause of death for men and women between 15 and 49 years of age. Demographic projections are even more troubling, showing that between 1990 and 2010, life expectancy could drop by 20 years. The second is historical. In it, two series of events are placed side by side: the end of the contemptible apartheid regime and the inexorable advance of AIDS, as if the latter were the result of the former, at least in part, as some suggest, or as though they were both part of the same eternal affliction of the African continent. The third is political. There have been a series of controversies in recent years over the viral etiology of AIDS and the toxicity of antiretroviral drugs, which has divided the tripartite alliance in power, opposing the first democratically elected government to its former allies in civil society, making the epidemic the greatest threat to a national unity that has hardly had the chance to be consolidated. The fourth is biographical. The life histories recorded by researchers and journalists, the fragments of history told in associations or at burials, the recordings and souvenirs placed in memory boxes as the sole legacy to children or relatives, are all ways to make exist what was, is still, and soon will be no longer. But how can this narrative weaving be understood without taking it apart thread by thread? For the narrative material to preserve its thickness and its truth, we can approach it as the voice of a condition and an experience.

The social condition of AIDS links the epidemiological and historical storylines while enriching the two others. To interpret the alarming advance of the infection, it must be approached in the light of history, which is a history of the most severe inequality, one with no way out because it justifies itself by differences in human nature which in turn are used to justify the most inhumane solutions. Apartheid, which became the official biopolitics of South Africa in 1948, extended and radicalized the policies of colonization, domination, exploitation and segregation whose racial and racist dimension has always existed. The speed with which AIDS has spread and its unequal distribution are the result of complex phenomena blending inequalities, violence, and migrations. Each of those factors is a legacy of the former regime, and paradoxically they were exacerbated precisely when it ended: socioeconomic and socioracial inequalities became far more apparent with the end of the official division of society along color lines; ordinary and sexual violence attributable to mechanisms of terror and exclusion became freed or were made visible by the drastic removal of extreme forms of control; displacements of people were directly provoked by wars carried out by the previous regime, or were accelerated by the freedom to travel and the lifting of international sanctions after

1994. The particularly high rates of infection among young men and women in the townships, in mining towns, and in the former homelands are evidence of the dynamic of this embodiment of the social order through the spread of AIDS. Therefore, an interpretation of the facts and, consequently, potential solutions cannot be found in the behavioral or cultural characteristics hastily referred to as "promiscuity," which has been used to explain the epidemiology of the infection. Instead, we must look at how each individual history has been marked by collective history. The scars of that recent past are borne in the relationships between individuals, between men and women, between citizens and state authorities.

The historical experience of AIDS links political and biographical narratives, but its painfulness is the result of the collision of the two others. Rather than speak of denial, as many do with regards to both governments in the choices they make and the population in the attitudes they have towards the disease, we need to analyze why so many view the connection between the end of apartheid and the beginning of the epidemic as intolerable and unthinkable. The proliferation of accounts that call scholarly or official truths into question is part of the logic of incredulity or incomprehension. But here again the presence of the past should not be underestimated as the most painful events are also the most recent. Just as the first racial segregation measures were implemented in the name of public health during the plague of 1900 and the flu of 1917, just as tuberculosis is both a product of the exploitation of miners and the reason given for importing new labor, under the former regime, AIDS led to discriminatory and stigmatizing discourses and practices by the medical system with respect to Africans. Suspicion of biomedical science and memories of violence perpetrated in the name of health, imaginary constructions of conspiracies, and proven plans for genocide thus constitute the historical legacy of the epidemic, which is reflected at the macrosocial level in the President's declarations concerning the virus or antiretrovirals and at the microsocial level in what people have to say concerning the current government's desire to rid itself of a useless population of poor and sick. For those who make them, such statements tell a truth that goes much deeper than the truth contained in statistics and health prevention messages.

The body, as it materializes the imprint of society and the work of time in each and every one of us, also bears witness through sickness as both a physical and material fact but also as an individual and collective narrative. The anthropology of violence, as it has been developed along diverse lines in Colombia (Taussig 1987), Ireland (Feldman 1991), India (Das 1995), and Sri Lanka (Daniel 1996), certainly echoes the epistemological and ethical concerns of any anthropology that strives to approach life as an objective fact and a subjective production.

Conclusion

An anthropology that takes the politics of life as its object goes far beyond the theoretical and empirical horizon of classical medical anthropology.[7] As I have shown, it is connected in many ways to what, in North America, is often called critical medical anthropology, as it shares a certain view of authoritative knowledge and the uses of power, and of structural violence and social inequality. However, there are three ways in which it may be distinguished. First, while it deals with the body, illness, and health, it analyses how they are constructed and produced, and therefore, how they can help to shed light on social worlds. Second, as it seeks to understand what the increasing importance of these expectations in contemporary societies means, it develops a criticism of the new forms of health or humanitarian legitimacy that are a result of that influence and seem to almost naturally impose themselves at the expense of other possible configurations. Third, it attempts to strike a balance between the anthropologist's interpretation and the perspective of those affected, with an attention to both the objective conditions and the subjective experiences of suffering, in an effort to avoid analyses that lack either a compassionate involvement or a critical distance. These three tendencies must not however be rigidly imposed, as they vary depending on the author and the work. The study of the politics of life opens spaces for anthropologists to discuss not only among themselves, as we have done here, but also with the men and women whose stories they tell.

Notes

1. Sylvie Fainzang's chapter in this book gives an accurate account of those combined orientations. There is no reason then to present a general overview which has already been done, but more suitable to focus on a specific research theme which has recently been developed in France.
2. Most obviously, anthropology shares those issues with other disciplines. It would then be quite easy to show the intellectual bridges which have actually been built in researches and workshops with historians (Wahnich 2003), sociologists (Memmi 2003), and philosophers (Brossat 2003).
3. The title of this chapter is a clear reference to the book published by Marc Augé and Claudine Herzlich (1984) which helped develop the anthropology of sickness in France. In the next pages I will follow up on three cases which, according to me, show the various dimensions and orientations of the political anthropology of health, though I would not dare say that they dig into all the questions that the social sciences face when dealing with health politics (Lock, 2002; Rabinow 1999; Rapp 2000).
4. Details and references on this particular theme will not be considered here. I would rather send the reader to my articles: "Les scènes locales de l'hygiénisme contemporain. La lutte contre le saturnisme infantile, une bio-politique à la française," in *Les Hygiénistes. Enjeux, modèles et pratiques*, P. Bourdelais éd. Belin, Paris, pp. 447–465; "Naissance d'une question de santé publique. Deux descriptions du saturnisme infantile à Paris (1987–1989)," *Genèses* 2003;53:139–153; "Public health as culture. The social construction of the childhood lead-poisoning epidemic in France," *British Medical Bulletin* 2004;69:167–177; "Plumbism reinvented. The early times of childhood lead poisoning in France 1985–1990" (with A.J. Naudé), *American Journal of Public Health* 2004;94:1854–1863.

5. On the administrative questions regarding migrants in France, the reader could refer to my articles: "The biopolitics of otherness. Undocumented immigrants and racial discrimination in the French public debate," *Anthropology Today. Journal of the Royal Anthropological Institute* 2001;17(1):3–7; "Une double peine. La condition sociale des immigrés malades du sida," *L'Homme. Revue française d'anthropologie* 2001;160:137–162; "Quand le corps fait loi. La raison humanitaire dans les procédures de régularisation des étrangers," *Sciences sociales et santé* 19(4):5–34; "Le corps exposé. Une économie morale de l'illégitimité," in *Le gouvernement des corps*, Didier Fassin and Dominique Memmi eds., Éditions de l'École des hautes études en sciences sociales, Paris, 2004.
6. Some elements on this issue can be found in my articles: "Le sida comme cause politique," *Les Temps modernes, L'Afrique et la mondialisation* 2002;620:429–448; "The South African politics of AIDS. Beyond the controversies," 2003, *British Medical Journal* 326:495–497; "The embodiment of inequality. A political anthropology of AIDS in Southern Africa," *EMBO Reports, Science and Society* 2003;4:S4–S9.
7. To illustrate the analyses of the French politics of life, I actually kept to my own researches. Of course, this is no equivalent to the whole intellectual panorama which I try to present here. The work done by the French researchers and students in the Centre de recherche sur les enjeux contemporains en santé publique (EHESS-Inserm-UP13) is a good example, amongst others, of issues related to the type of anthropology put forward here: Corinne Lanzarini, on the homeless in Paris; Estelle d'Halluin, on the use of psychic trauma as a means of asylum seeking in France; Paula Vasquez, on the management of a natural disaster in Venezuela; Karine Vanthuyne on the politics of remembrance in Nicaragua; Frédéric Le Marcis, on the AIDS patients' survival strategies in Southern Africa, to name but a few.

References

AGAMBEN G., 1997 [1995], Homo sacer. Le pouvoir souverain et la vie nue. Paris, Seuil.
AGIER M., 2002, Au bord du monde, les réfugiés. Paris: Flammarion.
ARENDT H., 1967 [1963], Essai sur la révolution. Paris: Gallimard.
AUGÉ M. and C. HERZLICH, 1984, Le sens du mal. Anthropologie, histoire, sociologie de la maladie. Paris: Éditions des archives contemporaines.
BERGER P. and T. LUCKMAN, 1966, The Social Construction of Reality. A Treatise in the Sociology of Knowledge. New York: Anchor Books.
BOURDIEU P., 1979, La distinction. Critique sociale du jugement. Paris: Minuit.
BROSSAT A., 2003, La démocratie immunitaire. Paris: La Dispute.
CANGUILHEM G., 1966, Le normal et le pathologique. Paris: Presses universitaires de France.
DANIEL V., 1996, Charred lullabies. Chapters in an Anthropology of Violence. Princeton: Princeton University Press.
DAS V., 1995, Critical Events. An Anthropological Perspective on Contemporary India. Oxford: Oxford University Press.
DOZON J. P. and D. FASSIN, eds, 2001, Critique de la santé publique. Une approche anthropologique. Paris: Balland.
FARMER P., 1992, AIDS and Accusation. Haiti and the Geography of Blame. Berkeley: University of California Press.

——, 1999, Infections and Inequalities. The Modern Plagues. Berkeley: University of California Press.

FASSIN D., 1998, Politique des corps et gouvernement des villes. *In* Les figures urbaines de la santé publique. Enquête sur des expériences locales. D. Fassin, ed. Pp. 7–46. Paris: La Découverte.

——, 2000, Entre politiques de la vie et politiques du vivant. Pour une anthropologie de la santé. Anthropologie et Sociétés 24(1):95–116.

FELDMAN A., 1991, Formations of Violence. The Narrative of The Body and Political Terror in Northern Ireland. Chicago: University of Chicago Press.

FOUCAULT M., 1976, La volonté de savoir. Histoire de la sexualité, vol. 1, Paris: Gallimard.

GOOD B., 1994, Medicine, Rationality and Experience. An Anthropological Perspective. Cambridge: Cambridge University Press.

HACKING I., 1995, Rewriting The Soul. Multiple Personality and The Sciences of Memory. Princeton: Princeton University Press.

——, 1999, The Social Construction of What? Cambridge: Harvard University Press.

KIM J. Y., J. MILLEN, A. IRWIN and J. GERSHMAN, eds, 2000, Dying For Growth. Global Inequality and The Health of The Poor. Monroe: Common Courage Press.

KLEINMAN A., 1988, The Illness Narratives. Suffering, Healing and The Human Condition. New York: Basic Books.

LANZARINI C., 2000, Survivre dans le monde sous-prolétaire. Paris: Presses universitaires de France.

LATOUR B., 1991, Nous n'avons jamais été modernes. Essais d'anthropologie symétrique. Paris: La Découverte.

LOCK M., 2002, Twice Dead. Organ Transplants and The Reinvention of Death. Berkeley: University of California Press.

MAUSS M., 1980 [1934], Les techniques du corps. *In* Sociologie et anthropologie. Pp. 363–386. Paris: Presses universitaires de France.

MCCULLOCH J., 1995, Colonial Psychiatry and the African Mind. Cambridge: Cambridge University Press.

MEMMI D., 2003, Faire vivre et laisser mourir. Le gouvernement contemporain de la naissance et de la mort. Paris: La Découverte.

PETRYNA A., 2002, Life Exposed. Biological Citizens After Chernobyl. Princeton: Princeton University Press.

RABINOW P., 1996, Essays on The Anthropology of Reason. Princeton: Princeton University Press.

——, 1999, French DNA. Trouble in Purgatory. Chicago: University of Chicago Press.

RAPP R., 2000, Testing Women, Testing the Fetus. The Social Impact of Amniocentesis in America. New York: Routledge.

SCHEPER-HUGHES N., 1992, Death Without Weeping. The Violence of Everyday Life in Brazil. Berkeley: University of California Press.

——, 2002, Bodies for Sale – Whole or in Part. *In* Commodifying Bodies. N. Scheper-Hughes and L. Wacquant, eds. Pp. 1–8. London: Sage Publications.

SINGER M. and H. BAER, 1995, Critical Medical Anthropology. Amityville, NY: Baywood.

TAUSSIG M., 1987, Shamanism, Colonialism, and the Wild Man. A Study in Terror and Healing. Chicago: University of Chicago Press.

WAHNICH S., 2003, La liberté ou la mort. Essai sur la terreur et le terrorisme. Paris: La Fabrique.

WITTGENSTEIN L., 1961 [1945], Investigations philosophiques. Paris: Gallimard.

YOUNG A., 1995, The Harmony of Illusion. Inventing Post-Traumatic Stress Disorder. Princeton: Princeton University Press.

CONCLUSION

Medical Anthropology: Intimations for the Future
Margaret Lock

Reciting Genealogies

It would be a mistake, I think, to write about the future of medical anthropology without giving some consideration to its past. Both the sciences and the social sciences map their futures on the basis of knowledge laid down in the past but, in contrast to the world of science, for the social sciences the fundamental questions can never be answered with finality but must be posed repeatedly in modified form from one epoch to another. Our ability to manipulate the natural world and our modes of sustaining human life in social groups have been massively transformed as the result of modernity, and more recently with globalization. This transformation is due in large part to sustained efforts to rationalize social life and to put into practice new technologies of all kinds, ranging from multinational driven agricultural practices to technologies of the self. But the fundamental issues that social scientists have attempted to confront for over a century now, whether they are concerned primarily with forms of representation or with social change, whether the theoretical approach is structural, materialist, or semiotic, remain the same (postmodernism may constitute an exception). The focus of attention is inevitably on the relationships among individuals, social and political ordering, modes of production, and the natural world. Anthropologists, to a much greater degree than other social scientists are, in addition, oriented towards documenting the lived experiences of individuals and to some extent subjectivity. Medical anthropology is, of course, primarily concerned with health, illness, and the body, but its orientation is fundamentally anthropological and, in my estimation, as we move into an ever more technologized world, its critical insights, past, present, and future, are of enormous value for the discipline as a whole.

When writing a 1982 review article, entitled "The Anthropologies of Illness and Sickness," for the *Annual Review of Anthropology*, Allan Young noted an explosion of publications in medical anthropology over the previous decade. Clearly, more than twenty years ago, this subdiscipline had already come of age. Young then went on in the same article to trace out a genealogy of eminent anthropologists whose work had gone unmarked as formative of medical anthropology. Not surprisingly, he noted that W. H. R. Rivers was a founding father. In addition he argued that, among others, E. E. Evans-Pritchard, Victor Turner, and Melford Spiro had routinely made use of analytical frameworks in which episodes of distress and sickness were conceptualized as vehicles for understanding broader constellations of knowledge and practices. In other words, by highlighting links between bodily experience and society writ large, these researchers revealed insights of relevance to anthropology as a whole.

Today this insight is commonplace among medical anthropologists, but in the early 1980s it proved to be somewhat of an inspiration for future research, and perhaps precluded an untimely entry of medical anthropology into the doldrums. Young argued that a crucial function of medical anthropology was not merely to consider the meanings attributed to sickness, but to lay bare how societal relations produce the forms and distribution of sickness characteristic of any given society. Young also insisted, as did Frankenberg (1980), that medical practices are products of ideologies, and that examination of the unquestioned assumptions embedded in medical knowledge and practice should be incorporated into the terrain of medical anthropological research. These questions about truth claims, power relations, and inequities associated with health, illness, and medicine, were brought to the fore in the same decade that feminist anthropologists were raising parallel questions in an overlapping domain where gender issues and reproduction were central (see Rapp 2001 for a summary of this research).

The 1982 Review contained a second pertinent article, the author of which was Peter Worsley, who argued, "the treating of bodily ills takes place in any culture within a 'metamedical' framework of thought" (Worsley 1982:315). This claim, for the existence of an overarching philosophy that guides the basic features of medical knowledge, as well as its organization and practice, provided further incentive to broaden the horizons of medical anthropology. Worsley argued that investigators should not be seduced into working only in institutions that are obviously part of the "health-care complex," nor should they necessarily start their investigations with "named" diseases, but rather assume that disease taxonomies are cultural constructions (1982:327).

It is clear today that medical anthropologists no longer regard biomedicine as a monolith, as was formerly often the case. Moreover, another tendency evident in the early publications of medical anthropology, namely to romanticize and essentialize the medical institutions and practices of non-Western societies, has long been superceded. Medical anthropology today can perhaps best be glossed as one in which "biopolitics" are central. Moreover, many researchers assume that neither the human body nor the medical sciences should be black boxed as though epistemologically privileged and therefore unavailable to social science investigation. A rigorous questioning of what are so often assumed to be "natural" categories of classification continues to be central to the majority of projects in medical anthropology, but further, going well beyond the social construction of medical knowledge, researchers examine how and why specific representations become dominant during certain epochs, and then unpack the hegemony they exert over everyday life. The influence of Michel Foucault, and to a lesser extent that of Antonio

Gramsci, and more recently that of Ian Hacking, is readily apparent in contemporary medical anthropology.

Rethinking the Body

One might assume that the body would inevitably take center stage in virtually all medical anthropological undertakings. But, oddly, it often remains notable for its absence. Farquhar and Lock (n.d.) argue that this absence is due in large part to the way in which the body is usually conceptualized:

> The individual body, from which societies are supposedly assembled, has been treated in the post Enlightenment West as a skin-bounded, rights-bearing, communicating, experience-collecting, biomechanical entity. Our common sense has attributed basic needs to this body along with fixed gender characteristics. In law it has been seen as the only possible locus for the citizen's responsibility to act and to choose. In the humanities it was long treated as the site of an originary consciousness that is "expressed" in voice and image.

One of the principal effects of this approach to the body was commented on some time ago by the philosopher Russell Keat when he pointed out that a good deal of time has been spent in the social sciences and humanities in discussing the distinctiveness of human beings, while at the same time holding to an assumption about the nondistinctiveness of the human body (Keat 1986:24). Even though there is currently an apparent turn towards materiality, notably in the field of cultural studies with its interest in the flesh and in body surfaces, the interiority of the body remains firmly "black boxed" (in the idiom of sociologists of science), an assumed universal that is fully consigned to the domain of the biological sciences. The literary critic Terry Eagleton suggests that these chic new bodies of cultural studies portray the sentiment of our times, and their primary purpose, he argues, is to decenter "the unhoused intellect favored by philosophers and others to whom . . . 'mind' is still a sexy notion" (Eagleton 1993:7). Talking and writing about bodies, body surfaces, that is – about "exteriority without depth" (Braidotti 1989:154) – is, it seems, a last ditch effort to dispose of the ghost in the machine. This is a move that, in Eagleton's opinion, risks settling for subjectivity itself as no more than a humanist myth. Meaning simply becomes the material.

Of course, well before cultural studies became fashionable, Michel Foucault recognized an essential tension between the lived body and its representation, a tension that became the point of departure for his genealogical method to which recognition of the fusion of power with knowledge is central. However, Foucault never made it clear as to where he stood with respect to the malleability or the interiority of the material body. His position is not one of universalism; what he terms the "validity" of his micro-physics of power is situated somewhere between the institutions and apparatuses of power and "the bodies themselves with their materiality and their forces" (Foucault 1979:26), but how this is accomplished is never elucidated.

Bruno Latour (1993), less concerned with relationships of power than was Foucault, and deeply interested in epistemologies of scientific knowledge, reminds us that, prior to the Enlightenment, nature was understood in Europe as an animated moral force and that only with the establishment of the biological sciences was nature made into an object for scientific experimentation. During classical and medieval times in certain circles it had already become pragmatically expedient to dismember human bodies but, with modernity, decontextualization of the human body in order to facilitate its manipulation became routinized (Lock 2002:40). Matter was thus made essentially independent of the moral order – in Latour's language it was "purified" (Latour 1993:10), and we continue to live today with this dilemma.

Throughout modernity, nature has been represented as the unassailable bedrock over which culture games are played (although there have been times, when the Behaviorists had their heyday in the postwar years for example, when society was briefly accorded a deterministic role). However, nature is not epistemologically free; its representation, even in contemporary times, is by means of socially informed categories; nature/culture boundaries are continually contested; and nature is called upon to do political and moral "work." In other words, nature can be and is used to create a value-laden commentary on social life. Such activities are acts of the imagination – frequently orthodoxies of the imagination, as many of the chapters in this book have shown. Unpacking this type of discourse is central to contemporary medical anthropology and will continue to be so for the foreseeable future.

It is now widely acknowledged that representation of the natural order is socially constructed, including among many scientists (e.g., see Rose 1997), but relatively few commentators are prepared to go further and open up the black box in order to challenge the universalism associated with biology. One exception is Judith Butler who has made the social construction of the material, in particular an argument for the recognition of gendered biological difference, a point of departure for much of her research. She critiques the assumption that "a culture or an agency of the social acts upon a nature, which is itself presupposed as a passive surface" (Butler 1993:4). Butler argues that the concept of nature has a history, and the "figuring of nature as the blank and lifeless page, as that which is, as it were, always already dead, is decidedly modern, linked perhaps to the emergence of technological means of domination" (Butler 1993:4).

The psychiatrist Laurence Kirmayer, in a somewhat different vein, has argued for "the body's insistence on meaning," for a recognition of how the body "presents" itself in "substance and action," rather than simply being an implement for reflection and imagination (1992). Kirmayer insists that subjective experience should not be conceptualized merely as an internalized response to discourse and practices external to the body. The body is not passive, but actively contributes to the production of individual experience and to socially shared discourse and practice.

In summary, if the above challenges are to be met and expanded upon by medical anthropologists as we move further into the 21st century, it is imperative that not only the culture concept be de-essentialized, a process that is well under way in anthropology as a whole, but also that our approach to biology and to the technologies that enable us to represent and manipulate biology be subjected to revision.

Rethinking Culture

Clifford Geertz has written that the task of "other-knowing" is a delicate business today (1995). As part of the escalating process of globalization, borders dissolve, and boundaries drawn to differentiate self from other, whether they are justified in terms of politics, economics, or culture, become less and less meaningful. Similarly, assigning individuals to named, essentialized cultures, on the basis of which it is assumed that certain behaviors can be predicted, is not a valid exercise. Under these circumstances it is questionable as to whether one can write with any confidence about culture as in effect accounting for variation among contemporary medical knowledge, practice, and technologies in diverse geographical locations.

In her edited book entitled *The Fate of Culture*, Sherry Ortner (1999) cites Geertz in his defense of his revised concept of culture:

> Everyone, everywhere and at all times, seems to live in a sense-suffused world, to be the product of what the Indonesian scholar Taufik Abdullah has nicely called a history of notion-formation . . . one can ignore such facts, obscure them, or pronounce them forceless. But they do not thereby go away. Whatever the infirmities of the concept of "culture" ("cultures," "cultural forms" . . .) there is nothing for it but to persist in spite of them.

Ortner is in agreement with Geertz, that we should not give up on "culture," but other contributors to her book are less content. Both George Marcus (1999) and Lila Abu-Lughod (1999), for example, while they are not ready to abandon the culture concept entirely, as some anthropologists would argue, take strong issue with the idea that culture is something that is acted out in a contained location. They are committed to a strong program for de-essentializing culture, so that attention can be better focused on discontinuities, global flows of information, hybridized identities, and massive, ceaseless social change.

Matters are made yet more complicated because emerging nationalisms more often than not draw self-consciously on the idea of a shared history and culture among a named group of people – such a move re-essentializes the anthropologically created culture concept, at a time when anthropologists themselves are voicing radical doubts about its misapplication. On the other hand, many people who formerly assisted in anthropological research react strongly today to being "treated as specimens of cultural difference and otherness" (Ortner 1999:8).

Ortner's position is that, rather than abandoning the concept of culture, it is imperative to reconfigure it so that it can be of use when applied to a transformed world and to the changing landscape of theoretical possibilities. At the very minimum, she suggests, the culture of the ethnographer should be brought to the fore and exoticized, first, to diminish the production of a stark portrayal of otherness and, second, to bring to light unexamined assumptions and biases on the part of the ethnographer. The process of active meaning-making should become a focus of attention, with special concern about the effects of situations of power and entrenched inequalities. Drawing on a static concept of a cultural system is no longer tenable Ortner argues and, further, a cultural analysis cannot be a thing in itself, but must be contextualized in history, politics, and economics.

A good number of medical anthropologists have in effect been taking this position for over a decade, some of them from before the publication of Ortner's article and others more recently (e.g., see Briggs and Mantini-Briggs 2003; Cohen 1998; Farquhar 2002; Inhorn 2003; Lock 1993; Rapp 1999; Scheper-Hughes 1992; Young 1995). In retrospect, it is clear that the challenge to medical anthropologists of de-centering and historicizing biomedical knowledge forced a critical examination of assumed natural categories, and ensured that they were among the first to rethink the cultural concept in productive ways.

In a recent essay, Didier Fassin highlights some of the real dangers inherent in failing to problematize culture. He discusses the situation in which health authorities of various kinds, including those employed by the WHO, frequently cite cultural beliefs as the reason why women apparently choose not to cooperate with the modernization of, for example, maternity practices: "In incriminating culture, as certain health authorities willingly do, sometimes supported by anthropological data, they are in fact blaming victims while masking their own responsibility in the matter" (2001:305). Fassin argues that "culturalism," by which he means a combination of a belief in reification of culture and cultural overdetermination (2001:302), ensures that the social and political origins of health-related behaviors and actual health status are easily pushed to one side when the focus of attention is on culturalism. Moreover, culturalism ensures that "target populations" are inevitably assumed to be the cause of difficulties encountered in trying to implement changes in health care. Further, culturalism denies the Other his "right to differences." Fassin decries the violence associated with culturalism, but concludes that it is possible to retain culture (in the form of shared values held by the Other) as a useful concept, provided that it is used as an explanation of last resort and then only as a politicized concept – a study of culture must move out of the realm of ideology and into the domain of politics. Such analyses then become accounts of culture in action and, when necessary, of culturalism in action.

From this point on, this essay will take up the topics of medical pluralism, the coproduction of biology and culture, and the technological manipulation of life. These research areas show clearly some of the new directions in which medical anthropology is moving, while at the same time illustrating how our ideas about culture, biology, and technology are undergoing major reformulations, largely on the basis of empirical findings, much of them produced as a result of extensive ethnographic research. At the same time, it is obvious that clear continuities remain as a result of insights obtained over the formative years of medical anthropology.

Medical Pluralism, Nationalism, Globalization, and Technology Transfer

It was Charles Leslie who first made use of the concept of medical pluralism; he was able to show how self-conscious attempts at revivalism of an "authentic" Ayurvedic tradition was closely associated with nationalism, and was in large part a response to perceived threats by forces for modernization and, by implication, "Westernization," emanating from both inside and outside India (Leslie 1973). Various forms of this tension persist to the present day and have been documented increasingly in recent years by medical anthropologists.

Most medical anthropologists are now at pains to collapse entirely the duality of "traditional" and "modern." They are also sensitive to the way in which, when studying medical practices, rigid boundaries of exclusion and inclusion are inevitably set up if one assumes the existence of a "system" or a "tradition" that can be clearly demarcated. For example, Ferzacca (2002) notes that the Indonesian government has used a commitment to "*pembangunan*" (development) as an ideological apparatus to govern the daily lives of its citizens. At the same time "traditional" values are lauded as essential to the state's vision of a reflexive and unique modernization. The modernity envisioned for Indonesia (and similarly by other countries) looks backward to find something recoverable – something felt to be lost in the present – but it does so for the sake of a better future (Adams 2002). Another example comes from the work of Stacy Pigg who argues that AIDS prevention is only welcomed by the state in Nepal when in the form of warnings about disease that reinforce "proper" conduct within traditional social hierarchies. Efforts at prevention become a threat to the state's moral identity when "sexual health" is addressed more broadly and openly (Pigg 2002).

Writing about the Senoi Temiar in Malaysia, Marina Roseman considers how ritual healing not only deals with the distress of individuals, but also mitigates the effects of colonialism and postcolonialism experienced by Temiars as a whole (Roseman 2002). In recent times, the Temiar have experienced a shift from semi-nomadic mobility and rainforest symbiosis to a sedentary, restricted lifeway based on an alien market economy. Roseman analyzes the way in which healing rituals are employed as a therapeutic means of mediating traumatic cultural change secondary to encounters with deforestation, Islamic religious evangelism, and economic transformation. Ritual becomes a means for reestablishing cultural integrity and resolving new types of illness/soul loss associated with disruption and dislocation.

Similar to Nichter's research on Kyasanur forest disease (1992) and Adelson's on the concept of well-being among the Cree (2000), Roseman's approach takes the form of a political ecological analysis that goes beyond a straightforward consideration of the impact of political economy on the physical environment. At stake is the Temiar's entire cosmos and sense of self, derived from their relationship to this cosmology. This type of research shows how environmental and medical anthropology are in some senses inseparable and points the way to future collaborations among ecologists, anthropologists, and individuals who take a critical stand towards the initiation from the top down of development projects that bring about massive social and environmental change.

One of the most comprehensive efforts to date to document postmodern medical pluralism appears in an edited collection by Laurent Pordié (n.d.). The transformation that Tibetan medicine is undergoing is examined from a number of points of view in this book, including practices of normalization and commoditization in addition to a turn towards neo-traditionalism. The practice of Tibetan medicine is examined simultaneously in multiple sites: Tibet, India, Nepal, Ladakh, Mongolia, China, the UK, and also from the point of view of healers, patients, tourists, and government officials of various kinds. Collaborative, multisited ethnographic work on pluralistic forms of medicine in practice is a key direction for future research, a move that suggests that the days of the lone, pioneering researcher are rapidly becoming a thing of the past, although the need for in-depth knowledge of local sites and contextualization of findings continues to be critical for medical anthropology.

Pluralism and the Social Life of Artifacts

It has been shown repeatedly that artifacts, including biomedical technologies, can be introduced successfully into different geographical locations without a simultaneous adoption of the use originally associated with them (Lock and Kaufert 1998; Van Der Geest and Reynolds Whyte 1988). New meanings and social relations coalesce around transported artifacts, whatever the direction of their travel.[1] This is not an argument for the autonomy of artifacts (or for that matter for the autonomy of culture), but rather for their inherent heterogeneity as social objects. Alternatively, some artifacts and technologies, notably when they threaten entrenched values, are actively rejected or, after attempted adoption, fail to take root or see their use severely restricted. Several of the best documented examples of cultural dissonance in connection with biotechnology transfer have to do with contraceptive and reproductive technologies, and with AIDS prevention (Bledsoe 2002; Ginsburg and Rapp 1995; Greenhalgh 1994; Inhorn 2003; Lock and Kaufert 1998; Nguyen 2005).

Current work by medical anthropologists focuses on the implementation of technologies in practice – their development, transfer, and application – and how these processes are influenced by the relationship of indigenous medicine to biomedicine, local political economies, national interests, dominant values, and the perceived impact of new technologies on individuals, communities, and societies at large. As with medical pluralism more generally, an ethnographic approach is central for effective research in connection with the social life of artifacts. There must be a two-way process involving an examination, not only of the importation of technologies associated with the biosciences, but also of the global movement of indigenous medicinals and local technologies in multiple directions. Research of this kind clearly reveals the metamedical context in which technologies of all kinds are mobilized and applied in practice. One of the most urgent areas for research is in connection with the global implementation of genetically modified organisms in agriculture, the multinational commodification of food sources, the patenting of plant materials, and the creation of immortalized cell lines of genetic material procured from humans, animals, and plants. Similarly, the globalized commodification of human organs and tissues, in which opportunities for massive exploitation of marginalized peoples with a resultant widening of inequities is an area that demands further rigorous investigation (Cohen 2001; Scheper-Hughes 2001).

Local Biologies

Medical anthropology has long been thought of as a specialty with the potential to transcend the nature/culture divide embedded in modernist thinking. I found it necessary to revise my own thinking in connection with the relationship between culture and biology and to argue for recognition of the coproduction of, on the one hand, the material, and on the other hand, representations about the material, when writing up ethnographic and survey research in connection with female aging and the menopausal transition. Before going into the field in the 1980s I had assumed that subjective differences in reporting about the menopausal experience, and the way in which this transition was represented in Japan, could be accounted for by drawing on a sophisticated concept of culture such as that outlined above. But, in fact, this approach turned out to be entirely inadequate. I will first summarize the research findings, and then set out why I believe that medical anthropologists should no longer set biological difference to one side.

Aging, and its potential cost to health-care systems, is of enormous political interest today, and this is in large part why menopause and its possible effects on women's health as they age is of concern beyond medical circles and the lives of women themselves. Medical knowledge about menopause has been created in large part out of the symptom reporting and experiences of small samples of women in clinical situations, almost all of whom live in Europe or North America. Most of these women have gone to visit doctors because of physical and emotional distress. In addition, many have had hysterectomies. As a result, medical knowledge about menopause is produced and circulated without reference to the lived experience of the majority of women, and as such is biased (Lock 1993).

Despite these shortcomings, the professional organizations of gynecologists in the United States, Canada, Australia, most European countries, and elsewhere have, until recently, made blanket recommendations to the effect that virtually all women once past menopause should take powerful hormone replacement therapy (HRT) until the day they die. These recommendations, that in effect make the body of a 30-year-old the norm for all women, are designed to counter what are believed to be the long term consequences of "estrogen starved bodies" including being at an increased risk for heart disease, osteoporosis, and possibly for stroke and Alzheimer's disease. But they ride roughshod over the considerable variation in incidence of these diseases across populations and socioeconomic groupings of women, and also over the iatrogenic effects that many women experience when taking HRT. On the basis of the findings from two major clinical trials conducted in the United States that showed that the risks associated with long term use of HRT are greater than its benefits, the recommendations have recently been withdrawn, causing a great deal of uncertainty and re-thinking on the part of numerous women and clinicians.

In order to counter received medical wisdom on the subject of menopause, comparative survey research was carried out in the mid-1980s with over 1,300 women in Canada, nearly 8,000 in the United States, and with over 1,300 women in Japan. They were aged between 45 and 55 inclusively, and were all drawn from the general population. The results of this research indicate strongly that the menopausal transition is not a difficult time for the majority (Avis and McKinlay 1991; Kaufert et al. 1992; Lock 1993). Of more significance for the present argument is that in Japan women going through *kônenki* (the term usually glossed as menopause) report relatively few of the "classical" symptoms of menopause, namely hot flushes and night sweats. Through extensive open-ended interviews with over 100 women I concluded that this difference has little to do with a lack of willingness to cooperate with the researcher. Nor is it to do with shyness on the part of women about reporting symptoms (as is often assumed to be the case by medical audiences). The fact that no clear and unambiguous signifier exists in Japanese that refers exclusively to hot flushes in female middle age does not appear to be a major stumbling block either. Those relatively few women in the study who had experienced hot flushes (12.5%) talked about them unambiguously, suggesting that the difference between Japan and North America is quantitative, not qualitative, but statistically significant.

Japanese doctors deal every day with middle-aged patients whose symptoms and experiences differ quite markedly from those that medical texts written in Europe or North America tell them are "normal" for menopause (Lock 1993). When I carried out this research virtually no doctors listed the hot flush as a "typical" symptom. After exposure to conferences and reading the proceedings of International Menopause Society meetings, together with other sources, a few of these doctors have come to believe that the low symptom reporting in Japan is due to the fact that Japanese women simply do not pay "proper" attention to their bodies. However, the majority of doctors prefer to hypothesize that a sufficiently marked biological difference – due perhaps to environment, diet, or genetics – results in a subjective experience at the end of menstruation for many (but not all) Japanese women that is different from that commonly experienced by women in North America. On the basis of my research findings I am in agreement with these physicians, and conclude that these embodied experiences produce an effect on (but do not determine) the production of medical and popular discourse about *kônenki* in Japan.

Japanese accounts about the end of menstruation sound bizarre to most North Americans and Europeans because emphasis is usually given to stiff shoulders, dizzyness, and other nonspecific symptoms. It is tempting to Orientalize this discourse and dismiss it as anomalous. The danger, of course, is that the white Euro-American body remains as the gold standard and the medical model of a universal menopause survives intact. Research conducted in Hong Kong, Singapore, Taiwan, China, Korea, the Philippines, Thailand, Malaysia, and Indonesia all reveal low reporting of hot flushes and night sweats (see Lock and Kaufert 2001 for details). Some of this research is methodologically weak, but the relative consistency of the results is nevertheless suggestive. Beyene, in a comprehensive study in the Yucatan (1989), found no reporting of the "typical" symptoms of menopause.

In all, these data strongly suggest that it is not appropriate to conceptualize the end of menstruation as an invariant biological transformation modified by culture alone. Similarly it should not be assumed that postmenopausal women are equally at increased risk for heart disease, osteoporosis, and other late onset chronic diseases. The coproduction of biology and culture are implicated both in embodied experience and in its representation by individual women. Where culture and shared biological attributes are widely shared across a group of people, then, embodied experience will, for the most part, also be reasonably similar.

In order to theorize about the above findings I created the concept of "local biologies" (Lock 1993). In using this concept I do not intend to convey the idea that the categories of the biological sciences are historically and culturally constructed (although this is indeed the case), nor does the concept indicate measurable biological difference across human populations. Rather, local biologies in part inform embodied experience – that is, the experience of physical sensations, including those of well-being, health, illness, and so on, *de facto* involve the material body, but this body is itself contingent upon evolutionary, environmental, and other factors.

Embodiment is also constituted by the way in which self and others represent the body, drawing upon local categories of knowledge and experience. If embodiment is to be made social, then history, politics, language, and local knowledge, including scientific knowledge to the extent that it is available, must inevitably be implicated. This means in practice that knowledge about biology is informed by the social and the social is in turn informed by the reality of the material. In other words, the biological and the social are coproduced and dialectically reproduced, and the primary site where this engagement takes place is the subjectively experienced, socialized body. The material body cannot stand, then, as an entity that is black-boxed and assumed to be a universal with so much sociocultural flotsam layered over it. The material and the social are both contingent, both local.

The embodiment of the coproduction of local biologies and culture is, by definition, internalized and individualized. Humans are unique in terms of both genetics and their lived experience, and to this extent embodiment is personal. At another level of abstraction, most embodied experiences are shared by us all – pain, immunological responses to infection, the biological changes of aging (although this last example is, of course, modified by sex), and so on. But even these most basic of biological events are contingent, as numerous studies have shown (e.g., see Good et al. 1992; Lock et al. 2005a; Worthman 1995). This contingency is due to individual biology and, of course, also to language as well as the social, environmental, and political contexts in which individuals live. Nevertheless, some types of embodied experience are relatively common across groups of people, due in part to shared environments, histories, language, behaviors, and values. Other contributing factors are biological attributes common to a good proportion of individuals who live in close proximity to one another and who for the most part have a shared biological ancestry.

Continuous migration from prehistoric times, accelerated today by globalization, ensures that people who share biological attributes are widely dispersed. Even so, until late in the last century, the majority of people other than those living close to major historical trade routes tended to live out their lives within a short distance of their birthplace. Biological attributes are used by population geneticists and others to ascribe people to populations that are, of course, not congruent with self-defined ethnic groups or communities. But the very fact that scientists are interested in documenting features of inclusion and exclusion based on biological attributes – formerly through anatomical taxonomies, blood typing, and so on, and now by means of DNA sampling – has made it relatively easy for prejudiced commentators to decontextualize the always provisional typologies of population biology and conflate them with social groupings to reproduce and naturalize a racist rhetoric. Certain population geneticists and biological anthropologists have actually encouraged this type of conflation (sometimes inadvertently) as ongoing criticism by anthropologists of the now defunct Human Genome Diversity Project make clear (Lock 1999; Marks 1995).

Under the circumstances it is not surprising that recognition of biological difference, and therefore of local biologies, has been an anathema to many social scientists but, given the speed with which the new genetics is revealing the complexity and significance for health of biological difference, to doggedly ignore these findings would be singularly unwise. Apart from anything else, the outrageous claims made by a few geneticists who appear disproportionately frequently in the media to talk about the way in which the new genetics will bring about the good life for us all need urgently to be countered (Lock et al. 2005b).

It goes without saying that there is no simple relationship between local biologies and societies, nation states, ethnicity, communities, or even families. Nevertheless, embodied subjectivity is shaped to *some extent* by the contingency of local biologies that may well be partially shared across groups of people living in close proximity to one another. These biological attributes have the potential to contribute to the creation of powerful, even hegemonic discourse in connection with health, distress, illness, and lifecycle transitions among both medical professionals and the public. When considering comparative research findings from Japan and North America in connection with menopause, such hegemonic discourse appeared to be at work, and I felt compelled to create the concept of local biologies in order to interpret the research findings (Lock 1993). The concept must, of course, be applied equally at all sites of investigation, including Europe and North America.

By drawing on such a concept, my hope was to prevent the Japanese findings from being treated as so much exotica, and at the same time to challenge the hegemony of the dominant disease-like medical model about the end of menstruation.

In sum, differences in local biologies partly account for, but do not determine, the cultural construction of menopause and, where relevant, its medicalization. There is no doubt that biological and genetic determinisms must be rejected outright. But it is also necessary to reject those equally deterministic arguments for the social and cultural construction of the body and related medical practices in which the material body is black-boxed. Truth claims about the body demand contextualization and critical appraisal, but to ignore the reality of biology entirely and its interdependence with history and culture is short sighted in the extreme.

Current research that takes up this challenge includes the work of Briggs and Mantini-Briggs (2003), Bledsoe (2002), Fulwiley (2004), Nguyen (2005), and Montana (2003).

After Nature: Biotechnologies and the Reinvention of the Normal

Medical anthropology has taken a leading role over the years in producing a critical commentary on "medicalization" and, more recently, on "geneticization." With some notable exceptions, this type of research has focused for the most part on clinical practice, support groups, and occasionally on family dynamics. The initial position taken by most researchers, that "medicalization" poses a threat to individual autonomy, has gradually been modified, particularly in light of empirical findings by medical anthropologists who have shown that many people actively seek out medical assistance in the hope that their distress can be given a medical diagnosis and either be treated or, in the case of lifecycle transitions, be efficiently managed. Moreover, people often find themselves, as a result of "medicalization," relieved of personal responsibility for their condition, and often of the stigma associated with it (see Lock 2004 for a summary of this literature).

A related emerging field of interest for medical anthropologists is the explosive world of genomics as well as other expanding and emerging biomedical technologies, making for challenging research projects in which basic science discourse and the politics of biomedical technologies must become part of the analysis. Moreover, the burgeoning bioethical commentary about these emerging technologies demands critical attention from medical anthropologists. The scale and depth of human manipulation of the material world in the 21st century, and the potential ramifications – technical, cultural, economic, and political – are enormous. Investigation of these changes by social scientists is significantly different from bioethical commentary about them.

Whereas bioethicists very often start out with an assumption that one can deduce right and wrong, good and harm, and cost and benefit associated with biomedical technologies by applying decontextualized moral principles to the situation, social scientists, particularly anthropologists, remain grounded, and examine not only competing discourse, but actual practices and their effects in context. Not surprisingly, emphasis is given by social scientists to competing truth claims, the politicized legitimation of dominant discourse, and frequently to the active suppression of less favored discourse; in connection with genetically modified organisms (GMOs) and genomics, this means a reluctance to apply the "precautionary principle" (see Nestle 2003). Medical anthropologists are beginning to examine the local and global effects of the application of these emerging technologies (Bibeau 2004; Franklin and Lock 2003; Fulwiley 2004; Rapp 2003). Above all, they are considering the challenges posed by such technologies to what has been assumed to be unassailable demarcations between nature and culture, and the need, therefore, to rethink what now will count as "normal." Alternatively, they may have to consider what normal might come to mean, as a result of the existence of enhancement technologies of many kinds.

As with all good anthropology, moral judgment is put on hold in favor of analyzing the stated positions and activities of the actors involved. This is not to argue, of course, for an unchallenged cultural relativism, nor to suggest that concern about the directions in which certain technologies may well take us, should they be freely applied, is not valid. Rather, it is clear that the moral implications of what is being brought about through technological means cannot be fully discerned in advance of or separately from actual knowledge production and its application in practice. One of the biggest challenges for the social scientist is to recognize that all knowledge associated with genomics, and with many other biomedical technologies, is knowledge in-the-making; it is provisional, unstable, and repeatedly subject to revision or abandonment. Moreover, the decontextualized "facts" of the basic sciences may be of little or no use for clinical practice, or for application in any site beyond a controlled laboratory setting.

One problem that arises is that the long term effects of many of the biomedical technologies – undergoing repeated use of reproductive technologies, being subjected to gene therapy (which remains as yet in the experimental stage), modifying the germ line (currently banned but believed to be taking place in experimental settings), or imbibing genetically modified food on a regular basis, to give a few examples – on individuals, families, society, future generations, and even the natural world, are unknown. The officially recommended widespread use of hormone replacement therapy that had to be reversed recently provides a cautionary tale in this respect.

Second, basic scientific knowledge is not stable and, further, is subject to competing interpretations. For example, risk estimates in connection with named diseases have been calculated for individuals who carry genes associated with the condition in question. These estimates are constantly subject to revision in light of new genomic knowledge that currently indicates that in only a few limited instances do genetic mutations follow a Mendelian pattern of inheritance and in effect determine disease. The action of virtually all of our genes is modified profoundly by mutual interactions among genes, by the proteins they produce, and above all by the environment, from conception to death. The gene no longer stands as the blueprint for life; in practice the gene has become, in effect, less and less knowable. In the interim, abortions of wanted pregnancies have been carried out, or else anxiety levels have soared in certain families, on the basis of knowledge about their genome that they have been given. People are not told that such knowledge is provisional, unstable, and in fact very often functions as disinformation. Moreover, there is always the problem of translating estimates of population-based risk to individual cases. Proposed routinization of testing for susceptibility genes (genes that may, under certain circumstances, put one at an increased risk but that do not determine disease onset) adds to public confusion (Lock et al. 2005b). A basic question demanding further attention is why so many of us living in contemporary society apparently believe that we can gain control over our lives through predictions made about our future health on the basis of printouts about our DNA. These probabilistic estimates of risk closely resemble more classical forms of divination.

The possibilities for anthropological research in this area are vast, but much of it cannot be done effectively without having considerable knowledge of the relevant scientific discourse, the politics of scientific practice, and the impact of the private sector on contemporary research. The best research will not be limited to examining the effects of geneticization on individuals and families, but will also examine the way in which these technologies and their associated discourse promise to bring about what we currently believe is the "good" society.

As early as 1992 Marilyn Strathern mapped the effects of the new reproductive technologies on what was assumed to be the "natural" domain of kinship. Among many things, this research involved the documentation of the widespread, calculated use of the concept of "choice" in connection with reproduction – what Strathern termed the "enterprising of kinship." More recently, in ongoing research, Paul Rabinow, is investigating several emerging DNA-related technologies using the concept of the "assemblage" to inform his approach – following Foucault, he is primarily interested in demonstrating how truth claims about "life," and its manipulation, are currently sustained through a discourse that draws upon knowledge, much of it provisional, created through innovations in biomedical technology (1996, 1999).

Charis Thompson in her work on changing ontologies that belong to what she describes as "the biotech mode of (re)production" under the sign of "promissory capital" gives us an inkling of the direction that some future research in medical anthropology may have to take. According to Thompson, the biotech mode of (re)production will have, and is already beginning to have, its own characteristic systems of exchange and value, its own notions of the dimensions we currently think of as time and space, its own epistemic norms, its hegemonic political forms, and its own hierarchies and definitions of commodities and personhood.

Similarly, the philosopher Hans Jorg Rheinberger's work has emphasized an epochal shift in the way new biotechnologies have altered the understanding of life itself.

With the advent of recombinant DNA technologies, a radical change of perspective ensued. The momentum of gene technology is based on the prospect of an intercellular representation of extracellular projects – the potential of "rewriting" life.

However, bringing an anthropological perspective to bear on biotechnology involves more than making claims about shifts in the meanings ascribed to nature and culture, or identifying changes in the way the biological is actually constituted for use as a technology (viral vectors for gene therapy; suspensions of immortalized cell lines; human organs for transplant). The emergence of technologies that have the potential to totally transform the "normal" requires close ethnographic attention for what they may do to society at large. Franklin and Lock (2003:22) argue:

> The cultural analysis of visual, textual, popular, discursive, and national forms of representation of the body require paying attention not only to embodiment itself, but to biology as a site of knowledge production, moral dispute, and economic worth. It is, for that matter, a site of aesthetic spectacle, heroic narrative, and imagined future. Situating the encounters between such emergent cultural formations and negotiations about their application in everyday life, constitutes the distinctive challenge of novel field sites where ethnographies of the contemporary worlds of the biological are mapped.

Into the Future

First, we should not forget our founding fathers and other theoreticians whose work has more than stood the test of time, including E. E. Evans Pritchard, Max Weber, Pierre Bourdieu, Michel Foucault, Georges Canguilhem, and others.

Clearly a medical anthropology of the future must continue to document inequities, discrimination, and above all, human rights abuses and the violence that so many people are subjected to as part of their everyday lives. We must insist that our findings, whether it be about the treatment of women and children, the political manipulation of medical knowledge, or the practices of certain NGOs (Nguyen 2005; Pandolfi 2002), are paid attention to in the worlds of politics, multinationals, and policy-making – this is a daunting challenge, of course, and one that Paul Farmer has been addressing for some time now (Farmer 2003). As Slavoj Zizek recently noted when writing about the Abu Ghraib jail in Iraq, it is above all the "unknown knowns" that must be brought to light; the "knowledge which doesn't know itself" – what we pretend not to know about (2004:19). Under these conditions, injustice and human atrocities run rife.

In addition, it is incumbent on medical anthropologists to counter arguments beginning to be made by certain policy-makers and bioethicists who support the idea of a technological fix for developing countries (whether this technology takes the form of GMOs, reproductive technologies, or some other emerging technology, such as gene chips) when basic hygiene, food, and clean water remain unattended to. Clearly technology has its place – vaccinations are indispensable, as are drugs that combat HIV/AIDS and other lethal diseases, and so too may be GMOs under certain conditions that are as yet unknown – but the robust evidence accumulated from many years of research cannot be overridden, that poverty causes the most sickness and is the greatest killer, and that public health is the best form of prevention. Intimately related to the political economy of health and illness is the area now demarcated as the politics of infectious disease. Some good work is being done in connection with HIV/AIDS but, with a few notable exceptions, among whom Paul Farmer is the best known, there are still relatively few medical anthropologists researching malaria, TB, and other infectious diseases that account for the greatest loss of human life.

Medical anthropologists are beginning to document the way in which a technological fix is actively sought after by certain members of the public in many countries, and that excessive use of medications, reproductive technologies, and other biomedical technologies cannot be put down entirely to the interests of doctors or even of pharmaceutical companies – although of course these actors are deeply complicit. For example, certain advocacy groups, concerned or disaffected parents, and individuals who wish to overcome infertility or to transform themselves in some fundamental way by means of technologies such as Prozac, have been shown to actively support a relatively uncontrolled use of technology. This trend needs careful ethnographic documentation and should take into account, as some research is already doing, what exactly such activists know and/or believe about the effects of the technologies they seek out. The public understanding of scientific knowledge, in particular awareness of the provisional nature of scientific knowledge, is an area demanding much more research attention. Similarly, the politics of nationwide advocacy groups such as Best Friends, a movement in the United States that promotes sexual abstinence among young people, is of great interest. Why, at this time, is such a group, largely composed of African American youth, being given millions of dollars in federal support?

Another expanding task for the future is to document the increasing use of human subjects for research purposes. Todeschini has written about the experimental use of data collected from victims of the atomic bombs dropped on Hiroshima and Nagasaki (2002), and Petryna has documented the biological politics associated with victims of the Chernobyl disaster (2002). With increasing regularity, residents of developing countries are being used as experimental subjects for drug, vaccine, and contraceptive testing, in large part because ethical controls over medical research in the developed world have been progressively tightened and simultaneously have become prohibitively expensive.

One of the features of many of the new biomedical technologies is that they make use not only of human subjects, but also of body organs, tissues, and cells for research purposes and as therapeutic tools. Mapping the rapidly expanding commodification of the human body and body parts, and the close links of these activities with increasing inequities between the poor and wealthy will be a major task for a medical anthropology of the future.

We live in an era of heightened nationalisms. The thrust of one part of the new genomics is towards a thorough documentation of biological difference at the level of DNA. It is urgent that medical anthropologists confront the political implications of this research while at the same time refusing to categorically deny biological difference. This will entail working closely together with scientists and with populations whose DNA has been procured or is targeted for research. The concept of race is highly evident once again in the scientific literature, and very often actively made use of by minority group scientists in the latest round of biopolitics. This turn of events presents an enormous challenge to medical anthropologists, first as to how they should situate themselves vis-à-vis research informants, and then in what form findings should be written up and distributed that actively counter well-grounded anthropological knowledge. It is possible that some anthropologists may find that they can no longer take a hard line about the concept of race.

One of the strengths of medical anthropology has been to document how the boundaries of normal and abnormal, nature and culture, self and other are continually challenged and modified by the biosciences. This documentation will increase exponentially in the coming years and decades. It is in this area, above all else, where unexamined morals and values lie exposed, and this type of research will continue to be, therefore, a rich seam for investigation; an area that, more than any other, builds bridges with the past and future of anthropology as a whole.

These are just a few of the areas where medical anthropology has a unique role to play. It is my belief that the discipline is entering a new era, an era that will continue to adopt a critical/interpretive approach, to make use of the techniques of ethnographic research and related empirical evidence, and to question the concepts and truth claims of the world of bioscience as well as those made by politicians and policy-makers. But there will also be a willingness to engage actively with the Other, whether this means with political activists, committed scientists, other social scientists, policy-makers, NGOs, or the media. For too long the remarkable insights resulting from so much good research in medical anthropology have been mainly unnoticed by society at large. This must change, and will only come about through our own concerted efforts.

Notes

1. This is as equally true for acupuncture and herbal medicines being imported and adopted for use in Europe and North America, as it is, for example, for vaccinations being administered throughout Africa.

References

ABU-LUGHOD L., 1999, The Interpretation of Culture(s) after Television. *In* The Fate of Culture: Geertz and Beyond. S. Ortner, ed. Pp. 110–135. Berkeley: University of California Press.

ADAMS V., 2002, Establishing Proof: Translating Science and the State in Tibetan Medicine. *In* New Horizons in Medical Anthropology: Essays in Honour of Charles Leslie. M. Nichter and M. Lock, eds. Pp. 200–220. New York: Routledge.

ADELSON N., 2000, Being Alive Well: Health and the Politics of Cree Well-Being. Toronto: University of Toronto Press.

AVIS N. E. and S. McKINLEY, 1991, A Longitudinal Analysis of Women's Attitudes Toward the Menopause: Results from the Massachusetts Women's Health Study. Maturitas 13:65–79.

BEYENE Y., 1989, From Menarche to Menopause: Reproductive Lives of Peasant Women in Two Cultures. Albany: State University of New York Press.

BIBEAU G., 2004, Le Québec Transgénique: Science Marché, Humanité. Montréal: Boréal.

BLEDSOE C. H., 2002, Contingent Lives: Fertility, Time, and Aging in West Africa. Chicago: The University of Chicago Press.

BRAIDOTTI R., 1989, Organs without Bodies. Differences: A Journal of Feminist Cultural Studies 1:147–161.

BRIGGS C. and C. MANTINI-BRIGGS, 2003, Stories in the Time of Cholera: Racial Profiling During a Medical Nightmare. Berkeley: University of California Press.

BUTLER J., 1993, Bodies That Matter: On the Discursive Limits of Sex. New York: Routledge.

COHEN L., 1998, No Aging in India: Alzheimer's, the Bad Family and Other Modern Things. Berkeley: University of California Press.

——, 2001, The Other Kidney: Biopolitics beyond Recognition. Body & Society 7(2–3):9–29.

EAGLETON T., 1993, It Is not Quite True that I Have a Body, and not Quite True that I Am One Either. London Review of Books May 27:7–10.

FARMER P., 2003, Pathologies of Power: Health, Human Rights, and the New War on the Poor. Berkeley: University of California Press.

FARQUHAR J., 2002, Appetites: Food and Sex in Post-Socialist China. Durham, NC: Duke University Press.

FARQUHAR J. and M. LOCK, n.d., Beyond the Body Proper: Reading the Anthropology of Material Life. Durham: Duke University Press. In press.

FASSIN D., 2001, Culturalism as Ideology. *In* Cultural Perspectives on Reproductive Health. C. M. Obermeyer, ed. Pp. 300–317. Oxford: Oxford University Press.

FERZACCA S., 2002, Governing Bodies in New Order Indonesia. *In* New Horizons in Medical Anthropology: Essays in Honour of Charles Leslie. M. Nichter and M. Lock, eds. Pp. 35–57. New York: Routledge.

FOUCAULT M., 1979, Discipline and Punish: The Birth of the Prison. A. Sheridan, trans. New York: Vintage.

FRANKENBERG R., 1980, Medical Anthropology and Development: A Theoretical Perspective. Social Science and Medicine 14:197–207.

FRANKLIN S. and M. LOCK, 2003, Remaking Life and Death: Toward an Anthropology of the Biosciences. Santa Fe: School of American Research.

FULWILEY D., 2004, From Discriminate Biopower to Everyday Biopolitics: Views of Genetic Testing in Dakar. Medical Anthropology 23:157–194.

GEERTZ C., 1995, Culture Wars. The New York Review of Books 42:4–6.

GINSBURG F. D. and R. RAPP, 1995, Conceiving the New World Order: The Global Politics of Reproduction. Berkeley: University of California Press.

GOOD DELVECCHIO M-J., B. J. GOOD, P. E. BRODWIN and A. KLEINMAN, 1992, Pain as Human Experience: An Anthropological Perspective. Berkeley: University of California Press.

GREENHALGH S., 1994, Controlling Birth and Bodies in Village China. American Ethnologist 21(1):3–30.

INHORN M. C., 2003, Local Babies, Global Science: Gender, Religion, and in Vitro Fertilization in Egypt. New York: Routledge.

KAUFERT P., P. GILBERT and R. TATE, 1992, Defining Menopausal Status: The Impact of Longitudinal Data. Maturitas 14:143–155.

KEAT R., 1986, The Human Body in Social Theory: Reich, Foucault, and the Representative Hypotheses. Radical Philosophy 42:24–32.

KIRMAYER L., 1992, The Body's Insistence on Meaning: Metaphor as Presentation and Representation in Illness Experience. Medical Anthropology Quarterly 6:323–346.

LATOUR B., 1993, We Have Never Been Modern. Cambridge, MA: Harvard University Press.

LESLIE C., 1973, The Professionalizing Ideology of Medical Revivalism. *In* Entrepreneurship and Modernization of Occupational Cultures in South Asia. M. Singer, ed. Pp. 16–42. Durham, NC: Duke University Press.

LOCK M., 1993, Encounters With Aging. Berkeley: University of California Press.

——, 1999, Genetic Diversity and the Politics of Difference. Chicago-Kent Law Review 75(1):83–111.

——, 2002, Twice Dead: Organ Transplants and the Reinvention of Death. Berkeley: University of California Press.

——, 2004, Biomedical Technologies, Anthropological Approaches. *In* Encyclopedia of Medical Anthropology: Health and Illness in the World's Cultures. Pp. 86–95. New York: Kluwer/Plenum.

——, 2005, Alzheimer's Disease: A Tangled Concept. *In* Complexities: Beyond Nature and Nurture. S. McKinnon and S. Silverman, eds. Pp. 196–222. New York: Routledge.

LOCK M. and P. KAUFERT, 1998, Pragmatic Women and Body Politics. Cambridge: Cambridge University Press.

——, 2001, Menopause, Local Biologies and Cultures of Aging. American Journal of Human Biology 13:494–503.

LOCK M., V-K. NGUYEN and C. ZAROWSKI, 2005a, Global and Local Perspectives on Population Health: Taking Contingency Seriously. *In* Social Inequalities and Health. C. Hertzman, J. Heyman and B. Evans, eds. Oxford: Oxford University Press.

LOCK M., J. PREST and S. LLOYD, 2005b, Genetic Susceptibility and Alzheimer's Disease: The Penetrance and Uptake of Genetic Knowledge. *In* L. Cohen and A. Leibing, eds. Thinking about Dementia. L. Cohen and A. Leibing, eds. Chap. 6. Pistcataway, NJ: Rutgers University Press.

MARCUS G. E., 1999, The Uses of Complicity in the Changing Mise-en-Scène of Anthropological Fieldwork. *In* The Fate of Culture: Geertz and Beyond. S. Ortner, ed. Pp. 86–109. Berkeley: University of California Press.

MARKS J., 1995, The Human Genome Diversity Project: Good For if Not Good As Anthropology? Washington, American Anthropological Association, Anthropology Newsletter 36:72.

NESTLE M., 2003, Safe Food: Bacteria, Biotechnology and Bioterrorism. Berkeley: University of California Press.

NGUYEN V. K., 2005, The Republic of Therapy: Biopolitics Before and After HIV in West Africa and Beyond. Durham: Duke University Press.

NICHTER M., 1992, Of Ticks, Kings, Spirits, and the Promise of Vaccines. *In* Paths to Asian Medical Knowledge. C. Leslie and A. Young, eds. Pp. 224–253. Berkeley: University of California Press.

ORTNER S. B., ed., 1999, The Fate of Culture: Geertz and Beyond. Berkeley: University of California Press.

PANDOLFI M., 2002, Moral entrepreneurs, souverainetés mouvantes et barbelés. Le bio-politique dans les Balkans postcommunistes. Pandolfi, M. and M. Abélès, eds. Special issue, "Politiques jeux d'espaces." Anthropologie et Sociétés 26(1):29–50.

PETRYNA A., 2002, Life Exposed: Biological Citizens after Chernobyl. New Jersey: Princeton University Press.

PIGG S. L., 2002, Too Bold, Too Hot: Crossing Culture in AIDS Prevention in Nepal. *In* New Horizons in Medical Anthropology: Essays in Honour of Charles Leslie. M. Nichter and M. Lock, eds. Pp. 58–80. New York: Routledge.

PORDIE L., n.d., Exploring Tibetan Medicine in Contemporary Context: Perspectives in Social Science. In press.

RABINOW P., 1996, Making PCR: A Story of Biotechnology. Chicago: University of Chicago Press.

——, 1999, French DNA: Trouble in Purgatory. Princeton, NJ: Princeton University Press.

RAPP R., 1999, Testing Women, Testing the Fetus: The Social Impact of Amniocentesis in America. New York: Routledge.

——, 2001, Gender, Body, Biomedicine: How Some Feminist Concerns Dragged Reproduction to the Center of Social Theory. Medical Anthropology Quarterly 15(4):466–477.

——, 2003, Cell Life and Death, Child Life and Death: Genomic Horizons, Genetic Diseases, Family Stories. *In* S. Franklin and M. Lock, eds. Remaking Life and Death: Toward an Anthropology of the Biosciences. S. Franklin and M. Lock, eds. Pp. 129–165. Santa Fe: School of American Research.

ROSE S., 1997, Lifelines: Life Beyond the Gene. Oxford: Oxford University Press.

ROSEMAN M., 2002, Making Sense out of Modernity. *In* New Horizons in Medical Anthropology: Essays in Honour of Charles L. M. Nichter and M. Lock, eds. Pp. 111–140. New York: Routledge.

SCHEPER-HUGHES N., 1992, Death Without Weeping: The Violence of Everyday Life in Brazil. Berkeley: California Press.

——, 2001, Commodity Fetishism in Organs Trafficking. Body and Society 7(2/3):31–62.

STRATHERN M., 1992, Reproducing the Future: Anthropology, Kinship and the New Reproductive Technologies. London: Routledge.

THOMPSON C., 2000, The Biotech Mode of Reproduction. Paper prepared for the School of American Research Advancement Seminar Animation and Cessation: Anthropological Perspectives on Changing Definitions of Life and Death in the Context of Biomedicine, Santa Fe, New Mexico.

TODESCHINI M., 2002, The Bomb's Womb: Women and the Atom Bomb. *In* Remaking a World: Violence, Social Suffering and Recovery. V. Das, A. Kleinman, M. Lock, M. Ramphele and P. Reynolds, eds. Pp. 102–156. Oxford: Oxford University Press.

VAN DER GEEST S. and S. REYNOLDS WHYTE, 1988, The Context of Medicines in Developing Countries: Studies in Pharmaceutical Anthropology. London: Kluwer Academic.

WORSLEY P., 1982, Non-Western Medical Systems. Annual Review of Anthropology 11:315–348.

WORTHMAN C., 1995 Hormones, Sex, and Gender. Annual Review of Anthropology 24:593–616.

YOUNG A., 1982, The Anthropologies of Illness and Sickness. Annual Review of Anthropology 11:257–285.

——, 1995, The Harmony of Illusions: Inventing Posttraumatic Stress Disorder. Princeton: Princeton University Press.

ZIZEK S., 2004, Between Two Deaths. London Review of Books 26:11.

INDEX

Aboriginal peoples *see* indigenous
abortion xix
   because of disease risk 281
   of female fetuses 236, 242–3
   Germany 149
Abraham, John 12
Abu-Lughod, Lila 271
access to health care *see* health care, access
   to
accountability 12
Ackerknecht, E. H. 42–3, 144–5
action, theories of 99
advocacy groups: support of medical
   technologies 283
Afghanistan 240
Africa
   development projects 98
   Dogon of Mali 132–3
   Dutch missionaries in 162
   German research in 149, 154
   HIV/AIDS 93, 98, 149, 151–2, 153, 154,
      240
   risk 94
   Spanish research in 105–6
African migrants: to France 255–6
Afro-Brazilian regions 65
Agamben, Giorgio xxvi, 5, 16, 257, 259
   bare life 132
aging people *see* elderly
agoraphobia 241
Aguirre-Beltrán, Gonzalo 73, 74, 76, 77,
      81
aid, humanitarian 96
   debates on xix
   and power relations 132
   Québec 26–7
AIDS *see* HIV/AIDS

alcoholism: in indigenous
      communities 78
Allcorn, Derek 185
Allen, D. R. 234
Allué, Marta 108, 111
alternative medicine
   Mexico 80
   UK 198–9
Amazon xxvii, 64, 152, 155
American Anthropological Association
   (AAA) 42, 46, 49
American Indian groups: Mexico 72–6
amniocentesis 236, 243
Andreu, A. 108
anorexia 241
anthropologists
   Spanish 106–7, 107–9
   UK 184
anthropology
   Germany 143–7, 153–5
   influence on medical anthropology xxi
   Italy 122–4
   links with medicine 103–4, 144–5
   novelistic 25
   Québec 26–8
   Spain 104–5
   US 42–3
   see also applied medical; critical
      medical; exotic; home; medical
Anthropology & Medicine 184
apartheid: South Africa 261–2
applied medical anthropology 93, 103
   Brazil 65
   Germany 147, 150, 155
   Netherlands 164, 174–5
   Spain 108
   UK 185, 195